DEVELOPING SPORT FOR WOMEN AND GIRLS

Women and girls are often excluded from organised sport or face challenges in accessing sport or developing within sport. This is the first book to focus on sport development for women and girls. It provides a theoretical and practical framework for readers in the emerging field of sport development.

Developing Sport for Women and Girls examines both the development of sport, and development through sport with expert contributions from Australasia, North America and Europe. It offers critical analysis of contemporary sport development, from high performance pathways to engaging diverse communities to the use of sport to empower women and girls. Each chapter explores various contexts of sport development and sport for development theory with a specific focus on women and girls. It covers key topics such as health, education, sexual orientation and participation across the lifecourse, and features international case studies in every chapter.

This is essential reading for students, academics, researchers and practitioners working in the area of sport development or sport management.

Emma Sherry is an internationally regarded expert in the field of sport development and access and inclusion within the sport and recreation environment with the Swinburne University Sport Innovation Research Group. Emma currently sits on the editorial boards of the *Journal of Sport Management, Sport Management Review,* the *Journal of Sport for Development, Communication and Sport Journal* and the *International Journal of Sport Business Management*.

Katie Rowe is Senior Lecturer in Sport Management and a member of the Centre for Sport Research at Deakin University, Australia. Katie's research focuses on sport and active recreation participation and community development through sport, with a particular emphasis on issues of relevance to women and girls.

ROUTLEDGE STUDIES IN SPORT DEVELOPMENT

Series Editors

Richard Giulianotti
Loughborough University, UK and University of Southeast Norway
B. Christine Green
George Mason University, USA

The *Routledge Studies in Sport Development* series showcases high-calibre work within the vibrant, diverse and rapidly expanding field of sport and development. It includes books in two broad areas. Firstly, the *development of sport*, focusing on the various ways in which sport is delivered, for example through building sport facilities, training coaches and athletes, improving sport performance, increasing public participation in sport, and strengthening the governance, management, marketing and delivery of sport. Secondly, *sport for development and peace* (SDP), examining how sport is used for different non-sporting social benefits, such as peace building and conflict reduction, health education, gender empowerment, community development, tackling crime, improving education, promoting 'positive youth development', and advancing the social inclusion of marginal populations. The series is committed to diversity in theory and method, is multi-disciplinary in approach, and includes work centring on local, national and transnational issues and processes, and on the global North and/or South.

Available in this series:

Routledge Handbook of Sport for Development and Peace
Edited by Holly Collison, Simon C. Darnell, Richard Giulianotti and P. David Howe

Sport, Development and Environmental Sustainability
Edited by Simon C. Darnell and Rob Millington

Developing Sport for Women and Girls
Edited by Emma Sherry and Katie Rowe

DEVELOPING SPORT FOR WOMEN AND GIRLS

Edited by Emma Sherry and Katie Rowe

LONDON AND NEW YORK

First published 2020
by Routledge
2 Park Square, Milton Park, Abingdon, Oxon OX14 4RN

and by Routledge
52 Vanderbilt Avenue, New York, NY 10017

Routledge is an imprint of the Taylor & Francis Group, an informa business

© 2020 selection and editorial matter, Emma Sherry and Katie Rowe; individual chapters, the contributors

The right of Emma Sherry and Katie Rowe to be identified as the authors of the editorial material, and of the authors for their individual chapters, has been asserted in accordance with sections 77 and 78 of the Copyright, Designs and Patents Act 1988.

All rights reserved. No part of this book may be reprinted or reproduced or utilised in any form or by any electronic, mechanical, or other means, now known or hereafter invented, including photocopying and recording, or in any information storage or retrieval system, without permission in writing from the publishers.

Trademark notice: Product or corporate names may be trademarks or registered trademarks, and are used only for identification and explanation without intent to infringe.

British Library Cataloguing-in-Publication Data
A catalogue record for this book is available from the British Library

Library of Congress Cataloging-in-Publication Data
A catalog record has been requested for this book

ISBN: 978-0-367-42654-5 (hbk)
ISBN: 978-0-367-42655-2 (pbk)
ISBN: 978-0-367-85420-1 (ebk)

Typeset in Bembo
by Taylor & Francis Books

CONTENTS

List of illustrations   *vii*
List of contributors   *ix*
Acknowledgements   *xiv*
Abbreviations   *xv*

1 Introduction   1
 Emma Sherry and Katie Rowe

2 Participation opportunities and pathways for women and girls   5
 Brianna L. Newland, Kim Encel and Pamm Phillips

3 Developing sport for girls and adolescents   19
 Rochelle Eime, Meghan Casey and Jack Harvey

4 Developing sport for mothers with dependent children   32
 Clare Hanlon, Tracy Taylor and Wendy O'Brien

5 Developing sport for older women   45
 Claire Jenkin

6 Developing sport for women and girls with a disability   57
 Andrew Hammond and Hannah Macdougall

7 Promoting LGBT+ inclusion in women's and girls' sport:
 Lessons from Australia   69
 Ryan Storr and Caroline Symons

8	Developing sport for culturally and linguistically diverse women and girls *Hazel Maxwell and Megan Stronach*	83
9	Developing sport for Indigenous women and girls *Megan Stronach and Hazel Maxwell*	95
10	Developing sport for women and girls in underserved and low socioeconomic communities *Katherine Raw*	110
11	Empowering women and girls through sport *Emma Seal*	121
12	Developing sport for women and girls: Education *Ruth Jeanes*	135
13	Gender, sport, and livelihoods *Rochelle Stewart-Withers*	147
14	Promoting health for women and girls through sport *Katie Rowe and Emma Sherry*	161
15	High-performance athletes *Lisa Gowthorp*	172
16	Coaches and officials *Donna de Haan and Stacy Warner*	185
17	Athlete protection and duty of care *Popi Sotiriadou and Pamela Wicker*	197
18	Regulating high testosterone in international women's sport *Madeleine Pape*	209
19	Professional women's sport leagues *Chelsey Taylor*	223
20	Developing sport for women and girls: Media influence *Merryn Sherwood*	236

Index *248*

ILLUSTRATIONS

Figures

1.1	The scope of sport development	2
5.1	Most successful advertisement for Walking Group initiative, London Sport (2018)	53
10.1	Socioecological model	112
15.1	FTEM framework	173

Tables

4.1	Building connections and support networks through sport	40
13.1	Some aspects which may impact women's livelihood opportunities	153
15.1	SSSM definitions	175

Boxes

	Case study: Ballarat women's and girls' cricket	27
	Case study: Soccer mums programme	41
	Case study: Digital marketing for walking groups	52
	Case study: Wheelchair Sport British Columbia (Canada)	63
	Case study: Promoting LGBTI+ inclusion in Australian Women's Cricket	73
	Case study: Australian Muslim women and Aussie Rules	92
	Case study: Ashleigh (Ash) Barty, Australian tennis player	105

Case study: The Good Wheel, a cycling programme for women and girls	117
Case study: Situating the case study: Pursuing empowerment of women and girls through an SFD programme in Papua New Guinea	126
Case study: Go Sisters, an SFD programme	142
Case study: Rugby Union and livelihoods in Fiji	157
Case study: This Girl Can	167
Case study: Talent identification and development in women's high-performance sport: A practitioner's perspective	181
Case study: UEFA Women's EURO	193
Case study: Bangladesh Weightlifting Federation – sexual assault allegation	204
Case study: Contemporary politics of testosterone regulation in track-and-field	213
Case study: Australian Women's Big Bash League	230
Case study: Changing traditional discourses through digital: *The Outer Sanctum* Podcast	243

CONTRIBUTORS

Meghan Casey is Senior Researcher and Lecturer in Sport Management and has extensive research experience in the sport and recreation field. She has informed programme and policy development on a range of sport management issues, including capacity, organisational change and programme development. A significant portion of Meghan's work has focused on sport participation and retention of females, and particularly adolescent girls.

Rochelle Eime is a Behavioural Epidemiologist with over 15 years of research experience specifically relating to the sport and recreation sectors in both public health and sport management. Rochelle is the Director of the Sport and Recreation Spatial programme of research (www.sportandrecreationspatial.com.au) which focuses on investigating sport and recreation.

Kim Encel is Associate Lecturer in Sport Management at Deakin University, Australia. He has researched, presented, and taught extensively in the management, psychology, health, and exercise science disciplines. The key findings of Kim's research will provide insights for developing women's professional sport leagues and organisations globally.

Lisa Gowthorp is Assistant Professor in Sport Management within the Bond Business School at Bond University, Australia. She has had over 14 years working in the high-performance sport industry, with organisations such as the Australian Institute of Sport (AIS), NSW Institute of Sport (NSWIS), Gymnastics Australia and Australian Canoeing, managing various Olympic teams. Lisa's research interests include sport governance, sport policy, high performance sport management, the Olympic Games and contemporary issues in high performance sport. Lisa continues to consult with industry and is the Vice-President of Sport Management Australia and New Zealand (SMAANZ) and a Director on the Board of Paddle Australia.

Donna de Haan is Principal Lecturer at the Hague University of Applied Sciences in the Netherlands. Her teaching and research expertise lies in the field of inclusion and diversity associated with issues of participation, coaching, leadership and governance in sport. She has been awarded grants for her work on gender equity from the International Olympic Committee, UEFA and Erasmus.

Andrew Hammond is Lecturer at the University of Essex, UK, where he contributes to teaching and research agendas in the departmental programmes relating to sports coaching, exercise science, sports therapy, and physiotherapy at both the graduate and undergraduate levels.

Clare Hanlon is the Susan Alberti Women in Sport Chair at Victoria University, Australia, as well as Director on the Oceania Gymnastics Union and Director of Gymnastics Australia. Her research focuses on sport, in particular to build community and organisational capacity to increase opportunities for women as leaders and participants in sport and physical activity. Clare's research has been translated into industry-based strategy, systems, policy, and programmes locally and internationally.

Jack Harvey is Senior Research Fellow in the School of Health and Life Sciences at Federation University, Australia, and the Institute of Health and Sport at Victoria University, Australia. He has particular expertise in the design and management of data collection processes, and in the design, management and analysis of large and complex data systems.

Ruth Jeanes is Associate Professor within the Faculty of Education and Director of Initial Teacher Education at Monash University, Australia. Ruth is a social scientist whose research interests focus on the use of sport and active recreation as a community development resource, particularly to address social exclusion amongst acutely marginalised groups. Ruth is also President of the Australian and New Zealand Association of Leisure Studies and is a member of several journal editorial boards including the *International Review for the Sociology of Sport*, *Sociology of Sport Journal*, *Managing Sport and Leisure* and *Qualitative Research in Sport, Exercise and Health*.

Claire Jenkin is Senior Lecturer in Sports Development at the University of Hertfordshire, UK. She is also a committee member of the UK Sports Development Network. Her research focuses on community sport for older adults, sport for social change, and sport diplomacy. She teaches on sport development and sport management courses, including UK based community sport, such as monitoring, evaluation, funding, and international sports development.

Hannah Macdougall is a dual Paralympian, previous World Record Holder, has captained the Australian Swimming Team at both a World Championships and Paralympic Games and completed a PhD in Athlete Well-Being. She is an inclusion advocate, mindfulness and wellbeing 'pracademic' and community engagement advisor at the Victoria State Emergency Service, Australia. With a focus on providing accessible and life-long tools based in mindfulness meditation Hannah inspires and empowers multiple communities to take positive action.

Hazel Maxwell is Senior Lecturer at the University of Tasmania, Australia. Her research and teaching focuses on physical activity, community sport, social inclusion and diversity management. She has been exploring social capital and diversity in not-for-profit organisations in sport and health promotion contexts.

Brianna L. Newland is Academic Director of Undergraduate Programs and Clinical Associate Professor in the Tisch Institute for Global Sport, USA. She is also the Editor of *Sport Entertainment Review* and sits on a number of other editorial boards for academic journals. Her research explores the long-term sustainability of sport participation by examining the sport development practices of sport organizations and events. She also explores the drivers of mass sport event participation to better understand how to leverage the economic, socio-cultural, and environmental impacts.

Wendy O'Brien is Adjunct Research Fellow in the Griffith Business School, Australia. Wendy's research interests include: the inequalities that impact women's well-being in the context of sport and leisure participation, elite athletes and environments that support their well-being and enhanced performance; the sociological implications of the rise of women's contact sport, volunteer management in sport and sport development systems.

Madeleine Pape is Postdoctoral Fellow in the Science in Human Culture programme and Department of Sociology at Northwestern University, USA. Her research and teaching interests include gender, Science and Technology Studies (STS), health and medicine, sociology of the body, political sociology, organizations, socio-legal studies, and physical cultural studies.

Pamm Phillips is Professor in the Sport Management Program at Deakin University, Australia. Pamm's research is focused on understanding sport organization development including formulating and testing intervention strategies that optimise an organisation's effectiveness and enhances the quality of life for individuals who participate and work in sport. Her recent research has focused on a range of issues related to sport development including the role of volunteers in creating and maintaining optimal sport environments for the development of individuals, groups and communities.

Katherine Raw is Lecturer in Sport Development at Western Sydney University, Australia. Her research focuses upon the use and management of sport as a vehicle to foster a variety of community outcomes, including social cohesion, gender equity, inclusion, health, prevention of domestic violence, and diplomacy. After six years of researching sport for development, her work has been conducted in partnership with a number of organisations, including Tennis Australia, the National Rugby League, Netball Australia, North Melbourne Football Club, and the Commonwealth Secretariat.

Emma Seal is Research Fellow in the Centre for Sport and Social Impact at La Trobe University, Australia. Emma's work draws on the sociology of sport, health and physical activity to understand sport as a tool for development and social change, and to explore how gender inequalities impact on women's sport and leisure participation, as well as their health and emotional wellbeing in society.

Merryn Sherwood is Senior Lecturer in the Department of Politics, Media and Philosophy and Coordinator of the Bachelor of Media and Communication at La Trobe University, Australia. She is a former award-winning Journalist and International Sport Media Manager, working at events such as the Rugby World Cup and London 2012 Olympic Games. Her research focuses on media disruption and change, and she is a CI on the ARC funded New Beats project, that explores redundancy and reinvention in Australian journalism.

Popi Sotiriadou is Associate Professor of Sport Management and the Director for Bachelor of Business Innovation at the Griffith Business School, Australia. Her research interests are in the area of managing high performance sport and elite athlete branding, sport development and policy, and gender equity and leadership. Her research has gained such acceptance that she has been invited to act as consultant to the International Olympic Committee, Sports Australia, Sarawak in Malaysia, and the Queensland Academy of Sport. Popi is also an Associate Editor of the *Journal of Sport Policy and Politics* and an editorial member for the *Journal of Sport Management*.

Rochelle Stewart-Withers (Te Āti Awa) is an Academic with the Institute of Development Studies at Massey University, New Zealand. She is an Indigenous scholar and broadly her research critically explores the potential of sport as a means for improving economic and social outcomes in developing countries, especially at the community and household level. She is also Chair of one of Massey University's Human Ethics Committees and member of the board with the New Zealand Mental Health Foundation.

Ryan Storr is Lecturer and Academic Course Advisor for the Sport Development undergraduate programme at Western Sydney University, Australia. His research interests focus on diversity and inclusion across different sport settings, with a specific focus on LGBT+ diversity. He is also Co-founder and Director of Proud 2 Play, a LGBTI+ youth sport charity, which aims to increase participation in sport for LGBTI+ youth, their friends and families.

Megan Stronach is Post-Doctoral Research Fellow at the University of Technology Sydney Business School, in an ARC-funded project which is focusing on entrepreneurship and people with disability in Australia. Megan worked for many years in sport management, in particular swimming management, along with teaching and coaching. In recent years she has developed a strong interest in the history of sport, women's and cultural issues in sport, and has written extensively about sport and physical activities among Indigenous Australian women.

Caroline Symons serves as Honorary Professor with Victoria University, Australia. She is the pioneering Researcher of homophobia in sport in Australia, leading the first comprehensive study to investigate the sporting experiences of LGBT people in the country: 'Come Out To Play', which won the prestigious VicHealth Research Translation award in 2011. Her most recent research has focused on the inclusion of LGBTI + people in Australian Cricket and the Olympic Games, and LGBTI+ Human Rights.

Chelsey Taylor commenced her PhD candidature at Swinburne University, Australia, in 2019, after successfully completing her honours degree investigating the first year of the Australian Women's Football League (AFLW). Chelsey has a wide range of experience as a Research Assistant with Deakin University, Australia, and Swinburne University, and recently completed a 6-month contract as a Research Analyst with Gemba. Chelsey's PhD studies focus on the social impact of the sport of AFL with Australian Aboriginal and Torres Strait Islander communities.

Tracy Taylor is Dean of Murdoch Business School, Australia. Tracy is also on the IOC Athlete 365 Advisory Board, and the Australian National Rugby League Research Committee. Tracy's research covers the areas of people management, diversity and equity management in sport, and volunteer management. Tracy's research with sport organisations has covered a range of areas including: disability participation in sport; volunteer retention in community sport; strategies to increase sport participation of women from culturally and linguistically diverse backgrounds; and risk and safety at sport events.

Stacy Warner is a Professor of Sport Management at East Carolina University, USA. Her research interests are primarily focused on the role that sport and sport culture plays in the lives of individuals through families, communities, work environments, and social networks. Warner is also a North American Society for Sport Management Research Fellow.

Pamela Wicker is Acting Professor for 'Sports Organizations' at Bielefeld University, Germany. Her primary research areas are (non-profit) sport organizations, including gender research; societal relevance of sport; sport participation and public health; and sport and the natural environment. Pamela is also Associate Editor of *Sport Management Review, European Sport Management Quarterly*, and the *Journal for Study and Teaching in Sport Science*, and she is an Editorial Board member at the *Journal of Sport Management, Journal of Sports Economics, International Journal of Sport Finance, European Journal for Sport and Society, Managing Sport and Leisure*, and *Journal of Sport & Tourism*.

ACKNOWLEDGEMENTS

We would like to sincerely thank all of our authors for their time and dedication, not only for their contribution to this book, but also for their ongoing research and advocacy for women and girls in sport. We would also like to acknowledge and thank our copy editor – Angela Osborne – for her careful eye and excellent work.

ABBREVIATIONS

ACA	Australian Cricketers Association
ACE	Athlete Career & Education Advisor
ACL	Anterior cruciate ligament
ADM	American Development Model
AIS	Australian Institute of Sport
AFL	Australian Football League
AFLW	Australian Rules football League for Women
B2N	Back to netball (Programme)
BBL	Big Bash League
BC	British Columbia
BCWCBS	British Columbia Wheelchair Basketball Society
BCWSA	British Columbia Wheelchair Sports Association
BME	Black, minority, ethnic
BMI	Body-mass-index
BWF	Bangladesh Weightlifting Federation
CA	Cricket Australia
CAAWS	Canadian Association for the Advancement of Women and Sport and Physical Activity
CALD	Culturally and linguistically diverse
CAS	Court of Arbitration for Sport
CEDAW	Convention on the Elimination of All Forms of Discrimination Against Women
CV	Cricket Victoria
CVD	Cardiovascular disease
DTE	Daily Training Environment
EI	Emotional intelligence
FATr	Female Athlete Triad

xvi Abbreviations

FTEM	FTEM model, comprising foundations, talent, elite, mastery
GET	Girl's Empowerment through Cricket
HAZ	Health Action Zones
HIC	High-income country
IAAF	International Association of Athletics Federations
ICC	International Cricket Council
INGO	International non-government organisation
IOC	International Olympic Committee
ISNA	Intersex Society of North America
IWG	International Working Group on Women's Sport
LGBT+	Lesbian, gay, bisexual, transgender
LIC	Low-income country
LMIC	Low- to middle-income country
LSRC	Lakemba Sport and Recreation Club
LTAD	Long-Term Athlete Development model
LTPA	Leisure time physical activity
M&E	Monitoring and evaluation
MOU	Memorandum of understanding
MVPA	Moderate-to-vigorous physical activity
NCAA	National Collegiate Athletic Association
NCD	Non-communicable disease
NFL	National Football League (US)
NGO	Non-government organisation
NSC	National Sports Council (Bangladesh)
NSO	National Sporting Organisations
ODI	One Day International cricket
OWSR	Office Women in Sport and Recreation, Victoria
PAR	Participatory action research
PE	Physical education
PFA	Professional Footballers Association
PGN	Practical gender needs
PNG	Papua New Guinea
SAWSF	South African Women and Sport Foundation
SDGs	Sustainable Development Goals (United Nations [UN])
SDP	Sport for development and peace
SES	Socioeconomic status
SFU	Simon Fraser University, Canada
SGD	Sport, gender and development
SGN	Strategic gender needs
SMA	Sports Medicine Australia
SSO	State sporting organisation
SSHRC	Canadian Social Science and Humanities Research Council
SSSM	Sport Science Sport Medicine
T20I	International Twenty-over Cricket

TID	Talent identification
TNC	Transnational corporation
TRC	Truth and Reconciliation Commission (Canada)
UK	United Kingdom
UN	United Nations
UNGA	United Nations General Assembly
UNOSDP	United Nations Office of Sport, Development and Peace
US	United States of America
USOC	United States Olympic Committee
USSF	US Football Federation
VAFCS	Vancouver Aboriginal Friendship Centre Society
WA	Western Australia
WADA	World Anti-Doping Agency
WAIS	Western Australian Institute of Sport
WBBL	Women's Big Bash League
WHO	World Health Organization
WNBL	Women's National Basketball League
WSF	Women's Sports Foundation
#fitspo	Fitness inspiration

1
INTRODUCTION

Emma Sherry and Katie Rowe

Introduction

Women's sport is an area of exponential growth in the international sport industry, via participation, high performance, focused initiatives and sport media. The increasing profile and reach of women's sport – and its use as a voice for gender equity – has brought sport into the spotlight as a vehicle to encourage dialogue and enact change with respect to the role and place of women in society.

Advocacy for increased opportunity for women and girls in sport has occurred in waves across the twentieth and twenty-first centuries, in the form of women participating in high profile sporting events, such as the Olympic Games, or long-distance runner Kathrine Switzer's defiant participation in the 1967 Boston Marathon, or the Battle of the Sexes tennis match with Billie Jean King. It has also taken the form of legislature, with the implementation of Title IX legislation in the US, pay equity negotiations in professional sport leagues in the US and Europe and the development of anti-discrimination legislation globally. Since the early twenty-first century, there has been an increased focus not just on the inequity in compensation and conditions and on gender-based violence but the focus has further expanded to the role of sport as a place and a mechanism for gender equity more broadly.

Opportunities for women and girls to participate and excel in sport are increasingly becoming focus areas of national governments, international sport federations, major events and sport business. Various stakeholders are recognising the value that women bring to the sport landscape through their participation, engagement, leadership and performance. Sport is responding to this growth by developing specific systems, programmes, pathways, protections and opportunities to further gender equity in sport globally. *Developing Sport for Women and Girls* provides a theoretical and practical framework for those engaging in this emerging field of expertise, via applying a global lens to examine how women and girls experience, participate, and excel in sport.

Throughout this book, the terms women and female will both be used. We understand that this is a contested area. The appropriate use of terminology to discuss sex (i.e. female) and gender (i.e. women and girls) has been selected by the chapter authors as appropriate to their specific context. In some chapters – most specifically those focused on sex-segregated sport competition – the term female has been used. In most cases throughout this book, we refer to women and girls as an overarching gender descriptor that is inclusive of gender diverse communities.

Conceptualising sport development for women and girls

The conceptualisation of sport development for women and girls within this book falls broadly within three themes: *participation and inclusion*, *development **through** sport* (*sport for development*) and *development **of** sport*.

Participation and access to sport opportunities underpins the broad nature of sport development for women and girls globally. This involves ensuring that women and girls have safe, inclusive and welcoming sport environments in which to participate. When speaking of participation, we do not simply imply participation on the field, instead we intend participation to be interpreted in its broadest sense, as participation in all aspects of the sport experience: playing, coaching, officiating, spectating, reporting, competing, administering and leading. We additionally recognise the importance of women as spectators, fans and consumers of sport. However, for the purposes of this book, the key focus areas are the forms of on-field participation – participants, athletes, coaches and officials.

In the context of sport development, we recognise that participation and inclusion strategies are fundamental building blocks that underpin both arms of sport development. Importantly, ensuring that women and girls have opportunities to engage in forms of sport that are welcoming and inclusive enables them to access both sport and non-sport outcomes in a sport setting.

Sport development, for the purposes of this book, includes *development **of** sport* (SD), through creating pathways for participation and talent identification, as well as *development **through** sport* or *sport **for** development* (SFD), where sport is used as a tool to engage the community for specific social outcomes.

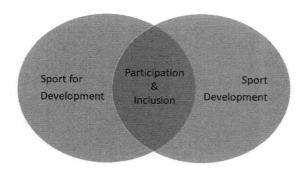

FIGURE 1.1 The scope of sport development

The two branches of sport development, SFD and SD, have much in common yet they differ in aspects of both purpose and focus. While SD emphasises pathways for professional participation and talent identification, SFD instead aims to use sport as a mechanism to contribute to specific social outcomes and overall community wellbeing. The focus of SD is predominantly individuals and groups participating in sport activity to achieve mastery and excellence. In comparison, the focus of SFD programmes and initiatives provides individuals and groups with opportunities to participate in sport-like activities to realise certain social, cultural, psychological, educational and/or economic goals (Schulenkorf, Sherry & Phillips, 2016).

About this book

This book is organised across three themes

1. Participation and inclusion
2. Sport for development
3. Sport development

Within the first focus area of participation and inclusion, the book begins with a chapter focused on mass participation and pathways in sport for women and girls. Chapter 2 sets the scene in which the context of women and girls sport participation is enacted and the role of organisations in facilitating opportunities for women's and girls' participation in sport. The following chapters in this section (Chapters 3–10) provide a specific focus on motivations and barriers experienced by specific populations of women and girls, and how organisations can adapt and develop programmes and opportunities to support each of these specific populations. The populations discussed within this section of the book include:

Chapter 3 – girls and adolescents
Chapter 4 – mothers with dependent children
Chapter 5 – older women
Chapter 6 – women and girls with a disability
Chapter 7 – same-sex attracted and gender diverse communities
Chapter 8 – culturally and linguistically diverse communities
Chapter 9 – Indigenous communities
Chapter 10 – low-socioeconomic and underserved communities.

Within the second focus area of sport for development, this section begins with a chapter focused on empowering girls through sport. This chapter sets the scene by explaining the concept of sport for development with a specific focus on women and girls. Chapters in this section (Chapters 11–14) then provide a specific focus on how sport can be used as a vehicle to support women's development, and how programmes and initiatives can be designed and delivered to support development outcomes for women and girls. The chapters within this section of the book specifically focus on:

Chapter 11 – empowering girls through sport
Chapter 12 – education
Chapter 13 – livelihoods
Chapter 14 – health.

Within the final focus area of sport development, the section begins with a chapter focused on high performance women athletes. This chapter lays the foundations by considering how sport develops successful women athletes. Chapters in this section (Chapters 15–21) provide a specific focus on issues identified that specifically impact women and girls within the sport performance landscape. The chapters within this section of the book provide insight into:

Chapter 15 – high-performance athletes
Chapter 16 – coaches and officials
Chapter 17 – athlete protection and duty of care
Chapter 18 – regulating high testosterone in international women's sport
Chapter 19 – professional sport
Chapter 20 – media influence.

Summary

Developing sport for women and girls is at exciting crossroads in the international sport landscape. This book has brought together expertise from across the globe, with authors drawing on a variety of cultural contexts and different national sport systems.

In this first chapter we have set the scene on why developing sport for women and girls has an increased focus and reach globally. We have discussed our conceptualisation of the two arms of sport development, namely the development *of* sport (SD) and the development *through* sport, or sport-for-development (SFD) and how these intersect with the overarching aim of participation and inclusion in sport for women and girls. In addition, we have outlined how this book – and its constituent sections and chapters – proposes to discuss the different aspects of developing sport for women and girls and their application to theory and practice.

We are confident that by using this book, readers will explore, learn and discuss the latest concepts and trends in developing sport for women and girls – including an understanding of the intersectionality of this population, the motivations and barriers for participation, challenges and opportunities in the sport performance context and how sport can contribute to the development of women and girls.

References

Schulenkorf, N., Sherry, E., & Phillips, P. (2016). What is sport development? In E. Sherry, N. Schulenkorf, & P. Phillips (eds). *Managing Sport Development: An International Approach* (pp. 3–11). London: Routledge.

2
PARTICIPATION OPPORTUNITIES AND PATHWAYS FOR WOMEN AND GIRLS

Brianna L. Newland, Kim Encel and Pamm Phillips

Introduction

Women's and girls' participation in sport has long been fraught with challenges. With the advent of the Title IX anti-gender discrimination law in the United States (US) in the 1970s, there was a shift in access and opportunity that spread globally. This chapter begins with a brief discussion of the history of sport participation for women and girls, continues with a critical examination of the current state of sport participation for women and girls, and goes on to discuss implications for the future of sport participation for women and girls. Through this account of participation, the chapter explores the roles and responsibilities of various sport organisations – including local and regional clubs, third party organisations, and education systems – in providing access and opportunities for women and girls to participate in all sports, as well as in designing and developing pathways to nurture continued involvement and participation in sport.

The way sport organisations can impact the participation of women and girls is exemplified by the following quote by gridiron footballer, Antoinette 'Toni' Harris:

> I first developed the interest in [gridiron] football between four and six years old. People around me weren't too fond of me playing football. They said I could get hurt easier by playing with guys. What motivates me most to play is people telling me I can't; I love to prove people wrong. I was kicked off a team when I was younger because I was a girl. But, once I got older and into high school … I mean it still was hard, but I just tried to pave my way through no matter what anybody said. It's my dream and I'm going to protect it at any cost. … A message that I would like to send to younger girls is to keep your dream alive, nothing is impossible.
>
> *(CBS News, 2019)*

Toni chose to play a sport that is traditionally dominated by men, both in its management and in participation. Her participation in this sport challenged a range of society norms. Perhaps not surprisingly, an historical exploration of women's sport illustrates a struggle wrought with misogyny, myth and fear that is even still apparent in 2019 as illustrated by the quote above from an interview with Toni Harris. Toni Harris dreams of being the first woman to play in the National Football League (NFL). She has recently been offered a football scholarship to play at the collegiate level. Despite being discouraged (at best) and prevented (at worst) from playing football, her journey provides a backdrop to explore and highlight a range of factors that impact the management of pathways and delivery of sport for women and girls and demonstrates the struggle for women to play invasion sports like gridiron (an example from the context of North America) or Australian Rules football (AFL) (in Australia).

Challenging myths and perceptions about women in sport

Women were once thought to be too frail and unsuited to participate in any form of sport (Hargraves, 1994) and this remains a prevailing attitude in relation to aggressive sports (or invasion sports), like gridiron football, as highlighted by the example provided at the beginning of this chapter. A common perception throughout history has been that playing *any* sport could harm reproductive function (McCrone, 1991), and women were cautioned not to participate due to the fear of 'neutering themselves by over-indulgencing in athletics' (Fletcher, 1985, p. 29).

Despite such myths and patriarchal views at the time, women took part in various sporting activities such as calisthenics and gymnastics (McCrone, 1991), as well as team sports like cricket (Fletcher, 1985). The late nineteenth and twentieth centuries ushered in a paradigm shift for women that began with the changes made possible by education systems, as well as by the introduction of sex discrimination laws like Title IX in the US. Title IX (20 US Code § 1681) stated that no discrimination should occur on the basis of sex in federally funded schools and that women and girls should have the same access and opportunities to engage in sport activities as men and boys.

However, sport to this day is still often described as a male-dominated institution because a large proportion of sport participation and management roles continue to be filled by men. For example, in the US, women represent less than 3% of the head coaches in men's sport and make up less than half (42.6%) of all coaches in women's sport (Walker & Bopp, 2011). Like other male-dominated institutions, women have been integral to the successful development of the sport and yet still find it difficult to be accepted (Adriaanse & Schofield, 2013; Velija, et al., 2014). What this means to women and girls like Toni Harris is that their first experience of sport is played under traditional rules designed for, delivered by, and, most often, coached by men. Further, decisions about the sport and the business of the sport are also mostly made by men.

Over the last century, women across the world have benefited from improved access and opportunity to participate in sport – but arguably only in some sports, and most often at the lower levels of sport, as opposed to in the higher levels of professional sport. That is: participation opportunities continue to be gendered (Baghurst, Tapps & Judy, 2014; Pfister, 2015). Women continue to be met with resistance from a male-dominated public culture and male-dominated sport institutions (Laurendeau & Sharara, 2008). In fact, Staurowsky, et al. (2006) noted that popular opinion persists that males are more naturally interested, and better suited physically, to play sport – even after decades of women and girls participating in and excelling at sport. Despite the continued challenges girls and women face, the increasing participation rates for women provides evidence that many have a deep interest in playing sport – across their lifespan.

The sport organisation's role in developing pathways

Over the last 25 years there has been increased emphasis on the importance of elite sport development, and much of this focus has been driven by access to funding, performance on the elite world stage and the benefits of international sporting success (e.g. De Bosscher, et al., 2009). When a nation's athletes dominate on world sport stages it can have economic, social and political advantages. Unfortunately, at the professional or elite levels of sport, women and girls continue to have fewer opportunities to play compared with their male counterparts (Anderson, 2009). Women's leagues do not necessarily command broadcasting rights or fan interest in the same way that men's sports do, which is largely due to pre-existing biases against women's sport (Fink, 2015).

One of the key ways that sport organisations have approached the development of their sports for women is to modify the rules. Rule modifications for women's sports have often been driven by societal understandings of women and their physical ability to participate in sport (Theberge, 1998). For example, Birrell (1988) noted that modifying sport specifically for women is built on sociological or cultural logics and understandings of the physical capacity of women. In the early 1900s, a small group of professional female physical activity educators, who were aligned with a male medical field, pioneered rule modifications because it was perceived that women needed to minimise physical overexertion to maintain their femininity and avoid commercial and violent male sport systems (Birrell, 1988). Thus, rule modifications for female athletes were based on gender expectations rather than physical abilities. Despite the rule modifications implemented regularly across a variety of sports, there is a lack of empirical evidence to demonstrate that the desired impact is being achieved.

In the sport development literature, delivery pathways have focused on two streams: elite development and mass participation. Mass participation has existed to provide a broad pool of athletes who can be developed into elite competitors (Green, 2005; Green & Collins, 2008; Houlihan & Green, 2008) or as a means to encourage and promote participation (Green & Collins, 2008) or health and well-being (Berg, Warner & Das, 2015). This sport performance metaphor – a pyramid illustrating the broad base of mass participation leading to the 'elite' peak – has long been used to describe how athletes are recruited, retained and transitioned to the next level of play (Eady, 1993; Green, 2005).

As the work in sport development evolved, talent identification and development have been the focus of a number of nations – particularly those focused on international elite performance (De Bosscher, et al., 2016; Houlihan & Green, 2008). Many sport organisations responsible for developing elite athletes to international standards have embraced the Long-Term Athlete Development (LTAD) model (Balyi, 2001). The LTAD was established to ensure optimum progress over the athletes' careers by teaching physical literacy – the skills, knowledge and behaviours that instil confidence in a range of physical activities and sports – and fundamental to the model is a recognition that there are various training stages that an athlete must master to achieve elite levels (Balyi, 2001; Ford, et al., 2011). In the US, the United States Olympic Committee (USOC), in partnership with the NGBs, created the American Development Model (ADM) to encourage youth to embrace healthy lifestyles and to realise their full potential through sport. The programme creates positive experiences at early stages of involvement that theoretically leads to longer engagement in sport. However, the ADM stops short of offering pathways for continued skill development for adults, including women. In the US, the pathways for adults and women are typically left to the free market to provide where third-party operators deliver adult sport participation opportunities – often in competition with governing bodies of sport – and most often for profit (Bowers, et al., 2011; Newland & Kellett, 2012; Phillips & Newland, 2014).

Unlike the US, many countries in Europe, as well as Canada and Australia, recognise the need for long-term programming and delivery of sport that extends into adulthood. For example, Sport Canada and the initiative Sport for Life – a multi-sport service organisation serving the NSOs by working across sport, recreation, and community. Sport for Life aims to build on high performance through recreation and participation while recognising that athletic development exists on a continuum. In Australia, the FTEM model (foundations, talent, elite, mastery), integrates three key pillars of active lifestyle, sport participation and sport excellence through ten stages of development (Gulbin, et al., 2013). Incorporating the tenets of the LTAD, including physical literacy, the FTEM model acknowledges the multiple pathways, including development, competition and continued skill development, to mastery. This broad, holistic approach to development aims to enable and support lifelong participation.

While elite pathways are important and necessary, many sport organisations have recognised the need to offer a range of options that support all athletes on the sport development journey (Sotiriadou, Shilbury & Quick, 2008). Pathways should include exit and re-entry points and allow for movement between higher and lower competitive levels to better accommodate a range of athletes in various stages of development and life. This concept of multiple entry and exit points is particularly important for women as they typically experience more interruptions to their sport participation, such as having children and families where they take substantial time away from work, leisure and other activities that they may have participated in. Sotiriadou and colleagues' (2008) were able so show that Australian sport organisations needed to consider pathways that allowed for movement in and out of sport, which would generate opportunities for all athletes – not just women. Further, Phillips and Newland (2014) recognised third-party operators as critical in creating and delivering additional pathways to provide programming that the NSOs or NFBs could not offer for participation in the sport of triathlon – particularly for women and girls.

How pathways differ, or whether they should differ, for girls and women has yet to be explored in the sport development literature. The LTAD has recognised that athletes develop differently based on the demands of the sport as well as an individual's physiological growth and development (Balyi, 2001). Canadian Sport for Life has recognised that female athletes have different physiological challenges, such as the Female Athlete Triad – disordered eating, amenorrhea, and reduced bone mineral health – that can influence their development in sport (Harber, 2007). Research has also shown that girls are less likely to participate in sport than boys (ABS, 2012; Shifrer, et al., 2015) and that participation of girls declines at twice the rate of boys by age 14 (Sabo & Veliz, 2008). It has also been reported that girls feel ashamed of their bodies (Evans, 2006) and are highly concerned about what others think (Kingsley & Spencer-Cavaliere, 2015) and experience discrimination based on sexual orientation – either real or perceived – and gender identity conflicts (Sabo & Veliz, 2008). Pressure to act and appear feminine continues to persist for women and girls, despite changing attitudes towards female athletes (Staurowsky, et al., 2006). These issues suggest that there are a range of managerial considerations in recruitment, retention and transition that need to be addressed in the design and development of pathways to facilitate the participation of women and girls in sport.

Additionally, there are continued challenges of access and equity in sport for women and girls. In Canada, the government has recognised a need to strengthen the sport system where women and girls are full and valued participants and leaders. The Canadian sport policy, 'Actively Engaged: A Policy on Sport for Women and Girls' is designed to foster sport environments through funding and programming to ensure women and girls are provided with quality sport experiences and equitable support by sport organisations to address systemic inequities for women and girls (Canadian Government, 2009). For example, Darroch, et al. (2019) found that governing bodies and sponsors failed to provide support to pregnant or postpartum elite runners causing undue stress around strategizing when to start a family. A clear gap in the literature is how pathways can accommodate both family planning and high performance for elite-level female athletes. Female athletes should not have to choose between an elite career and a family. Sport organisations should provide pathways that accommodate unique requirements of the female athlete. To that end, Netball Australia (the Australian governing body of Netball) has introduced pregnancy and parental support provisions in its collective bargaining agreements removing childbirth as a roadblock for professional women athletes in the sport (George, 2017).

The role of local and regional clubs in providing participation opportunities and pathways

The role of local and regional clubs is to provide access to sport programmes at the grassroots level, as well as provide opportunities for athletes to pursue elite development opportunities if they desire, as well as to offer adult programming. In this way, community-based clubs are the foundation for participation and involvement in sport. For girls and women in Europe, Canada and Australia, sport is delivered through coordinated systems that theoretically start in local communities, and clubs are connected through a structured network in regions and states that allows for movement and transitions within and across various levels of a sport (Sotiriadou, et al., 2008; Vail, 2007). As the foundation to the sport system, clubs play a key role in providing for participation, as well as pathways for elite development. Clubs not only facilitate and enable opportunities for high performance, but they provide a place for women to continue to participate as they transition through the sport system – whether they transition down from elite levels of the sport to more recreational or social involvement, or re-enter a sport system that they may have left for other reasons. Clubs enable lifelong participation by providing facilities, programming and events for continued play at various levels of skill and age.

In the US, however, the club system does not operate in this way. Sport delivery is driven by both the free market and the educational system. Some sports, like swimming and gymnastics, have a very strong club sport network and provide a clear pathway to high performance. For most other sports, the pathway to elite participation varies widely by sport and can often be unclear and ambiguous, especially if the sport is not offered the education system (Bowers, Chalip & Green, 2011). To complicate matters even further, an athlete could start a sport at a club, play for her high school team, earn a scholarship to a university, and advance to a national team for international competition. Or, she could join a club and advance to an elite national team without ever entering the educational sport system. This process is even more complex as many select club teams and high school teams compete with one another for athletes (Newland & Bowers, 2013). Because the sport system is so competitive and has little to no governmental oversight, programming, delivery and standards vary greatly by community, region, state and institution. Parents who can afford the best 'select' club teams will ensure their child can develop to the elite ranks, whereas those who are less fortunate – either due to geography or income level – do not have the same access.

For women, access to sport clubs and participation opportunities as an adult in the US can be difficult, depending on the sport. The club system for swimming is very well developed and offers opportunities for adults to continue to train and race through a well-supported and developed master's network. However, access to sport will depend on the community and its infrastructure. Women often describe lack of facilities, programming, and time are barriers to continued participation (Cerin, et al., 2010). Many have turned to sports like triathlon, running, or CrossFit because these sports provide a pathway to competition and events (Newland & Kellett, 2012; Newland, 2019) and more flexible skill development and training opportunities in facilities that are female-friendly and cater for social environments that women desire (Laurendeau & Sharara, 2013; Newland, 2019). In fact, the growth of women-only events has demonstrated that women experience participation in sport differently from men. Sport organisations have been forced to reconsider how they deliver sport for women and have thus developed new products. For example, Newland (2019) found that women participated in women-only events because they were less intimidating, provided a social community inspired by support and enabled advocacy for empowerment, health, and charity. In other words, those sport organisations that provided a pathway catering more specifically for the needs and motivations of women were rewarded with greater participation, and therefore sport business success.

The role of education system in providing participation opportunities and pathways

More than any other nation in the world, the US has relied heavily on its educational system to deliver sport participation opportunities. Often touted as a means to educate through sport (Newland, Dixon & Green, 2013), school sport in the US has shifted from a means to promote the values and interests of education to a viable pathway for high performance sport. Family spending data illustrates that nearly 20% of US families spend more than US$12,000 a year per child on sport, and the majority (63%) spend between US$100–499 per child, per month (Shell, 2017). While many parents have the means to afford pay-for-play sport, many US families do not have the same access to, nor ability to pay for, such programmes (Edwards, et al., 2014; Shifrer, et al., 2015). Therefore, the US education system provides facilities, access and opportunity to those often underserved by the free market system, especially minority athletes (Edwards, Kanters & Boccaro, 2014). American interscholastic and intercollegiate sports – although publicised as amateur sport systems (worth billions of dollars) – serve as an elite sport development pathway to some national teams and professional leagues. But while interscholastic school sport missions promote that their programmes provide opportunities for physical development, health and participation, the reality is that many programmes are competitive and exclusionary due to limited space on the rosters (Kingsley & Spencer-Cavaliere, 2015). Therefore, those who do not have the means to pay for private sport are often left behind. This can be devastating for girls in lower socioeconomic and minority groups (Shifrer, et al., 2015).

Like the US, the Canadian sport system offers competitive pathways for sport development in the school system, but the athletic financial awards are not nearly as competitive as US scholarships, although they are increasing (Won, 2017). Unlike the US, Canada offers specialised sport schools at the interscholastic level access to experienced coaches and competitive leagues (Our Kids, 2018). These specialised schools also provide a pathway to university sport, which is a competitive pathway to higher performance. In other countries like Australia and England, sport in the school provides opportunity for physical literacy, health and participation. While still offering opportunities for performance development, school sport in Australia is intended to be inclusive and collaborative, fostering lifelong participation.

Sport Australia, the government agency that oversees Australian sport, partners with NSOs to deliver sport in the schools at little or no cost to children in order to increase sport delivery and opportunities for participation (SportAUS, 2018).

Opportunities for future research

A number of issues have been identified within the course of this chapter that offer opportunities for future research. First, what is not understood is how the current pathways for athlete development are working, if at all, for girls and women. The need for and utility and design of multiple entry, re-entry and exit points for women and girls in sport is yet to be explored by scholars. Sport scientists and policymakers in some countries have identified that female athletes have different needs than their male counterparts. However, do these needs warrant different sport delivery requirements that sport managers need to be cognisant of? Such thinking could reinforce the biological ideologies and lead us further down the path of sex segregation in sport (Anderson, 2009). Researchers have extolled the virtues of sex integration in sport (Anderson, 2008), but would such a change improve pathways of sport delivery for women and girls? Programmes that have successfully integrated women and men should be examined, along with high performance outcomes for both women and men. Further, women should be at the table when discussing the design and delivery of sport for them. As policymakers, coaches, event operators or club owners, women's voices are critical in discussions about how sport should be developed and delivered for women and girls.

Future work should explore how elite sport pathways can accommodate family planning and high performance for elite-level female athletes. Research is needed that examines what programmes exist to support elite development and family planning for female athletes, as well as how family planning should be incorporated into the elite development plan. Athletes should not be forced to retire from sport or lose their sponsor support to have children during their competitive years.

The research demonstrates a clear challenge for female athletes in lower socioeconomic and minority groups. There are many sport for development (SFD) programmes that focus on sport participation, education and obesity, among other issues faced by young girls. However, there is a paucity of work that addresses high performance pathways for these girls. Future research should examine existing programmes that provide access and opportunity to girls who exhibit signs of talent in sport.

Practical actions to address issues

Research has identified that girls most frequently drop out from sport around the age of 14 years. Programmes should focus on this age demographic, in particular, to try to retain girls at this time, or to provide ways and reasons for them to re-enter their sport at a later time. Studies have found that girls are very sensitive to what others think about their sport participation, especially in the sensitive adolescent years. Many girls are insecure about their abilities, their bodies and perceptions of their abilities. Programmes should be sensitive to how girls perceive themselves as well as how they think others perceive them. Perhaps campaigns that attempt to deal with these insecurities by addressing confidence and self-esteem could be helpful. Girls also worry about the perception of their sexuality and femininity. The societal norms pressure girls and women to align to certain ideals. While this is slowly changing, girls still feel this pressure to conform to these ideals. Programming that attempts to address this by making girls feel confident in their athletic prowess as well as what it means to be a woman or a girl in today's culture could be helpful. Many of these practical actions are more focused on education, rather than the sport delivery; however, given the reasons for why women and girls leave sport, they are critical aspects of the developmental pathway, especially if the goal is to deliver the best programming to support elite development.

Case study

Women in invasion sports: The case of AFL Women's (AFLW)

As a result of the growing popularity of women's participation, the AFL prioritised the establishment of the semi-professional Australian Football League Women's (AFLW) competition. This case study explores pathways and participation for women and girls in the AFLW competition.

Football codes are invasion sports where the aim is to attack an opponent's territory (Gye, 2015; Hess, 2000), and have been described as masculine institutions (Lennon, 2013). Invasion sports have traditionally been the domain of men – and sport organisations that deliver such sports have traditionally not provided opportunities for women to participate in their sports, largely due to the perception that the sports require strength and masculinity for their execution, they are dangerous and can cause injury. As such, it has been commonly accepted that invasion sports should be exclusively for men (Bullingham, et al., 2014), and this has extended to governance, management and administration, meaning that if women and girls wanted to play such sports, they were typically the only woman on the team, as seen with the example of Toni Harris and her sport of gridiron that opened this chapter. In recent years, however, women's participation in football has increased rapidly, including women's tackle football in Canada (Liechty, et al., 2015), women's flag football in the US (Xing, et al., 2014) and Australian Rules football. In fact, the Australian Football League reported an increase of approximately 46% in participation by women and girls in 2015 and, at that time, women reportedly made up 23% of overall participation in the sport (AFL, 2015).

The AFL is the governing body of the largest and arguably most successful (men's) football code in Australia (Stewart, et al., 2016). From a participation perspective, Australian Rules football is one of the most popular sports in Australia, with over 1.6 million participants, which is approximately 6% of the Australian population. Since 2016, most of the increase in participation in the sport has been due to the increased participation of women and girls (AFL, 2019). In the second season of AFLW, where there were 28 matches in the season, the total attendance was 171,312, with an average of 6,118 attendees to match – although all matches were free (non-ticketed). The AFLW competition represents the first time the AFL has embraced, supported and established a semi-professional competition for women. Originally intended to begin in 2020, the official launch date of the AFLW competition season was brought forward to 2017 due to industry pressure from the increase in opportunities for women to play professional sport in Australia – such as cricket and netball – and increased participation rates of women and girls in AFL (Colasimone, 2016).

Prior to the introduction of the AFLW competition, girls had been participating alongside boys in development and competitive programmes, despite empirical evidence that suggests that girls and women often desire different benefits from sport than men and boys, meaning that organisation, management and delivery structures may need to be adapted to cater for such needs (Green & Chalip, 1998; Rowe, et al., 2016). Participation by women and girls in Australian Rules football has burgeoned since the announcement of the AFLW competition, increasing by 86%, with women currently making up 32% of all participation (AFL, 2019).

Despite the rapid growth of women's participation in Australian Rules football, there is little empirical knowledge about how it might be managed, structured and played by women. These different structures are particularly important, given that girls often have their first experience of the sport in teams that consist predominantly of boys and are most often coached by men, in programmes delivered by men. Further, when women and girls do play in female-only teams, those clubs and leagues are embedded in existing football structures that may not necessarily be resourced or equipped to understand and offer women the experiences that they enjoy.

Much of the academic literature and empirical evidence that exists about women in Australian Rules football has been focused on marketing to women as spectators or fans (Mewett & Toffoletti, 2011), women as sexual objects for male elite football players (Waterhouse-Watson, 2012), women as part of the supporting structures and administration of AFL (Gye, 2015; Hess, 2000), and relationships that form between women (Sanders, 2015). Most football codes around the world have traditionally been dominated by men in participation, organisation, management, delivery and representation in the media (Pfister, 2015). That is, they are male-dominated institutions. The AFL is no exception (Lennon, 2013), which is what makes the introduction of the AFLW competition interesting and significant. There are a few concerns that warrant attention as it relates to women participating in invasive sport:

1. How should invasion sport be developed and delivered for women and girls?
2. Should the women's game have different rules?
3. Do the rule changes effect women's interests in the sport and do rule changes impact the legitimacy of the sport?
4. Does the perception of invasion sport as too masculine or dangerous hinder development and delivery? And,
5. Have we even bothered to ask girls and women what they think?

References

ABS (2012, June). Australian social trends: Who participates in organised sport or dancing. Australian Bureau of Statistics. Retrieved from www.abs.gov.au/AUSSTATS/abs@.nsf/Lookup/4102.0Main+Features40Jun+2012#WP

Adriaanse, J. A., & Schofield, T. (2013). Analysing gender dynamics in sport governance: A new regimes-based approach. *Sport Management Review*, 16(4), 498–513.

AFL (2015). Women's participation in AFL Soars. Retrieved from www.afl.com.au/news/2015-10-13/womens-participation-in-afl-soars-in-2015

AFL (2019). Females lead big rise in football participation rate. Retrieved February 21, 2019 from https://womens.afl/news/16754/females-lead-big-rise-in-football-participation-rate

Anderson, E. (2008). 'I used to think women were weak': Orthodox masculinity, gender segregation, and sport. *Sociological Forum*, 23(2), 257–280.

Anderson, E. (2009). The maintenance of masculinity among the stakeholders of sport. *Sport Management Review*, 12(1), 3–14.

Baghurst, T., Tapps, T., & Judy, A. (2014). A comparison of sport commitment in female-only versus co-recreational intramural basketball leagues. *Recreational Sports Journal*, 38(2), 143–152.

Balyi, I., Way, R., & Higgs, C. (2001). Sport system building and long-term athlete development in British Columbia, Canada. *Coaches Report*, 8(1), 22–28.

Berg, B. K., Warner, S., & Das, B. M. (2015). What about sport? A public health perspective on leisure-time physical activity. *Sport Management Review*, 18(1), 20–31.

Birrell, S. J. (1988). Discourses on the gender/sport relationship: from women in sport to gender relations. *Exercise and Sport Sciences Reviews*, 16(1), 459–502.

Bowers, M. T., Chalip, L., & Green, B. C. (2011). Beyond the façade: Youth sport development in the United States and the illusion of synergy. In B. Houlihan and M. Green (eds), *Routledge Handbook of Sports Development* (pp. 173–183). Oxfordshire, UK: Routledge.

Bullingham, R., Magrath, R., & Anderson, E. (2014). Sport and a cultural shift away from homohysteria. In B. Houlihan and M. Green (eds), *Routledge Handbook of Sports Development* (pp. 275–280). Oxfordshire, UK: Routledge.

Canadian Government (2009, January 1). Actively engaged: A policy on sport for women and girls. *Canadian Heritage*. Retrieved from www.canada.ca/en/canadian-heritage/services/sport-policies-acts-regulations/policy-actively-engaged-women-girls.html#a4

CBS News (2019, January 29). Toni Harris, featured in Super Bowl ad, aspires to be 1st female NFL player. New York, NY: CBS this Morning. Retrieved from www.cbsnews.com/news/super-bowl-toyota-ad-features-toni-harris-woman-who-wants-to-be-first-female-nfl-player/

Cerin, E., Leslie, E., Sugiyama, T., & Owen, N. (2010). Perceived barriers to leisure-time physical activity in adults: an ecological perspective. *Journal of Physical Activity and Health*, 7(4), 451–459.

Colasimone, D. (2016). Women's AFL competition could spark turf war with netball, cricket, W-League and rugby. Retrieved from www.abc.net.au/news/2016-09-15/turf-war-in-womens-sport-would-be-great-for-female-athletes/7844516

Darroch, F. E., Giles, A. R., Hillsburg, H., & McGettigan-Dumas, R. (2019). Running from responsibility: athletic governing bodies, corporate sponsors, and the failure to support pregnant and postpartum elite female distance runners. *Sport in Society*. doi:10.1080/17430437.2019.1567495

De Bosscher, V., Shibli, S., Westerbeek, H., & van Bottenburg, M. (2016). Convergence and divergence of elite sport policies: Is there a one-size-fits-all model to develop international sporting success? *Journal of Global Sport Management*, 1(3–4), 70–89.

De Bosscher, V., De Knop, P., Van Bottenburg, M., Shibli, S., & Bingham, J. (2009). Explaining international sporting success: An international comparison of elite sport systems and policies in six countries. *Sport Management Review*, 12(3), 113–136.

Eady, J. (1993). *Practical Sports Development*. London: Pitman.

Edwards, M. B., Kanters, M. A., & Bocarro, J. N. (2014). Peer reviewed: Policy changes to implement intramural sports in North Carolina middle schools: Simulated effects on sports participation rates and physical activity intensity, 2008–2009. *Preventing Chronic Disease*, 11. doi:10.5888/pcd11.130195

Evans, B. (2006). 'I'd feel ashamed': Girls' bodies and sports participation. *Gender, Place & Culture*, 13(5), 547–561.

Fink, J. S. (2015). Female athletes, women's sport, and the sport media commercial complex: Have we really 'come a long way, baby'? *Sport Management Review*, 18(3), 331–342.

Fletcher, F. (1985). The making and breaking of a female tradition: women's physical education in England 1880–1980. *The International Journal of the History of Sport*, 2(1), 29–39.

Ford, P., De Ste Croix, M., Lloyd, R., Meyers, R., Moosavi, M., Oliver, J., Till, K., & Williams, C. (2011). The long-term athlete development model: Physiological evidence and application. *Journal of Sports Sciences*, 29(40), 389–402.

George, E. (2017). Childbirth no longer roadblock to professional netball careers. Retrieved from www.theaustralian.com.au/life/health-wellbeing/childbirth-no-longer-roadblock-to-professional-netball-careers/news-story/852cc64eee39b025d3029af3414b2887

Green, B. C. (2005). Building sport programs to optimize athlete recruitment, retention, and transition: Toward a normative theory of sport development. *Journal of Sport Management*, 19, 233–253.

Green, B. C., & Chalip, L. (1998). Antecedents and consequences of parental purchase decision involvement in youth sport. *Leisure Sciences*, 20(2), 95–109.

Green, M., & Collins, S. (2008). Policy, politics and path dependency: Sport development in Australia and Finland. *Sport Management Review*, 11(3), 225–251.

Gulbin, J.P., Croser, M. J., Morley, E.J., & Weissensteiner, J. R. (2013). An integrated framework for the optimisation of sport and athlete development. *Journal of Sports Sciences*, 31(12), 1319–1331.

Gye, L. (2015). Mission statements and cake stalls: The women's supporter group in Australian Football League clubs. *The International Journal of the History of Sport*, 32(18), 1–13.

Harber, V. (2007). The female athlete perspective: Coach, parent, administrator guide. *Canadian Sport for Life*. Retrieved from http://sportforlife.ca/wp-content/uploads/2016/11/The-Female-Athlete-Perspective-1.pdf

Hargraves, J. (1994). *Sporting Females: Critical Issues in the History and Sociology of Women's Sports*. London: Routledge.

Hess, R. (2000). 'Ladies are specially invited': women in the culture of Australian rules football. *The International Journal of the History of Sport*, 17(2–3), 111–141.

Houlihan, B., & Green, M. (eds). (2008). *Comparative Elite Sport Development*. London: Routledge.

Kingsley, B. C., & Spencer-Cavaliere, N. (2015). The exclusionary practices of youth sport. *Social Inclusion*, 3(3), 24–38.

Laurendeau, J., & Sharara, N. (2008). "Women Could Be Every Bit As Good As Guys" Reproductive and Resistant Agency in Two "Action" Sports. *Journal of Sport and Social Issues*, 32(1), 24–47.

Lennon, S. (2013). Journalism, gender, feminist theory and news reporting on the Australian Football League. *eJournalist*, 13(1), 20–39.

Liechty, T., Sveinson, K., Willfong, F., & Evans, K. (2015). 'It doesn't matter how big or small you are… there's a position for you': Body image among female tackle football players. *Leisure Sciences*, 37(2), 109–124.

McCrone, K. E. (1991). Class, gender, and English women's sport, c. 1890–1914. *Journal of Sport History*, 18(1), 159–182.

Mewett, P., & Toffoletti, K. (2011). Finding footy: Female fan socialization and Australian rules football. *Sport in Society*, 14(5), 670–684.

Newland, B. L. (2019). The delivery and management of women-only sport events and their future sustainability. In N. Lough & A.N. Geurin (eds), *Routledge Handbook of the Business of Women's Sport* (pp. 95–100). London: Routledge.

Newland, B. L., & Bowers, M. T. (2013). Managing a confederation of rivals. *Sport Management Review*, 16(3), 388–396.

Newland, B. L., & Kellett, P. (2012). Exploring new models of elite sport delivery: The case of triathlon in the USA and Australia. *Managing Leisure*, 17(2–3), 170–181.

Newland, B. L., Dixon, M. A., & Green, B. C. (2013). Engaging children through sport: Examining the disconnect between program vision and implementation. *Journal of Physical Activity and Health*, 10(6), 805–812.

Our Kids (2018). Sports schools and programs. Our Kids. Retrieved from www.ourkids.net/sports-schools.php

Pfister, G. (2015). Assessing the sociology of sport: On women and football. *International Review for the Sociology of Sport*, 50(4–5), 563–569.

Phillips, P., & Newland, B. (2014). Emergent models of sport development and delivery: The case of triathlon in Australia and the US. *Sport Management Review*, 17(2), 107–120.

Rowe, K., Shilbury, D., Ferkins, L., & Hinckson, E. (2016). Challenges for sport development: Women's entry level cycling participation. *Sport Management Review*, 19(4), 417–430.

Sabo, D., & Veliz, P. (2008). *Go Out and Play: Youth Sports in America*. East Meadow, NY: Women's Sports Foundation.

Sanders, K. (2015). Mean girls, homosociality and football: an education on social and power dynamics between girls and women. *Gender and Education*, 27(7), 887–908.

Shell, A. (2017, September). Why families stretch their budgets for high-priced youth sports. *USA Today*. Retrieved from www.usatoday.com/story/money/2017/09/05/ why-families-stretch-their-budgets-high-priced-youth-sports/571945001/

Shifrer, D., Pearson, J., Muller, C., & Wilkinson, L. (2015). College-going benefits of high school sports participation: Race and gender differences over three decades. *Youth & Society*, 47(3), 295–318.

Sotiriadou, K., Shilbury, D., & Quick, S. (2008). The attraction, retention/transition, and nurturing process of sport development: Some Australian evidence. *Journal of Sport Management*, 22(3), 247–272.

SportAUS (2018). Sporting schools: About. Retrieved from www.sportingschools.gov.au/about

Staurowsky, E. J., Hogshead-Makar, N., Kane, M. J., Wughalter, E., Yiamouyiannis, A., & Lerner, P. K. (2006). Gender equity in physical education and athletics. Retrieved from www.feminist.org/sports/18%20Physical%20Ed%20%20Athletics.pdf

Stewart, M. F., Stavros, C., Phillips, P., Mitchell, H., & Barake, A. J. (2016). Like father, like son: Analyzing Australian Football's unique recruitment process. *Journal of Sport Management*, 30(6), 672–688.

Theberge, N. (1998). 'Same sport, different gender.' A consideration of binary gender logic and the sport continuum in the case of ice hockey. *Journal of Sport and Social Issues*, 22(2), 183–198.

Title IX of the Education Amendments Act, 20 U.S. Code § 1681 (1972).

Vail, S. E. (2007). Community development and sport participation. *Journal of Sport Management*, 21(4), 571–596.

Velija, P., Ratna, A., & Flintoff, A. (2014). Exclusionary power in sports organisations: The merger between the Women's Cricket Association and the England and Wales Cricket Board. *International Review for the Sociology of Sport*, 49(2), 211–226.

Walker, N., & Bopp, T. (2011). The under representation of women in the male dominated sport workplace: perspectives of female coaches. *Journal of Workplace Rights*, 15(1), 47–64.

Waterhouse-Watson, D. (2012). Framing the victim: Sexual assault and Australian footballers on television. *Australian Feminist Studies*, 27(71), 55–70.

Won, S. (2017, October 18). Canadian universities have a game plan for wooing top athletes. Canadian University Report. Retrieved from www.theglobeandmail.com/news/national/education/canadian-university-report/canadian-universities-have-a-game-plan-for-wooing-top-athletes/article36634827/

Xing, X., Chalip, L., & Green, B. C. (2014). Marketing a social experience: how celebration of subculture leads to social spending during a sport event. *Sport Marketing Quarterly*, 23(3), 138–148.

3
DEVELOPING SPORT FOR GIRLS AND ADOLESCENTS

Rochelle Eime, Meghan Casey and Jack Harvey

Introduction

This chapter aims to provide an understanding of the motivations for sport participation among young and adolescent girls, as well as an understanding of the barriers to participation that young and adolescent girls face. Motivations to participate in sport do not work in isolation from barriers to participation – the two domains are often linked in a complex web of influences and preferences. The chapter also provides enlightening examples of sport programming that support inclusion of and engagement with girls and adolescents in sport. We present and discuss sport participation trends among girls and adolescents and investigate the key drivers for participation in sport across the intrapersonal, interpersonal, and organisational/ environmental domains of the socioecological model (McLeroy, et al., 1988).

Internationally, the definition of sport is not uniform or universal, and for this chapter we have focused on organised and generally competitive, community-level, club-based activities; we do not include other recreational leisure-time physical activities, such as non-competitive running, swimming or going to the gym. By this definition, the majority of sport opportunities for girls and adolescents involve traditional competitive sport models. However, it is important to note that there are also many entry-level modified sport programmes offered to girls, which focus on the development of sport skills in a fun and inclusive environment, rather than a focus on competition and winning (Eime, et al., 2018b).

Participation trends

A sport participation rate is the proportion of a population – or a sub-population defined by characteristics like age or gender – who participate in sport at a particular time, for example in a particular season or year. Sport participation rates differ according to many factors, including gender, age and residential location of participants; they also vary in terms of the types of sport programmes and other sport and non-sport activities that are available. Women and girls are consistently reported to participate in sport at lower rates than men and boys across the lifespan (Eime, et al., 2016a; Eime, et al., 2018c; Somerset & Hoare, 2018). Girls are also less likely than boys to start participating in sport at a very early age (Eime, et al., 2016b), with a higher proportion of boys than girls participating among children aged 4–7 (Eime, et al., 2016a).

Recent research suggests that there are optimum ages of entry into sport that facilitate continued sport participation. In a four-year study of 13,760 girls, the optimal age of entry into junior modified sport programmes for continued participation and transition into club competition was found to be 7–9 years (Eime, et al., 2018b). Another study, which included boys and girls participating in modified sport programmes, reported that the majority of children withdrew from participation in the sport during the four-year period, rather than transitioning from the modified sport programme to club competition (Eime, et al., 2015a). Across the ages 4–12, 24.5% of girls and 13.6% of boys transitioned to club sport competition within the four-year period. Furthermore, two-thirds of children (67.4%) withdrew from participation in their sport after the first year/season of the study (Eime, et al., 2015a).

Beyond childhood, many changes occur in participation in sport throughout the lifespan, beginning with a sharp decline during adolescence (Crane & Temple, 2015; Eime, et al., 2016a). While participation in sport is popular amongst young girls, particularly those aged 5–14, after this age, girls often drop out of competitive sport and choose to be physically active in non-competitive forms of leisure-time physical activity, such as going for a run or to the gym, or they become inactive (Eime, et al., 2016c). Girls' participation rates in sport peak at ages 10–14 and then drop by half in the ages of 15–19 years and drop by half again during the ages of 20–24 years (Eime, et al., 2016b). Internationally, girls and boys are more likely to play team sports, whereas adolescents are more likely to participate in non-sport activities such as walking, running and athletics (Hulteen, et al., 2017).

Several factors contribute to this drop-off in sport participation. The competitive nature of sport is not attractive to many adolescent girls and some indicate a preference for more social options (Rowe, et al., 2018). Furthermore, some feel that they do not have the necessary sport skills to gain a position in a team (Casey, et al., 2009; Eime, et al., 2015b). The increasing importance of other life priorities may also decrease the capacity or inclination of some to fit in with the organised structures and time commitments imposed by many sports (Eime, et al., 2010). Girls report that increasing levels of school education pressure, socialising with peers, part time work, as well as body image concerns, make engaging in sport more difficult (Rowe, et al., 2018). Some recommendations for retaining adolescent girls in sport include the provision of social sport options, having women and girls-only sessions, keeping friendship groups together, devising strategies to develop sport specific skills, and identifying and promoting women role models (Rowe, et al., 2018).

There are also regional differences in participation in sport, with higher rates of participation observed in regional and rural areas compared to metropolitan areas, particularly in traditional sports (Eime, et al., 2017). It has been suggested that this increased participation in regional areas relates to the significant social role that community sport plays in non-metropolitan regions (Eime, et al., 2017); the choice of traditional sports is argued to be related to the limited offerings in regional areas, which sees traditional sports dominate, as opposed to the vast array of leisure activities available within metropolitan areas (Eime, et al., 2017).

Socioecological determinants of sport participation for young and adolescent girls

Following the model used in previous studies (for example, Casey, et al., 2009 and Vella, et al., 2014), in this chapter, we categorise the determinants of sport participation – the motivations and barriers – into the domains of the socioecological model (McLeroy, et al., 1988), specifically the intrapersonal, interpersonal, and organisational/environmental domains. While these are discussed separately here, it is acknowledged that the determinants are interrelated across each domain. For example, for young girls and adolescents, a key determinant of participation is enjoyment (intrapersonal), which is often motivated by playing with friends (interpersonal), and a barrier to enjoyment might be some aspect of club culture (organisational/environmental).

Intrapersonal

At the core, a primary internal motivation for children and adolescents to participate in sport is fun and enjoyment (Eime & Harvey, 2018a; Rowe, et al., 2018). At the core, a primary internal motivation for children and adolescents to participate in sport is fun and enjoyment (Eime & Harvey, 2018; Rowe, et al., 2018); when girls are not having fun playing sport, they often drop out. Girls' enjoyment in sport can often be enhanced by women and girls-only participation (Rowe, et al., 2018) or by the specific type or structure of the activity (Eime & Harvey, 2018a). The main other intrapersonal motivator for girls and adolescents to be physically active is overall health and fitness (Rowe, et al., 2018; Rowe, et al., 2015).

A common barrier to participation in sport is a perceived and/or actual lack of skills or competency (Eime, et al., 2015b; O'Neal, et al., 2015). Women and girls often have fewer opportunities to acquire fundamental movement skills and sport specific skills early in life (O'Neal, et al., 2015). Not being good at sport can also relate to a fear of being judged (Somerset & Hoare, 2018). A recent study reported that the peak entry age into modified sports programmes, with the highest rates of transition into club competition, was 7–9 years (Eime, et al., 2018b). A person starting to play sport at age ten or older may be limited in their competency, compared with those who have played for several years (Eime, et al., 2015a). Feeling self-conscious while playing sport may be related to playing with boys, a lack of competency or to girls' body image and the uniform requirements (O'Neal, et al., 2015).

While not gender-specific, the cost of participation and continued participation across childhood can be a barrier to participation (O'Neal, et al., 2015; Somerset &

Hoare, 2018), especially for those in socioeconomically disadvantaged areas (Basterfield, et al., 2015; Eime, et al., 2018b). More specifically, it has been recognised that the transition from modified sport to club competition is associated with increased participation costs, such as club memberships, uniforms and other associated costs, such as travel to home-and-away games (Eime, et al., 2015a). It may be that modified sports programmes provide a value-for-money sporting opportunity, but then club competition becomes too costly for families with low socioeconomic status (Eime, et al., 2015a). A lack of time is also commonly reported as a barrier to participation in sport (O'Neal, et al., 2015; Somerset & Hoare, 2018), and for adolescent girls this can relate to other competing activities and changes in priorities for their use of leisure time (Crane & Temple, 2015; Eime, et al., 2015b).

Interpersonal

An important contributing factor to fun and enjoyment for girls playing sport is support from their friends, peers and family (Eime, et al., 2015b; Hayoz, et al., 2017). Girls generally enjoy playing sport with their friends, often in women and girls-only activities and social settings (Eime & Harvey, 2018a; Howie, et al., 2018). Girls often take up playing sport because they have been encouraged by family, and this is often because parents or older siblings have played the particular sport (Rowe, et al., 2018). Parental support can include financial support, transport and role modelling, as well as emotional support (Howie, et al., 2018; Somerset & Hoare, 2018). However, in general, support from family and peers for participation in sport significantly decreases during late adolescence for girls (Eime, et al., 2015b).

In contrast to levels of peer support, however, girls in their adolescent years are often becoming increasingly concerned about being judged negatively by their peers (Slater & Tiggemann, 2010;Somerset & Hoare, 2018), or are teased by boys for their ongoing participation in sport (Eime, et al., 2010). Girls want to comply with the norms of their peer group, including the image of what is seen as cool to participate in, and they do not want to be embarrassed amongst their peers (Rowe, et al., 2018). This also relates to gender stereotypes, and there is evidence that girls and women participating in stereotypical 'feminine' sports, such as netball and gymnastics, are often given higher status, as rated by their peers, compared to those participating in stereotypical 'masculine' sports, such as football (Howie, et al., 2018). Often, boys and girls do not enjoy playing sport together; the boys can dominate the play or game and fail to engage with the girls (Somerset & Hoare, 2018). Competitive rivalry and poor culture can lead to teasing and a lack of enjoyment for girls (Rowe, et al., 2018).

Organisational and environmental

The onset of adolescence, a period marked by many personal and social changes, is time of transition, one of the most significant of which is the transition from primary to secondary school. At this point, a clear distinction in trends in participation and barriers to participation in sport for women and girls is noted (Basterfield, et al., 2015;

Eime, et al., 2016c). Adolescent girls are likely to drop out of competitive sport and replace it with non-competitive forms of physical activity (Eime, et al., 2016c). Much research attention has been aimed at raising the low levels of participation in sport and physical activity in this group, mostly focused on the school environment (Mooney & Casey, 2014; Okely, et al., 2017). However, most of the school interventions have not been successful, sometimes due to failures in implementation of the intervention (Okely, et al., 2017), and participation in school physical education also decreases sharply in late adolescence for girls (Eime, et al., 2016c).

An important aspect of the organisational/environmental domain is the issue of female-friendly environments; this relates not only to the design and availability of suitable change rooms, and associated access and safety issues in local sports clubs (O'Neal, et al., 2015), but also to the general support and provision of opportunities for girls' participation (Rowe, et al., 2018). A three-year longitudinal study of adolescent girls showed that health-promoting sports club characteristics, such as smoke-free and injury prevention strategies, along with a welcoming environment, were important positive influences on participation in club sport (Casey, et al., 2017).

Regarding the broader issue of gender inequalities evident within sport and sports clubs, there has been extensive research highlighting the social construction of sport, the power differences between men's and women's sport, and the lower value society places on the participation of girls and women in sport (Alsarve, 2018; Spaaij, et al., 2015). Sports clubs are socially constructed and there is deep history of power relations associated with gender and politics of identity within sports clubs. Furthermore, there is often a male-dominated culture in sport that is a barrier to girls' and women's involvement (Rowe, et al., 2018) and many sports have traditionally been male dominated (Eime & Harvey, 2018a). Despite considerable development in sport participation opportunities for women and girls, there is still strong gender stereotyping in sport, which is culturally shaped and embedded, and to which girls often feel the need to conform (Somerset & Hoare, 2018; Crane & Temple, 2015).

Despite increased opportunities for women and girls to play sport, they are still much under-represented in all levels of leadership positions, including executive officer and board positions, as well as among coaches and officials (Burton, 2015). The challenge is how to change systems and culture to normalise women in leadership positions. The gender imbalance is also apparent in the limited representation of women's sport and of women role models in the media (O'Neal, et al., 2015; Rowe, et al., 2018). Other gender equity issues include women and girls teams and individual participants not receiving equal access to playing spaces, training venues and other resources, such as coaching and equipment, and 'unfriendly' scheduling of matches and training sessions late in the evening or very early in the morning (O'Neal, et al., 2015).

The construction of sports club in Australia and other countries is that they are governed and run by volunteers. With recent policy and investment strategies aimed at increasing opportunities for women and girls throughout a wider range of sports, there may be issues related to volunteer capacity at clubs to cater for an influx of participants (Eime & Harvey, 2018a).

Approaches to increase sport participation for adolescent girls

The challenges facing the engagement and retention of adolescent girls in sport are increasingly recognised by various levels of government around the world (Parliament of Canada, 2017; Sport and Recreation Victoria, 2015; Sport England, 2006) and various health and sports organisations (Brunette, et al., 2016; VicHealth, 2015). As such, deliberate policies, investment, programmes and strategies have been created in an attempt to improve levels of sport participation by women and girls. For example, in 2015 Sport England launched a nationwide campaign in the United Kingdom (UK) This Girl Can to encourage more women to be active. Likewise, the Victorian Health Promotion Foundation (VicHealth) invested in Changing the Game (2015) in Victoria, Australia, which provided funding to sports to develop and implement modified recreation sport programmes for women and girls. VicHealth has also invested in the Active Women and Girls for Health and Wellbeing programme (2017), which included funding for sporting organisations to create opportunities for women and girls in sport and physical activity and funding to promote gender equality and increase the profile of women's sport.

Many campaigns, including those identified above, have tended to target women and girls in general and not specific age groups or gender identities. Further, the various campaigns and programmes to encourage more women and girls to participate in sport have not been fully or independently evaluated to determine their effectiveness. For instance, the media campaign This Girl Can has been linked to an increase of 250,000 women participating in sport by Sport England (Sport England, 2016), but the evidence base for this claim is not strong, due to the lack of detailed and published evaluation reports. Media campaigns – including those which use social media platforms – are often used as a strategy to encourage people to be physically active (Craig, et al., 2015; Zhang, et al., 2015). These types of campaigns have been shown to increase awareness of the messaging and the brand, and sometimes self-efficacy, but they are often not associated with significant increases in levels of activity (Craig, et al., 2015; Zhang, et al., 2015).

There is an absence of high-quality evidence on the outcomes of policies, programmes and interventions that are designed and delivered by sporting organisations to increase sport participation (Allison, et al., 2017; Priest, et al., 2008). Research on the effectiveness of programmes and interventions targeting adolescent girls has tended to focus on physical activity and as such has examined physical activity outcomes rather than sport participation (Pearson, et al., 2015; van Sluijs, et al., 2007). In addition, many interventions have used sport settings such as school sport and physical education to try and improve adolescent girls' physical activity levels (Casey,, et al. 2014; Lonsdale, et al., 2013; Lubans, et al., 2012). These interventions have reported outcomes associated with physical activity and/or health. For example, interventions have resulted in increases in the proportion of time students spend in moderate-to-vigorous physical activity (Lonsdale, et al., 2013), changes in body composition (Lubans, et al., 2012), and maintenance of the level of health-related quality of life, against a background of a general decline during adolescence (Casey, 2014). Others have found limited success in school-based programmes, predominantly due to lack of implementation by intervention schools (Okely, et al., 2017). There is also research that has used sport as a vehicle for social change to promote health, academic success or develop life skills (Bruening, et al., 2009; Hemphill & Richards, 2016). Again, these studies tend not to specifically target sport participation and retention or measure sport-related outcomes.

Physical activity research has found that multicomponent interventions and interventions based on theory have strong intervention effects on behaviour for adolescent girls (Pearson, et al., 2015; van Sluijs, et al., 2007). For instance, Pearson, et al. (2015) concluded that multicomponent interventions that contain a 'combination of support components (i.e. family, friends, etc.), individual components (i.e. specifically tailored programmes for individuals/groups), choice components (different options to facilitate behaviour change), and educational and environmental components targeting during- and after-school behaviours' (p. 13) were almost twice as effective when compared with programmes designed to focus on singular components. The results suggested that different agencies – e.g. schools, community organisations – might need to work together rather than rely on one setting, such as the school or family.

Effectiveness of programmes and interventions addressing adolescent girls' sport participation

Only a small number of studies, programmes and interventions have specifically addressed adolescent girls' sport participation and examined their effectiveness and programme features. For instance, in a systematic review that examined evidence for the effectiveness of team sport interventions for adolescent girls, only four studies were found. These studies were found in the 'grey literature', which refers to studies that have not gone through a formal, peer review process, a process that verifies the reliability of the research outcomes (Allison, et al., 2017). Although the review was limited to studies in the UK, it supports the view that there is a lack of evidence-based research on sport participation programmes (Allison, et al., 2017). The review reported on participation outcomes and identified several areas for consideration in terms of facilitating girls' participation in sport (Allison, et al., 2017). The authors identified the importance of consulting with girls about all aspects of their sport participation: programme design and format; the importance of encouraging girls to try new sports and sustain participation; the need for relatable, healthy role models in the media; and the role of the coach, who is a key factor in the enjoyment, motivation and attendance in sports programmes by adolescent girls. Reported participation outcomes were mostly positive, although limited to assessing programme reach and perceptions of physical education teachers about changes in girls' physical activity (Allison, et al., 2017).

An Australian intervention study conducted in an organised youth sports setting – a school holiday basketball programme – aimed to increase adolescent girls' moderate-to-vigorous physical activity (MVPA) levels via education sessions for coaches (Guagliano, et al., 2015). The authors found that brief coach education sessions (2 x 2hr sessions) that focused on strategies to increase MVPA and decrease inactivity during practice can increase MVPA without effects on players' motivation to participate

(Guagliano, et al., 2015). The organised youth sport setting provides an opportunity to encourage youth to accumulate MVPA and meet physical activity guidelines. However, Guagliano and colleagues' study (2015) targeted girls already involved in organised youth sport and not those who do not participate or have dropped out. Furthermore, the outcome measures were not specifically sport related.

More recent intervention studies have examined the effects of a ball skill intervention on preschool-age girls' ball skill performance (Veldman, et al., 2017), which might contribute to future sport participation. This study found that girls in the intervention experienced significant gains in ball skills at both post-test and retention (after nine weeks), indicating that early childhood interventions that focus on the development of ball skills in young girls might help improve girls' ball skill performance (Veldman, et al., 2017), which is likely to be important for perceived sport competence and future sport participation.

Conclusion and recommendations

Girls and women participate in sport at much lower rates than boys and men. This is related historically to the cultural norms associated with girls and women playing sport. Historically, there were few opportunities for girls and women to play certain sports, for example, soccer, cricket or Australian Rules football. In recent years, opportunities for girls and women to play a sport of their choice have increasingly become available. Sport policies and investment, specifically targeting the growth of women's and girls' participation in sport, have increasingly been observed. However, there are still barriers which limit their participation in sport.

The development of physical literacy early in life is very important and opportunities for girls to obtain fundamental movement skills and competency are needed, in the home, at school and through community sport. Young women and girls need to have support from family, friends, teachers and coaches to develop their sport skills and competency. The sport programmes and offerings need to be enjoyable for girls and young women, particularly their motivations for participation. People need to have a choice of what sports they play. This includes sport opportunities that cater for those who desire to play competitively and for those who wish to play non-competitive sport. It is also recommended that sports specifically focus on retention of girls and young women, and to achieve this, different sport offerings across the lifespan are required. Women and girls-only programmes, teams and physical education sessions should be encouraged, especially in school-based settings.

At the broader level, there will not be significant changes to women and girls' participation in sport without strategic policy and investment to increase capacity of facilities and club volunteers, as well as continued cultural change regarding gender equity, attitudes, media focus and representation in sport organisational structures. Broader sport and public health policy should include multiple components and not rely solely on mass media campaigns without specific strategies to increase participation for those who are inactive or least active. Strategies to implement cultural change within sports clubs are required. Furthermore, there should be rigorous, independent evaluation of all interventions and investments to better identify what kind of strategies and interventions are most effective.

CASE STUDY

Ballarat women's and girls' cricket

In recent years, in Australia, there have been strategic developments to introduce more opportunities for women and girls to play cricket, which has long been a traditionally male dominated sport. For example, Cricket Australia recently developed the Growing Cricket for Girls Fund, which was an investment initiative to support the development of girls' community level cricket competitions. This funding supported a competition coordinator, equipment costs, marketing and promotional materials, and coach accreditation.

The available funding prompted the cricket community in the regional city of Ballarat, Victoria, Australia to develop a women and girls-only competition that aimed to provide young girls with the opportunity to play competitive cricket in female-only environments.

Development took place in 2016 and the competition was launched in Summer 2016/2017. The developmental phase included discussions with a wide range of stakeholders, including academic researchers in the field of girls' and women's participation in sport, women cricketers, and all levels of cricket administration and governance. This consultation provided guidance on the format of the competition and a smaller working party was formed. Participant recruitment was conducted through schools, and cricket clubs and associations, with entry level and come-and-try programmes offered.

Participation has grown considerably within a short period of time. In the first season there was one competition with nine clubs. In the second season, this grew to two competitions with different junior game formats. The third season saw investment and improvement of women and girls-friendly facilities. Now that the demand for the different competitions and programmes is strong and growing, the Ballarat Cricket Association has developed the inaugural women's senior cricket club and competition in the region. This now provides a true pathway for female cricketers in the region.

Having all teams and participants (from multiple clubs), play at the same location/facility worked well to create a vibrant atmosphere and allowed the participants and their parents to see a clear cricket pathway with different levels of programmes and competitions being played. Initially, due to lack of capacity and availability of infrastructure including facilities and ovals, the facilities and playing surface were sub-standard. However, this was soon recognised, and improved facilities have now been provided, including suitable change rooms and toilets.

Women and girl participants simply wanted access to try sports like cricket, which traditionally had not been made available to women and girls at club level. Initially, the women and girls played in existing clubs which also had teams for men and boys. However, in a recent development, a new female-only club was created in 2018 to assist with breaking down the barriers to women's and girls' participation in cricket. The Ballarat Women's Cricket Club facilitates entry level and open-age competition programmes with the aim to build a complete cricket pathway for women and girls in cricket in the coming seasons/years. For girls' and women's participation in sport to develop, it is important that they have a voice and are heard.

References

Allison, R., Bird, E. L., & McClean, S. (2017). Is team sport the key to getting everybody active, every day? A systematic review of physical activity interventions aimed at increasing girls' participation in team sport. *AIMS Public Health*, 4(2), 202–220.

Alsarve, D. (2018). Addressing gender equality: Enactments of gender and hegemony in the education textbooks used in Swedish sports coaching and educational programmes. *Sport Education and Society*, 23(9), 840–852.

Basterfield, L., Reilly, J., Pearce, M., Partkinson, K., Adamson, A., Reilly, J., & Vella, S. (2015). Longitudinal associations between sports participation, body composition and physical activity from childhood to adolescence. *Journal of Science and Medicine in Sport*, 18(2), 178–182.

Bruening, J. E., Dover, K. M., & Clark, B. S. (2009). Preadolescent female development through sport and physical activity. *Research Quarterly for Exercise and Sport*, 80(1), 87–101.

Brunette, M., Scarapicchia, T., & Micay, R. (2016). Women in sport: Fuelling a lifetime of participation. A report on the status of female sport participation in Canada. Canada's Dairy Farmers and The Canadian Association for the Advancement of Women and Sport and Physical Activity (CAAWS). Retrieved from www.womenchampions.ca/bundles/dfcwomenchampions/dist/pdf/research-short.pdf

Burton, L. (2015). Underrepresentation of women in sport leadership: A review of research. *Sport Management Review*, 18(2), 155–165.

Casey, M., Eime, R., Payne, W., & Harvey, J. (2009). Using a socioecological approach to examine participation in sport and physical activity among rural adolescent girls. *Qualitative Health Research*, 19(7), 881–893.

Casey, M., Harvey, J. T., Telford, A., Eime, R. M., Mooney, A., & Payne, W. R. (2014). Effectiveness of a school-community linked program on physical activity levels and health-related quality of life for adolescent girls. *BMC Public Health*, 14(649), 1–15.

Casey, M., Eime, R., Harvey, J., Sawyer, N., Craike, M., Symons, C., & Payne, W. (2017). The influence of a healthy welcoming environment on participation in club sport by adolescent girls: A longitudinal study. *BMC Sports Science, Medicine and Rehabilitation*, 9(12).

Craig, C. L., Bauman, A., Latimer-Cheung, A., Rhodes, R. E., Faulkner, G., Berry, T. R., … Spence, J. C. (2015). An evaluation of the My ParticipACTION campaign to increase self-efficacy for being more physically active. *Journal of Health Communication*, 20(9), 995–1003.

Crane, J., & Temple, V. (2015). A systematic review of dropout from organized sport among children and youth. *European Physical Education Review*, 21(1), 114–131.

Eime, R., & Harvey, J. (2018a). Sport participation across the lifespan: Australian trends and policy implications. In R. Dionigi & M. Gard (eds), *Sport and Physical Activity across the Lifespan* (pp. 23–43). UK: Palgrave Macmillan.

Eime, R., Harvey, J., & Charity, M. (2018b). Girls' transition from participation in a modified sport program to club sport competition – a study of longitudinal patterns and correlates. *BMC Public Health*, 18(718).

Eime, R. M., Harvey, J. T., Charity, M. J., & Nelson, R. (2018c). Demographic characteristics and type/frequency of physical activity participation in a large sample of 21,603 Australian people. *BMC Public Health*, 18(1), 692.

Eime, R., Harvey, J., Charity, M., & Payne, W. (2016b). Population levels of sport participation: Implications for sport policy. *BMC Public Health*, 16(1), 1–8.

Eime, R., Payne, W., Casey, M., & Harvey, J. (2010). Transition in participation in sport and unstructured physical activity for rural living adolescent girls. *Health Education Research*, 25(2), 282–293.

Eime, R. M., Casey, M. M., Harvey, J. T., Charity, M. J., Young, J. A., & Payne, W. R. (2015a). Participation in modified sports programs: A longitudinal study of children's transition to club sport competition. *BMC Public Health*, 15(649).

Eime, R. M., Casey, M. M., Harvey, J. T., Sawyer, N. A., Symons, C. M., & Payne, W. R. (2015b). Socioecological factors potentially associated with participation in physical activity and sport: A longitudinal study of adolescent girls. *Journal of Science and Medicine in Sport*, 18(6), 684–690.

Eime, R., Harvey, J., Charity, M. J., Casey, M., Westerbeek, H., & Payne, W. R. (2017). The relationship of sport participation to provision of sports facilities and socioeconomic status: a geographical analysis. *Australian and New Zealand Journal of Public Health*, 41(3), 248–255.

Eime, R., Harvey, J., Charity, M., Casey, M., Westerbeek, H., & Payne, W. (2016a). Age profiles of sport participants. *BMC Sports Science, Medicine and Rehabilitation*, 8(6).

Eime, R., Harvey, J., Sawyer, N., Craike, M., Symons, C., & Payne, W. (2016c). Changes in sport and physical activity participation for adolescent females: A longitudinal study. *BMC Public Health*, 16(533).

Guagliano, J. M., Lonsdale, C., Kolt, G. S., Rosenkranz, R. R., & George, E. S. (2015). Increasing girls' physical activity during a short-term organized youth sport basketball program: A randomized controlled trial. *Journal of Science and Medicine in Sport*, 18(4), 412–417.

Hayoz, C., Klostermann, C., & Schmid, J. (2017). Intergenerational transfer of a sports-related lifestyle within the family. *International Review for the Sociology of Sport*, 54(2). 182–198.

Hemphill, M. A., & Richards, K. A. R. (2016). Without the academic part, it wouldn't be squash": Youth development in an urban squash program. *Journal of Teaching in Physical Education*, 35(3), 263–276.

Howie, E. K., Daniels, B. T., & Guagliano, J. M. (2018). Promoting physical activity through youth sports programs: It's social. *American Journal of Lifestyle Medicine*. doi:10.1177/559827618754842

Hulteen, R. M., Smith, J. J., Morgan, P. J., Barnett, L. M., Hallal, P. C., Colyvas, K., & Lubans, D. R. (2017). Global participation in sport and leisure-time physical activities: A systematic review and meta-analysis. *Preventive Medicine*, 95, 14–25.

Lonsdale, C., Rosenkranz, R., Peralta, L., Bennie, A., Fahey, P., & Lubans, D. (2013). A systematic review and meta-analysis of interventions designed to increase moderate-to-vigorous physical activity in school physical education lessons. *Preventive Medicine*, 56(2), 152–161.

Lubans, D. R., Morgan, P. J., Okely, A. D., Dewar, D., Collins, C. E., Batterham, M., ... Plotnikoff, R. C. (2012). Preventing obesity among adolescent girls: One-year outcomes of the nutrition and enjoyable activity for teen girls (NEAT Girls) cluster randomized controlled trial. *Archives of Pediatrics & Adolescent Medicine*, 166(9), 821–827.

McLeroy, K., Bibeau, D., Steckler, A., & Glanz, K. (1988). An ecological perspective on health promotion programs. *Health Education Quarterly*, 15(4), 351–377.

Mooney, A., & Casey, M. (2014). 'Girls get going': Using games sense to promotion physical activity amongst adolescent girls in rural and regional contexts in Australia. In R. Light, S. Harvey, J. Quay, & A. Mooney (eds), *Contemporary Developments in Games Teaching* (pp. 103–117). Abingdon: Routledge.

Okely, A., Lubans, D., Morgan, P., Cotton, W., Peralta, L., Miller, J., ... Janssen, X. (2017). Promoting physical activity among adolescent girls: the Girls in Sport group randomized trial. *International Journal of Behavioral Nutrition and Physical Activity*, 14(81).

O'Neal, P., Barnett, N., Hanlon, C., Jacobs, K., Jones, M., Keating, M., ... Talalla, D. (2015). Inquiry into women and girls in sport and active recreation: A five year game plan for Victoria. Retrieved from www.sport.vic.gov.au/sites/default/files/documents/201704/Inquiry%20into%20women%20and%20girls%20in%20sport.pdf

Parliament of Canada. (2017). *Women and Girls in Sport. A Report of the Standing Committee on Canadian Heritage*. Retrieved from www.ourcommons.ca/DocumentViewer/en/42-1/CHPC/report-7

Pearson, N., Braithwaite, R., & Biddle, S. J. H. (2015). The effectiveness of interventions to increase physical activity among adolescent girls: A meta-analysis. *Academic Pediatrics*, 15(1), 9–18.

Priest, N., Armstrong, R., Doyle, J., & Waters, E. (2008). Interventions implemented through sporting organisations for increasing participation in sport. *Cochrane Database of Systematic Reviews*, 3, Art. No.: CD004812.

Rowe, K., Sherry, E., & Osborne, A. (2018). Recruiting and retaining girls in table tennis: Participant and club perspectives. *Sport Management Review*, 21(5), 504–518.

Rowe, K., Shilbury, D., Ferkins, L., & Hinckson, E. (2015). Challenges for sport development: Women's entry level cycling participation. *Sport Management Review*. doi:10.1016/j.smr.2015.11.001

Slater, A., & Tiggemann, M. (2010). 'Uncool to do sport': A focus group study of adolescent girls' reasons for withdrawing from physical activity. *Psychology of Sport and Exercise*, 11(6), 619–626.

Somerset, S., & Hoare, D. J. (2018). Barriers to voluntary participation in sport for children: a systematic review. *BMC Pediatrics*, 18(1), 47. doi:10.1186/s12887-018-1014-1

Spaaij, R., Farquharson, K., & Marjoribanks, T. (2015). Sport and social inequalities. *Sociology Compass*, 9(5), 400–411.

Sport and Recreation Victoria. (2015). *Inquiry into Women and Girls in Sport: A Five Year Game Plan for Victoria*. Retrieved from www.sport.vic.gov.au/sites/default/files/documents/201704/Inquiry%20into%20women%20and%20girls%20in%20sport.pdf

Sport England. (2006). *Understanding Participation in Sport: What Determines Sport Participation among 15–19 Year Old Women?* Retrieved from www.paha.org.uk/Resource/understanding-participation-in-sport-what-determines-sports-participation-among-15-19-year-old-women

Sport England. (2016). Record number of women get active. Figures show surge in the number of women playing sport and getting active. Retrieved from www.sportengland.org/news-and-features/news/2016/december/8/record-numbers-of-women-getting-active/

van Sluijs, E. M. F., McMinn, A. M., & Griffin, S. J. (2007). Effectiveness of interventions to promote physical activity in children and adolescents: Systematic review of controlled trials. *BMJ*, 335(7622), 703–707.

Veldman, S., Palmer, K., Okely, A., & Robinson, L. (2017). Promoting ball skills in preschool-age girls. *Journal of Science and Medicine in Sport*, 20(1), 50–54.

Vella, S., Cliff, D., & Okely, A. (2014). Socio-ecological predictors of participation and dropout in organised sports during childhood. *International Journal of Behavioral Nutrition and Physical Activity*, 11(62).

VicHealth. (2015). Female participation in sport and physical activity. Retrieved from www.vichealth.vic.gov.au/media-and-resources/publications/female-participation-in-sport-and-physical-activity-a-snapshot-of-the-evidence

Zhang, J., Brackbill, D., Yang, S., & Centola, D. (2015). Efficacy and causal mechanism of an online social media intervention to increase physical activity: Results of a randomized controlled trial. *Preventive Medicine Reports*, 2, 651–657.

4

DEVELOPING SPORT FOR MOTHERS WITH DEPENDENT CHILDREN

Clare Hanlon, Tracy Taylor and Wendy O'Brien

Introduction

The aim of this chapter is to provide an understanding of the motivations and barriers specific to women who have dependent children – mothers – that enable or impede their participation and volunteering in sport and leisure time physical activity. Issues and opportunities for further research evolving from the literature are identified and examples of sport programmes that have acted to address issues for mothers are discussed; this is followed by recommendations to further advance organisations in the quest to increase opportunities for mothers in sport and leisure time physical activity. Finally, a case study on a sport development programme is presented to illustrate some of the considerations in getting mothers actively involved and connected through sport.

Many women with dependent children also have other caring roles, including looking after parents and grandchildren, and/or sociodemographic characteristics that impact on their sport and physical activity options and behaviours. While acknowledging the intersection of these factors and other roles, the focus of this chapter is on women as mothers.

A range of studies spanning more than 30 years has provided consistent evidence that mothers commonly prioritise the physical activity needs of their family before their own (Currie, 2004; Lewis & Ridge, 2005). However, research specifically on why mothers participate in organised sport and the benefits that they accrue from this participation is somewhat limited. Therefore, the literature presented in this chapter takes a broad view of sport involvement and covers mothers' leisure time physical activity (LTPA, encompassing active recreation) as well as their involvement in formally organised sport. Mothers are not a homogeneous group, and clearly their involvement in sport will be influenced by individual, cultural, economic, environmental and societal considerations. However, the extant literature suggests that mothers' level and type of involvement can be explained by considering two key aspects: i) motivations; and ii) barriers. It is important to acknowledge the body of work pertaining to gender-based leisure constraints and related theory; however, this literature tends to mainly refer to women in general rather than women as mothers.

Involvement in LTPA and sport

Research suggests that the motivation of mothers to participate in LTPA and play sport can be classified into four main factors:

1. Sense of belonging
2. Body awareness
3. Health and wellbeing
4. Identity

Assuming a role in sport as a volunteer is underpinned by a different set of motivations, related to parenting and motherhood.

Sense of belonging

Numerous studies have found that the primary motivation of mothers' participation in LTPA and sport is related to gaining and retaining a sense of belonging and social networks (Hanlon, Morris & Nabbs, 2010). For example, it has been found that social interaction and camaraderie of being a team member can attract working mothers to sports programmes, and accountability to team members can motivate them to continue (Dixon, 2009). Similarly, meaningful connections to others was created in a netball programme for mothers, and weekly commitment encouraged longer term involvement (Walsh, et al., 2018). Likewise, collective social spaces to belong and "fit in" with other women retained mothers in a study on climbing (Dilley & Scraton, 2010). Evidence suggests that emotional and relational connections add value to mothers' participation in sport (Spowart, Burrows & Shaw, 2010).

In their research on recreational runners McGannon, McMahon and Gonsalves (2017) found that blogging offered mothers the opportunity for social connection that worked to keep them committed to activity. The social connection gained through blogging allowed mothers to express how they felt about, in this case running, noting a sense of strength, confidence, accomplishment and pride in their achievements (McGannon, et al., 2017). Blogs afforded an opportunity to share stories of empowerment and thus encouraged other mothers to become runners (McGannon, et al., 2017).

Belonging to a group can provide women with opportunities to collectively challenge and disrupt ideals of motherhood. For example, having an identity alongside that of a mother, developing an ethical self-stylization that was akin to a lifestyle, and valuing feelings of enjoyment and fulfilment were found to be important aspects of women's involvement in surfing (Spowart, et al., 2010). Traditional gendered identities and roles were challenged by mothers who climbed and found space in which to 'be' and 'be different' (Dilley & Scraton, 2010, p. 136). Leisure time physical activity provided the opportunity to disassociate from the demands of motherhood and its expectations (O'Brien, Lloyd & Riot, 2016). Motivations to reframe discourses of a good mother and prioritise their own needs for physical activity can include recognising the importance of time out for mental health, placing an emphasis on health and social benefits and engaging in 'pleasure, play, transgression, social interaction and release' (Lewis & Ridge, 2005, p. 2304).

Body awareness

Engaging with the physicality of one's body is another important contributor to mothers' involvement. Engagement with activity can be tracked from when a woman is pregnant. In a study of pregnant women who exercised, women described sensuous embodied connections, coupled with negotiated 'biomedical discourses of risk, health and maternal responsibility' (Nash, 2011, p. 62). In O'Brien and colleagues' (2016) research, recognition of post-childbirth changes in physical strength and capability led mothers with young children to alter their activity patterns to engage previously unused muscles and create an embodied sense of self. Changes in physicality from surfing was evident from mothers and in turn this contributed to their feeling of wellbeing (Spowart, et al., 2010).

Tensions exist, however, for many mothers who engage in LTPA to meet coercive body ideals (Currie, 2004). For example, in one study, pregnant women were motivated to exercise by the belief it would benefit the foetus and assist with maintaining their physical appearance (Nash, 2011). However, issues of body image – particularly post-baby body image – evoke feelings of shame and embarrassment that negatively impacted on women engaging in physical activity. This included mothers who did not want to exercise around '20-year old babes in their midriffs' (Nash, 2011, p. 40).

Running is often linked to providing a way to change body shape or appearance (Bond & Batey, 2005). In the study of recreational running mentioned earlier, running was empowering for the mothers involved, as it was a sport in which they were doing the activity for themselves, rather than to achieve limiting normative ideals of women's bodies (McGannon, et al., 2017). Transformative connections have been identified in studies where mothers found their running led to them discovering previously unknown capacities (Bond & Batey, 2005; McGannon, et al., 2017).

Health and wellbeing

Health and wellbeing motivations of mothers to be physically active can be associated with the life cycle as a mother. For example, pram walking was found to encourage mothers with babies to get out of the house (Currie & Develin, 2002) and mothers with older children often engage in LTPA programmes with their children to spend more time together (Ransdell, et al., 2001). In contrast, Dixon

(2009) identified that having family members involved in a mother's activity could constrain their enjoyment and influence their choice of activity.

Physical activity has been used to reframe women's view of themselves as better mothers, improve their mood and provide an avenue of relaxation (Lewis & Ridge, 2005). Actively negotiating time for the 'self' has been found to motivate mothers to sustain their participation and raise their confidence to cope with life as a mother. Mothers who play sport can temporarily escape the ethic of care and create 'time and space for themselves' (Bond & Batey, 2005, p. 77). In a study of mothers who snowboard, the passion of snowboarding and experiences of freedom were major driving factors that underpinned the mothers' active persistence for negotiating time to participate (Spowart, Hughson & Shaw, 2008). Similarly, O'Brien, et al. (2016) argue that participation in physical activity allows mothers to feel different to their everyday lives through experiencing pleasure and enjoyment. Mothers in their study described emotions such as 'feeling good', and a sense of 'peace and quiet', and feelings of excitement and being energised (O'Brien, et al., 2016, p. 228). The feeling of pleasure was also an incentive in a study of mothers who surfed, as their sense of an embodied identity allowed them to be a 'different self' (Spowart, et al., 2010, p.1193).

The unequal division of domestic labour in heterosexual relationships has long been identified as a barrier for mothers to access leisure (see, for example, Brown, et al., 2001). Therefore, having good support networks provides mothers with the motivation and opportunity to devote time to the 'self' and participate in LTPA and/or play sport. Support from partners, family members and friends enables mothers to negotiate time for themselves (Spowart, et al., 2008) and to access LTPA and sport (Brown, et al., 2001; Dixon, 2009; Dilley & Scraton, 2010; Hamilton, Cox & White, 2012). This includes support from husbands/partners with their schedules to enable access and assist mothers who juggle work and school schedules to negotiate time for sport and provision of childcare facilities (Bond & Batey, 2005; Dixon, 2009).

Identity

Through participating in sport, women can see themselves as more than simply a mother (Appleby & Fisher, 2009; McGannon, et al., 2015; McGannon, et al., 2017). Participating in LTPA and sport reinforced their self-definition in positive ways, encouraged them to pursue activities such as running (Bond & Batey, 2005), and recognise themselves as a 'role mother/advocate' and 'resilient mother runner' (McGannon, et al., 2017, p. 129). For some mothers, a sense of identity is gained through exercise; this might be as an elite athlete or as a role model. For others, exercise considerations regarding their cultural identity are important.

Elite athlete

Mothers who play sport can fulfil competitive goals and maintain an athletic identity (McGannon et al., 2017; McGannon, et al., 2018; Nash, 2011) but may need to negotiate work-family balance in order to meet specific sport performance goals (McGannon, et al., 2018). For elite women athletes with children, sport provides the opportunity to achieve athletic goals, think positively and improve their focus (McGannon, et al., 2015). The identity of motherhood can also temper performance pressures, while an athletic identity helps manage the demands of motherhood (Appleby & Fisher, 2009; Palmer & Leberman, 2009). The ability to train and compete gave mothers in McGannon and colleagues' (2018) study a sense of balance in their lives, reduced their stress and allowed them to be better mothers through 'compatible competitive athlete-mother identities' (p. 45).

The social expectations, however, of motherhood – selflessness, self-sacrificing, feelings of guilt – can impede elite athlete's re-entry into their sport, with many having to balance and juggle expectations of motherhood with training and competing (Appleby & Fisher, 2009). The guilt mothers experience intensifies when they return to sport (Palmer & Leberman, 2009; McGannon, et al., 2015; Ronkainen, Watkins & Ryba, 2016), particularly when they relied on support to enable them to train and compete (Gierc, et al., 2016). Other research on elite athletes who are mothers has suggested that an athletic identity is incompatible with motherhood, resulting in withdrawal from sport (Ronkainen, et al., 2016).

Role models

Physically active mothers have been portrayed as role models for their children (Batey & Owton, 2014; McGannon, et al., 2017; McGannon, et al., 2018; Nash, 2011). For example, playing netball allowed mothers to feel as if they were a role model for the family, reinforcing their 'good mother' role (Walsh, et al., 2018).

Elite athletes reframed the ethic of care, suggesting that a return to sport allowed them to role model for their children while blending 'their identities as mothers and athletes' (Darroch & Hillsburg, 2017, p. 67). Similarly, Appleby and Fisher (2009, p. 8) argue that through role modelling women both accepted and resisted the social construction of motherhood and in this way, sport offered a 'transformative process of embodying, resisting and negotiation'. Sport became a site of empowerment where women developed new identities and capabilities, such as a complex understanding of self, 'deploying this construct to legitimize their desire to train and compete' (Darroch & Hillsburg, 2017, p. 67). By extension, elite athletes also saw themselves as role models for other women to encourage them to continue being active after childbirth (Palmer & Leberman, 2009).

Culture and ethnicity

While there is a growing body of work on the various cultural and ethnic dimensions of participation of women in LTPA and sport, few studies have explored the specific subgroup of mothers.

Generic research with women has identified that the support of family and friends is of critical importance to motivate mothers from culturally diverse backgrounds to participate in LTPA and sport. For example, Latina women suggest that exercising with their husbands and other friends provides motivation for them to engage in LTPA (Skowron, Stodolska & Shinew, 2008). In many cultures with strong traditions of family responsibility, conforming to cultural expectations around family takes precedence over individual needs and may lead to women experiencing guilt and shame if they focus on themselves in sport (Stronach, Maxwell & Taylor, 2016).

Organisations that actively support the provision of culturally appropriate programmes, facilities, childcare and norms of culturally appropriate behaviour have been found to influence the decision of mothers to engage in LTPA (Skowron, et al., 2008) and sport (Sawkrikar & Muir, 2010). However, some ethnic minority groups can feel marginalised or excluded from sport participation. For example, in Australia, mothers from culturally and linguistically diverse (CALD) backgrounds have reported that they feel sport is 'exclusively a white institution' (Sawkrikar & Muir, 2010, p. 366) where racism occurs (Stornach, et al., 2016). Feelings of exclusion, coupled with a lack of belonging, and discomfort from not knowing the rules of the game can lead to mothers opting out of participation (Sawkrikar & Muir, 2010).

Volunteering mothers

In many high-income countries (HIC), where youth sport systems rely on volunteer labour to survive, there is a significant level of parental volunteering, often across multiple roles such as coach, manager, board member etc. In Australia more than 20% of mothers of children 5–14 years old volunteer for a sport and recreation organisation (ABS, 2009). There are a range of intrinsic reasons why mothers volunteer including spending time with their children, personal and career development, and developing social networks (Women in Sport, 2017). The motivations to volunteer also overlap with some of the above stated motivations for participation, namely for a sense of belonging and identity.

In study of working coach-mothers, taking on the role of coach provided an opportunity to spend time with their children, helped their children and others to develop life skills, and role model behaviour – particularly for their sons – which enriched their involvement (Leberman & LaVoi, 2011). The mothers in this study also noted the passion for the sport they coached provided motivation for their involvement.

Sport leadership volunteering can assist mothers to form a strong sport identity, and it can be coupled with a motivation to mentor and develop others, while also bringing about change (Leberman & Palmer, 2009). Mothers who coach see it as an opportunity to challenge 'perceptions about women in positions of power and leadership' (Leberman & LaVoi, 2011, p. 481).

Volunteering can generate positive feelings that have the potential to transfer to women's other roles as workers and mothers. Through sport leadership roles, mothers have acquired greater tolerance, become organised and have focused on personal growth to enable them to be better leaders (Leberman & Palmer, 2009). The mothers in Leberman and Palmer's (2009) study believed that more women would volunteer to coach if organisations recruited using the tactic of translating mothering skills onto coaching.

Support networks provide motivation and enablers for mothers to volunteer in sport. Strong social supports, including a supportive partner, can be drawn on to overcome societal disapproval of assuming leadership roles, and to counter organisational resistance to accepting the presence of children in a sport setting (Leberman & Palmer, 2009). Mothers recommended that organisations support co-coaching approaches as this reduces time commitments and may entice more mothers to coach (Leberman & Palmer, 2009). Sharing the load meant women are more able to manage worker-mother-coach roles, reducing the feelings of inadequacy, guilt and stress (Leberman & LaVoi, 2011).

Identification of issues and opportunities for further research

While there is a growing body of research on women in sport in general, our specific knowledge about mothers playing or volunteering in sport is relatively sparse. This is particularly notable within different subgroups across dimensions, such as culture, ethnicity, religion, (dis)ability and gender identification, and within different participation populations, such as recreational participants, elite athletes and volunteers. A prime opportunity exists to advance knowledge in this field to identify how sport can develop and be more inclusive to women who are mothers across this diverse range of circumstances and situations.

Establishing and retaining connections is a pervasive theme throughout the literature. This presents an opportunity to further develop our understanding of mothers' participation through a lens of various conceptualisations of embodied connections through sport.

There is an opportunity to further examine ways in which sport can enable mothers who may feel ill-at-ease with their bodies after childbirth to feel more comfortable in a sporting environment. Other research opportunities include exploring what mothers need in order to be able to play or volunteer in sport within their particular life cycle stage, identifying how sport makes women feel external to being a mother, a mother's identity associated with engaging in sport – both at amateur and elite level – and role modelling. A deeper examination of the physicality of sport could provide insights into how sport can assist mothers capitalise on opportunities for health and wellbeing and/or develop in terms of body-mind connections.

The reliance on support networks provides an opportunity for research to focus on how the sport environment can connect women to groups who are also mothers. In addition, research is required to understand the strategies and support networks of family and friends that enable acceptance and access for mothers to be physically active and volunteer in sport. For example, mothers' exercising identity is interesting as it points towards relying on social networks to assist with physical activity becoming part of life or a habit, rather than a chore.

A connected environment that brings people together provides an opportunity to explore how sport organisations can build connections to enable mothers gain a sense of belonging in group programmes and it also helps them to access programmes and volunteer roles through the provision of family-friendly facilities. Findings could be translated to new knowledge on practical implications for management in sport on strategies and programmes required to strengthen connections to recruit and retain mothers in general and within the different subgroups.

The new knowledge gained from these research opportunities could be used to develop policies, strategies and initiatives to assist organisations in the quest to attract and retain mothers as participants and volunteers in sport.

Practical actions taken to address the need to connect mothers to sport

There are many practice-based instances of mothers or sport organisations across the globe taking action to embed connections through sport for mothers. Examples include blogging, creating an exercise identity, and providing a female friendly programme and a connected school environment.

Belonging through blogging (Australia)

Blogging can provide a sense of belonging to a group, it is low cost, and available to mothers regardless of the time of day. A Cycling Mums Australia website (www.cyclingmumsaustralia.com.au/) was created by a mother who struggled to find a training space she felt comfortable with after having children. The site contains stories posted by mothers and seven ambassadors were appointed to share their stories to help women achieve their cycling goals.

Sport creating an exercise identity (England)

Mothers can also be encouraged to re-engage in sport through focused interventions (Cramp & Brawley, 2006). An example of a focused intervention is Back to Netball (B2N), a programme to re-engage inactive mums in England. B2N allows mothers to explore their exercising identity and as a result 'participants begin to view exercise as central to their weekly routines and an important part of who they are' (Walsh, et al., 2018, p. 615). The programme emphasises social connection, rather than skills, and feedback on the programme indicated that women developed a sense of competence, confidence and capabilities (Walsh, et al., 2018).

Family friendly programmes (Australia)

Mums Who Ball and Baby Ballers programmes are two interconnected programmes conducted by Basketball ACT (Australia). Mums Who Ball (www.playbytherules.net.au/resources/case-studies/basketball-act-mums-who-ball) is a mothers' daytime weekly competition focused on the fundamentals of basketball and game play. Weekly commitment is optional and there are no requirements for ongoing registration. The competition runs for four 10-minute quarters. On the court adjacent to the mothers playing is the Baby Ballers programme where their children, aged six months to four years, experience visual and kinaesthetic learning.

Support network through school settings (United States)

To encourage social connections and camaraderie with other mothers, districts and parishes of schools have come together to create a sport environment for mothers. A mothers' volleyball league, located within the Jasonville School district (United States), has run for over 40 years and comprises close to 300 mothers (http://the-source.net/mothers-volleyball-league-celebrates-40th-anniversary/). The Archdiocese of Baltimore (United States), created a similar programme that has been running for over 10 years (www.archbalt.org/ihm-moms-basketball-league-scores-big/). Both examples involve the mothers fund raising for the hosting schools.

Recommendations

In addition to the research opportunities identified in this chapter, we provide five practical recommendations for governing sport bodies and schools. These recommendations presented in Table 4.1 are based on the findings identified in the literature reviewed, and they focus on education, policy and practice to provide women greater opportunities as mothers to build connections and support networks.

TABLE 4.1 Building connections and support networks through sport

Recommendation	Implications
Government health, school and sport bodies to educate younger women before they become mothers about the importance of maintaining a connection to sport	Increased awareness by women on the connection sport provides for their mental and physical wellbeing as a mother
Sport organisations to increase understanding on what mothers need to play and volunteer in their sport	Increased understanding will enable amendments to infrastructure, policies, strategies and programs that are more inclusive to a broader range of members
Sport organisations to create a blog on their social media for mothers who play or volunteer in their sport	Assist mothers to identify strategies for managing the demands of motherhood and involvement in sport, how sport helps them as a mother (e.g. role model to their children), and how they feel as an individual playing or volunteering in sport
Sport organisations to create family-friendly scheduling and programs, e.g., the option for mothers to participate in sport at the same time and venue as their child, mother and child programs	Increased number of mothers playing instead of sitting while their child plays sport, children see their mothers playing sport (role model), exercise identity formed
Schools in collaboration with sport organisations to initiate sport programs targeted to mothers at convenient times, e.g., just after 'school drop off' or prior to 'school pick up', in return mothers organise a fundraiser event for the school	Schools represent a safe and familiar space to play sport where embodied connections are made for mothers
Sport organisation to introduce 'shared volunteering' to assist with work, domestic and family responsibilities	Prevalence of co-coaching, co-officiating, and being a co-committee member in sport, e.g., alternating weeks of coaching or officiating for half a season

CASE STUDY

Soccer mums programme

Australia https://soccermums.com.au/

The following case study is an example of sport for development (SFD), in which soccer (football) is used as a tool to engage mothers in the community and to provide an opportunity for the participants to achieve connections relating to intrapersonal, interpersonal and organisational aspects.

Aim

An introductory football programme designed specifically for less active mothers – particularly those with children school aged or younger – to increase their physical activity, have fun, meet others, and learn basic football skills. No experience required.

Initiative

Created by Football Federation Victoria, partnered with Melbourne City Football Club, and funded from VicHealth.

Programme

The length of the programme varies from 4–10 weeks, depending on venue availability. Each weekly session is 30–45 minutes, tailored to the needs of the participants and conducted by Programme Deliverers who understand the demands of being a mother and the need to create a social and fun environment. The hashtags typify the focus of the programme: #nojudgement #noexperiencerequired #jointhefun.

Sessions are conducted on training nights at the club where mothers can deliver their child/ren to training and then participate in their own session that is completed before their child/ren's session. Mothers who do not have a child playing football or associated with a club can still join the programme.

Website

The website provides options for women to register for a programme, a free come-and-try session, and/or attend a Melbourne City Football Club Match Day. The site also allows people to register to be a Programme Deliverer; the recruitment process includes the need for potential deliverers to understand and appreciate the life of a mother and to create a fun and social environment for participants. Clubs can also register interest to host a programme and are supported by a Programme Project Manager and can request/nominate a person to be a Programme Deliverer for their club.

> The site provides a video link to a soccer mums programme, including responses and a photo gallery of women's experiences.
>
> ### Soccer mums Programme Deliverer
>
> The Programme Deliverer is a paid position. The person needs to complete a Programme Deliverer's course or one-on-one training depending on the launch of the programme at the club. A manual provides support for the Programme Deliverer on programme delivery and activities to use.
>
> ### Cost
>
> The cost to participate in each session was AUS $10 in metropolitan areas and AUS $5 in regional areas, with discounts advertised at various times for different programmes. Each programme has two free sessions included in the upfront registration fee.
>
> ### Value-add
>
> A women's football festival for participants is held annually to provide the opportunity for mothers to network and play football. Half-time at Melbourne City matches include exhibition games by participants.
>
> ### Outcomes
>
> In the first 18 months there has been an overwhelming number – 680 – of registered participants. It is expected the second 18 months will result in 2,500 participants. Satisfaction with the programme remains high, with interest in rolling out this programme nationally from other member Federations. Amendments to enhance the programme based on participant feedback include inserting to the Programme Deliverer manual more challenges for the mothers, e.g., more skill-based and technical information and upskilling the leadership of Programme Deliverers.

References

Appleby, K. M. & Fisher, L. A. (2009). Running in and out of pregnancy: Elite distance runners' experiences of returning to competition after pregnancy. *Women in Sport and Physical Activity Journal*, 18(1), 3–17.

Australian Bureau of Statistics (ABS). (2009). *Voluntary Work, Australia*. Catalogue No. 4441.0

Batey, J., & Owton, H. (2014). Team mums: Team sport experiences of athlete mothers. *Women in Sport and Physical Activity Journal*, 22, 20–36.

Bond, J., & Batey, J. (2005). Running for their lives: A qualitative analysis of the exercise experience of female recreational runners. *Women in Sport and Physical Activity Journal*, 14(2), 69–82.

Brown, P. R., Brown, W., Miller, Y., & Hansen, V. (2001). Perceived constraints and social support for active leisure among mothers with young children. *Leisure Sciences*, 23(3), 131–144.

Cramp, A. G., & Brawley, L. R. (2006). Moms in motion: A group-mediated cognitive behavioural physical activity intervention. *International Journal of Behaviour Nutrition & Physical Activity*, 3(23), 1–9. doi:10.1186/1479-5868-3-23

Currie, J. (2004). Motherhood, stress and the exercise experience: Freedom or constraint? *Leisure Studies*, 23(3), 225–242.

Currie, J., & Develin, E. (2002). Stroll your way to well-being: A survey of the perceived benefits, barriers, community support, and stigma associated with pram walking groups for new mothers, Sydney, Australia. *Health Care for Women International*, 23(8), 882–893.

Darroch, F., & Hillsburg, H. (2017). Keeping pace: Mother versus athlete identity among elite long distance runners. *Women's Studies International Forum*, 62, 61–68. https://doi.org/10.1016/j.wsif.2017.03.005

Dilley, R. E., & Scraton, S. J. (2010) Women, climbing and serious leisure. *Leisure Studies*, 29(2), 125–141.

Dixon, M. (2009). From their perspective: A qualitative examination of physical activity and sport programming for working mothers. *Sport Management Review*, 12(1), 34–48.

Gierc, M., Locke, S., Jung, M., & Brawley, L. (2016). Attempting to be active: Self-efficacy and barrier limitation differentiate activity levels of working mothers. *Journal of Health Psychology*, 21(7), 1351–1360.

Hamilton, K., Cox, S., & White, K. M. (2012). Testing a model of physical activity among mothers and fathers of young children: Integrating self-determined motivation, planning, and the theory of planned behavior. *Journal of Sport and Exercise Psychology*, 34(1), 124–145.

Hanlon, C., Morris, T. & Nabbs, S. (2010). Establishing a successful physical activity program to recruit and retain women. *Sport Management Review*, 13(3), 269–282.

Leberman, S., & Palmer, F. (2009). Motherhood, sport leadership, and domain theory: Experiences from New Zealand. *Journal of Sport Management*, 23(3), 305–344.

Leberman, S. I., & LaVoi, N. M. (2011). Juggling balls and roles, working mother-coaches in youth sport: Beyond the dualistic worker-mother identity. *Journal of Sport Management*, 25(5), 474–488.

Lewis, B. S., & Ridge, D. (2005). Mothers reframing physical activity: Family oriented politicism, transgression and contested expertise in Australia. *Social Science and Medicine*, 60(10), 2295–2306.

McGannon, K., Gonsalves, C., Schinke, R., & Busanich, R. (2015). Negotiating motherhood and athletic identity: A qualitative analysis of Olympic athlete mother representations in media narratives. *Psychology of Sport and Exercise*, 20(1), 51–59

McGannon, K. R., McMahon, J., & Gonsalves, C. A. (2017). Mother runners in the blogosphere: A discursive psychological analysis of online recreational athlete identities. *Psychology of Sport and Exercise*, 28, 125–135. doi:10.1016/j. psychsport.2016.11.002

McGannon, K. R., McMahon, J., & Gonsalves, C. A. (2018). Juggling motherhood and sport: A Qualitative study of negotiation of competitive recreational athlete mother identities. *Psychology of Sport and Exercise*, 36, 41–49.

Nash, M. (2011). "You don't train for a marathon sitting on the couch": Performances of pregnancy "fitness" and "good" motherhood in Melbourne, Australia. *Women's Studies International Forum*, 34, 50–65.

O'Brien, W., Lloyd, K., & Riot, C. (2016). Exploring the emotional geography of the leisure time physical activity space with mothers of young children. *Leisure Studies*, 36(2), 220–230.

Palmer, F. R., & Leberman, S. I. (2009). Elite athletes as mothers: managing multiple sport identities. *Sport Management Review*, 12(4), 241–254. doi:10.1016/j.smr.2009.03.001

Ransdell, L. B., Dratt, J., Kennedy, C., O'Neil, S., & DeVoe, D. (2001). Daughters and mothers exercising together (DAMET): A 12-week pilot project designed to improve physical self-perception and increase recreational physical activity. *Women & Health*, 33(3–4), 113–129.

Ronkainen, N. J., Watkins, I., & Ryba, T. V. (2016). What can gender tell us about the pre-retirement experiences of elite distance runners in Finland?: A thematic narrative analysis. *Psychology of Sport and Exercise*, 22, 37–45. doi:10.1016/j. psychsport.2015.06.003

Sawrikar, P., & Muir, K. (2010). The myth of a "fair go": Barriers to sport and recreational participation among Indian and other ethnic minority women in Australia, *Sport Management Review*, 13(4), 355–367.

Skowron, M. A., Stodolska, M., & Shinew, K. J. (2008). Determinants of leisure time physical activity participation among Latina women, *Leisure Sciences*, 30(5), 429–447. doi: doi:10.1080/01490400802353174

Spowart, L., Burrows, L., & Shaw, S. (2010). 'I just eat, sleep and dream of surfing': When surfing meets motherhood. *Sport in Society*, 13, 1186–1203. doi:10.1080/17430431003780179

Spowart, L., Hughson, J., & Shaw, S. (2008). Snowboarding mums carve out fresh tracks: Resisting traditional motherhood discourse? *Annals of Leisure Research*, 11(1–2), 187–204.

Stronach, M., Maxwell, H., & Taylor, T. (2016) 'Sistas' and Aunties: sport, physical activity, and Indigenous Australian women, *Annals of Leisure Research*, 19(1), 7–26. doi:10.1080/11745398.2015.1051067

Walsh, B., Whittaker, E., Cronin, C., & Whitehead, A. (2018). 'Net mums': a narrative account of participants' experiences within a netball intervention. *Qualitative Research in Sport, Exercise and Health*, 10(5), 604–619.

Women in Sport (2017). Good sports: Why sports need to engage female volunteers. Retrieved from www.womeninsport.org/wp-content/uploads/2017/06/Good-Sports.pdf?x99836

5

DEVELOPING SPORT FOR OLDER WOMEN

Claire Jenkin

Introduction

The global population is ageing (World Health Organisation, 2015), with predictions that by 2050, one in five people will be over 60 years old (World Health Organisation, 2017). Older age is often associated with a decline in health (Haskell, et al., 2007). As poor health often results in a lower quality of life (Djärv, Wikman, Johar & Lagergren, 2013) and an increased burden on health services (Rechel, Doyle, Grundy & McKee, 2009), an increasing international focus is being placed on improving health for older adults. This is particularly pertinent for older women, as women tend to have a longer life expectancy than men (United Nations, 2017). As physical activity can improve health (Toepoel, 2013), there is a need to ensure there are diverse and appropriate opportunities for older women to be physically active.

This chapter examines trends in relation to sport participation of older women, potential motivations and benefits for older women to participate in sport, potential barriers that may deter their participation and their relationship with volunteering in sport. Opportunities for future research into older women and sport, examples of practical actions to service this population and recommendations for practitioners wishing to engage older women will be discussed, before a case study of an innovative older women's physical activity programme is presented.

The sport for health movement

The links between physical activity and health have been long established, with sport in particular being increasingly used as a vehicle to improve health (Edwards & Rowe, 2019). With ageing populations and the associated health concerns, public health organisations have increasingly turned to sport to try to increase physical activity levels. For older adults, this concept is often called 'active ageing'. Whilst the relationship between older adults and physical activity can often be multifaceted and complex, there is strong medical evidence to suggest physical activity can mitigate some of the effects of numerous illnesses and diseases associated with old age (see, for example, Haskell, et al., 2007). Therefore, it is important to encourage and enable older women to be physically active, in an accessible activity they enjoy, to enhance their quality of life.

Who are older adults?

Globally, there is no definitive age when someone becomes an 'older adult'. The World Health Organisation defines older adults as people aged 65 years old and over, which is widely accepted. However, a move away from chronological age has been suggested, as it does not always reflect perceptions of ageing in different parts of the world. The more subjective concept of social age – where people act the age that is deemed socially acceptable in their respective society – has been mooted instead.

In Masters sport, age categories can vary widely, often dependent on the sport. For example, in gymnastics, Masters events commence at 20 years of age, while in athletics, there are categories for 100 years and older. In community sport, New Zealand and Australian sporting policies define older adults as 65 years and older, while Sport England now focuses on adults over the age of 55 (previously it was 50+ years). To cover all possible definitions, this chapter will focus on sport for women over the age of 50 years.

What is sport for older adults?

This chapter will largely focus on Masters sport, community sport and physical activity for the general older female population, rather than those with specific medical issues and diseases associated with old age, such as dementia.

Sport participation trends

Whilst participation in sport is often dependent on life stage, and thus tends to fluctuate during people's lives; it typically decreases with age (Eime, et al., 2016). In Australia, it is estimated that only 32% of older women (55+ years) meet the recommended physical activity guidelines (minimum of 30 minutes of activity per day) (Sport Australia, 2018). Historically, most of the activity options for older women have focused on general, low-impact physical activity, such as walking or swimming, and traditional sports, such as bowls, which are enjoyed by many older women. However, with the ageing global population, and the increased focus on using sport to improve health, alternative and diverse activity options are being explored to encourage older women to be active.

Potential motivations and benefits of sport participation

Older women may choose to participate in sport for many different reasons and may derive a number of benefits.

Health

Public health messages detailing the importance of improving health in older age have been well publicised. Thus unsurprisingly, playing sport to improve health is a major motivating factor for older women (Cedergren, et al., 2007) and also a key potential benefit (Jenkin, et al., 2017). Motivations include, for example, to become fitter and improve muscle strength and flexibility (Jenkin, Hilland & Eime, 2018a; Heo, et al., 2013), to prevent weight gain (Eman, 2012), and to mitigate disease/disability (Siegenthaler & O'Dell, 2003), in addition to using sport to rehabilitate after injury (Jenkin, et al., 2018b).

Social health is an umbrella term that can cover a multitude of interactions. Within social health, developing social support and connections are significant determinants of participation. Social aspects can be especially important for this age group, as social isolation tends to increase with age (Grenade & Boldy, 2008). Using sport to reduce social isolation, in particular, as a reason to leave the house (Cedergren, et al., 2007), for company and to make friends (Berlin, et al., 2018; Jenkin, et al., 2018a), and to give a purpose in life (Berlin, et al., 2018), are key motivators to participation.

It has been reported that older women are more motivated by the potential social health benefits of sport than older men (Kolt, Driver & Giles, 2004). These benefits can include meeting new friends and increasing social support (Berlin, Kruger & Klenosky, 2018; Heo, et al., 2013), reinforcing social identity (Heo, et al., 2013) and decreasing social isolation (Jenkin, et al., 2018b; Naar, et al., 2017). Research has also suggested that older women enjoyed being part of a team (Jenkin, et al., 2018a; Kirby & Kluge, 2013). Similar to other population groups, enjoyment and to have fun are other reasons why older women may want to play sport (Berlin, et al., 2018; Naar, et al., 2017).

For mental and psychological health motivations, older women report they wanted to play sport to relax (Naar, et al., 2017) and relieve stress (Berlin, et al., 2018), in addition to enjoying the mental stimulation of playing sport (Jenkin, et al., 2018a; Wong, et al., 2018). Developing their self-confidence (Jenkin, et al., 2018a; Naar, et al., 2017), in addition to achieving goals (Berlin, et al., 2018), have also been identified as potential mental and psychological benefits of playing sport.

Negotiating the ageing process

Using sport to negotiate the ageing process is a specific motivator for the older population. This can be split into two subsections: the positive ageing discourse; and to mitigate the negative stereotypes of ageing. A positive ageing discourse relates to the social motivations of participation, as older women often play sport to develop or maintain their self-, and social, identity (Heo, et al., 2013; Litchfield & Dionigi, 2011; Pfister, 2012). For example, they may have played sport all their life and see it as an important component of their identity. Some older women may also use sport to mitigate societal stereotypes that sport is the domain of younger people (Dionigi, 2006; Naar, et al., 2017), to minimise the effects of ageing (Jenkin, et al., 2018b), to not feel 'old' (Horton, et al., 2018; Pfister, 2012) and to differentiate themselves from the often negative image of an older adult (Kelley, et al., 2014).

Potential barriers to sport participation

Health is a particularly important determinant for participation. Improving health can motivate people to participate and can be derived as a benefit. However, poor health can also deter participation. Poor physical health, in particular, can be a barrier (Jenkin, et al., 2017; Wong, et al., 2018), for example, older women may be contending with disease, pain and injury (Horton, et al., 2018), and that the body takes longer to recover after exercise at an older age (Jenkin, et al., 2018b; Naar, et al., 2017). Poor psychological health, such as low self-confidence (Women in Sport, 2017), is another potential barrier. Research has identified that to enable older women to be active, social support is needed (Kirby & Kluge, 2013). Therefore, a lack of social support – for example, resistance or apathy from family members (e.g. Horton, et al., 2018; Naar, et al., 2017), particularly their concerns about the perceived risk of injury for their older relatives (Jenkin, et al., 2018a; Kirby & Kluge, 2013) – can deter participation.

Societal expectations, ageist stereotyping and negative comments (Gayman, Fraser-Thomas & Baker, 2017; Jenkin, et al., 2018b; Pfister, 2012) are other age-specific barriers older women often experience. In particular, Kirby & Kluge (2013, p. 291) describe that older women not only face ageist discrimination, but that this is compounded with negative gender stereotypes: 'Gender shapes lived experience, intersects with age, and can result in older women, in particular, thinking they are too old and too unfit to become physically active or try something new later in life'.

Finally, access to few appropriate opportunities (Jenkin, et al., 2017; Pfister, 2012) and lack of organisational resources (van Uffelen, et al., 2015) can be organisational barriers to older women's participation, as sporting organisations have historically focused on engaging younger population groups. As detailed in this chapter, more participation opportunities are emerging; however, these are often ad hoc and are dependent on local providers, in addition to relying on external, largely short-term, funding.

Volunteering in sport

In England, it is estimated that 6.3m adults (16+ years) volunteered in sport and physical activity between May 2017 and May 2018 (Sport England, 2018). While this data does not provide specific information on older women, it suggests that adults aged 45–54 years old were more likely to volunteer than any other age group (apart from 16–24-year-olds), while women of all ages tended to volunteer less than men. Research has suggested that older adults are often more likely to volunteer in club committee or other administrative roles (Jenkin, et al., 2016a; Nichols, et al., 2016) than younger people. Most research on volunteering and older adults tends to examine mixed gender groups. General motivations for their volunteering can include supporting their children/grandchildren's participation (Cuskelly, 2004; Jenkin, et al., 2016a); staying involved in a sport and to 'give back' – especially if they no longer actively participate (Nichols, et al., 2016) – and to contribute to society (Misener, Doherty, & Hamm-Kerwin, 2010).

Many of the benefits associated with volunteering reflect those of active participation, including health (Thoits & Hewitt, 2001), social interaction (Misener, et al., 2010) and social inclusion (Nichols & Ralston, 2011). Other identified benefits could be the chance to interact/bond with children/grandchildren (Jenkin, et al., 2018b) and to develop/enhance a sense of identity (Nichols & Ralston, 2011). For sporting organisations, engaging older women to volunteer could also help increase local sport club capacity (Adamson & Parker, 2006; Jenkin, et al., 2016a). This research demonstrates that engaging older women to volunteer in sport can bring benefits for both older women and sporting organisations.

Opportunities for future research

In the past ten years, more diverse sporting opportunities have been developed for this age group, in particular, modified sports. Research in this area has largely focused on the potential physiological benefits of walking football, with minimal consideration of the potential psychological and social aspects of these activities. Furthermore, this is a sport mostly participated in by men. Whilst this preliminary research has provided useful starting points, future research should review different forms of modified sport. In particular, to explore potential motivations to participate and social benefits that can be derived; whilst also specifically focusing on older female participation.

Another opportunity for research would be to look specifically at culturally and linguistically diverse (CALD) older women. Whilst CALD covers a plethora of ethnicities and cultural backgrounds, research shows lower than average participation by CALD women of all ages (Long, et al., 2015). Furthermore, diseases that can be somewhat mitigated by physical activity, such as Type 2 diabetes, are often more prevalent in older CALD women. Therefore, it would be beneficial to further understand CALD older women and their relationship with sport.

Practical actions taken to address the issue and service the population

Some sporting organisations have developed products to provide useful advice on how to service this population. For example, Sport England has created market segmentation profiles to identify key attributes of different population groups, including older women. Some sporting bodies have established specific policies and funding to engage older adults in sport, such as Sport England's Active Ageing fund and Sport Australia's Better Ageing Grant programme, whilst some activities are run by charities and social enterprises.

In Masters sport, the International Masters Games Association holds a multisport event every four years for women and men participants aged 35 years and over. As per most Masters events, participating athletes compete against others within their five- or ten-year age bracket (e.g. 50–55 years). For this competition, there are no further specific entry requirements, enabling any appropriately aged athlete to enter as an individual (rather than on behalf of their country), regardless of ability level. Some regions, such as Europe, the Americas and Asia-Pacific, run continental tournaments, and most individual countries also host local, regional and national age specific competitions, such as the Senior Games in the US. For all types of Masters events, there is an emphasis on social interaction, in addition to the competitive element.

In community sport, some areas have local, age-specific competitions. However, a more recent initiative is modified sports for older adults. While some sports were originally modified to introduce accessible versions of sports to young children, this concept has now been extended to older adults. The first version of this was walking football, established in the UK in 2011; now, walking versions of netball, basketball, rugby and hockey, amongst other sports, have been developed and utilised in different countries. Some of these programmes run independently; however, modified sport has also been used as a health referral pathway. For example, the award-winning Active Herts programme, in Hertfordshire in the UK, offers walking football for those with cardiovascular disease (CVD) risk factors and those with mental health issues. Another version of a modified sport that has been used in residential care homes in London is sitting netball (London Sport, 2017), where participants sit in a circle around a standing hoop and shoot balls into the hoop.

One sport that has become popular for older adults is pickleball. Originating in the US in the 1960s, the sport is played on a badminton court using a type of tennis net and a paddle racket. It is now played across the world and while it is not a sport specifically designed for older adults, it is popular with this age group, as it a slower and often more accessible form of racket sport. Many other types of programmes and initiatives, such as the Love to Dance programme and the second This Girl Can campaign in the UK, try to motivate and provide opportunities for older women to be physically active.

Designing and promoting sport for older women

A range of recommendations can be posed based on findings from numerous sources (for example, Jenkin, et al., 2016b; Jenkin, et al., 2018a; Kirby & Kluge, 2013; Women in Sport, 2017; Wong, et al., 2018). However, the 50+ age range spans a range of ages/life stages, and it is important to recognise that the group referred to as older women – as with any population group – is a very heterogeneous group. For example, some older women are still working, while others are retired, and some might care for their children or grandchildren during weekdays. Therefore, these recommendations may not be applicable to all older women or all activities that are aimed at this population group, but they are a useful starting point from which to design and deliver activity programmes.

- *Fun & enjoyment*: Focus on the fun and social element of sport in designing and promoting programmes. This includes making the sessions fun but also providing opportunities for participating women to socialise outside of the session. For example, visiting a local café after a session or regular social outings.
- *Engage with family members*: Older women may want to use sport to interact with family members that already play that sport. Family members also often provide older women with social support, both of which demonstrate positive family engagement. However, family members can also sometimes deter their participation, especially based on concerns about injury risk. Engaging with family members may mitigate some of this resistance and encourage older women to participate.
- *Peer support*: Some older women may lack confidence to attend sessions or try a new activity. Utilising peer support could include attending with a friend or asking more experienced members of the group to support newer members and also less abled participants.
- *Competition*: The opportunity to be competitive has been identified as a key reason for Masters and community sport participation. Some may want competitive fixtures against external teams and be part of a formal league structure, while some may want 'fun' competition within their weekly session.
- *Marketing*: Engage with older women when designing and disseminating marketing materials, specifically on language and imagery. For example, an older participant in Jenkin and colleagues' (2018a) study wrote an article to publicise a programme she was involved in. This participant used phrases and language that were likely to resonate with other older women, such as focusing on the social interactions and that participating was fun, rather than a focus on health (Jenkin, et al., 2018a). Furthermore, some older women do not like being identified as 'older', as it can sound derogatory; involving older women in the marketing and promotion of these activities ensures the messaging is appropriately phrased and avoids unhelpful stereotypes that have been shown to represent a barrier to participation.

  a   Imagery is also very important. Research has shown that getting the right imagery can be difficult and that in two example programs (Jenkin, et al. 2018a; London Sport, 2018) some women who eventually participated were initially discouraged if they felt the women portrayed in images looked older or frailer than they felt but decided to participate for other reasons. It is likely, though, that the imagery deterred other women from taking part. In these programmes, older women were not part of the initial consultation on imagery.

- *Age specific opportunities*: As people age, they may feel uncomfortable playing against younger, and sometimes more physically capable, opponents. Chronological age categories are standard in Masters competitions, but often are not available in community sport.
- *External partnerships*: In sport development generally, developing high quality and relevant partnerships is key for programmes to be successful. For

programmes for older women, sporting organisations need to develop relationships with partners such as Age UK, University of the Third Age, local older adult charities/organisations, religious organisations and, if appropriate, local residential villages and homes.

Finally, it is vital that older women are not patronised or stereotyped. Many older women are likely to be more physically capable than younger women and some may be far more competitive than other age groups. Some older women may enjoy traditional older adult sports and physical activity, such as walking or bowls. Some may want – and are more than capable – to continue to play sports they have played their whole lives. Some may still want to play sport but would prefer to play a modified version, or only participate against peers of their own age or ability level. Some might want a combination of all these options. Others might want to formally compete at regional, national and/or international level. As with any population group, it is important to provide a variety of physical activity options to enable participation in an activity that they enjoy. Therefore, it is essential to engage with older women throughout the whole programme life cycle – the design, marketing, implementation and evaluation of a programme – to ensure it is suitable and attractive for the target audience.

Conclusion

With the rising average life expectancy for women, there is a greater emphasis on their quality of life in old age. As physical activity can positively contribute towards quality of life, providing a diversity of appropriate physical activity options for this population group is extremely important. As detailed in this chapter, there are numerous organisations around the world that offer such activities. However, participation levels are generally lower for older women than at any other age. Thus, there is a need for a greater focus on continuing to mitigate the participation barriers women may encounter as they age.

CASE STUDY

Digital marketing for walking groups

This case study will focus on a 'digital marketing pilot for Walking Groups' (London Sport, 2018), a project designed to use social media to engage older women and encourage them to join free, local, existing walking groups. Technology and social media are often seen as the domain of younger people. However, even in these age groups, using technology to encourage participation in sport is still greatly underutilised. It is often assumed that older adults rarely use social media or technology, therefore using digital marketing to engage with this population group was an exciting initiative. This programme was devised and led by London Sport, which is the Active Partnership for

London in the UK. At present, Sport England, and consequently, the Active Partnerships, has a strategic focus to use behaviour change techniques to engage inactive people in physical activity.

The project was piloted in 2018 and worked with partners, including The Ramblers, Make Sport Fun and ten London boroughs (suburbs). The purpose was to utilise Facebook Lead Generation adverts, to specifically target older women (55+) residing in these ten boroughs. The programme organisers used social media, as they felt traditional marketing methods, such as posters and leaflets, were not particularly effective in engaging those who are inactive and often socially isolated. Older women who lived within one mile of a walking group were targeted in the Facebook adverts. Using existing activity sessions meant the programme was likely to be more sustainable and provide the women with a long-term activity to engage in.

Different messages and images on Facebook were used throughout the pilot to determine which type of advert worked best. Figure 5.1 was deemed to be the most successful advert. The messaging provided a clear call to action,

FIGURE 5.1 Most successful advertisement for Walking Group initiative, London Sport (2018)

meaning woman saw a purpose to sign up and made it easy for them to take the next step. It was determined that the most attractive images were close up shots of attendees' faces, people looking happy and of people in the 'younger old' older adults' category, generally those aged 55–65 years old.

A number of communication methods were then used to mitigate common barriers for older women to exercise. Text messages were used to firstly welcome the women and also to provide details of a nearby walk. Participants were also sent an automated text reminder before the walk and after four weeks; a final text message asked if they had attended any walks. Emails were sent regularly over that first two-week period, post–sign up – to provide information, such as what to wear – and case studies of group attendees, who they could relate to. The women could also communicate with London Sport staff via Facebook Messenger and text messages to ask specific questions, enabling programme staff to alleviate concerns and mitigate some potential barriers.

In the pilot phase over a three-month period, 2,799 women signed up via Facebook and 360 reported that they had joined a local walk (13%). The majority of those who signed up (71%) were classed as less active, with 55% of those deemed inactive, which demonstrated the success of using digital marketing to engage with inactive older women. Those who had yet to attend a walk were provided with behaviour change support by the programme, either through being encouraged to download a physical activity app (NHS Active 10 app) or through continuing conversations with the team to discuss other activity options in their local area. To understand the longer-term impact of this programme, older women who joined the walking groups were to be contacted after six months, to determine if their activity levels had improved.

In 2019, London Sport is expanding this programme to all 33 London boroughs, to encourage more older women in the capital city to increase their physical activity.

The use of technology to engage older women to be more physically active was an innovative idea and will hopefully be used in other types of physical activity programmes. Longer term academic evaluations of technology use will enable practitioners to understand best practice for the effective use technology and social media to increase activity levels for this population group.

References

Adamson, L., & Parker, G. (2006). "There's more to life than just walking": Older women's ways of staying healthy and happy. *Journal of Aging and Physical Activity*, 14(4), 380–391.

Berlin, K., Kruger, T., & Klenosky, D. B. (2018). A mixed-methods investigation of successful aging among older women engaged in sports-based versus exercise-based leisure time physical activities. *Journal of Women & Aging*, 30(1), 27–37.

Cedergren, A., King, K. A., Wagner, D. I., & Wegley, S. (2007). Perceived social health benefits among participants in a countywide senior chair volleyball program. *Activities, Adaptation & Aging*, 31(4), 23–36.

Cuskelly, G. (2004). Volunteer retention in community sport organisations. *European Sport Management Quarterly*, 4(2), 59–76.

Dionigi, R. (2006). Competitive sport as leisure in later life: Negotiations, discourse, and aging. *Leisure Sciences*, 28(2), 181–196.

Djärv, T., Wikman, A., Johar, A., & Lagergren, P. (2013). Poor health-related quality of life in the Swedish general population: The association with disease and lifestyle factors. *Scandinavian Journal of Public Health*, 41(7), 744–753.

Edwards, M. B., & Rowe, K. (2019). Managing sport for health: An introduction to the special issue. *Sport Management Review*, 22(1) 1–4.

Eime, R. M., Harvey, J. T., Charity, M. J., Casey, M. M., Westerbeek, H., & Payne, W. R. (2016). Age profiles of sport participants. *BMC Sports Science, Medicine and Rehabilitation*, 8(6), 1–10.

Eman, J. (2012). The role of sports in making sense of the process of growing old. *Journal of Aging Studies*, 26(4), 467–475.

Gayman, A. M., Fraser-Thomas, J., & Baker, J. (2017). Relational developmental systems metatheory: A conceptual framework to understand and promote older adults' involvement in sport. *European Review of Aging and Physical Activity*, 14(12).

Grenade, L., & Boldy, D. (2008). Social isolation and loneliness among older people: issues and future challenges in community and residential settings. *Australian Health Review*, 32(3), 468–478.

Haskell, W. L., Lee, I. M., Pate, R. R., Powell, K. E., Blair, S. N., Franklin, B. A., Macera, C. A., Heath, G. W., Thompson, P. D., & Bauman, A. (2007). Physical activity and public health: Updated recommendation for adults from the American College of Sports Medicine and the American Heart Association. *Circulation*, 116(9), 1081–1093.

Heo, J., Culp, B., Yamada, N., & Won, Y. (2013). Promoting successful aging through competitive sports participation: Insights from older adults. *Qualitative Health Research*, 23(1), 105–113.

Horton, S., Dionigi, R. A., Gard, M., Baker, J., & Weir, P. (2018). "Don't sit back with the geraniums, get out": The complexity of older women's stories of sport participation. *Journal of Amateur Sport*, 4(1), 24–51.

Jenkin, C. R., Hilland, T. A., & Eime, R. M. (2018a). *Walking Basketball Program: Evaluation Report for Basketball Victoria*. Australia.

Jenkin, C. R., Eime, R. M., Westerbeek, H., & van Uffelen, J. G. Z. (2018b). Sport for adults aged 50+ years: Participation benefits and barriers. *Journal of Aging and Physical Activity*, 26(3), 363–371.

Jenkin, C. R., Eime, R. M., Westerbeek, H., O'Sullivan, G., & van Uffelen, J. G. Z. (2016a). Are they "worth their weight in gold"? Sport for older adults: benefits and barriers of their participation for sporting organisations. *International Journal of Sport Policy and Politics*, 8(4) 663–680.

Jenkin, C., Eime, R., Westerbeek, H., & Van Uffelen, J. (2016b). *Why don't Older Adults Participate in Sport?* Report prepared for the Australian Sports Commission by Victoria University, Institute of Sport, Exercise and Active Living (ISEAL). Australia.

Jenkin, C. R., Eime, R. M., Westerbeek, H., O'Sullivan, G., & van Uffelen, J. G. Z. (2017). Sport and ageing: A systematic review of the determinants and trends of participation in sport for older adults. *BMC Public Health*, 17(976), 1–20.

Kelley, K., Little, S., Lee, J. S., Birendra, K. C., & Henderson, K. (2014). Articulating meanings of positive adjustment to aging through physical activity participation among older adults. *Journal of Park & Recreation Administration*, 32(1), 63–79.

Kirby, J. B., & Kluge, M. A. (2013). Going for the gusto: Competing for the first time at age 65. *Journal of Aging and Physical Activity*, 21(3), 290–308.

Kolt, G. S., Driver, R. P., & Giles, L. C. (2004). Why older Australians participate in exercise and sport. *Journal of Aging and Physical Activity*, 12(2), 185–198.

Litchfield, C., & Dionigi, R. A. (2011). The meaning of Sports participation in the lives of middle-aged and older women. *International Journal of Interdisciplinary Social Sciences*, 6(5), 21–39.

London Sport. (2017). *Sitting Netball Shoots and Scores*. Retrieved from https://data.londonsport.org/insights/sitting-netball-shoots-and-scores/

London Sport. (2018). *Using Facebook to Recruit New Participants for Walking Groups: A Digital Behaviour Change Pilot*. Retrieved from https://londonsport.org/wp-content/uploads/2018/11/Digital-Behaviour-Change-Pilot-Interim-Report-Nov-18-Online.pdf

Long, J. A., Dashper, K., Fletcher, T., & Ormerod, N. (2015). *Understanding Participation and Non-Participation in Sport amongst Black and Minority Ethnic Groups in Wales*. Report prepared for Sport Wales by Leeds Beckett University.

Misener, K., Doherty, A., & Hamm-Kerwin, S. (2010). Learning from the experiences of older adult volunteers in sport: A serious leisure perspective. *Journal of Leisure Research*, 42(2), 267–289.

Naar, J. J., Wong, J. D., West, S. T., Son, J. S., & Liechty, T. (2017). A socioecological approach to women's participation in competitive softball during middle and late adulthood: Implications for the future. *Topics in Geriatric Rehabilitation*, 33(3), 170–181.

Nichols, G., & Ralston, R. (2011). Social inclusion through volunteering: The legacy potential of the 2012 Olympic Games. *Sociology*, 45(5), 900–914.

Nichols, G., Knight, C., Mirfin-Boukouris, H., Uri, C., Hogg, E., & Storr, R. (2016). *Motivations of Sport Volunteers in England: A Review for Sport England*.

Pfister, G. (2012). It is never too late to win – sporting activities and performances of ageing women. *Sport in Society*, 15(3), 369–384.

Rechel, B., Doyle, Y., Grundy, E., & McKee, M. (2009). Health systems and policy analysis: How can health systems respond to population aging? Retrieved from https://apps.who.int/iris/bitstream/handle/10665/107941/E92560.pdf

Siegenthaler, K. L., & O'Dell, I. (2003). Older golfers: Serious leisure and successful aging. *World Leisure Journal*, 45(1), 45–52.

Sport Australia. (2018). *AusPlay National Data Tables*. Retrieved from www.clearinghouseforsport.gov.au/research/smi/ausplay/results/national

Sport England. (2018). *Active Lives Adult Survey*. November 16/17 Report. London.

Thoits, P. A., & Hewitt, L. N. (2001). Volunteer work and well-being. *Journal of Health and Social Behavior*, 42(June), 115–131.

Toepoel, V. (2013). Ageing, leisure, and social connectedness: How could leisure help reduce social isolation of older people? *Social Indicators Research*, 113(1), 355–372.

United Nations. (2017). *World Population Prospects: 2017* (Population Division, Department of Economic and Social Affairs). New York.

van Uffelen, J. G. Z., Jenkin, C. R., Westerbeek, H. M., Biddle, S. J. H. & Eime, R. M. (2015). *Active and Healthy Ageing through Sport*. Report prepared for the Australian Sports Commission: Victoria University, Institute of Sport, Exercise and Active Living (ISEAL).

Women in Sport. (2017). *Silver Linings – Engaging Women in Sport in Later Life*. London. Retrieved from www.womeninsport.org/wp-content/uploads/2017/10/Silver-Linings-report.pdf?x99836

Wong, J. D., Son, J. S., West, S. T., Naar, J. J., & Liechty, T. (2018). A life course examination of women's team sport participation in late adulthood. *Journal of Aging and Physical Activity*, 27(1), 73–82.

World Health Organisation. (2015). *World Report on Ageing and Health*. Geneva.

World Health Organisation. (2017). *Global Strategy and Action Plan on Ageing and Health*. Geneva.

6

DEVELOPING SPORT FOR WOMEN AND GIRLS WITH A DISABILITY

Andrew Hammond and Hannah Macdougall

Introduction

Women with disabilities are among some of the most disadvantaged groups in our society. In Canada, for example, of the 6.2 million people who experience disability, it is reported that more women (24%) than men (20%) have an impairment (Statistics Canada, 2017). Furthermore, women and girls who have a disability face double disadvantage – disablism and sexism – when seeking to participate in sport and organised physical activity (Anderson, et al., 2008; Olenik, et al., 1995; Rolfe, et al., 2012). Thus, it would appear that new approaches are required from policy makers, sport practitioners and researchers to engage more women and girls with disabilities in sport and physical activity, especially at the community level. Practitioners are encouraged to consider female disability sport as an expansionary opportunity, which is yet to have been fully appreciated and actualised.

This chapter comes at an exciting time and has allowed us to review recent research that has examined the intersection between gender and disability. This chapter is divided into four sections: a) an outline of the feminist disability studies perspective underpinning the chapter; b) a review of research that has explored the motivations and barriers to sports participation for participation for women and girls with a disability;(c) a real-world example of how sport leaders have supported the inclusion of women and girls with a disability in Vancouver, British Columbia; and d) practical recommendations to policy makers and sport leaders on how to improve the provision of sport for women and girls with disability.

A note on language: where possible 'person first' terminology is used (i.e. 'people with disabilities') in this chapter. This terminology is preferred because the authors, Hannah and Andrew, are Australian, and Andrew is working in Canada where this is also the preferred nomenclature. Governments and key disability advocacy groups in both Canada and Australia see person first terminology to be least offensive by the vast majority of people with a disability. However, this terminology is not universal, and it would be foolish to assume all people who experience, or are labelled as disabled, prefer this terminology in Australia or Canada. Indeed, there are some scholars, such as Fiona Kumari-Campbell who is Australian, who prefer the terminology disabled people in their writing.

Feminist disability studies

According to one of the key pioneers of feminist disability studies, US scholar Rosemarie Garland-Thomson, a key focus of feminist disability studies is to augment the terms used to discuss disability, and to confront the limits of the ways we understand human diversity, the materiality of the body, multiculturalism, and the social formations that interpret bodily differences (Garland-Thomson, 2002, p. 3).

Central to Garland-Thomson's thesis is how the *integration* and *transformation* of disability and feminist theory can expand and deepen analyses that are of concern for both disability and feminist scholars. In relation to sport, a feminist disability lens considers a dual analysis of the body and sporting practices from a gendered and ability perspective. This thinking allows us to think, for example, both about what kind of bodies are accepted in sporting contexts, but also, to consider what practices are acceptable to perform. For example, a feminist disability studies lens prompts us to question why wheelchair rugby and sledge hockey are predominantly male-dominated sports at the Paralympic Games. Also, why women and women's competitions are excluded or have not gained prominence in these spaces? And why sport and physical cultures research has (at times) ignored the perspectives of women with disability? The feminist disability studies lens allows considerations of these novel ideas, while not losing sight of traditional questions, such as why men's football (soccer) dominates women's and disability forms of the sport? We argue that an analysis of disability shifts the conceptual framework of feminism to strengthen our understanding of how oppression works along multiple lines – such as race, sexuality, ethnicity or gender – to infect institutions, such as sport. We argue that such an analysis provides a vantage point from which to explore and unpack how normativity is produced through power and privilege (Garland-Thomson, 2002).

Motivations for participation for women and girls with a disability

Motivation is a topic that explores what moves people to act, think, and develop (Deci & Ryan, 2008); it is a construct used to describe 'the internal and external forces that produce the initiation, direction, intensity, and persistence of behaviour' (Vallerand & Thill, 1993, p. 18, translated from French). Much of the sport psychology research for women and men competing in Paralympic sports during the 1990s and 2000s focused upon participation motives (Perreault & Vallerand, 2007). Indeed, the topic of motivation within Paralympic sport has seen various theories applied, such as Self-Determination Theory (Banack, Sabiston & Bloom, 2011; Perreault & Vallerand, 2007),

Achievement Goal Theory (Pensgaard, Roberts & Ursin, 1999), Social Cognitive Theory, and the Sport Commitment Model (Martin, 2006). It is beyond the scope of this chapter to clearly define and explore specific motivational concepts (see Ryan & Deci, 2000; Nicholls 1984, 1989); instead, this chapter focuses on explicitly investigating the motivations for sport participation for women and girls with a disability.

Reflecting the feminist disability theory discussion above, the common trend of Parasport research has predominantly focused on male athletes with a disability (Martin, Malone & Hilyer, 2011). There is a lack of research focusing on the motivations for sport participation for female athletes with a disability. Evidence of this exists strongly in two systematic reviews that explored wellbeing and motivation for women and men with a physical disability in elite sport and injured combat veterans (Caddick & Smith, 2014; Macdougall, et al., 2015). Within the review by Caddick and Smith (2014), only three out of 11 studies included veterans who were female. While the review by Macdougall and colleagues (2015) saw 75% of studies include women and girls, the studies reviewed typically saw disproportionate ratios of women to men; for example, Dorogi, Szabo and Bognár's (2008) study included 46 men, but only 13 women. This theme of disproportionate ratios extends to studies beyond those included in the reviews (see, for example, Pensgaard, Roberts & Ursin (1999)).

Like the general population, people with disabilities – men, women and non-binary – are motivated to participate in sport for many different reasons (Cottingham, et al., 2018). For instance, in a study that explored physical activity participation in Pacific adolescent girls with a physical disability in New Zealand, it was found that adolescent girls with disabilities wanted to participate in sport for intrinsic reasons such as 'for fun and enjoyment' or 'feeling good' (Dickson, 2018). In contrast, adult women who played competitive wheelchair basketball reported higher levels of intrinsic motivation – that is, motivation from sources inherent in the activity itself – than their male counterparts (Perreault & Vallerand, 2007). Thus, it would appear, regardless of age or sport level, women and adolescent girls seem to be more self-determined than men in sport (Brière, et al., 1995; Perreault & Vallerand, 2007).While intrinsic motivations have been key themes, Anderson (2009a) included participant voices where sport promotes the competitive spirit and athletic identity for girls with a disability. For athletic identity to be affirmed, participants need to develop competence, which in turn, reinforces potential. For example, the statement 'a lot of my friends, they always forget I have disabilities', implies that a certain degree of competence has been achieved in the eyes of her peers and that she fits in. There are consistent themes in the research literature around intrinsic and task-oriented motivation for women and girls with a disability to participate in sport. The importance of social connections and social support has also been emphasised.

Also highlighted in a study from the United States, where Anderson (2009a) investigated the involvement of 12 adolescent girls in disability sport, was the theme of support and role models. The majority of girls indicated it was the influence of *multiple* social agents, such as parents, friends, peers and role models; girls heard about sport 'from a friend… she used to be on the team' (Anderson, 2009a, p. 437). Similarly,

Ruddell and Shinew (2006) in their study, which explored the socialisation process for women into elite disability sport, indicated the relative importance of multiple influential people – 'significant others' – not just one singular source. These significant others included a mother, father, sibling, therapist, coach, friend, or peer, but not those from educational settings (Ruddell & Shinew, 2006). External factors – especially the influence of a coach's expectations and equipment – have also been shown to contribute to success and the task goal-belief dimension within goal achievement motivation theory for both men and women wheelchair basketball athletes (White & Duda, 1993). On the other hand, Page, Connor and Peterson (2001) found that it may not necessarily be purely influential people, significant others or role models who encourage sport participation; rather, it was the perception of others that influenced motivation to participate in sport. As such, role models within sport for girls with a disability have influenced sporting definitions and perceptions through demonstrating that they *could* participate and *how* to participate (Ruddell & Shinew, 2006).

Additionally, women and girls with disabilities see access to participation as important if they are to be motivated in sport and physical activity (Dickson, 2018). In one of the few North American studies of engagement in sport and physical activity at the recreational level, many women positioned sport and physical activity as something that made life worth living (Dickson, 2018). Similarly, in their study of 12 American women with disabilities, Blinde and McCallister (1999) found three main reasons for participation: maintaining functionality, social factors and psychological factors. These motivations were highly related to outcomes, which were intrinsic gains through an enhanced view of capabilities, their body became a source of strength and participation provided a sense of control in life. Women in their study were quoted as saying that recreational sport and physical activity was 'a reason "to get out of the apartment" and be "with other people." [...] [And] "something to look forward to when [they] wake-up in the morning"' (Blinde & McCallister, 1999, p. 308). Indeed, in the quantitative analysis of wheelchair basketball athletes by Skordilis and colleagues (2001), women athletes were found to approach sport participation with a greater focus on personal goals when compared to their male counterparts. It was found that men had a greater propensity to approach sport with goals related to competition (Skordilis, et al., 2001). These results are not aligned with research that has found the most relevant sources of motivation and incentives for both men and women with physical disabilities were 'enjoying the sport' and 'improving one's performance level' (Kampfe, et al., 2014).

Barriers for participation for women and girls with a disability

Women and girls with disabilities face double exclusion from sport when compared with the general population. From a gender perspective, social norms around masculinity and femininity dictate how girls and boys, women and men, can and cannot use their bodies. And in high-income countries (HIC), sport is positioned as masculine heteronormative and thus promotes and embraces physicality, aggression, risk taking and dominance (Connell, 2008; Cottingham, et al., 2018; Jeanes, 2006; Vertinsky, 1990). According to Blinde and McCallister (1999), people with disabilities – and women with disabilities in particular – are juxtaposed against traditional masculine notions of sport and are thus assumed to be weak, passive, dependent and to have varying degrees of physical inability. Thus, socialisation of gender appropriate roles creates various barriers such as marginalisation, trivialisation and stigmatisation (Bryson, 1987). However, according to some of the participants in the study by Blinde and McCallister (1999), the greatest effect and limiter of this 'double whammy' was felt through having a disability, rather than being a woman. This was reflected in the study conducted by Page and colleagues (2001); barriers described by participants relating to perceived incompetence and discrimination were due to disability rather than gender. Both women and men with disabilities – while they felt they were an athlete first and disabled second – were faced with labels such as 'courageous', 'special', 'brave' by non-disabled individuals (Page, et al., 2001).

Additionally, an aspect of having a disability and being female is that overcoming the barriers from membership in one group may not assist in tackling the difficulties associated with membership in the other group (Anderson, Wozencroft & Bedini, 2008). Thus, it is not a simple case of transferring skills from one area of life to another area. For instance, in a report commissioned by the Office for Women in Sport and Recreation (OWSR) in Victoria, Australia, Phillips and colleagues (2018) found that sporting leaders have difficulty isolating factors that specifically impacted women and girls with a disability. This was a rather disappointing finding, given that a vast body of research (for example, Anderson, Bedini, & Moreland, 2005; Anderson, et al., 2008; Appleton, et al., 1994; French & Hainsworth, 2001; Page, et al., 2001; Phillips, et al., 2018) has suggested that barriers for women and girls with disabilities to sport and physical activity occurs due to:

- low levels of social support
- gender stereotypes
- lack of funding, lack of appropriate programming and
- a lack of role models.

In addition to the above barriers, Anderson and colleagues (2009) have suggested that the family and friends of girls with disabilities typically assume a spectator role. Thus, significant role models for girls with a disability, through their behaviour modelling, or lack thereof, are negatively impacting sport participation (Brittain, 2004; Kristen, Patriksson & Fridlund, 2002).

While we have focused extensively on how external organisations or factors can create barriers to sport participation, it is important that girls with disabilities and parents of people with disabilities can also create internal barriers through a lack of awareness or information. For instance, research has explored the 'cotton wool ball' effect of overprotective parents and carers of children with disabilities. Research into this style of parenting highlights how participation barriers have been created (Kristen, et al., 2002). Additionally, in Ruddell and Shinew's (2006) study, the barriers of lack of education and awareness were espoused by a number of participants who played wheelchair basketball. As such, agencies, such as education systems, hospitals, physical education teachers, through their lack of awareness, have contributed to specific barriers for women and girls with disabilities. The following section provides a practical example of the steps that sports leaders in British Columbia, Canada, have taken to address some of these issues illuminated in the chapter above.

Recommendations

As the chapter has progressed, there has been a shift between 'a green cape' and a 'red cape' approach to investigating the participation in sport for women and girls with disability. The green and red cape approach metaphor was espoused by Pawelski (2016). Pawelski (2016) discussed that a red cape approach is one where we use our power to fight the undesirable and unjust things in our world, such as the discrimination and entrenched masculine cultures within sport. In contrast, a green cape approach suggests that we use our talents to help grow the desirable things in our world (Pawelski, 2016). For example, using a well-being and strengths-based approach to grow the participation of women and girls with a disability in sport. The recommendations below are a mixture of both, a reversible cape if you will, and briefly summarise and synthesise key practical points made in other reviews.

While geographically specific to Victoria, Australia, we want to highlight the recommendations made by Phillips and colleagues from the Women in Sport and Recreation (OWSR) in Victoria, Australia, with regards to their recommendations to address barriers faced by women and girls with a disability. These included:

- Focus and development of champions / role models / buddy systems – these systems need to include an ability for an individual to walk the journey with that person
- Look to cater for all abilities, rather than just the physical disability
- Engage with parents of girls with a disability to encourage participation
- Sports to share narratives of women and girls with a disability in their sport
- Ensure the OWSR ambassadors include women and girls with a disability.

We also argue that there is a need for governing bodies to lead the way in demonstrating collaboration with traditional media to create the role models that women and girls with a disability sorely need. An example of how a media and government partnership can be made to rectify the role model issue is the Victorian iteration of This Girl Can. The campaign originated in the UK, and has since been adopted by VicHealth (2018) in Victoria in Australia (a government funded organisation). The campaign crosses age, ethnicity, disability etc. This Girl Can – Victoria celebrates and supports Victorian women to embrace physical activity in a way that suits them (VicHealth, 2018). We acknowledge that this campaign is far from perfect (see for example commentary by Depper, Fullagar & Francombe-Webb, 2019) however to its credit it did shine a light on promoting women with disabilities in sport[2]. A key role model for women and girls with a disability in the This Girl Can,

Victoria, campaign include Janelle, who during her teenage years found she was embarrassed about her prosthetic leg. However, two years ago she started running with a blade and decided to tackle her insecurities. Similarly, Neslihan was discouraged from playing sport when she was younger due to vision impairment; her parents feared she would get hurt. In her thirties, Neslihan began to run and has since enjoyed the freedom this brings. While these campaigns are not perfect, we argue that it is important to provide role-models for women and girls with disabilities – especially those that cut across age and ethnicity. It would also be encouraged for This Girl Can style campaigns in future to also include women and girls with disabilities who have less function or 'invisible' disabilities too.

To sum up, this chapter has illustrated the motivations and barriers that women and girls with a disability face to participate in sport. The chapter has also presented a detailed case study to provide an example of how a programme that targets women and girls with a disability can assist in participation, motivation, and a reduction of barriers. It also became evident throughout the writing of this chapter, there are multiple layers, problems and motivations when looking to enhance the participation of women and girls with a disability in sport. As such, there is not a one-size-fits-all solution or approach. Based on the recommendations above, multiple solutions, stakeholders, and collaboration will be needed to create equity and equality for women and girls with a disability in the future.

CASE STUDY

Wheelchair Sport British Columbia (Canada)

A number of disability sporting organisations in British Columbia (BC) have identified the lack of participation of Women and girls in disability sports as an issue. For instance, organisations such as the British Columbia Wheelchair Sports Association (BCWSA) and the British Columbia Wheelchair Basketball Society (BCWCBS) have been proactively trying to engage more woman and girls in the programmes they manage. For BCWSA, these sports include wheelchair tennis, wheelchair rugby, wheelchair athletics. In contrast, BCWCBS focuses on wheelchair basketball. In this chapter, BCWSA provides a case study that demonstrates how organisations and sports managers are proactively working to increase opportunities for women and girls with disabilities to participate in sport. Presented below are the strategies BCWSA has used to increase the participation of women and girls with a disability in sport.

The BCWSA is an independent sporting organisation that utilises office space at the Spinal Cord Injury BC offices in South Vancouver. The BCWSA is a multisport organisation and provides support and programming for individuals in wheelchairs who wish to play wheelchair tennis, wheelchair rugby and wheelchair athletics, specifically catering for athletes with physical disabilities who can use manual, self-propelled wheelchairs. The BCWSA is affiliated with the national governing body of wheelchair rugby, and works in partnership with the provincial sporting organisations, BC Athletics and BC Tennis. The BCWSA provides Para Sport programming at competitions and tournaments, taking some shared responsibility for the integration of people with disabilities into the broader sport system, but in many respects, BCWSA takes a standalone, segregated, and dedicated approach to its role, mission, and purpose.

According to its website (www.bcwheelchairsports.com), 'BC Wheelchair Sports Association knows that girls with disabilities face unique barriers to getting active'. This is one of the possible reasons why they developed the Girls Only Wheelchair Tennis programme in 2018. According to the website, the programme was coached by Paralympian Sarah Hunter, and aimed to provide a 'supportive environment for […] girls to learn wheelchair tennis, make friends and get mentored by women with disabilities'. The webpage features numerous pictures of girls enjoying themselves playing wheelchair tennis and testimonials from girls and parents of girls with disabilities. One testimonial is highlighted in the example of Nikki and her mum, Kim:

> Before I met Megan and Judy, I'd never had a friend with a disability before. I can talk to them about stuff that I wouldn't talk to other people about. I definitely feel that we have more of a bond because we all have disabilities. (Nikki, aged 11)
>
> The idea of bringing girls in a similar situation together was amazing because a lightbulb went on in Nikki where she realised that she's not the only one. There are all these other women playing wheelchair tennis. It's opened her eyes to all the possibilities of what's out there.
>
> *(Nikki's mum, Kim)*

While the above quotes show motivations for girls with a disability to participate in sport, it needs to be provided in context. Specifically, BCWSA was using the quotes as part of a broader marketing strategy around 'give it up for the girls this giving Tuesday' to raise and elicit more donations for their programmes. Nevertheless, the quotes highlight and echo the findings of the research reviewed in this chapter that asserts how strong social support is critical to the success of sport participation for women and girls with a disability. It is clear that with some thoughtful planning, programmes such as BCWSA's Girls Only Wheelchair Tennis programme can lead to genuine feelings of community connectedness and social cohesion that improves the lives of the girls participating. Indeed, sport for Nikki became a little less intimidating when her friends were also going to activities such as basketball or sailing.

The BCWSA case study also offers further insights into role model visibility. For example, through conducting its own research, BCWSA determined that girls being able to see other girls participating in sport is important to counter the dominance of masculine discourses and practices that characterise sport. As noted by one anonymous sport development officer who worked at BCWSA,

> One of the things that we learned through interviewing these parents was that ... there is one little girl, whose mom drove up her to the track programme and she looked at the track and she saw boys and she did not see anybody that looked like her or she would identify with, so she refused to get out of the car. It was not until we held a girls-only programme, with two or three girls with a female mentor as a leader that she could be convinced to go.

As such, it is critical for girls and women to be able to see themselves in sporting spaces and connect with others like them. It is also important to note how the BCWSA's positioned girls with disabilities as being physically inactive and at risk of developing low self-esteem aligning with a charity and medical model discourse of disability. This suggests that,

> We know that girls with disabilities who are physically active have greater self-esteem, more self-confidence, more friends and a higher likelihood of going to university and getting a job.

While there is no doubt that disability sport charitable societies are enhancing opportunities for girls and women to engage in sport and physical activities, such statements in their marketing could be considered potentially problematic by disability studies researchers and disability rights advocates such as Garland-Thomson, based on the perspectives discussed in this chapter. This is because disability sport charitable societies (such as BCWSA) are drawing upon medical and charity discourses to elicit donations. In so doing, they risk positioning disabled girls as helpless and in need of assistance and charity from others (Moore & Slee 2012). Although such notions and discourses of dependency and charity are potentially harmful to women and girls with disability, without alternative funding streams, it seems that disability sport charitable societies will likely continue to draw on these discourses in their marketing in order to decrease barriers and costs to participate in disability sport, which remain reasonably high.

A positive outcome of more government funding for disability sport charitable societies might be that there is less pressure on these groups to position their athletes as helpless victims in order to attain charity dollars. This case study, therefore, draws attention to the need for sport developers to be cognisant of the messages that can be implied or inferred in the pursuit of funding and how such messages might, albeit unintentionally, be disempowering for the communities they are seeking to empower.

Acknowledgements

Andrew wishes to acknowledge the financial contributions from viaSport British Columbia, MITACS Canada and the Canadian Social Science and Humanities

Research Council (SSHRC) that funded his postdoctoral research fellowship as part of a broader partnership development grant held and led by Dr Andrea Bundon at the University of British Columbia. His postdoc funding led to the development of the case studies in this chapter.

Hannah and Andrew wish to thank Marni Abbott-Peter (BCWCBS), Gail Hamamoto (BCWSA and Canadian Paralympic Committee) and Lisa Hingh (viaSport British Columbia) for their assistance in developing the case studies.

References

Anderson, D. (2009). Adolescent girls' involvement in disability sport: Implications for identity development. *Journal of Sport and Social Issues*, 33(4), 427–449.

Anderson, D. M., Bedini, L. A., & Moreland, L. (2005). Getting ALL girls into the game: Physically active recreation for girls with disabilities. *Journal of Park and Recreation Administration*, 23(4), 78–103.

Anderson, D. M., Wozencroft, A. & Bedini, L. A. (2008). Adolescent girls' involvement in disability sport: A comparison of social support mechanisms. *Journal of Leisure Research*, 40(2), 183–207.

Anderson, E. D. (2009). The maintenance of masculinity among the stakeholders of sport. *Sport Management Review*, 12(1), 3–14.

Apelmo, E. (2012). (Dis) Abled bodies, gender, and citizenship in the Swedish sports movement. *Disability & Society*, 27(4), 563–574.

Appleton, P. L., Minchom, P. E., Ellis, N. C., Elliott, C. E., Boll, V., & Jones, P. (1994). The self-concept of young people with spina bifida: A population based study. *Developmental Medicine and Child Neurology*, 36(3), 198–215.

Banack, H. R., Sabiston, C. M. & Bloom, G. A. (2011). Coach autonomy support, basic need satisfaction, and intrinsic motivation of paralympic athletes. *Research Quarterly for Exercise and Sport*, 82(4), 722–730.

Bandura, A. (1996). *Self-Efficacy: The Exercise of Control*. New York: Freeman.

Blinde, E. M. & McCallister, S. G. (1999). Women, disability, and sport and physical fitness activity: The intersection of gender and disability dynamics. *Research Quarterly for Exercise and Sport*, 70(3), 303–312.

Brière, N. M., Vallerand, R. J., Blais, M. R., & Pelletier, L. G. (1995). Développement et validation d'une mesure de motivation intrinsèque, extrinsèque et d'amotivation en contexte sportif: l'Échelle de motivation dans les sports [On the development and validation of the French form of the Sport Motivation Scale] (EMS). *International Journal of Sport Psychology*, 26(4), 465–489.

Brittain, I. (2004). The role of schools in constructing self-perceptions of sport and physical education in relation to people with disabilities. *Sport, Education and Society*, 9(1), 75–94.

Bryson, L. (1987). Sport and the maintenance of masculine hegemony. *Women's Studies International Forum*, 10, 349–360.

Caddick, N., & Smith, B. (2014). The impact of sport and physical activity on the well-being of combat veterans: A systematic review. *Psychology of Sport and Exercise*, 15(1), 9–18.

Connell, R. W. (2008). Masculinity construction and sports in boys' education: A framework for thinking about the issue. *Sport, Education and Society*, 13(2), 131–145.

Cottingham, M., Hums, M., Jeffress, M., Lee, D., & Richard, H. (2018). Women of power soccer: exploring disability and gender in the first competitive team sport for powerchair users. *Sport in Society*, 21(11), 1817–1830.

Deci, E. L., & Ryan, R. M. (2008). Facilitating optimal motivation and psychological well-being across life's domains. *Canadian Psychology/Psychologie canadienne*, 49(1), 14–23.

Depper, A., Fullagar, S., & Francombe-Webb, J. (2019). This Girl Can? The limitations of digital do-it-yourself empowerment in women's active embodiment campaigns. In Parry, D., Johnson, C., & Fullagar, S. (eds) *Digital Dilemmas*. Basingstoke: Palgrave Macmillan, 183–204.

Dickson, C. (2018). Physical activity participation in Pacific adolescent girls with a physical disability. *Pacific Health*, 1(1). doi:10.24135/pacifichealth.v1i1.3

Dorogi, L., Szabo, A., & Bognár, J. (2008). Goal orientation and perceived motivational climate in Hungarian athletes with physical and visual disabilities and in able-bodied athletes. *Kinesiology*, 40(2), 163–170.

French, D., & Hainsworth, J. (2001). "There aren't any buses and the swimming pool is always cold!": Obstacles and opportunities in the provision of sport for disabled people. *Managing Leisure*, 6(1), 35–49.

Gardner, F. L., & Moore, Z. E. (2012). Mindfulness and acceptance models in sport psychology: A decade of basic and applied scientific advancements. *Canadian Psychology*, 53(4), 309–318.

Garland-Thomson, R. (2002). Integrating disability, transforming feminist theory. *NWSA journal*, 14(3), 1–32.

Garland-Thomson, R. (2005). Feminist Disability Studies. *Signs: Journal of Women in Culture and Society*, 30(2), 1557–1587.

Houghton, E. J., Pieper, L. P., & Smith, M. M. (2017). *Women in the 2016 Olympic and Paralympic Games: An Analysis of Participation, Leadership, and Media Coverage*. East Meadow, NY: Women's Sports Foundation.

Kabat-Zinn, J. (1994). *Wherever You Go, There You Are: Mindfulness Meditation in Everyday Life*. New York: Hyperion Books.

Kämpfe, A., Höner, O., & Willimczik, K. (2014). Multiplicity and development of achievement motivation: A comparative study between German elite athletes with and without a disability. *European Journal of Adapted Physical Activity*, 7(1), 32–48.

Kristen, L., Patriksson, G., & Fridlund, B. (2002). Conceptions of children and adolescents with physical disabilities about their participation in a sports programme. *European Physical Education Review*, 8(2), 139–156.

Macdougall, H., O'Halloran, P., Shields, N., & Sherry, E. (2015). Comparing the well-being of Para and Olympic sport athletes: A systematic review. *Adapted Physical Activity Quarterly*, 32(3), 256–276.

Martin, J. J. (2006). Psychosocial aspects of youth disability sport. *Adapted Physical Activity Quarterly*, 23(1), 65–77.

Martin, J. J., Malone, L. A., & Hilyer, J. C. (2011). Personality and mood in women's Paralympic basketball champions. *Journal of Clinical Sport Psychology*, 5(3), 197–210.

Moore, M., & Slee, R. (2012). Disability studies, inclusive education and, exclusion. *Development in Practice*, 4(1), 23–34.

Nicholls, J. G. (1984). Achievement motivation: Conceptions of ability, subjective experience, task choice, and performance. *Psychological Review*, 91, 328–346. doi:10.1037//0033–0295X.91.3.328

Nicholls, J. G. (1989). *The Competitive Ethos and Democratic Education*. Cambridge, MA: Harvard University Press.

Olenik, L. M., Matthews, J. M., & Steadward, R. D. (1995). Women, disability and sport: Unheard voices. *Canadian Woman Studies*, 15(4), 54–57.

Page, S. J., O'Connor, E., & Peterson, K. (2001). Leaving the disability ghetto: A qualitative study of factors underlying achievement motivation among athletes with disabilities. *Journal of Sport and Social Issues*, 25(1), 40–55.

Pawelski, J. O. (2016). Defining the 'positive' in positive psychology: Part II. A normative analysis. *The Journal of Positive Psychology*, 11(4), 357–365.

Pensgaard, A. M., Roberts, G. C., & Ursin, H. (1999). Motivational factors and coping strategies of Norwegian Paralympic and Olympic winter sport athletes. *Adapted Physical Activity Quarterly*, 16(3), 238–250.

Perreault, S., & Vallerand, R. J. (2007). A test of Self-Determination-Theory with wheelchair basketball players with and without disability. *Adapted Physical Activity Quarterly*, 24(4), 305–316.

Phillips, P., Rowe, K., Brown, H., & Grogger, H. (2018). Office for Women in Sport and Recreation: Diversity and inclusion forums. Deakin University.

Rolfe, D. E., Yoshida K., Renwick R., & Bailey C. (2012). Balancing safety and autonomy: structural and social barriers affecting the exercise participation of women with disabilities in community recreation and fitness facilities. *Qualitative Research in Sport, Exercise and Health*, 4(2), 265–283.

Ruddell, J. L., & Shinew, K. J. (2006). The socialization process for women with physical disabilities: The impact of agents and agencies in the introduction to an elite sport. *Journal of Leisure Research*, 38(3), 421–444.

Ryan, R. M., & Deci, E. L. (2000). Self-determination theory and the facilitation of intrinsic motivation, social development, and well-being. *American Psychologist*, 55(1), 68.

Skordilis, E. K., Koutsouki, D., Asonitou, K., Evans, E., Jensen, B., & Wall, K. (2001). Sport orientations and goal perspectives of wheelchair athletes. *Adapted Physical Activity Quarterly*, 18(3), 304–315.

Taub, D. E., Blinde, E. M., & Greer, K. R.. (1999). Stigma management through participation in sport and physical activity: Experiences of male college students with physical disabilities. *Human Relations*, 52(11), 1469–1484.

Statistics Canada. (2017). Canadian Survey on Disability Reports: A demographic, employment and income profile of Canadians with disabilities aged 15 years and over, 2017. Retrieved from www.150.statcan.gc.ca/n1/pub/89-654-x/89-654-x2018002-eng.htm

Vallerand, R. J., & Thill, E. E. (1993). Introduction au concept de motivation. In R. J. Vallerand & E. E. Thill (eds), *Introduction à la psychologie de la motivation* (pp. 3–40). Laval, QC: Etudes Vivantes.

Vertinsky, P. A. (1990). *The Eternally Wounded Woman: Women, Doctors, and Exercise in the Late Nineteenth Century*. Manchester: Manchester University Press.

VicHealth. (2018). Campaign page. Victorian Health Promotion Agency. Retrieved from www.vichealth.gov.au/thisgirlcan

White, S. A., & Duda, J. L. (1993). Dimensions of goals and beliefs among adolescent athletes with physical disabilities. *Adapted Physical Activity Quarterly*, 10(2), 125–136.

7
PROMOTING LGBT+ INCLUSION IN WOMEN'S AND GIRLS' SPORT

Lessons from Australia

Ryan Storr and Caroline Symons

Introduction

In this chapter, we discuss lesbian, gay, bisexual, and transgender (LGBT+) inclusion within the context of women and girls sport in Australia. Our aim is to present an overview of the current landscape for LGBT+ inclusion in relation to women and girls in particular, using a case study of women's cricket. Although intersex is often used within the LGBTI+ acronym, this chapter does not focus on intersex participants; this group will be addressed in a subsequent chapter.

There has been a rise in opportunities at both the grassroots and elite levels of sport in Australia for women and girls. With increased media and sociopolitical commentary across media platforms in Australia, awareness has been raised and debates have been fuelled around the inclusion of women of diverse genders and sexualities in women's sport. Sport is a pastime enjoyed by many, with participation often driven by people seeking fun, social interaction, enjoyment and health benefits. However, if LGBT+ people do not have access or are unable to participate in sport, they miss out on these benefits, most concerningly, the social aspect of sport.

In the broader Australian society, LGBT+ rights have been a prominent concern, with major attitudinal changes being observed. In both society and sport, there is evidence to suggest that there has been a growing acceptance of LGBT+ people and a reduction in homophobia (Cashmore & Cleland, 2012; Hart-Brinson, 2018). This is reflected in Australia's 2017 marriage equality debate and postal vote, with 61.6% of the Australian population voting in support of marriage equality. This is not to say that LGBT+ discrimination does not occur anymore, however.

The marriage equality campaign in Australia prompted many sports organisations to take a stance and promote inclusion and equality for all Australians, by communicating that their sport would be voting yes and advocating to change the law to allow same sex couples to legally marry in Australia. This also led to sports actively engaging with LGBT+ inclusion, through participation in the Pride in Sport Index, which is a national benchmarking system to rate the level of inclusion for LGBTI athletes, coaches and fans (www.prideinclusionprograms.com.au/psi/). How this more directed focus and awareness of LGBT+ inclusion in sport has filtered down to promote participation and engagement within grassroots communities remains to be seen. One thing we can conclude, however, is that in the last five years in Australia, there has been increased focus and awareness of LGBT+ inclusion in sport, across all levels of competition.

New polices have been developed enabling the participation of transgender and intersex athletes in women's sport, alongside national debates around unfair advantages and an often-cited myth of the 'level playing field'. We note that inclusive policies have been developed in some sports, but in other sports, such as AFL, the transgender policy for elite athletes – centred around strength, speed and stamina, in particular – falls short and actually excludes transgender athletes, a point discussed later in the chapter. In this chapter, we argue that developments for some women, heterosexual or cisgender women, should not be to the detriment to women who may sit outside these rigid gender binaries and traditional understandings of women. Developing opportunities for all women, regardless of sexual orientation and gender identity, should be central to both sport policymakers and administrators to make equal access to sport a reality for all Australian women. We provide a short review of literature and evidence around LGBT+ inclusion in the context of women and girls sport, followed by a case study of Australian Women's cricket. We conclude with some recommendations for future research and a summary of the chapter for the reader.

Evidence: What do we know about LGBT+ inclusion?

LGBT+ inclusion: Which abbreviation?

To begin, we draw attention to the use of the 'LGBT+' acronym, and the use of inclusion. First, we use LGBT+ inclusion as this is the most commonly cited term in Australia, specifically in policies, programmes and marketing material. We use the '+' to include all the different identities which come under the rainbow umbrella and relate to sexual orientation and gender identity. This can include: 'Q' which represents questioning or queer; 'A' which represents asexual; or 'P' which represents pansexual. From here onwards, we use the term LGBT+, but will highlight to the reader when we focus on a particular letter; for example, the latter half of this chapter focuses on the 'L' for lesbian. We do not include 'I' in the acronym in this chapter as we do not focus on intersex.

Second, on the use of inclusion: use of this term also shows a move away from language which may not be as appealing to policymakers or sporting bodies, most notably homophobia, discrimination, equality and so forth. Ahmed (2012; 2017) refers to this kind of linguistic practice as 'happy talk', words and phrases that are used in policy documents and rhetoric to be comforting, akin to the lip service model of diversity. Ahmed (2017, p. 100) observes 'The word diversity has become mobile partly as it does less: the words that travel more are the ones that do less [diversity], while the words that travel less do more [racism]'.

Although this chapter serves as a brief introduction to the topic of LGBT+ inclusion within the context of women and girls sport, we do specifically focus on lesbian women. We make a cautionary note and distinction about this for several reasons. As Worthen (2013) notes, generalising and grouping all people within the LGBT+ acronym homogenises the experience of LGBT+ people. There are distinct differences between sexual orientation (LGB) and gender identity (T) and between the experiences of these communities in sport. Research on gay male athletes within the theoretical boundaries of masculinity (Anderson, 2010) has dominated scholarship in the field, whereas research on lesbians in sport is far less common. This is a concern because women in sport often have to contend with both sexism and homophobia. As Griffin (2014: 269) notes,

> Addressing the differences in how homophobe and heterosexism are manifested in women's and men's sport is an important challenge that needs attention from LGBT sports advocates and allies. Simply put, sexism and how it effects women in sports must be factored into any comprehensive understanding of homophobia and heterosexism.

Further, Caudwell (2014) notes that much research has focused on lesbian and gay people, and because LGBTI is synonymous with gay and lesbian people, bisexual, transgender and intersex people are often ignored. Caudwell (2014) also notes transgender people, in particular, do not share common experiences or transition, and this differs significantly between transgender men and transgender women. The differences in transgender men's and transgender women's experiences is exacerbated by increased media attention around transgender women in competitive sport, whereas seldom do issues of transgender men gain attention. Having noted this, however, we observe from our research in Australia that many sports organisations view LGBT+ inclusion and diversity as one box of difference and a fixed identity, and often homogenise and conflate the letters of the LGBT+ acronym. One theme that runs across the LGBT+ acronym, however, is gender, and the strict policing of gender expression and identity in sporting environments. This can be illustrated through various examples: women not demonstrating appropriate femininity, men being targeted with homophobic abuse for not 'manning up' or having a certain haircut, to a transgender woman being perceived as having an unfair advantage in women's sport competition.

LGBT+ inclusion in Australian Sport

A large body of work on LBGT+ inclusion in sport organisations originates from the US (see, for example, Kauer & Krane, 2006; Sartore & Cunningham, 2010), and also from the UK from Anderson and colleagues, who focus on homophobia and LGBT+ athletes (Anderson, 2011; Anderson, McGrath & Bullingham, 2016).

Research documents issues around women's sexuality within sport, in particular, around the perceived stigma the lesbian label brings to both the sport and the athlete (Caudwell, 1999; Griffin, 1992; Melton & Bryant, 2017; Sartore & Cunningham, 2009, 2010). Hickey, Harrison, Ollis and Mooney (2016) highlighted problems around homophobia and female athletes through their research into the commercialisation of Australian women's cricket. They noted that there was 'some evidence that early career players were struggling with a lingering public perception of a culture of lesbianism within women's cricket' (Hickey, et al., 2016, p.17). The same report also noted concerns associated with the marketing of certain players and 'photo friendly' women athletes, which 'strategically works against the lesbian stereotype that exists around the women's game' (Hickey, et al., 2016, p.3). Interestingly, Fink (2012) also draws attention to the challenge of promoting marketing efforts around female athletes in a climate of homophobia and sexism.

In Australia, there have been several pieces of research that have documented both the experiences of LGBT +athletes, and the discrimination and barriers to participation in sport they experience. The Come out to Play study (Symons, O'Sullivan & Polman, 2017) documented the experiences of LGBT+ Australians and found that 42% of participants reported experiencing homophobic harassment and abuse. Further, 43% reported experiencing sexism in their mainstream sport. Lesbian women experienced both sexism and homophobia, which had negative impacts on their sport involvement (Symons, et al., 2017). The Equal Play study (Symons, et al., 2014), which was funded by Beyond Blue, a peak mental health organisation in Australia, investigated the mental health impact of discrimination in physical education (PE) and sport on young LGBT+ Victorians. The main finding in the study was that more frequently experienced verbal homophobic abuse in PE and sport settings contributes to higher levels of depression, anxiety and stress in LGBT+ youth (Symons, et al., 2014). The Out in the Fields study (Denison & Kitchener, 2015) was an international study on homophobia in sport that used a large Australian sample. Eighty per cent of Australian participants – of all sexualities, including heterosexual people – reported they had witnessed or experienced homophobic behaviour in sport. Only 13% of gay men and 25% of lesbians under the age of 22 years were 'out' to their entire team when participating in team sport (Denison & Kitchener, 2015).

This is an important point because playing in a team where you are not able to be your authentic self and have to conceal or hide your sexuality, can have a negative impact on performance and overall enjoyment. Moreover, welcoming and accepting LGBT+ people – in both sports teams and organisations – can lead to better results with everyone feeling accepted so they can perform at their best (Cunningham, 2011).

Inclusion based on gender identity

For the purpose of this chapter we do not have the opportunity to discuss the 'T' in any great detail, not because it is not important, but because we have little data to report on it. There is a significant gap in up to date knowledge and research related to transgender athletes. Often, when these issues are reported in the media, they are done so with factually incorrect information, and not based on evidence, but rather, on assumptions and stereotypes. For recent discussions around the inclusion of transgender athletes, see Anderson and Travers (2017) and Buzuvis (2016).

In Australia, an example of a transgender athlete's experience of inclusion is found in the AFL Women's competition. In 2017, the AFL did not allow transgender footballer Hannah Mouncey entry into the draft for the country's elite women's competition, the AFLW. With the league in only its second year, the adjudicating committee decided that other players would be at a physical disadvantage due to 'available data on transgender strength, stamina, physique along with the specific nature of the AFLW competition' (AFL, 2017). The AFL statement indicated the Mouncey would be allowed to 'nominate for future drafts and was able to compete in other Australian Football competitions' (AFL, 2017). During this time, there was much public transphobia directed toward Hannah and other transgender athletes, with opinion polls on media outlets around whether she should be allowed to play, whether transgender athletes have an unfair advantage.

However, the most notable outcome – of the decision not to allow Hannah to be drafted – was that it resulted in anti-transgender discrimination and vilification, especially on social media. Hannah publicly talked about receiving constant transphobic abuse, and even death threats. In addition to the potential damage to the sport of AFL as it became a vehicle for promoting transphobia in the Australian sport landscape, the toll on this to Hannah was significant; her emotional and mental health were severely impacted. So much so, that after considering to be nominated for the draft in the second year in 2018, Hannah decided not to nominate herself for the draft for the 2018 season.

The lead-up to the AFL's decision to not allow Hannah to be drafted involved the AFL developing a gender diversity policy on their own to specifically address trans women and non-binary athletes, and not athletes with intersex variations. The AFL's new policy was developed outside of a national consultation and policy on transgender and gender diversity, being spearheaded by the Australian Human Rights Commission and Sport Australia. It is hoped that sports will be able to use the standardised policy to ensure consistency, and to be in line with the law surrounding gender identity and anti-discrimination law. The final version of the guidelines is yet to be released. In the next section, we move on to discuss a case study of women's cricket and lesbian inclusion.

CASE STUDY

Promoting LGBTI+ inclusion in Australian Women's Cricket

In 2016, alongside other colleagues at Victoria University, we conducted an evaluation of LGBT inclusion in Australian cricket (Storr, et al., 2017) for both Cricket Australia (CA) (the national sport organisation [NSO] for cricket in Australia), and Cricket Victoria (CV) (the state sport organisation [SSO] in Victoria). The research was prompted by both organisations wanting evidence-based research to inform policies and practices within the sport. Both organisations were also members of the Pride in Sport Index and required data to help them design participation and education programmes to promote LGBT+ inclusion.

We conducted a mixed methods study which involved a national survey with over 300 responses, and seventeen key stakeholder interviews (women=9, men=8) from across Australian Cricket. Eleven of the participants were administrators, across CA, CV and Women's Premier Cricket, and were a combination of administrators who were specifically responsible for the development of women's cricket, and cricket in Australia more generally.

Several themes arose from the data, but in this next section and for the purpose of this chapter we focus on one key area: gender and sexuality in women's cricket. We discuss both the exclusion and inclusion of women involved in the sport of cricket in Australia through key three themes. First, we present data on historical prejudices towards lesbians in cricket; then, we document some of the discrimination and prejudice associated with lesbian stigma, experienced by lesbian cricketers and administrators. Finally, we outline some conclusions around celebrating and championing the contributions of lesbian cricketers.

Historical prejudice against lesbians in cricket

In 1994, a player on the Australian Women's cricket national side, Denise Annetts, was not selected for the tour of New Zealand. What followed was a media storm, as she made an official complaint to the Human Rights Association on the grounds of positive discrimination, asserting that she was not selected because she was not a lesbian (Burroughs, Seebohm & Ashburn, 1995). The incident had powerful repercussions for many lesbians in the team and further afield in cricket.

A number of administrators interviewed in the 2016 study experienced the negative effects of this incident, including one administrator (Administrator 5) who stated that, 'I remember when I first started playing cricket, I think it was Denise Annetts, the ex-Australian player, came out and said, "I didn't get selected in the Australian team because I'm married to a bloke"'. In the two months following these damaging comments, 140 news media articles were written, and the incident occupied talkback radio for several weeks (Burroughs, et al., 1995). There was significant media attention around the incident and the tour in New Zealand because it highlighted social biases and prejudice towards lesbians within the cricket community. One cricket administrator in the 2016 study explained that,

> A previous coach of a women's team was a male coach and a mature aged Anglo-Saxon male coach. And just casually … you know talked about the players and sexuality, sexual preferences of players and … he quite casually said, 'well no, I think we've been able to weed out the lesbians'. And

talking to a group where probably half the group were lesbians as well and just said, 'this guy's got no idea', and that's the sort of thing we're facing now.

The Annetts incident was significant for many cricket administrators. Another administrator commented that:

How she [Annetts] got air because of that.... Even though it was 20 years ago, there were still some really good things that came out of it. So, at the time, *Frontline* was a very big satirical current affairs show, and they parodied it on the show to just show how stupid it was. But it still … it forced the women's game further into the closet.

Lesbian stigma and discrimination

Several respondents in the 2016 study discussed an abiding public perception that women playing cricket were probably lesbian, unless they could demonstrate their heterosexuality. A female player summed up the nature and impact of this negative and homophobic stereotyping well:

So I have always participated in cricket since I was very, very young, where I wouldn't understand the idea or this general perception that if you are a women and you play cricket that you're probably going to be gay until you prove you're not. And this is a public perception. And as I got older, I became more and more aware of this perception, and this belief, and that that was negative in some way. So, it brought a negative, the way it was spoken about was in a negative way. So, there was hesitation for me to I guess add fuel to the fire, and almost prove people right that I turned out to be gay, and I play cricket, and I'm female.

(Player, Female)

This female player went on to discuss the personal toll that negativity and prejudice about being a lesbian in the sport caused for her. She denied her sexuality to herself and internalised the homophobia, which resulted in self-shaming. Another administrator commented,

This whole notion of homophobia and that women that play cricket are gay, it still has a lot of stigma to it. It's a bit … because of the popularity of the sport, the growing popularity of the sport, that's being diluted, which is good. But then this whole transition of the girls that are … that was a safe environment for them to play in where they could play with other gay, or gay friendly people, girls. And then progress if they needed to through national competitions.

Another player discussed the pressure she experienced as a nineteen-year old to disclose the number of gay women who were on the Australian team:

> Like at networking events, when the team has to be at events and there's all sorts of business people, and high flyers, administrators, and people from the media, and you just get these, often I would get the question, as a young member of the Australian team, I played at (age) for the Australian team, so how many girls are gay? And it was a really unfair thing to have to do.

It is important to acknowledge that homophobia in women's cricket works on a number of levels, with direct personal impact on young same sex attracted women, as well as acting as a potential challenge for heterosexual girls who are affected by the 'lesbian label'. To complicate matters further, it appeared that women's cricket was also going through some major changes.

One male administrator commented that through the growing popularity of cricket for women – as well as the more fulsome acceptance of lesbian and gay people more broadly in society – the homophobic stigma had reduced considerably, and that women's cricket was in a transition period. He made the important point that many same sex attracted girls and women historically have found cricket to be a safe space in which to experience a gay-friendly and supportive environment to play well the sport they love. So, these girls and women are transitioning with the growth of cricket as their clubs are also being transformed. The following quote captures his nuanced and informed perspective well:

> Now we're transitioning, trying to open it up and get mass participation. Some of those girls are really struggling with the transition, particularly at club level because their club is a little niche market. And now we're trying to make it broad. Some have really embraced it, but the older ones are struggling with it ... and there's transition issues that we're working through now.

Nearly all the administrators and players interviewed advocated for full acceptance and an honest and open recognition of lesbian players' contribution to the success of the sport of cricket. This sentiment is evident in the following reflection by a male administrator on cricket's inclusion of lesbian players:

> I think on the women's side is there is a very it's established, acceptance. We've got gay, we've got straight players, couldn't tell you what the balance is in terms of proportions. I wouldn't know and don't care. We encourage players to bring their partners along to social events. It's not a problem. I think cricket has been ... it's an advantage for our sport to have

that experience of embracing our women's game in all its dimensions, and all its characters and its people that have enriched the sport.

This administrator goes on to mention the outstanding Australian female cricketers who are lesbian, acknowledging their important contribution to the success of the Australia women's team, as well as to coaching and administration of the sport. This positive valuation of lesbian/bisexual women's contribution to cricket was also reflected in the survey data. For instance, 91% of LGBT survey respondents and 67% of non-LGBT respondents agreed that lesbian/bisexual players of cricket had made a positive impact in cricket. Furthermore, 94% of LGBT survey respondents and 84% on non-LGBT respondents were happy with the number of lesbian/bisexual players in cricket or believed that this population was under-represented (36% LGBT and 18% non-LGBT).

However, this overall acceptance and positive valuation is not reflected in the responses received on how accepted openly lesbian/bisexual players are in cricket, with 47% of LGBT respondents and 52% of non-LGBT respondents indicating that openly lesbian/bisexual players were not accepted. This discrimination needs to be addressed for lesbian/bisexual players to be able to enjoy and achieve in their chosen sport in a safe and inclusive environment.

One area of prejudice discussed by some interviewees was the persistence and impact of negative and destructive myths around lesbians' predatory behaviour on young players and/or potentially 'turning' young players into lesbians. According to one administrator, these are the concerns of some parents, who are not keen to let their daughters play cricket because they believe these myths and do not want their daughters to be influenced by, or become, lesbians. Women's cricket teams are often multi-aged and fifteen-year-old girls can play on the same team with women aged in their thirties.

Adult relationships and concerns can be part of the team experience, and openly lesbian players may be on these teams. It is important to acknowledge the concerns of parents and ensure a safe environment for young people; however, there is no evidence whatsoever that the team environment is unsafe due to the existence of openly lesbian players, nor is there evidence that lesbian sexual orientation can be caused directly by playing a particular sport or by being on a sport team with lesbian players. Sexual attraction and identity are complex. Furthermore, homophobic prejudice underlies the belief that being a lesbian is somehow inferior undesirable, or deviant. To take the sting out of the 'lesbian label', this prejudice needs to be identified and all sexualities need to be affirmed in a sport that treats all as equal.

Researcher Lynne Hillier (2005) observed the upside of lesbian involvement in women's football, which she asserted included the provision of a safe and positive environment for same sex attracted and gender diverse women to explore non-traditional and heteronormative sexuality and gender, as well as being able to play a sport that involves more physical contact and assertion. As observed by a previous interviewee in the 2016 study, cricket has also provided a safe space for lesbians to play the sport they love and do well in.

Championing lesbian contributions to women's cricket

One of the key messages from the data within the 2016 study around women and girls and those who identify as LGB, was that they should have a safe and inclusive experience playing cricket and should be celebrated and thanked for their contributions to cricket (especially at the elite level). The data we collected showed that cricket as an institution, has been biased against LGBT+ people, but in particular lesbian women. Theoretically, institutional work (Lawrence & Suddaby, 2006) provides an explanation as to the social change that has occurred in the past decade around women's sport and the inclusion of lesbian athletes in Australian cricket. Lawrence and Suddaby (2006, p. 125) state that institutional work is, 'the purposive action of individuals and organizations [sic] aimed at creating, maintaining and disrupting institutions'. Lesbian women involved in cricket at all levels, from administration to elite players, have worked to disrupt the institution of cricket, so they are better included and experience less prejudice and discrimination.

In 2019, much progress has occurred, and we now also see several women cricketers speaking publicly and being visible about their sexuality. One example is former Australian Women's captain, Alex Blackwell, who has done lots of advocacy and media engagement promoting LGBTI+ inclusion in sport. It is the work of these players, administrators and women working in cricket who have engaged in institutional work to open it up and make it more accessible and inclusive for lesbian women.

Working to make cricket more inclusive for all people of diverse sexualities and genders is reflected by many people working in cricket. Administrators in cricket believe they have a responsibility to ensure that everybody has an opportunity to play cricket, regardless of sexual orientation or gender identity. One administrator stated,

> So, what responsibility do we have? We've got a responsibility to the kids that love the game, to make sure that whether they're a boy or a girl, whether they're gay, straight, transgender or gender diverse, whether they're from a multicultural background, indigenous, or have some form of disability, that they can play their game knowing that they are welcome, that they are worth something, and that whatever their background is it doesn't really matter. Because when they step on the cricket field, they're a cricketer, and that's … and when they're in life they're a person. That's the responsibility that we have.

This quote summarises the positive role that sport can play across Australian communities, and that each sport organisation has a role to play in ensuring every person, regardless of their sexual orientation, gender identity, or sex characteristics, has a safe and enjoyable experience in their respective sport. The case study of lesbian inclusion in women's cricket has provided a good case study to position our discussions around women and girls sport in Australia within the context of LGBT+ inclusion. The approach taken here responds to calls to not generalise the LGBTI experience (Cauldwell, 2014), hence, we have focused on lesbian inclusion. We now offer some recommendations and thoughts on future research in the area of LGBTI inclusion and the advancement of women and girls in sport.

Recommendations and future research: blurring the binary

More LGBT+ inclusion research is needed surrounding transgender and gender diverse inclusion. In particular, research is needed about the 'T' groups in the LGBT+ acronym/abbreviation to advance the knowledge base. More research that documents the benefits and social impact sport and exercise can have on LGBT+ communities – beyond studies of homophobia, biphobia and transphobia – would also be beneficial. School and PE have been shown to be particularly unwelcome environments for young transgender and gender diverse people (Symons, et al., 2010; 2014), and we therefore encourage researchers to focus on ways in which young LGBT+ people can be better included in PE and youth sporting environments. We conclude the chapter with some key recommendations for improving LGBT+ inclusion within the context of women and girls and for advancing the inclusion of all types of women in sporting environments, regardless of sexual orientation, gender identity or sex characteristics.

Institutional support

It is important that leaders within sports organisations support the efforts of LGBTI+ inclusion. A key component to this is educating leaders within sport and giving them the skills and tools to be able to lead by example, and drive culture change from the top. Engaging in current research, policy and programmes will facilitate this. Research by Cunningham (2011) outlines the extent to which LGBTI+ inclusive sports organisations can drive social change and lead to higher organisation outputs. Also see the advice provided in Krane and Symons (2014) for promoting LGBT+ inclusive sports teams cultures.

Inclusive language

Changing the language used – especially in communications across sport and in the media – can result in more inclusive practices and a sense of inclusion. This is particularly significant for gender diverse women, and includes adopting gender neutral terms where possible; for example, using the term 'partner' avoids the assumption that someone is heterosexual or has a wife or husband. Similarly, recognition for diverse families and understanding that there are a wide range of rainbow families in society can be achieved with appropriate language use. Diverse families include those with same sex parents, a transgender parent, or any family that includes a LGBTI+ person.

Marketing and communications

It is essential to use a diverse range of athletes and employees, participants and volunteers in media, marketing and communications across organisations. This is especially critical for promoting diverse sexualities and genders, and avoiding the promotion of traditional gender stereotypes through the use of 'heterosexy' – heterosexual and sexy – imagery to appeal to the masses. Fink (2012) notes the important role homophobia plays in the marketing of female athletes and women's sport, and how these athletes are perceived and portrayed.

Affirming lesbian, bisexual, trans and intersex athletes

Times are changing and with a greater acceptance of lesbian and gay athletes and evidence of a reduction in homophobia in sport (Anderson, 2015), sports are encouraged to celebrate and affirm their LGBTI+ athletes. Although research has shown the stigma around lesbian athletes (Sartore & Cunningham, 2009) and has identified sports actively trying to conceal and manage lesbians in sport – as discussed in the case study – sports should start to celebrate their lesbian and bisexual athletes. Within the context of respectful relationships, administrators need to tackle myths about lesbians in sport, and these discussions should be aligned with equality issues linked to homophobia and sexism.

Building and supporting allies

Allies are important to the LGBTI+ community as they can actively support, speak out, affirm and use their platform to raise awareness about inequalities in sport. For example, the English cricket captain, Joe Root, and the Wallabies captain, David Pocock, have spoken out against homophobia and discrimination directed towards the LGBT+ community and raised awareness about such discrimination in sport and society. It can also be effective and have significant impact when high profile male athletes speak out about these issues and how they relate to women's sport. Andy Murray, the British Tennis player and former World Number 1, provided an excellent example of an LGBT+ ally when he spoke out against criticism of his coach Amelie Mauresmo, who is also openly gay.

Seek support and guidance

LGBTI+ inclusion can be a complex and challenging topic, and there are support services and organisations out there to assist sports organisations who might not feel confident or have the expertise to engage in the area. Proud 2 Play is one such organisation which helps facilitate participation and engagement in sport for LGBTI+ communities. Similarly, looking at best practice in relation to inclusive polices and sporting cultures is paramount. The Flying Bats, a women's football/ soccer club in Sydney, has a widely praised inclusive policy around women and gender diversity. Further, Roller Derby has an inclusive culture around gender diverse women that celebrates and affirms all women regardless of gender identity, expression, or sex characteristics. Finally, the Victorian Equal Opportunities and Human Rights Commission released their Guidelines for Trans and Gender Diverse Inclusion in Sport in 2018, and this is a great resource to facilitate the inclusion of trans and gender diverse participants.

References

AFL. (2017). AFL statement on AFLW draft eligibility of Hannah Mouncey. Retrieved from www.afl.com.au/news/2014-07-08/afl-statement-on-aflw-draft-eligibility-of-hannah-mouncey

Ahmed, S. (2012). *On Being Included Racism and Diversity in Institutional Life*. Durham: Duke University Press.

Ahmed, S. (2017). *Living a Feminist Life*. Durham: Duke University Press.

Anderson, E. (2010). *Inclusive Masculinity: The Changing Nature of Masculinities*. Oxon: Routledge.

Anderson, E., & Travers, A. (2017). *Playing Against Gender: Transgender Athletes in Sport*. Oxon: Routledge.

Anderson, E., McGrath, R., & Bullingham, R. (2016). *Out in Sport: The Experiences of Openly Gay and Lesbian Athletes in Competitive Sport*. Oxon: Routledge.

Burroughs, A., Seebohm, L., & Ashburn, L. (1995). 'A leso story': A case study of Australian women's cricket and its media experience. *Sporting Traditions*, 12(1), 27–46.

Buzuvis, E. (2016). As who they really are: Expanding opportunities for transgender athletes to participate in youth and scholastic sports. *Law & Ineq.*, 34, 341.

Caudwell, J. (ed.). (2007). *Sport, Sexualities and Queer Theory*. Oxon: Routledge.

Caudwell, J. (2014). [Transgender] young men: Gendered subjectivities and the physically active body. *Sport, Education and Society*, 19(4), 398–414.

Cashmore, E., & Cleland, J. (2012). Fans, homophobia and masculinities in association football: Evidence of a more inclusive environment. *The British Journal of Sociology*, 63(2), 370–387.

Cunningham, G. B. (2011). The LGBT advantage: Examining the relationship among sexual orientation diversity, diversity strategy, and performance. *Sport Management Review*, 14(4), 453–461.

Denison, E., & Kitchen, K. (2015). Out on the fields. The First International Study on Homophobia in Sport, Sydney, Australia. Retrieved from www.outonthefields.com/

Fink, J. S. (2012). Homophobia and the marketing of female athletes and women's sport. In G. B. Cunningham (ed.), *Sexual Orientation and Gender Identity in Sport: Essays from Activists, Coaches, and Scholars* (pp. 49–60). College Station, TX: Center for Sport Management Research and Education.

Griffin, P. (1992). Changing the game: Homophobia, sexism, and lesbians in sport. *Quest*, 44(2), 251–265.

Griffin, P. (2014). Overcoming sexism and homophobia in women's sports. In J. Hargreaves & E. Anderson (eds), *Routledge Handbook of Sport, Gender and Sexuality* (pp. 265–274). Oxon: Routledge.

Hart-Brinson, P. (2018). *The Gay Marriage Generation: The Evolution of the LGBTQ Movement and the Transformation of American Culture. How the LGBTQ Movement Transformed American Culture*. New York: NYU Press.

Hickey, C.Harrison, L., Ollis, D., & Mooney, A. (2016). *The Professionalisation of Australian Women's Cricket: New Times and New Opportunities*. Research Report. Melbourne: Deakin University.

Kauer, K. J., & Krane, V. (2006). 'Scary dykes' and 'feminine queens': Stereotypes and female collegiate athletes. *Women in Sport & Physical Activity Journal*, 15(1), 42–55.

Krane, V., & Symons, C. (2014). Gender and sexual orientation. In A. Papaioanniou & D. Hackfort (eds) *Routledge Companion to Sport and Exercise Psychology. Global perspectives and fundamental concepts*. London: Routledge.

Lawrence, T., & Suddaby, R. (2006). Institutions and institutional work. In S. Clegg, C. Hardy, T. Lawrence, & W. R. Nord (eds) *Handbook of Organization Studies* (pp. 215–254). London: Sage.

Melton, E. N., & Bryant, M. J. (2017). Intersectionality: the impact of negotiating multiple identities for women in sport leadership. In *Women in Sport Leadership* (pp. 76–96). Oxon: Routledge.

Sartore, M., & Cunningham, G. (2009). The lesbian stigma in the sport context: Implications for women of every sexual orientation. *Quest*, 61(3), 289–305.

Sartore, M., & Cunningham, G. (2010). The lesbian label as a component of women's stigmatization in sport organizations: An exploration of two health and kinesiology departments. *Journal of Sport Management*, 24(5), 481–501.

Symons, C. M., O'Sullivan, G. A., & Polman, R. (2017). The impacts of discriminatory experiences on lesbian, gay and bisexual people in sport. *Annals of Leisure Research*, 20(4), 467–489.

Symons, C., O'Sullivan, G., Borkoles, E., Andersen, M.B., & Polman, R. C. (2014). *The Impact of Homophobic Bullying During Sport and Physical Education Participation on Same Sex Attracted and Gender-Diverse Young Australians' Depression and Anxiety Levels 'The Equal Play Study'*. Melbourne: Institute of Sport, Exercise and Active Living (ISEAL) and the School of Sport and Exercise at Victoria University.

Symons, C., Sbraglia, M., Hillier, L., & Mitchell, A. (2010). *Come Out to Play: The Sports Experiences of Lesbian, Gay, Bisexual and Transgender (LGBT) People in Victoria*. Melbourne: ISEAL, Victoria University.

Victorian Equal Opportunities and Human Rights Commission. (2017). *Guidelines: Trans and Gender Diverse Inclusion in Sport*. VEOHRC. Retrieved from www.humanrightscommission.vic.gov.au/home/our-resources-and-publications/eoa-practice-guidelines/item/1560-guideline-trans-and-gender-diverse-inclusion-in-sport-complying-with-the-equal-opportunity-act-2010

Worthen, M. G. (2013). An argument for separate analyses of attitudes toward lesbian, gay, bisexual men, bisexual women, MtF and FtM transgender individuals. *Sex Roles*, 68(11–12), 703–723.

8

DEVELOPING SPORT FOR CULTURALLY AND LINGUISTICALLY DIVERSE WOMEN AND GIRLS

Hazel Maxwell and Megan Stronach

Introduction

Sport has increasingly been posited as a vehicle for confronting racism and sexism in traditional patriarchal cultures – via the promotion of cultural diversity and gender equity (Adair, Fox, Hollman, & Maxwell, 2018; Agergaard, 2016; Benn, Pfister & Jawad, 2011; Maxwell, 2012). Foley, Taylor & Maxwell (2011) argue that in the twenty-first century, traditions of male Anglo privilege and exclusivity in sport are being challenged by women at a greater frequency. This chapter investigates the processes, practices and policies of sport for development globally in relation to gender equity and cultural diversity. The intersecting challenges of sexism and racism are examined in the context of experiences and barriers to participation of a marginalised population group: women and girls from culturally and linguistically diverse (CALD) backgrounds. Culturally and linguistically diverse (CALD) is the preferred term in Australia to refer to migrants from diverse backgrounds. The focus is primarily on women in Australia, particularly Muslim women, with some examination of women from the Indian subcontinent (Sawrikar & Muir, 2010) and China (Tsai & Coleman, 1999). A range of global examples are also included (Benn, et al., 2011; Long, Hylton, Spracken, Ratna & Bailey, 2009).

The paucity of research about women from other geographical and cultural origins somewhat limits our exploration of the participation of migrant women from CALD backgrounds in sporting activities and their propensity and opportunity to participate to women living in neoliberal Western democracies such as Australia, Canada, Denmark, New Zealand, Norway and the UK. Nevertheless, the groups of women discussed have a wide range of countries of origin, including countries in North Africa, Eastern Europe, the Middle East, as well as some Asian countries. Additional to their ethnic diversity, it is acknowledged that while these women may be linked by overarching religious faith, their interpretation of their faith varies widely.

The following sections provide an overview of the motivations for participation in sporting activities for women and girls in CALD communities globally, along with an exploration of the barriers and obstacles facing these women when they participate in sport. Finally, an examination is made of contemporary initiatives that seek to provide appropriate sporting experiences for these women. Exemplar sporting programmes are described, and contemporary strategies currently employed by government, non-profit, health and sporting organisations for overcoming any negative or exclusionary issues that these women may otherwise experience are detailed. The chapter concludes with recommendations for improving access and inclusion for girls and women from CALD backgrounds in sporting activities and for further research in this key area.

Understanding CALD women and girls

Pfister (2011), in her Danish studies, found that the characteristics of gender relations and sports tastes are shaped particularly by Islamic laws and the cultures of the countries of origin, and these are reproduced in ethnic communities in the new countries of settlement. New cultural identities and practices emerge with new migrants from diverse cultural backgrounds, including different social and cultural constructions of gender identity, which are then passed on to the next generation (Pfister, 2011). Life as an immigrant woman offers specific opportunities and contestations (Delavari, Sønderlund, Mellor, Mohebbi & Swinburn, 2015), such as challenges to women's traditional roles and language constraints within the new country. It can also include male family members wishing to protect the women in their family and social groups because they think women need to be kept away from a new and potentially dangerous culture – especially in mixed-sex settings – and can lead to the banning of sport participation for women family members or to close supervision of their sporting activities.

Pfister (2011) recognises that many migrants, especially in the second and third generations, may no longer identify with the home country of their parents or grandparents and will develop hybrid cultures that show a negotiation of a mixture of cultural traditions. These cultural factors need careful consideration in sport development (SD) contexts to enable appropriate participation opportunities for CALD women and girls.

The place of sport in the lives of migrant women

Sport as a social connector has been found to have powerful development attributes as individuals from diverse cultures can come together and develop community values through civic engagement (Maxwell, 2012). However, while evidence suggests that community sport has the potential to develop mutuality and grow multicultural and diverse communities, it can also contribute to negative outcomes and exclusion, i.e. division, social disintegration, lack of trust and lack of community cooperation. It may even lead to feelings of alienation for some marginalised individuals and groups (Maxwell, 2012; Tonts, 2005).

A review of the involvement of Black and Minority Ethnic (BME) communities in the UK found evidence of discrimination against BME groups in community sport settings, owing to the lack of provision for particular religious and cultural beliefs (Long, et al., 2009). The report stated that 'testimonies of racism provide evidence of the pervasiveness of this exclusionary process' (Long, et al., 2009, p. 36) and that 'despite years of initiatives, research consistently demonstrates the damaging impact racism in sport has on participation of people from BME communities' (Long, et al., 2009, p. 43). Evidence of discrimination is linked to the exclusion of many BME groups – including CALD women – from participation in sport in non-Islamic countries.

In an Australian study of CALD women's experiences of community sport, Cortis, Sawrikar & Muir (2007) argue that sport is in a particularly good position to provide an environment that encourages social inclusion through the processes of social integration and civic participation. Claims have also been made that community sport can be used to construct individual and group identity for Muslim women (Palmer, 2009). However, Coalter (2007) warns that marginalisation and exclusion may also be reflected in access to and participation in sport. In Australia, many minority groups – including the CALD community – are underrepresented in community sport involvement. Women of Islamic faith have, in particular, been identified as one community group with low sport participation rates and specific inclusion considerations across the globe (Cortis, et al., 2007; Walseth & Strandbu, 2014).

Motivations to participate in sport

CALD women identify a range of mental, physical and social benefits of participation in sporting activities. These include:

  i feeling good and keeping fit
 ii managing weight
iii recovering from illness or injury
 iv social benefits such as making friends
  v opportunities for personal development and personal time
 vi self-development
vii mixing with other cultures, and
viii retaining their own cultural identity.

(Cortis, et al., 2007)

However, CALD women face significant health risks and challenges as they adapt to new cultures that can be exacerbated by their limited participation in sport – which may otherwise be used as a preventative behaviour (Hagarty, Maxwell, Burridge & Gholizadeh, 2015; O'Driscoll, Banting, Borkoles, Eime & Polman, 2014).

A recent Australian research report around Muslim women's motivations to play sport uncovered a love of sport and a passion and joy for playing specific sports, for example football (soccer) (Bahfen, Helal & K-Hassan, 2017). Bahfen and colleagues (2017) further identified the importance of the task of developing and improving new skills and excelling in a chosen sport as important incentives for these women. Women also spoke about their eagerness to play and succeed in sport in order to be role models for others in their communities and to combat negative stereotypes. These findings substantiate research carried out by Palmer (2009) with a group of Australian Muslim refugees, which uncovered the young Muslim women's strong desire for to participate in soccer. Moreover, research by Summers, Hassan, Ong and Hossain (2018), focusing on the fitness choices of Muslim women, uncovered a positive attitude towards fitness and regular exercise. The importance of a healthy body and mind was paramount, and the participants also confirmed that their religion supported this view.

Factors which may exclude participation

The systemic underrepresentation of women from CALD groups in community sport has been linked to non-inclusive practices and programming of sport organisations, restrictive community attitudes and values, lack of appropriate venues and/or opportunities allowing culturally appropriate clothing to be worn and the scarcity of women-only sporting environments (Benn, et al., 2011; Maxwell, 2012). In particular, sociocultural barriers, such as experiences of racism and discrimination, issues of dress, modesty, body image and perceived gender roles, have been highlighted (McCue & Kourouche, 2010). A specific example of such a sociocultural constraint involved a community sport organisation banning Muslim women from wearing the hijab (headscarf). Consequently, non-inclusive practices may lead in some circumstances to the exclusion and underrepresentation of women from CALD groups in community sport.

Despite the strong motivations to participate in sport discussed previously, Bahfen, et al. (2017) found additional factors which may act as a deterrent to CALD women playing sport; these include injuries (or perceptions of injury), study, work and family commitments, negative attitudes from family and community members, personal safety concerns, racial discrimination and financial cost. To this list of barriers to participation, Caperchione, Kolt, Tennent and Mummery (2011) added psychological trauma related to the migration process. Personal safety was a key concern for CALD women as many migrant groups found themselves living in areas of higher-than-average crime rates and therefore found it difficult to feel safe in their new country (Caperchione, et al., 2011).

In New Zealand, Guerin, Abdi and Guerin (2003) discovered that language was a major constraint to sport participation, mirroring earlier Australian research with Chinese migrants (Tsai & Coleman, 1999). When interpreters were available, the content and instructions of a training session were simplified, making it easier for the women to understand directions. Guerin, et al. (2003) also found that religious and cultural factors, such as the need for some Muslim women to pray five times each day, made it difficult to participate. Khalil (2018) discovered in Canada that Islamophobic interactions occurred on occasion with teammates. The hypervisibility of the hijab made Muslim women immediately recognisable targets for Islamophobia, causing exclusion and alienation of some Muslim sportswomen, a fact that needed to be carefully navigated by hijab-wearing athletes (Khalil 2018).

Sawrikar and Muir (2010) identified multiple barriers operating for Indian women in sporting settings; these involved sociocultural, access and resource and interpersonal constraints, combining to form a powerful exclusionary force. Evidence was found of stereotyping and of ignorance of the needs of CALD women on the part of sport providers, and of informal institutional practices that could be considered culturally inappropriate; in addition, findings revealed participants experienced a lack of family support and feelings of not belonging and 'otherness' in sporting environments. Participation in sport can still be alienating even when these constraints are overcome, especially if it involves a misalignment or conflict of values and expectations (Spaaij, Magee & Jeanes, 2014). Spaaij, Magee and Jeanes (2014) express concern that experiences of discrimination, aggression and violence on the playing field can lead to reinforcement of group boundaries experienced by individuals outside of sport, which have negative implications for community engagement and settlement.

Sport practices and programmes as enablers

On a more positive note, inclusive sporting practices, such as flexible uniform requirements, can be developed either in a top-down manner – emanating from policy change at the highest levels of sporting organisations – or from a bottom-up approach – from the 'grassroots' of individual clubs and spread upwards. Spaaij, Magee and Jeanes (2014) raise concerns about the capacity of top-down policy to facilitate the important cultural shifts deemed necessary for the development of inclusive sporting opportunities. Instead, they articulate the advantages of the adoption of a bottom-up community development approach, founded on local empowerment, participation, change from below and enhanced local capacity. This approach better provides the target group the opportunity to express its views (Spaaij, Magee and Jeanes, 2014). In this case, the target group is CALD women, who may feel more comfortable communicating those activities they would like to take part in, and expressing their concerns regarding any constraints that they experience, in a low-key, local setting. A local, community approach may also develop personal and collective capacity among the group through partnerships with service providers in organising and managing appropriate sporting activities. The active engagement of CALD women who are the intended beneficiaries of these services is a critical enabler of their inclusion.

A positive example of an Australian community sport organisation using a bottom-up approach to engage Muslim women in a soccer club, in both participation and administration roles, was described in 2010 by Maxwell and Taylor. The transformation of a soccer club, Lakemba Sport and Recreation Club (LSRC), from its origin as a traditional Australian club with members from the majority Anglo culture and no CALD women or girl participants to a situation where these women are integral members of the club at all levels is detailed below as a case study. The club became a focus for community activities, and the local CALD population of the

Sydney suburb of Lakemba is represented in the club membership, with members born in countries such as Vietnam, Greece, Italy, Indonesia, Lebanon and Australia (LSRC, 2006). Nine key practices were identified as fostering this inclusion (Maxwell, Foley, Taylor & Burton 2013). These are outlined below:

Key practice 1: Accommodating clothing. Previous research indicates that the adoption of flexible dress codes (Benn, et al., 2011) and the introduction of specific Islamic sportswear (McCue & Kourouche, 2010) are practices that can ease access restrictions for CALD women playing sport. Headgear and clothing that covered knees, ankles, elbows and wrists was permitted and even encouraged at LSRC.

Key practice 2: Gender segregation. Providing gender-segregated sporting sessions for CALD women in community sport settings is an important factor in facilitating their inclusion (McCue & Kourouche, 2010). Gender segregation and provision of women coaches were adopted at LSRC in 2006 by managers at the request of the local community.

Key practice 3: Culturally sensitive facilitators. Using cultural facilitators to liaise with CALD groups in community sport settings has been identified as a positive way to facilitate the participation of individuals from diverse backgrounds (Long, et al., 2009). This practice was adopted at LSRC for coaches, managers and administrators. These facilitators were recruited by the club from the local community. An understanding of the values and belief systems of the local community provided a basis for understanding the religious requirements in matters such as uniform, fasting during religious events (e.g. Ramadan), diet and participants going on religious events or pilgrimages.

Key practice 4: Culturally appropriate food and non-alcoholic beverages. Offering culturally appropriate food to meet specific dietary requirements assists with the development of cultural awareness and cultural affinity within sporting organisations and is a practice which facilitates inclusion of CALD women (Amara, 2008). Culturally-appropriate food, fulfilling Islamic dietary requirements, was made available at LSRC through the canteen during and after matches. This included halal meat and gelatine-free products. The exclusionary effect of serving alcohol in sport clubs is an issue highlighted by McCue & Kourouche (2010), as the Muslim faith does not encourage the consumption of alcoholic beverages. No alcohol was served LSRC.

Key practice 5: Building competencies and leadership positions for CALD women participants. Previous research has identified that individuals from CALD communities are keen to develop competencies through the development of skills in community sport settings (Crabbe, et al., 2006). The development of sport specific skills among individuals from CALD communities is a recognised vehicle in promoting their social inclusion in sporting contexts (McCue & Kourouche, 2010). At LSRC, this was also found to also be the case.

Key practice 6: Assistance with finance and transport. Cost is shown to be a key factor in promoting social inclusion in community sport settings for individuals from CALD communities (Cortis, et al., 2007), particularly for those from lower socioeconomic backgrounds (McCue & Kourouche, 2010). At LSRC, assistance was provided with uniform and registration costs, as well as with transport to and from games.

Key practice 7: Provision of team building activities. The formation of social bonds is demonstrated as a central feature of social inclusion for individuals from CALD communities in community sport settings (Maxwell & Taylor, 2010). LSRC deployed a range of off-the-field team building activities to build inclusion, including social events, leadership camps, family fun days, coaching courses and barbeques.

Key practice 8: Positive images of CALD women and role models. The portrayal of images of Muslim women playing sport distinguishes their unique social identity and provides young Muslim women in the community with relatable role models (McCue & Kourouche, 2010). Images of Muslim women participating in soccer were promoted regularly by LSRC through the local community newspaper to build a sense of collective social identity and community pride.

Key practice 9: Building partnerships. Social networks are identified as valuable in encouraging the social inclusion of women from CALD communities in community sport settings (Cortis, et al., 2007; Maxwell & Taylor, 2010). The LSRC put partnerships in place with local schools, community health services, mosques, community advocacy groups, the local council and businesses.

It is important to note that the LSRC represents just one example of a sports club rising to the challenge of understanding and responding to its local CALD community. Sports clubs and other organisations are tasked with understanding the differing needs and interests of women from extremely varied CALD backgrounds. This makes imperative the adoption of a grass-roots, community development approach which seeks to understand the needs of CALD communities. A case study illustrating an inclusive engagement approach is discussed at the end of this chapter.

Policy approaches

A key feature of government policy in most high-income neoliberal democracies is the use of sport as an avenue for social inclusion (Toffoletti & Palmer, 2017). For example, Caperchione, et al. (2011) outline the establishment of Health Action Zones (HAZ) in deprived communities in the UK, where many CALD communities reside. These tackle environmental factors, such as safety concerns and access to facilities, which lie at the heart of inclusive opportunities. The HAZ provide improved lighting, well maintained paths, access to indoor facilities and, importantly, programmes at the centre of local neighbourhoods within walking distance of community members.

However, sustainable long-term approaches are required for CALD communities and these need policies and practices that are embedded beyond the life of dedicated projects. This capacity building approach aligns with strategies adopted and recommended for SD programmes with refugee and asylum seekers (Bunde-Birouste, Bull & McCarroll, 2010), and those used by community empowerment projects (Partington & Totten, 2012). In summary, strategies need to be developed with local community support and control, and to be built on established sport and social inclusion approaches. Such approaches should incorporate practices which acknowledge the importance of the development of individual and collective social identity and the agency of marginalised groups, without alienating others with different social identities (Maxwell, 2012).

New directions and opportunities

Currently, within sport for development (SFD) contexts, there is a shift from a deficit model, in which CALD women must adapt to the white majority to participate in sporting activities, to a challenging stereotypes model, in which Muslim sportswomen are considered role models of how Muslim women can be (Agergaard, 2016; Bahfen, et al., 2017; Cheng, 2018). Cheng (2018) proposes a Muslim sportswoman model, which focuses on the sporting interest and prowess of Muslim women participants. Cheng's (2018) research involved interviews with ten Muslim women who were members of the Swim Sisters group in Sydney, Australia. The group was set up so that Muslim women could gain confidence in public swimming situations, improve their swimming technique and participate in swimming events. The women did not view themselves as role models; they simply wanted to express their love of swimming in a supportive environment. The women's experience of swimming in a setting that is sometimes hostile to Islamic swimwear (clothing that covers the body) and the provision of women-only pools or swimming opportunities is the significant part of their story. Cheng (2018) explains that while the challenging stereotypes model seems positive, it reaffirms the stereotype of Muslim women as submissive and isolated by presenting those who are not as exceptions. By focusing on Muslim women's sporting abilities, achievements and ambitions, Cheng (2018) argues that progress can be made in eliminating harmful stereotypes.

A change of sports policy towards enabling and facilitating, rather than working from a framework that positions Muslim women as problematic or in deficit is proposed (Knez, Macdonald & Abbott, 2012). Organisations have a role under this approach in helping CALD women to contest social norms and narrow stereotypes and encouraging them to be physically active in their communities. Knez and colleagues (2012, p. 118) support this claim, suggesting that 'it is important to highlight examples of difference to offer an alternative to the homogenous stereotype that dominates public discourse'.

It is necessary for sport organisations to discuss the specific requirements of CALD women with the women themselves, their parents and other members of their families and communities. Cultural intermediaries within community sport settings can invite parents and local community leaders to community sporting venues and community sporting events to develop relationships and to gain the support of local diverse communities. This is critical as it is inadequate to consider CALD 'women' as a homogenous category, with certain mechanisms of social exclusion being more problematic for some groups of women than for others (Palmer, 2009).

Future research

A range of future research directions is proposed by Khalil (2018), who argues that a better understanding of barriers to sports participation for CALD women, particularly around sporting costs, is an important, and as yet, under-explored avenue. Looking at specific inclusionary practices, such as flexible uniform requirements, family friendly practices, or the provision of gender-segregated sporting environments across a range of community sport settings, physical activity contexts and physical education settings for different CALD groups, could also provide useful avenues for future research.

Furthermore, the role of referees who act as maintainers, gatekeepers and enforcers of the sporting community, needs to be more closely examined in relation to the sporting experiences of CALD women, particularly in the light of research that revealed officials questioning players about their hijabs or asking women to leave a game because of their clothing (Khalil, 2018). Summers (2018) indicates that future studies could explore the relationship between religiosity, identity, notions of femininity and the role of body image to better understand CALD women as consumers of health and fitness products and services. Toffoletti and Palmer (2017) argue that examining the consumption and representation of Muslim women as sports writers, sport policymakers and sports fans is also required to enhance understanding. Currently, much of the research involves young women and school-aged children, with the attitudes of older women receiving little attention. Indeed, the different experiences and requirements of first and second generational CALD women have also, as yet, been largely ignored. Further research into these CALD women's sporting experiences would be beneficial.

There are also a number or practical steps that can be taken. For example, there is an identified need for increased power sharing opportunities for CALD women in mainstream sport organisations in order to increase their social inclusion in these contexts. The inclusionary challenge involves increased awareness of the motivations, barriers and sporting programmes targeted at this group and a consideration of how this extends globally to all countries looking to provide equal opportunities for CALD women to participate in sport on an equal footing with men and women from the majority culture.

Conclusion

The research presented in this chapter has shown how it is possible to change sporting contexts to foster greater inclusion for CALD women and encourage women who are often on the fringes of our societies to feel more connected to the dominant social group and within their own communities. However, the challenges and resources needed for bottom-up community development cannot be underestimated. Sport can provide an opportunity to challenge both racism and sexism within society and to promote social justice. This is a real necessity as statistics worldwide continue to demonstrate that girls and women with an immigrant background still participate in organised sports to a lesser extent than other women in these societies and thus find themselves excluded from the important economic, social and health benefits that sports can bring.

CASE STUDY

Australian Muslim women and Aussie Rules

In the last decade, the choice of sports and the type of sporting opportunities available to Muslim women and girls in Australia have expanded. The sport of Australian Rules football (AFL) has been extending its reach into the culturally diverse Western Suburbs of Sydney using a strategy which aims to provide greater opportunity for young migrants and refugees to feel a sense of 'Australian culture' (Bahfen, 2013). This includes encouraging opportunities for Muslim women and girls to become involved and the establishment of the women's Aussie Rules team, the Auburn Tigers. According to Bahfen (2013), increasing discussion around Muslim minority populations and sport has led to gendered discourses on the permissibility of involvement in secular sporting traditions, raising some public sentiment against hijab-wearing Muslim women participating in sport. Fakier (2012) writes, 'I've identified this attitude as one of the greatest barriers preventing women and girls from taking up sport for fun or as a career'. Fakier (2012) describes two key barriers faced by Muslim women: i) one from fellow Muslims who believe participation is un-Islamic; and ii) a wider barrier from the global sporting community with its preconceived notions of a 'united sporting world' that does not include women wearing headscarves.

In this context, Amna K. Hassan co-founded the women's Aussie Rules team, the Auburn Tigers. Bahfen (2013) explains that Amna sought religious advice before setting up a Muslim team for women and was given an opportunity to make her own decision. She decided that within her Islamic faith there was no contradiction between playing sport in an all-women competition and remaining loyal to her religious beliefs. The AFL made a decision to work with members of the Muslim community. Furthermore, by catering for specific religious needs, the sports administrators were able to facilitate the Auburn Tiger to attract players and increase Muslim women's involvement (Bahfen, 2013). The experience of playing AFL was described by Muslim women participating in the Auburn Tigers as having tremendous impact on overcoming stereotypes about women and sport because its full contact nature involves tackling and because AFL could cater for all sizes of girls and women (Bahfen, et al., 2017). Bahfen and colleagues (2017) recommend that Australian sport and government organisations expand their existing work with Muslim community organisations to facilitate greater participation of Muslim women in sport.

References

Adair, D., Fox, C., Hollman, J., & Maxwell, H. (2018). *Raising the Bar for All*. Paper presented at the 2018 AIHL Women in Sport Summit, Melbourne, Australia. Plenary Presentation. Retrieved from http://ecite.utas.edu.au/128552

Agergaard, S. (2016). Religious culture as a barrier? A counter-narrative of Danish Muslim girls' participation in sports. *Qualitative Research in Sport, Exercise and Health*, 8(2), 213–224.

Amara, M. (2008). An introduction to the study of sport in the Muslim world. In B. Houlihan (ed), *Sport and Society: A Student Introduction* (pp. 532–552). Los Angeles: Sage.

Bahfen, N. (2013). Embracing footy: The sporting dimensions of Australian Muslim identity in Greater Western Sydney. *Islam and Christian–Muslim Relations*, 24(4), 445–457. doi:10.1080/09596410.2013.816468

Bahfen, N., Helal, A., & K-Hassan, A. (2017). 'Community and camaraderie': an exploration of Australian Muslim women's involvement in organized sport. In D. Kilvington & J. Price (eds), *Sport and Discrimination* (pp. 102–118). Oxon: Routledge.

Benn, T., Pfister, G., & Jawad, H. (2011). *Muslim Women and Sport*. London: Routledge.

Bunde-Birouste, A., Bull, N., & McCarroll, B. (2010). Moving beyond the 'lump-sum': A case study of partnership for positive social change. *Cosmopolitan Civil Societies: An Interdisciplinary Journal*, 2(2), 92–114.

Caperchione, C. M., Kolt, G. S., Tennent, R., & Mummery, W. K. (2011). Physical activity behaviours of Culturally and Linguistically Diverse (CALD) women living in Australia: A qualitative study of socio-cultural influences. *BMC Public Health*, 11(26).

Cheng, J. E. (2018). *Moving Beyond the 'Challenging Stereotypes' Model of Muslim Women's Sports Participation*. Paper presented at the Proceedings of The Australian Sociological Association (TASA) Conference, Deakin University, Burwood Campus, Melbourne.

Coalter, F. (2007). *A Wider Social Role for Sport: Who's Keeping the Score?* London: Routledge.

Cortis, N., Sawrikar, P., & Muir, K. (2007). *Participation in Sport and Recreation by Culturally and Linguistically Diverse Women*. Sydney, Australia: Social Policy Research Centre, University of New South Wales.

Crabbe, T., Blackshaw, T., Brown, A., Choak, C., Gidley, B., & Mellor, G. (2006). *Knowing the Score. Positive Futures Case Study Research. Final Report*. Retrieved from www.sportdevelopment.org.uk/index.php/subjects/53-crime/147-knowing-the-score-positive-futures-case-study-research-final-report

Delavari, M., Sønderlund, A. L., Mellor, D., Mohebbi, M., & Swinburn, B. (2015). Migration, acculturation and environment: Determinants of obesity among Iranian migrants in Australia. *International Journal of Environmental Research and Public Health*, 12(2), 1083–1098. doi:doi:10.3390/ijerph120201083

Fakier, F. (2012). How do we decide what is acceptable sports for public participation? Key is modesty. Friniggi. Retrieved from https://friniggisportswear.blogspot.com/2012/12/how-do-we-decide-what-is-acceptable.html

Foley, C., Taylor, T., & Maxwell, H. (2011). Gender and cultural diversity in Australian sport. In J. Long & K. Spraken (eds), *Sport and Challenges to Racism* (pp. 167–182). United Kingdom: Palgrave Macmillan.

Guerin, B., Abdi, A., & Guerin, P. (2003). Experiences with the medical and health systems for Somali refugees living in Hamilton. *New Zealand Journal of Psychology*, 32(1), 27–32.

Hagarty, D., Maxwell, H., Burridge, N., & Gholizadeh, L. (2015). *Exploring the nature of physical activity participation among Middle Eastern and North African Born Women living in Australia*. Paper presented at the Australia New Zealand Leisure Studies Association 12th Biennial Conference, Adelaide, Australia.

Khalil, A. A. A. (2018). *In and out: Exploring inclusion and alienation within the sport experiences of hijabi athletes in Ontario*. (Master of Science), University of Toronto, Toronto.

Knez, K., Macdonald, D., & Abbott, R. (2012). Challenging stereotypes: Muslim girls talk about physical activity, physical education and sport. *Asia-Pacific Journal of Health, Sport and Physical Education*, 3(2), 109–122.

LSRC (Lakemba Sport and Recreation Club). (2006). *Lakembaroos Annual Report 2006*.

Long, J., Hylton, K., Spracken, K., Ratna, A., & Bailey, S. (2009). Systematic review of the literature on black and ethnic minorities communities in sport and physical recreation. In *Conducted for Sporting Equals and the Sports Councils*. Leeds: Carnegie.

Maxwell, H. (2012). *An exploration of social inclusion in Australian community sport: The case of Muslim women*. (PhD). Retrieved from http://ecite.utas.edu.au/102289

Maxwell, H., & Taylor, T. (2010). A culture of trust: Engaging Muslim women in community sport organizations. *European Sport Management Quarterly*, 10(4), 465–483. doi:10.1080/16184742.2010.502745

Maxwell, H., Foley, C., Taylor, T., & Burton, C. (2013). Social inclusion in community sport: A case study of Muslim Women in Australia. *Journal of Sport Management*, 27(6), 467–481. doi:10.1123/jsm.27. 6. 467

McCue, H., & Kourouche, F. (2010). The identity of the 'Australian Muslim woman' in sport and recreation. In S. Akbarzadeh (ed.), *Challenging Identities: Muslim Women in Australia* (pp. 130–158). Melbourne, Australia: Melbourne University Press.

O'Driscoll, T., Banting, L. K., Borkoles, E., Eime, R., & Polman, R. (2014). A systematic literature review of sport and physical activity participation in culturally and linguistically diverse (CALD) migrant populations. *Journal of Immigrant and Minority Health*, 16(3), 515–530.

Palmer, C. (2009). Soccer and the politics of identity for young Muslim refugee women in South Australia. *Soccer and Society*, 10(1), 27–38. doi:10.1080/14660970802472643

Partington, J., & Totten, M. (2012). Community sport projects and effective community empowerment: A case study in Rochdale. *Managing Leisure*, 17(1), 29–46.

Pfister, G.U. (2011). Muslim women and sport in diasporas: Theories, discourses and practices – analysing the case of Denmark. In T. Benn, G. Pfister & H. Jawad (eds), *Muslim Women and Sport* (pp. 41–76). Oxon: Routledge.

Sawrikar, P., & Muir, K. (2010). The myth of a 'fair go': Barriers to sport and recreational participation among Indian and other ethnic minority women in Australia. *Sport Management Review*, 13(4), 355–367.

Spaaij, R., Magee, J., & Jeanes, R. (2014). *Sport and Social Exclusion in Global Society*. Oxon: Routledge.

Summers, J., Hassan, R., Ong, D., & Hossain, M. (2018). Australian Muslim women and fitness choices – myths debunked. *Journal of Services Marketing*, 32(5), 605–615

Toffoletti, K., & Palmer, C. (2017). New approaches for studies of Muslim women and sport. *International Review for the Sociology of Sport*, 52(2), 146–163.

Tonts, M. (2005). Competitive sport and social capital in rural Australia. *Journal of Rural Studies*, 21(2), 137–149. doi:10.1080/17430431003587947

Tsai, E.H.-L., & Coleman, D. J. (1999). Leisure constraints of Chinese immigrants: an exploratory study. *Society and Leisure*, 22(1), 243–264.

Walseth, K., & Strandbu, Å. (2014). Young Norwegian-Pakistani women and sport: How does culture and religiosity matter? *European Physical Education Review*, 20(4), 489–507.

9

DEVELOPING SPORT FOR INDIGENOUS WOMEN AND GIRLS

Megan Stronach and Hazel Maxwell

Introduction

This chapter explores the distinctive experience that Indigenous women in two high-income, English-speaking countries – Canada and Australia – have with sport. The term 'Indigenous' refers to anyone who traditionally occupied a territory that is or was threatened by colonisation. It may be considered more inclusive than terms like 'Aboriginal' because it refers to common experiences rather than legal status or designation. In Canada, Indigenous refers to the descendants of the original inhabitants of North America and includes First Nations, Inuit and Métis groups. Australia officially has two groups of Indigenous peoples: Aboriginal and Torres Strait Islander peoples. Canada and Australia share a mutual heritage on a number of fronts, and, for the purposes of this chapter, perhaps one of the greatest parallels between these two countries is a shared colonial history, with government by white settler societies and cultures, resulting in extensive exploitation and dispossession of Indigenous traditional land.

Indigenous societies are found in every inhabited climate zone and continent of the world. Since Indigenous peoples are often faced with threats to their sovereignty, economic wellbeing and access to the resources on which their cultures depend, political rights have been set forth in international law by organisations such as the United Nations (UN). Formal recognition of the rights of Indigenous peoples is legislated, but that does not mean that all activities of all Indigenous peoples are similarly recognised and protected. One of these contested areas is sport.

The following sections present an exploration of the barriers and obstacles facing Indigenous women and girls when they wish to participate in sport, as well as a discussion of motivations of these women for participation in sporting activities. Some strategies currently employed by government, not-for-profit, health and sporting organisations to overcome negative or exclusionary issues that Indigenous women may otherwise experience are detailed. Finally, contemporary initiatives, including examples of sporting programmes that seek to provide appropriate sporting experiences for Indigenous women, are examined. The overarching position adopted by the authors throughout is that Indigenous women deserve support to be able to change their current situations as they see fit, thereby taking control of their own health and wellbeing through sport and physical activity.

Indigenous women in society today

In Canada and Australia, issues surrounding sport and physical activity for Indigenous women have lately received significant attention, signalling a potential for more careful consideration of what role sport could play in the lives of these women and girls. Indeed, in recent years, most research relating to sport programmes and Indigenous people has been conducted in high-income, English-speaking countries such as Canada, the US, New Zealand and Australia – all countries with a British colonial heritage. A catalyst for these inquiries has been a realisation that almost every health indicator suggests that Indigenous peoples in these countries – and women in particular – are over-burdened with ill-health. Indigenous women are less physically active than Indigenous men, and Indigenous people overall have statistically reported lower levels of physical activity than non-Indigenous people (ABS, 2012; Browne, McDonald, & Elliott, 2009; Public Health Agency of Canada, 2011). Of course, such disparities are of major concern in well-developed nations such as Australia and Canada, where Indigenous communities are viewed as marginalised groups due to ongoing effects of dispossession and the consequences of colonisation (Burnette, Sanders, Butcher, & Rand, 2014; Chilisa, 2012; Tsui, 2004). Colonisation is an act of colonialism and begins with taking over an area and sending people to live there. Colonisation continues when one group or society imposes their values or ways of life on another group in order to suppress the group. Colonised groups are expected to assimilate or adopt the colonial ways of living. It has often been argued that the underlying causes of Indigenous women's disproportionate burden of ill health in both countries are directly related to the impacts of colonisation (Bourassa, McKay-McNabb, & Hampton, 2004; Loppie Reading & Wein, 2009).

Given that Indigenous women in both Australian and Canada have higher incidences of non-communicable diseases such as diabetes and cardiac ailments (Australian Institute of Health and Welfare, 2015; Reading, 2009), for which low physical activity is a risk factor, we believe that for Indigenous women, exercise and sport are more than simply fun and games. Sport and physical activity are important factors in efforts to improve health (Foulds, Bredin, & Warburton, 2011; Lavallée, 2007; Reiner, Niermann, Jekauc, & Woll, 2013) and sport has the capacity to contribute to both health and social engagement in society (MacDonald, Abbott, & Jenkins, 2012; Stronach, Maxwell, & Pearce, 2018).

When collecting data on the situations of Indigenous people, researchers must acknowledge cultural differences (Burnette, et al., 2014; Chilisa, 2012). As well – to ensure that Indigenous research is carried out in a sensitive, respectful and ethical manner – many authors insist that Indigenous voices should be included in processes within which researchers embrace 'Indigenous knowledges, languages, metaphors, worldviews, experiences, and philosophies' (Chilisa, 2012, p. 101). The importance of historical, political, economic and social contexts when researching and discussing the situations of Indigenous people needs also to be acknowledged (Burnette, et al., 2014; Rousseau & Fried, 2001; Tsui, 2004), as Indigenous people today are strongly influenced by their precolonial traditions, and in some communities, have resisted tremendous pressures to assimilate. For example, for many years Indigenous women have rejected efforts to encourage them into westernised forms of sport, preferring instead activities such as music, dance, craft work and physical activities that are non-competitive, exciting, creative and more culturally acceptable (Fredericks, Croft, & Lamb, 2002).

In summary, Indigenous women's involvement in sport and physical activity in both Canada and Australia has reduced over time, seemingly due to external factors beyond their control. Arguably, these factors remain the effects of colonisation, which continue to impede Indigenous women's capacity to participate in sport and be physically active.

Historical background

A significant body of knowledge explores the status of sport in Indigenous populations. Much of this work notes that, despite the potential benefits of sport participation, there are significant cultural and institutional constraints limiting participation (Mason & Koehli, 2012). It seems incongruous that even in the twenty-first century, the legacy of colonisation continues to affect Indigenous minds (Wilson & Yellowbird, 2005), diminishing Indigenous values, destroying Indigenous community ethics (Alfred, 2005) and reducing chances of reconciliation (Coulthard, 2014). Despite important differences, but in strikingly similar circumstances, past racist legislation in both Canada and Australia – the Canadian *Indian Act* (1876) and the Australian *Aboriginal Protection Act* (1869) – caused great harms to Indigenous peoples, and neocolonial and neoliberal forms of domination and oppression continue to subjugate and negatively impact the lives of Indigenous peoples (Hayhurst, Giles, & Wright, 2016).

The Australian context

Australia has two core groups of Indigenous peoples: Aboriginal and Torres Strait Islander peoples. Together, they constitute approximately 649,200 people, equating to 2.8% of the total population (ABS, 2016). The majority live in urban areas, with only about 25% living in remote or very remote areas. Until the late eighteenth century, Australian Indigenous people largely led a 'hunter–gatherer' lifestyle. Day-to-day activities included moving across the land, sourcing and obtaining required resources. Indigenous people's use of land and resources reflect their cultural values and beliefs linking spirit to country and to person. At that time, sport was a crucial element in the lives of Australian Indigenous women, as they engaged in sophisticated games with rules, and tournament-like 'sports' competitions with other tribes (Edwards, 2009; Stronach, Adair, & Maxwell, 2018). Sport provided competition, fun and recreation in gendered spaces, and gave women special status in communities (Haebich, 2016). As well as cultural and economic importance, sport and games were generally played solely for enjoyment, with victory of minor importance. Participation was high, with many activities of a group nature (Edwards, 2009). Prior to colonisation, 'Aboriginal sport ... did not exist as a separate compartment [it] ... was inseparable from ritual and daily life' (Cashman, 1995, p. 13). Like physical activity, sport was embedded in a complex web of meanings about family and communities, described by Indigenous scholar Judy Atkinson:

> a group of women on a gathering excursion could also be teaching the younger members of the group, giving instruction and passing on skills necessary for survival ... such activities can be very much recreational.
>
> *(1991, p. 1)*

When Europeans settled in Australia from 1788, the lifestyles of Indigenous people underwent forced change. Agricultural practices introduced by the settlers progressively led to a reduction in access to natural resources, as Indigenous people were displaced from their lands. Dispossession meant that many Indigenous people had to rely on the provision of food from the Europeans – often to their detriment in terms of health and wellbeing. Indeed, this was an established system of segregation that:

> removed Aboriginal people into closed reserves, whilst operating a labour bureau to provide cheap servile labour for white employees. It [was] against this backdrop young Aboriginal women were dispatched as domestic servants to pastoral properties, farms and urban households.
>
> *(Goodall, 1995, pp. 81–82)*

Reduction in the activity levels of Indigenous people over time, combined with poor nutrition practices associated with dispossession, became embedded in the social foundations and determinants of health (Gray, Macniven, & Thomson, 2013). Health disadvantages therefore can be viewed as historical in origin, but they continue and are reflected today in the various social determinants of health, such as lower life expectancy, and higher incidences of chronic conditions (for example, Type II diabetes and cardiovascular disease) compared with non-Indigenous populations (Gray, et al., 2013).

Over twenty years ago, Colin Tatz, the most prolific Australian author to have focused on the nature of involvement of Indigenous athletes in the nation's physical culture, recognised the diabolical situation of Indigenous women. He claimed that:

> what black Australian woman has endured, no white woman – native or migrant – has ever endured or come close to enduring. The gradations of discrimination, the scales and dimensions of injustice, are enormous.... In sporting terms, if white women are having difficulty getting to first or second base in sport, then, by comparison, their black sisters are not coming within 'cooee' of the ballpark ... Of all such Cinderellas, black women's sport has the strongest case for encouragement, change, and a fair go.
>
> *(Tatz, 1995, pp. 98–100)*

The Canadian context

For thousands of years, Indigenous peoples in Canada played their own sports to teach survival and other life skills, and for fun and competition. While historians know relatively little about the lives of Aboriginal women in the precolonial period, it is likely that women participated in some games and contests, including the precursors of shinny (a version of hockey played outdoors on a flooded, home-made rink or a frozen body of water such as a pond or lake), lacrosse, and football. In many tribes, the games were reserved for men only, but in others, certain games were played by women alone, or by both men and women.

As in Australia, colonisation in Canada by white settler societies and cultures resulted in extensive exploitation and dispossession of Indigenous traditional land. Colonisation led to a cultural genocide for First Nations peoples and impacted the health of First Nations populations over several generations (Schiffer, 2016). Opportunities for First Nations women were restricted, as they were increasingly confined to small settlements and subjected to European ideas about appropriate behaviour for women. First Nations communities across North America were progressively restricted to settlements, and were subject to new laws and regulations, as well as a European worldview which was largely hostile to First Nations culture, beliefs and practices. Women were particularly affected by the imposition of European ideas, with their status and autonomy undermined by European patriarchal views about women's place in society. First Nations women lost not only power and position, but also the opportunity to participate in games and sports (Marshall, 2015).

The contributions of First Nations peoples to Canadian sport are visible today in sports such as kayaking, canoeing, and snowshoeing (Collier & Blackshaw, 2018). However, First Nations peoples' accomplishments – of both men and women – and contributions to sport are often overlooked and remain largely unrecognised by Canadians. In addition, throughout Canada's history, athletic competitions have barred First Nations athletes from participating, or have relegated them to separate divisions. Canada's Truth and Reconciliation Commission (TRC), in its Call to Action 87 (TRC, 2015), called upon all levels of government, in collaboration with First Nations peoples and other organisations, 'to provide public education that tells the national story of Aboriginal athletes in history' (TRC, 2015, p. 10).

Despite these exclusionary policies and other forms of discrimination, numerous First Nations athletes have excelled in sports on the regional, national and international stage (Collier & Blackshaw, 2018), representing their own nations at both Indigenous and global sporting competitions.

Enablers and barriers

Despite the negativity of colonisation that still impacts Indigenous societies, there is good reason to feel optimistic as Indigenous women and girls take up these challenges and participate more in sport. In trying to understand their endeavours, and to examine the connections between Indigenous women and girls and sport, it is essential to embrace a strengths approach (Brough, Bond, & Hunt, 2004; Paraschak & Thompson, 2014), rather than adopt a focus on deficits. A strengths approach places the voices of Indigenous women at the centre of the research process. A focus on Indigenous peoples' positive experiences also means it is possible for practitioners to identify resources and strengths for promoting wellbeing (Coppola, Dimler, Letendre, & McHugh, 2016).

Across these two countries, remarkably similar stories emerge. For Indigenous women, sport provides important cultural benefits and pride. While supporting a healthy lifestyle, sport also strengthens Indigenous identity and contributes to self-confidence and dignity. Indigenous scholars, such as Cheryl Kickett-Tucker, have noted how sport contributes to Indigenous children valuing themselves positively more than in any other school activity, stating 'sport is an area that Aboriginal children often excel in at school. Participation helps to motivate children to attend school and helps foster positive self-esteem' (Kickett-Tucker, 1999, p. 35).

Indigenous women have positive feelings towards being involved in sport, and as Kickett-Tucker's words illustrate, many do experience active younger lives where sport plays an important role (McGuire-Adams, 2017; Stronach, Maxwell, & Taylor, 2015). The challenge, of course, is determining how this early active lifestyle may continue into later years. Indigenous women see sport as a means of improving life, strengthening communities and maintaining culture. Sport appears to provide a social meeting place, and so is a means of participating in cultural activity. It is a central element for developing family and community, and one that provides very real opportunities for women. In particular, sport is a positive force in relation to a number of social issues, such as to:

i   reduce crime
ii rebuild community
iii prevent girls and young women engaging in unhealthy and unsafe behaviours
iv reduce obesity
v   provide a pathway out of poverty
vi provide a career path for Indigenous women to the highest level, and
vii challenge negative stereotypes

(Hayhurst, Audrey, Radforth, & The Vancouver Aboriginal Friendship Centre Society, 2015; McGuire-Adams, 2017; Stronach, et al., 2015)

An important enabler for this is the concept of the 'natural' athlete. Biological, genetic, and 'racial' explanations for innate sporting acumen are pervasive in the context of non-white popular culture, whether in Australia or Canada (Adair, 2012). Even if there is no scientific evidence to sustain folkloric theories that Indigenous people, as a group, have 'natural' ability in sport, the fact of this perception has real significance (Godwell, 2000). Women participants in a study by Stronach and colleagues (2015) acknowledged the stereotype of Indigenous people as instinctive, naturally talented, magical, inventive, even having a 'sixth sense' in sport. One woman interviewed in the study commented: 'Black fellas were only ever seen as being "deadly" sportspersons. Genetically the black fellas are just generally athletic'.

Sport allows Indigenous women to develop agency by taking ownership and leadership roles in programmes and associated activities, provided that they are given opportunities and support (House of Representatives Standing Committee on Aboriginal and Torres Strait Islander Affairs, 2013). There is no doubt that Indigenous women can and will take control of their sport engagement whenever and wherever possible. The ability of Indigenous women to develop strength through sporting accomplishments – and indeed their resilience against adversity – enables them to develop greater self-confidence and resist negative stereotypes. As socially disadvantaged groups, the 'sisterhood' of Indigenous women in sport is based on shared understandings and common experiences, perceptions, values and goals. Being part of a sporting group or team helps women to develop agency and ultimately empowers them. Team building and creating partnerships can empower women through working with others (McDonald, 2015; Stronach, et al., 2018).

Yet there are caveats to these positive forces, for example, it has been shown that through sport, women develop distinct identities as enablers for their families (McGuire-Adams, 2017; Stronach, et al., 2015). While sport can rally a society, all too often this results in women setting up a barbecue or canteen or participating in administrative roles rather than participating in the sport itself. Performance of this valuable enabling role may be at the expense of women's own participation. Other barriers, particularly in remote areas, are the costs associated with sports participation, including costs to play, register, travel, and buy equipment and uniforms (Hayhurst, et al., 2016). Another barrier is found in the time involved in getting to a centre with enough of a population base to field a team to compete against – depending on demographics, there simply may not be enough people of the right age to field teams.

Ware and Meredith (2013) caution against expecting too much from sports programmes for Indigenous people, for example, expecting that a sport programme can, on its own, eliminate substance abuse or antisocial behaviour. The authors suggest that sport and physical activity may be powerful and transformative but note that these effects tend to be indirect. Their suggestion is that such programmes tend to reduce antisocial behaviours through diversion, providing safe alternatives to risk-taking and providing opportunities to build healthy relationships with community and culture (Ware & Meredith, 2013). Nevertheless, there are many examples of sports programmes where Indigenous women are empowered, and where women have grasped opportunities for leadership and management roles.

Sport programming

To support the inclusion and engagement of Indigenous women and girls, strategies need to include knowledge and awareness of the history, experience, culture and rights of Indigenous women. The most successful programmes see participants not as mere consumers but as active agents and producers of social, cultural and political change for themselves, on their own terms and in their own communities (McGuire-Adams, 2017; Samie, Johnson, Huffman, & Hillyer, 2015). It has been repeatedly shown that Indigenous women in Canada and Australia want involvement in sport programme design to reflect their unique strengths and community requirements. Furthermore, they are both willing and able to be influential in programme design (McGuire-Adams, 2017; Samie, et al., 2015; Stronach, et al., 2018).

A number of factors may assist with this overall aim. These include:

i strong community involvement in sport programmes (Blodgett, et al., 2008; Giles & Lynch, 2012)
ii female role models such as family members, peers and or/other sports people to promote women's participation in sport programmes (Adriaanse & Crosswhite, 2008; McGuire-Adams, 2017), and
iii the provision of safe spaces, which often means women's-only environments, which can 'diminish the presence and effect of lateral violence and to enhance the habits of respect' (Bulman & Hayes, 2011, p.21).

In Australia, many successful partnerships have been developed between established organisations involving national, state and local sporting codes, health promotion and Indigenous communities, resulting in appropriate sporting programmes for Indigenous women. Exemplars include the Onkaparinga Women's Rugby Club, Softball Australia, Hockey Queensland, and David Wirrpunda Foundation (Maxwell, Stronach, Adair, & Pearce, 2017), all of which demonstrate innovation and creativity. Another successful partnership is that between Softball Australia and the Indigenous organisation Red Dust to deliver the Indigenous Softball Programme to 7,800 Indigenous participants in Australia's Northern Territory.

The Grassroots Sites Netball Programme provides opportunities to increase netball participation and development for Indigenous women and girls living throughout Western Australia (WA), with a strong focus on targeting players who do not currently play in an affiliated competition on a regular basis. Netball WA began the initiative 15 years ago in Bunbury, as part of a state government initiative seeking to boost regional sport participation (George, 2018). The programme was initially piloted as the Moorditj Noongar Yorgas Development Programme. In 2004, the programme evolved into the Aboriginal Grassroots Programme, and was introduced to the Midwest, Wheatbelt and Goldfield Regions of WA in early 2005. The programme has continued to evolve, and is now operating in seven regional areas, with over 300 athletes and a large number of coaches and officials engaging in and progressing through the Netball WA pathway (Netball WA, 2018).

Canada has similar initiatives; for example, the Canadian Association for the Advancement of Women and Sport and Physical Activity (CAAWS) programme, Building on Our Strengths (2018), is delivered by CAAWS, in collaboration with the Aboriginal Sport Circle and a working group of female Indigenous leaders from across Canada. The programme provides personal and professional development opportunities to Indigenous women and girls and aims to increase the skill level and confidence of Indigenous women, with a view to making a difference in their community (CAAWS, 2018). Another programme, Team Spirit: Aboriginal

Girls In Sport, funded by Sport Canada, is geared specifically to young Indigenous women and girls, and is designed to give them similar opportunities as boys (CAAWS, 2015; Laskaris, 2005).

The Vancouver Aboriginal Friendship Centre Society (VAFCS) is a non-governmental organisation established in 1956, which provides Indigenous and non-Indigenous people with a vast array of community services, including activities for youth and Elders in areas such as health, education, human rights, culture and recreation. The VAFCS' recreation department aims to 'provide the urban aboriginal community a safe and positive space to participate in sport and recreation activities' (Simon Fraser University, 2012), with recreation programmes that are 'designed to meet the physical, educational and cultural needs of the community by offering a multitude of programmes indiscriminate of age, sex, status, income or (dis)ability' (VAFCS 2014). The VAFCS underpins its activities with an understanding that 'sport and recreation activities have the power to transform people into healthy, happy and expressive individuals; adding tremendous value to the community as a whole' (VAFCS 2014). The recreation programme is funded by Nike and also receives support from federal and provincial governments (Hayhurst, et al., 2016). Specific women and girls-only programmes include a Because we are Girls Group, which aims to focus on better engaging young Indigenous women and girls in VAFCS' sport and recreation activities.

Implications for policy and future practice

In both Australia and Canada, Indigenous peoples have overcome many barriers, such as a lack of infrastructure and resources, and racism, to achieve greatness in sport. Recognising these barriers, the TRC and Sport Australia (formerly the Australian Sport Commission) have called for the development of national sports programmes and initiatives inclusive of Indigenous peoples, the creation of elite development programmes for Indigenous athletes and anti-racism awareness programmes. Canada's TRC Report (2015) identifies sport and recreation as tools for social development to improve the health and wellbeing of individuals and communities. Sport Australia's Reconciliation Action Plan January–December 2018 (2018) commits the organisation to the Australian Government's goal to make significant and measurable improvements in Indigenous health and wellbeing, and acknowledges the important role that sport plays in achieving this goal.

When considering the implications for sport management practice, it is apparent that practitioners ought to understand the role of Indigenous women in sport and the development of agency in the context of Indigenous culture, family networks, gender norms and history. Sport managers need to comprehend Indigenous women's own understanding of how they can improve their health and wellbeing, and that of their societies, through sport and physical activity. Without specific policies and programme development at the sport club or code organisation level, Indigenous women and girls may continue to miss out. In a nutshell, Indigenous women need support to develop agency, become empowered, and, wherever possible, to influence policy.

Sport for Indigenous women is not detached from other spheres of life. Therefore, programmes promoting sport should be incorporated into holistic approaches to developing health and wellbeing objectives. Some examples are the projects delivered through Netball WA and the VAFCS that involve positive female Indigenous role models, personal mentoring for girls, positive social interaction through sporting activities, combined with an asset-based approach linked to good communication, and self-discipline.

Programmes need to include and engage Indigenous women in the type of activities that they feel are appropriate – regardless of whether they involve organised, competitive sport. Sport managers should embrace the different and unique attributes that Indigenous women can bring to sport and exercise and encourage the potential of Indigenous women as leaders in playing, coaching and managing roles. Strengths-based, community-led approaches, such as those outlined above, provide excellent exemplars of programmes that encourage inclusivity and foster empowerment and self-management for Indigenous women and girls.

Future research

In researching this chapter, the authors have identified a number of opportunities for future research. This chapter, along with many others in recent times, has explored the experiences of Indigenous women and girls in two high-income, English-speaking countries, Australia and Canada. However, the experiences of Indigenous women around participation in sport in other countries appears to be under-researched. In other countries the situation is often quite different for Indigenous people as, for example, Indigenous people might not be recognised as such officially by their governments (IWGIA, 2018; Tsui, 2004). In Communist or former Communist countries, Indigenous organisations can be seen as a challenge to government power and authority, leading to the stifling of Indigenous voices and even to threats of physical violence to those who draw attention to Indigenous issues (Belousov, et al., 2007; Tsai, 2010). Hence, an understanding of such unique contexts – including the historical and political development of each country – is essential for an understanding of the experiences of Indigenous women and girls in these societies. Finally, much of the current research involves sporting activity for young women and school aged children, with the attitudes and experiences of older women receiving little attention.

Conclusion

Canada and Australia share a mutual heritage on a number of fronts, with one of the most profound parallels being a shared British colonial history, with government by white settler societies and cultures resulting in extensive exploitation and dispossession of Indigenous traditional land. Indigenous women's involvement in sport and physical activity in both Canada and Australia has reduced over time, seemingly due to the effects of colonisation, which continue to impede Indigenous women's capacity to participate in sport and be physically active. Nevertheless, Indigenous women and girls see many positive results in being physically active. Sport and physical activity provide Indigenous women with opportunities to preserve culture and to develop distinct identities as both enablers and participants. Indigenous women want culturally safe spaces to participate in their sports and for other Indigenous females to act as role models. Government, sporting and community organisations can be proactive in facilitating Indigenous women's efforts to overcome entrenched social, historical and health inequalities.

CASE STUDY

Ashleigh (Ash) Barty, Australian tennis player

Twenty-two-year-old Ashleigh (Ash) Barty is an Australian Indigenous woman, a rising superstar of tennis. Barty grew up in Springfield, in Queensland, Australia. Her father, Robert, is an Indigenous Australian, and her mother, Josie, is the daughter of English immigrants. Instead of following in the footsteps of her netball-playing sisters, Ali and Sara, Ash chose tennis.

Years ago, the Barty girls learned about their Indigenous background, which derives from their great-grandmother, a member of the Ngarigo people from southern NSW and north-eastern Victoria. They began the process of registering with the clan and learning what they could. They found that the clan language itself is nearly extinct, but a dictionary of key words exists, which could be used to describe Barty's game. Her forehand is like 'malub', lightning. Her smash is like 'miribi', thunder; her backhand slice is like 'djuran', running water. And she glides lightly on the court like a 'mugan', a ghost. Ash says her heritage is really important to her. She refers to her olive complexion and 'squished nose' and says, 'I just think it's important to do the best I can to be a good role model'.

Barty's mentor is Evonne Goolagong Cawley, Australia's most famous Indigenous tennis icon, a former world number one who won 14 grand slams. 'Evonne has absolutely created the pathway, not just for Indigenous boys and girls, but kids across the nation', Barty says. 'She is just such a special person, and I'm incredibly lucky to share heritage with her. That is a very special part of me that I'm extremely proud of, and I know she is as well.'

Three years ago, getting to where Barty is now might not have been predicted. At that time, she was known as a prodigy who, unable to cope with the rigours of the circuit, had given the game away. She was exhausted, confused and depressed. She quit tennis, took a break, did some coaching, and in 2015 tried her luck in the cricket Women's Big Bash League for the Brisbane Heat, proving her versatility as an athlete.

She received nothing but support for her decision to step away from tennis from family, friends and coaches. Evonne Goolagong Cawley sent her a text message: 'Hey darl. Good decision. Go and wet a line'. And so, she did. She

> went fishing, travelled to northern NSW for a few weeks at the beach and the pub, and had a new home built, only five minutes' drive from her parents and her sisters. 'I was so relieved', she says, 'it was a weird time, but as soon as I got it off my chest, I was so much better'.
>
> Now Ash Barty is back and, as a disciplined, gifted and emotionally mature Indigenous woman – who loves tennis, plays it exceptionally well and regards that as a privilege – she looks set to become the hero that Australian tennis needs.

References

ABS (Australian Bureau of Statistics). (2012). *Participation in Sport and Physical Recreation Australia, 2011–12*, cat. no. 4177.0. Retrieved from www.abs.gov.au/ausstats/abs

ABS (Australian Bureau of Statistics). (2016). *Census: Aboriginal and Torres Strait Islander Population*. Retrieved from www.abs.gov.au/ausstats/abs

Adair, D. (2012). Ancestral footprints: Assumptions of "natural" athleticism among Indigenous Australians. *Journal of Australian Indigenous Issues*, 15(2), 23–35.

Adriaanse, J., & Crosswhite, J. (2008). David or Mia? The influence of gender on adolescent girls' choice of sport role models. *Women's Studies International Forum*, 3(5), 383–389.

Alfred, T. (2005). *Wasáse: Indigenous Pathways of Action and Freedom*. Toronto: University of Toronto Press.

Atkinson, J. (1991). *Recreation in the Aboriginal Community*. A report to the Department of the Arts, Sport, the Environment, Tourism and Territories. Canberra: AGPS.

Australian Institute of Health and Welfare. (2015). *The Health and Welfare of Australia's Aboriginal and Torres Strait Islander Peoples*, cat. no. IHW 147. Canberra: AIHW.

Belousov, K., Horlick-Jones, T., Bloor, M., Gilinskiy, Y., Golbert, V., Kostikovsky, Y., & ... Pentsov, D. (2017). Any port in a storm: Fieldwork difficulties in dangerous and crisis-ridden settings. *Qualitative Research in Sport, Exercise and Health*, 7(2), 155–175.

Blodgett, A. T., Schinke, R. J., Fisher, L. A., George, C. W., Peltier, D., Ritchie, S., & Pickard, P. (2008). From practice to praxis: Community-based strategies for Aboriginal youth sport. *Journal of Sport & Social Issues*, 32(4), 393–414.

Bourassa, C., McKay-McNabb, K., & Hampton, M. (2004). Racism, sexism, and colonialism: The impact on the health of Aboriginal women in Canada. *Canadian Woman Studies Journal*, 24(1), 23–29.

Brough, M., Bond, C., & Hunt, J. (2004). Strong in the city: Toward a strength-based approach in Indigenous health promotion. *Health Promotion Journal of Australia*, 15(3), 215–220.

Browne, A. J., McDonald, H., & Elliott, D. (2009). *First Nations Urban Aboriginal Health Research Discussion Paper*. Retrieved from www.naho.ca/documents/fnc/english/UrbanFirstNationsHealthResearchDiscussionPaper.pdf

Bulman, J., & Hayes, R. (2011). Mibbinbah and spirit healing: Fostering safe, friendly spaces for Indigenous males in Australia. *International Journal of Men's Health* 10(1), 6–25.

Burnette, C. E., Sanders, S., Butcher, H. K., & Rand, J. T. (2014). A toolkit for ethical and culturally sensitive research: An application with indigenous communities. *Ethics and Social Welfare*, 8(4), 364–382.

CAAWS (Canadian Association for the Advancement of Women and Sport and Physical Activity). (2015). *Team Spirit: Aboriginal Girls in Sport*. Retrieved from www.caaws.ca/onthemove/e/aboriginal/index.htm

CAAWS (Canadian Association for the Advancement of Women and Sport and Physical Activity). (2018). *Aboriginal Women and Leadership*. Retrieved from www.caaws.ca/aboriginal-women-and-leadership/
Cashman, R. (1995). *Paradise of Sport: The Rise of Organised Sport in Australia*. South Melbourne: Oxford University Press.
Chilisa, B. (2012). *Indigenous Research Methodologies*. Thousand Oaks: Sage Publications.
Collier, B., & Blackshaw, M. (2018). *Indigenous Peoples and Sport in Canada*. Retrieved from https://hillnotes.ca/2018/06/21/indigenous-peoples-and-sport-in-canada/
Coppola, A. M., Dimler, A. J., Letendre, T. S., & McHugh, T.-L. F. (2016). 'We are given a body to walk this earth': The body pride experiences of young Aboriginal men and women. *Qualitative Research in Sport*, 9(1), 1–14. doi:10.1080/2159676X.2016.1174727
Coulthard, G. S. (2014). *Red Skin, White Masks: Rejecting the Colonial Politics of Recognition*. Minneapolis, MN.
Edwards, K. (2009). Traditional games of a timeless land: Play cultures in Aboriginal and Torres Strait Islander communities. *Australian Aboriginal Studies*, 2, 32–44.
Foulds, H., Bredin, S., & Warburton, D. (2011). The effectiveness of community based physical activity interventions with Aboriginal peoples. *Prev Med*, 53, 411–416. doi:10.1016/j.ypmed.2011.09.008
Fredericks, B., Croft, P., & Lamb, N. (2002). Talkin' up sport and gender: Three Australian Aboriginal women speak. *Canadian Woman Studies*, 21(3), 140–142.
George, E. (2018, 23 November). Massive boost for girls' game. *The Australian*, 34. Retrieved from www.theaustralian.com.au/sport/massive-boost-for-girls-game/news-story/9055c0060b9272b6e67f8c6ecbba3aa9
Giles, A. R., & Lynch, M. (2012). Postcolonial and feminist critiques of sport for development. In R. J. Schinke & S. J. Hanrahan (eds), *Sport for Development, Peace, and Social Justice* (pp. 89–104). Morgantown, WV: Fitness Information Technology.
Godwell, D. (2000). Playing the game: Is sport as good for race relations as we'd like to think? *Australian Aboriginal Studies*, 1&2, 12–19.
Goodall, H. (1995). Assimilation begins in the home: The state and Aboriginal women's work as mothers in New South Wales, 1900s to 1960s. *Labour History*, 69(1), 89–95.
Gray, C., Macniven, R., & Thomson, N. (2013). *Review of physical activity among Indigenous people*. Canberra: Australian Indigenous Health InfoNet.
Haebich, A. (2016). Aboriginal women. In S. Swain & J. Smart (eds) *The Encyclopedia of Women & Leadership in Twentieth-Century Australia*. Melbourne: University of Melbourne.
Hayhurst, L., Audrey, G., Radforth, W., & The Vancouver Aboriginal Friendship Centre Society. (2015). "I want to come here to prove them wrong": Using a post-colonial feminist participatory action research (PFPAR) approach to studying sport, gender and development programmes for urban Indigenous young women. *Sport in Society*, 18(8), 952–967.
Hayhurst, L., Giles, A., & Wright, J. (2016). The benefits and challenges of girl-focused Indigenous SDP programs in Australia and Canada. In L.N.C. Hayhurst, T. Kay, & M. Chawansky (eds), *Beyond Sport for Development and Peace: Transnational Perspectives on Theory, Policy and Practice* (pp. 111–127). Abingdon, United Kingdom: Routledge.
House of Representatives Standing Committee on Aboriginal and Torres Strait Islander Affairs. (2013). *Sport – More Than Just a Game: Contribution of sport to Indigenous wellbeing and mentoring*. Retrieved from https://catalogue.nla.gov.au/Record/6492621
IWGIA. (2018). *The Indigenous World 2018*. Retrieved from www.iwgia.org/images/documents/indigenous-world/indigenous-world-2018.pdf
Kickett-Tucker, C. S. (1999). *School Sport Self-Concept of Urban Aboriginal School Children: Teacher Influences*. Paper presented at the Joint Conference of the Australian Association

for Research in Education and the New Zealand Association for Research in Education, Melbourne, Australia.
Laskaris, S. (2005). Opportunities for women increased. *Alberta Sweetgrass*, 12(11), 9.
Lavallée, L. (2007). Physical activity and healing through the medicine wheel, Paper 2 *Social Work Publications and Research*, 5(1), 127–153.
Loppie Reading, C., & Wein, F. (2009). *Health Inequalities and Social Determinants of Aboriginal Peoples' Health*. Retrieved from www.nccah-ccnsa.ca/docs/social%20determinates/nccah-loppie-wien_report.pdf
MacDonald, D., Abbott, R., & Jenkins, D. (2012). Physical activity of remote Indigenous Australian women: A postcolonial analysis of lifestyle. *Leisure Sciences*, 34, 39–54.
Marshall, T. (2015). *The History of Canadian Women in Sport*. Retrieved from www.thecanadianencyclopedia.ca/en/article/the-history-of-canadian-women-in-sport
Mason, C., & Koehli, J. (2012). Barriers to physical activity for Aboriginal youth: Implications for community health, policy, and culture. *Pimatisiwin: A Journal of Aboriginal and Indigenous Community Health*, 10(1), 97–107.
Maxwell, H., Stronach, M., Adair, D., & Pearce, S. (2017). Indigenous Australian women and sport: Findings and recommendations from a parliamentary inquiry. *Sport in Society (Online)*, 1–29. doi:10.1080/17430437.2017.1284802
McDonald, M. (2015). Imagining neoliberal feminisms? Thinking critically about the US diplomacy campaign, 'Empowering Women and Girls Through Sports'. *Sport in Society*, 18(8), 909–922.
McGuire-Adams, T. (2017). Anishinaabeg women's stories of wellbeing: Physical activity, restoring wellbeing, and confronting the settler colonial deficit analysis. *Journal of Indigenous Wellbeing*, 2(3), 90–104.
Netball WA. (2018). *Aboriginal Grassroots Netball Program*. Retrieved from https://wa.netball.com.au/indigenous/aboriginal-grassroots-netball-program/
Paraschak, V., & Thompson, K. (2014). Finding strength(s): Insights on Canadian Aboriginal physical cultural practices. *Sport in Society*, 17(8), 1046–1060.
Public Health Agency of Canada. (2011). *Diabetes in Canada: Facts and Figures from a Public Health Perspective*. Retrieved from www.phac-aspc.gc.ca/cd-mc/publications/diabetes-diabete/facts-figures-faits-chiffres-2011/chap2-eng.php
Reading, J. (2009). *A Life Course Approach to the Social Determinants of Health for Aboriginal Peoples*. Retrieved from https://sencanada.ca/content/sen/Committee/402/popu/rep/appendixAjun09-e.pdf
Reiner, M., Niermann, C., Jekauc, D., & Woll, A. (2013). Long term health benefits of physical activity – a systemic review. *BMC Public Health*, 13, 1–9. doi:10.1186/1471-2458-13-813
Rousseau, D. M., & Fried, Y. (2001). Location, location, location: Contextualizing organizational research. *Journal of Organizational Behavior*, 22(1), 1–13.
Samie, S., Johnson, A., Huffman, A., & Hillyer, S. (2015). Voices of empowerment: Women from the Global South re/negotiating empowerment and the global sports mentoring programme. *Sport in Society*, 18(8), 923–937. doi:10.1080/17430437.2014.997582
Schiffer, J. J. (2016). Why Aboriginal peoples can't just 'Get over it'. *Visions – Indigenous People: Reconciliation and Healing*, 11(4), 10–11.
Simon Fraser University (SFU). (2012). *Vancouver Aboriginal Friendship Centre*. Retrieved from www.sfu.ca/olc/stories/topic/vancouver-aboriginal-friendship-centre
Sport Australia. (2018). *Reconciliation Action Plan January – December 2018*. Retrieved from www.sportaus.gov.au/__data/assets/pdf_file/0006/677337/ASC_Reconciliation_action_plan.pdf
Stronach, M., Adair, D., & Maxwell, H. (2018). "Djabooly-djabooly: why don't they swim?": The ebb and flow of water in the lives of Australian Aboriginal women. *Annals of Leisure Research*. doi:10.1080/11745398.2018.1503086

Stronach, M., Maxwell, H., & Pearce, S. (2018). Indigenous Australian women promoting health through sport. *Sport Management Review*. doi:10.1016/j.smr.2018.04.007

Stronach, M., Maxwell, H., & Taylor, T. (2015). 'Sistas' and aunties: Sport, physical activity and Indigenous Australian women. *Annals of Leisure Research*. doi:10.1080/11745398.2015.1051067

Tatz, C. (1995). *Obstacle Race: Aborigines in Sport*. Kensington: NSW University Press.

TRC (Truth and Reconciliation Commission of Canada). (2015). *Truth and Reconciliation Commission of Canada: Calls to Action*. Retrieved from www.trc.ca/websites/trcinstitution/File/2015/Findings/Calls_to_Action_English2.pdf

Tsai, L. L. (2010). Quantitative research and issues of political sensitivity in rural China. In A. Carlson, M. E. Gallagher, K. Lieberthal, & M. Manion (eds), *Contemporary Chinese Politics: New Sources, Methods, and Field Strategies* (pp. 246–265). Cambridge: Cambridge University Press.

Tsui, A. S. (2004). Contributing to global management knowledge: A case for high quality indigenous research. *Asia Pacific Journal of Management*, 21(4), 491–513.

VAFCS (Vancouver Aboriginal Friendship Centre Society). (2014). *Recreation*. Retrieved from www.vafcs.org/programs/recreation/

Ware, V., & Meredith, V. (2013). *Supporting Healthy Communities through Sports and Recreation Programs* (Vol. 26). Canberra: Australian Institute of Health and Welfare.

Wilson, A. C., & Bird, M. Y. (eds). (2005). *For Indigenous Eyes Only: A Decolonization Handbook*. Santa Fe: School of American Research.

10

DEVELOPING SPORT FOR WOMEN AND GIRLS IN UNDERSERVED AND LOW SOCIOECONOMIC COMMUNITIES

Katherine Raw

Introduction

This chapter focuses upon populations of women who are of low socioeconomic status (SES), and/or have typically lower levels of engagement with physical activity and sport. As such, we examine a diverse population of women and girls who have not necessarily been represented in the other chapters of this book. First, this chapter provides a literature review as a means of establishing a background and context, before turning to examine the concept of 'low SES' in relation to sport and physical activity among women. Following this, the barriers to engagement in sport among low SES and underserved communities of women are discussed, and research issues and opportunities are considered. The chapter then explores the potential practical actions and strategies that can be implemented as a means of enhancing engagement with this population. Finally, a case study provides an example of these strategies in action.

Literature review

Through engaging women and girls in sport and physical activity, sport development (SD) and sport for development (SFD) programmes not only provide the opportunity to promote the health and wellbeing of participants (Hamilton, Foster, & Richards, 2016), but they also have the capacity to play a substantial part in the social lives of individuals and communities. For individuals, engaging in these activities can provide opportunities to express physical actions, social identities and develop closeness to other people (Spaaij, 2015). In addition to individual outcomes, sport has also been noted for its capacity to teach life lessons, to instil values, such as honesty, respect, and trust, and to build character (Oxford & Spaaij, 2017). Despite the plethora of positive outcomes associated with sport and physical activity, many barriers faced by girls and women – particularly those with low SES – reduce the frequency of their participation

(Missy Wright, Griffes, & Gould, 2017). Further, despite efforts to address this issue, certain subgroups within this community typically display even lower levels of participation in sport and physical activity. In particular, research has pointed to those within the adolescent age group (Eime, Harvey, Craike, Symons, & Payne, 2013), those who have generally low access to sporting facilities and opportunities (Eime, et al., 2017; Missy Wright, et al., 2017), and/or those who are generally marginalised or excluded from participating in sport (Sherry, 2010).

Before examining these barriers to participation in sport and physical activity, however, it is important to first explore what the term 'low SES' means and examine how this terminology might relate to a number of different sociocultural groups and communities. Specifically, SES is defined as a person or community's social and economic status (Baker, 2014; Galobardes, Shaw, Lawlor, Lynch, & Davey Smith, 2006). There are variety of indicators that are taken into account when determining a person or community's SES, such as wealth, neighbourhood disadvantage and home ownership. While there is no single or best indicator of SES, the three most commonly utilised measures are education, income and occupation (Baker, 2014). Typically, a high SES is associated with better health and education and vice versa (Baker, 2014; Galobardes, et al., 2006). Given the broad range of indicators associated with SES, this chapter focuses on women and girls that are of low SES, and/ or, have decreased levels of access to sport and physical activity. Therefore, the intersectionality of these women should also be considered, as they might be associated with a number of societal groups, such as those living in rural or regional communities, homeless persons, those struggling with drugs or alcohol, incarcerated populations, and/or, those living in poverty.

Marginalised populations are frequently excluded from participation in sport and physical activity, and as such, these groups typically struggle to benefit from sport's associated health and social benefits (Sherry, 2010). In particular, people with low SES are less likely to be engaged in physical activity or sport than those with higher SES (Eime, Charity, Harvey, & Payne, 2015; Eime, et al., 2013; Federico, Falese, Marandola, & Capelli, 2013; Pan, et al., 2009; Steenhuis, Nooy, Moes, & Schuit, 2009). This reduced participation is to such an extent that a number of studies have consistently evidenced this association between SES and physical activity across a range of international contexts (Eime, et al., 2015). For example, in an Australian study of physical activity participation among adolescent girls, findings indicated that both younger and older adolescent girls were more likely to participate in sport if they were living in high SES neighbourhoods and metropolitan areas (Eime, et al., 2013). Similarly, in the US, research into girls' sport participation in urban school environments found that engagement in high school sport was significantly greater in schools situated in communities with high SES, when compared with those of low SES (Johnston, Delva, & O'Malley, 2007). Further, in an investigation of socioeconomic differences in sport and physical activity among Italian adults, results demonstrated that those with higher SES were more frequently engaged in sport compared with those with lower SES (Federico, et al., 2013). Consequently, the association between low SES and decreased levels of participation in physical activity and sport is a phenomenon that occurs across range of global contexts (Lim, et al., 2011).

In order to improve participation levels, researchers have examined the factors influencing physical activity among those women with low SES, and/or, those with typically lower levels of engagement in sport. The socioecological model has been particularly useful in such research, as it provides a framework from which to determine and understand a variety of interrelated personal and environmental factors that affect human behaviours (Stokols, 1996). While the model can vary between different research projects and contexts, in its most fundamental form, there are three factors that are thought to influence health related behaviours, including intrapersonal (e.g. individual), interpersonal (e.g. social), and environmental factors (Glanz, Rimer, & Lewis, 2008). Figure 10.1 provides an example of a rudimentary three-layered version of a socioecological model. Using this socioecological model as a lens, the next part of this chapter discusses the barriers that often reduce sport and physical activity engagement among women and girls with low SES.

In terms of *intrapersonal influences*, research has suggested that there are a number of socioecological factors that can influence sport participation among women, including employment status, income and level of education. In particular, with regard to adolescent girls, a perceived lack of competence in sport (Eime, et al., 2015) and a lack of self-esteem are thought to play a part in whether or not an individual engages in physical activity (Slater & Tiggemann, 2010). Further, personal priorities are another intrapersonal factor that can also influence participation. For instance, if an individual views sport or physical activity as a lesser priority, other priorities, such as study, family or work responsibilities, can often take precedence (Missy Wright, et al., 2017). Longitudinal research into sport participation among

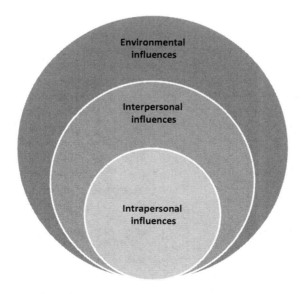

FIGURE 10.1 Socioecological model

adolescent girls has highlighted how such intrapersonal factors can influence physical activity behaviours. In particular, research has illustrated how barriers, such as a perceived lack of energy or time, often increase as adolescence progresses. These barriers are often reinforced when individuals begin to prioritise their work, career and/or education over sport and physical activity (Eime, et al., 2015).

Interpersonal influences, such as the education level or income of family, can also have a significant affect upon physical activity levels. An example of this was highlighted in a study of the association between SES and girls' engagement in sport, undertaken by Eime and colleagues (2013). Findings from this research indicated that girls with increased levels of parental engagement, assistance and support exhibited higher levels of sport participation (Eime, et al., 2013). In addition, unemployment can be an influential interpersonal factor, with research suggesting that those with unemployed family members, particularly parents or caregivers, are less likely to participate in sport (Toftegaard-Støckel, Nielsen, Ibsen, & Andersen, 2011). Further, adolescents are thought to be more likely to participate in sports and be physically active if their parents engage in sport and exercise (Toftegaard-Støckel, et al., 2011). Similarly, peer support can also play a part in hindering or encouraging engagement in physical activity. In particular, research has demonstrated how those with friends who like to play sport are thought to be more likely to participate themselves (Casper, Bocarro, Kanters, & Floyd, 2011).

More broadly, *environmental factors*, such as neighbourhood income and provision of sporting facilities, can also influence the extent to which women and girls of low SES engage in sport and physical activity (Missy Wright, et al., 2017). Research has suggested that accessibility in the form of transportation (e.g. car-pooling or buses) and proximity to sporting facilities are particularly common barriers for those with low SES. It has been proposed that this might occur because those from low SES backgrounds are more likely to reside in communities where there is a lack of facilities, or that existing facilities are of poor quality (Casper, et al., 2011). These environmental barriers have been evidenced in both urban environments and geographically remote areas. For example, in one study, a lack of access to affordable physical activity opportunities in urban environments meant that girls of low SES families were less likely to participate in sport (Missy Wright, et al., 2017). Likewise, geographical remoteness (Eime, et al., 2015) and provision of sport facilities in these locations (Eime, et al., 2017) have also been identified as contributing factors. A number of strategies and initiatives have been developed and implemented to help reduce these barriers and encourage physical activity among these populations. However, before examining these, we now turn to consider research issues and opportunities in this field.

Research issues and opportunities

There are a number of potential challenges that researchers face when examining physical activity among women and girls in underserved and low SES communities. In particular, given the broad range of people who are considered to be of low SES and or generally underserved by sport, it can be difficult for researchers to account for the effects of various sociocultural factors. For instance, in a study that examined sport participation in relation to the provision of sport facilities and SES, scholars noted that one limitation of their research was its ability to simultaneously account for the effects of SES, geographical region, sport memberships and population density upon research findings (Eime, et al., 2017). Similarly, in a study of socio-ecological factors associated with participation in physical activity and sport among adolescent girls, researchers examined a wide range of sport facilities, but in doing so, were limited by the extent to which they could account for road and personal safety, walkability and the aesthetics and quality of facilities (Eime, et al., 2015). Therefore, controlling for all potential factors in a population that represents such a broad intersection of sociocultural groups and geographic locations can be difficult. Consequently, to completely account for their impact upon research findings remains a challenging task for researchers.

In addition to the intersectionality of this cohort, recruitment and small sample sizes can also be challenging for researchers. At the most fundamental level, small sample sizes can limit the applicability and generalisability of findings (Casper, et al., 2011; Slater & Tiggemann, 2010). Further, when comparing groups within this population, if one group of participants is bigger than another, it can impact the statistical significance of results and thereby sway research findings (Eime, et al., 2015). In order to address this challenge, some researchers provide incentives (e.g. vouchers or movie tickets) to participants as a means of encouraging recruitment. However, this can be a double-edged sword, as it can result in selection bias and sway results, as participants might potentially opt in to be a part of studies even if they were not initially motivated to do so (Missy Wright, et al., 2017).

Despite these challenges, scholars have provided a number of suggestions to help future researchers better understand participation patterns and engagement. Given the variety of sociocultural and socioecological factors associated with researching underserved and low SES groups, researchers have suggested that future studies should look to further examine and unpack potential variations in the relative impact of different social and environmental factors on physical activity (Toftegaard-Støckel, et al., 2011). In particular, it has been suggested that future researchers should investigate the differences between more structured forms of sport in comparison to leisure activities (Casper, et al., 2011). In addition, given that adolescent girls have some of the lowest rates of physical activity, researchers have highlighted the importance of understanding how sport participation might be impacted by the transition from primary school to high school (Slater & Tiggemann, 2010). Furthermore, opportunities exist for researchers to investigate the complexities and social realities of facility usage in relation to participation levels. For example, while the scheduling of activities at one facility might accommodate some participants, it could also discourage others (Eime, et al., 2017). It has also been suggested that the social realities of women and girls should be examined, particularly in relation to how the notion of 'girly girls' is viewed by those that manage sporting programmes and opportunities (Missy Wright, et al., 2017). The following section now turns to discuss the practical actions and strategies that can help to address physical inactivity among underserved and low SES women.

Practical actions taken to address the issue and service the populations

A variety of practical actions and strategies can be implemented in order to increase sport and physical activity engagement among underserved and low SES communities of women. For instance, research has highlighted the value of ensuring healthy and welcoming sport club environments when looking to engage adolescent girls. In particular, findings demonstrated that sport clubs should promote a positive and supportive club culture through fostering welcoming and inclusive environments, promoting the prevention of sports injuries, providing sun protection, encouraging healthy eating, providing a smoke-free environment and ensuring alcohol is served responsibly (Casey, et al., 2017). Similarly, other research has suggested that women and girls in low income, urban environments are more likely to participate in activities if they are enjoyable, and if financial and logistical barriers are removed (Missy Wright, et al., 2017). In addition, the timing and type of physical activities should align with the needs of prospective participants. For example, when designing physical activities and sporting programmes for women and girls with low SES, programme accessibility and local neighbourhood safety should be a core consideration (Ball, Salmon, Giles-corti, & Crawford, 2006). Likewise, study, family and the overall life stages and priorities of prospective participants should also be considered (Missy Wright, et al., 2017).

In addition to promoting engagement in sport and physical activity, if designed appropriately, programming can also help to foster positive social outcomes among underserved and low SES groups. To that end, women prison populations are examples of a typically underserved community that can benefit from engaging sport and recreation programming. Research into the management of such programming in an Australian women's prison found that a softball initiative helped to reduce inmates' stress and anxiety levels and improve physical and mental health (Gallant, Sherry, & Nicholson, 2015). In addition, the programme also served as an incentive for the good behaviour of inmates, with those involved ensuring they maintained appropriate behaviour so that they did not lose the privilege of participation (Gallant, et al., 2015). In order to encourage the engagement of incarcerated women populations in such sporting programmes, there are a number of practical considerations that should be taken into account. For instance, it has been suggested that practitioners should work to reduce institutional barriers to participation, including poor communication about programmes, a lack of variety in sporting activities, conflicts with other regimes and responsibilities (e.g. work) and too few women on staff (Meek & Lewis, 2014). Further, programme managers should look to encourage innovative programming and employ enthusiastic and supportive staff who focus upon the inmates' strengths (Meek & Lewis, 2014). In doing so, programmes have the potential to impact the quality of life of women in custody, promote their physical and mental health and enhance their chances of rehabilitation (Meek & Lewis, 2014).

Research has also demonstrated how homeless populations can benefit from engaging in physical activity and sport for development (SFD) programming. For example, Back on My Feet is a non-profit, US-based organisation working with volunteers to engage the homeless community via an early morning running group (Filo, Funk, & Jordan, 2014). The organisation aims to break down stereotypes of homelessness, foster confidence and self-esteem, and link participants into employment and housing initiatives (Back on My Feet, 2019). Similarly, Street Soccer USA is an SFD organisation that uses soccer to engage with homeless individual and families, special needs populations and people in recovery from alcohol and substance abuse. The organisation aims to reduce poverty and empower underserved communities through providing safe places to play sport. The organisation employs a number of strategies to promote positive outcomes for its participants. An example of one of these strategies is training and employing coaches and staff to help participants foster their communication skills, self-esteem, independence and mutual respect for one another (Street Soccer USA, 2019). Research into this initiative has demonstrated how programming contributed to positive social outcomes among participants. Specifically, findings illustrated how one woman participant was particularly successful in the programme, as it helped her move beyond homelessness and addiction. Eventually, this pathway culminated this particular participant becoming a community activist, working with Street Soccer USA, and in turn, enabled her to give back to her own community (Cohen & Welty Peachey, 2015).

Recommendations

In summary, there are several considerations that should be taken into account when working with populations of women and girls with low SES, and/or those who have typically lower levels of engagement with physical activity and sport. First, it is worth noting that this population represents a broad variety of sociocultural groups that differ across a wide range of factors, such as age, education, employment, living conditions, geographic location, and more. Consequently, it is imperative that efforts are made to understanding target populations – for example, adolescents, homeless women, incarcerated groups – when designing or implementing programming for low SES and underserved communities of women and girls. In doing so, barriers to engagement in sport and physical activity can be identified and addressed appropriately. Logically, given the diversity represented within this population, there is a plethora of potential barriers to engagement in sport and physical activity. These barriers could include, but are not limited to, self-esteem, confidence, level of education, family or peer support, housing, employment, income, neighbourhood safety, provision of sporting facilities, transportation and access. In addition to reducing barriers, practical actions can be taken to encourage engagement in sport and physical activity. Examples of these include promoting inclusive environments through fostering welcoming and healthy club cultures, ensuring activities are enjoyable for participants, employing skilled coaches or volunteers to work with participants, and linking sporting activities into other programming – for example, vocational, educational and/or health programmes – to empower participants and promote positive social development outcomes. The following case study provides an example of how sport programming can be designed to engage with underserved populations of women and girls.

CASE STUDY

The Good Wheel, a cycling programme for women and girls

The focus of this case study is a Melbourne-based initiative known as the Good Wheel bike programme. Conducted from 2013 to 2016, the initiative aimed to give young women and girls the opportunity to develop cycling skills and knowledge, learn about traffic safety, promote confidence, increase physical activity, improve access to cycling, and in turn, enable access to other life pursuits – for example, education and employment (The Squeaky Wheel, 2014). The initiative conducted programming in Melbourne's inner north-west and targeted those who were not typically engaged in cycling or physical activity. While not specifically targeting low SES communities, the initiative's aims and location meant that many participants lived in local public housing, and as such were considered as low SES. The programme's participants faced a number of barriers to participating in sport and physical activity, some of which included access and transport (particularly during the evenings and in winter), financial challenges, substantial family responsibilities, a lack of time due to study or work and minimal access to equipment, such as bikes, helmets, lights (Raw, 2018).

In order to address these challenges, the three founding organisations – two SFD initiatives and one social enterprise – worked together to design and implement programming that minimised these barriers and encouraged engagement as much as possible. For example, programming was conducted indoors on basketball courts. This meant that programme activities were implemented in a safe space where riding conditions were more predictable and lighting was sufficient. In addition, programming was scheduled during late afternoons, and as such, clashes with study, work, and or family responsibilities were reduced, and feelings of safety when participants departed from the venue were increased. Further, the three partner organisations worked together to source funding and equipment, and as a result, participants did not have to pay any fees to take part in programming, and they were provided with refurbished bikes and new helmets (Raw, 2018).

Initially, programme sessions revolved around familiarising participants with equipment and short stints of riding around the indoor basketball court. These preliminary sessions were facilitated by local women volunteers, all of whom were confident cyclists. Following this, sessions progressed with traffic safety, bike maintenance and increasingly independent cycling activities. The final session involved a practical safety excursion, whereby participants and volunteers rode in a single file with staff and volunteers. Provided they attended all sessions – particularly the educational and safety sessions – participants were able to keep their bikes and helmets at the conclusion of the programme. Research demonstrated that the initiative helped to promote a number of positive outcomes, including improvements in confidence, increased physical activity, enhanced cycling knowledge and improved access to school, work and other community programmes (Raw, 2018).

References

Back on My Feet. (2019). *Back on My Feet: About Us*. Retrieved from www.backonmyfeet.org/about-us/

Baker, E. H. (2014). Socioeconomic status, definition. In W. C. Cockerham, R. Dingwall, S. Quah, & E. H. Baker (eds), *The Wiley-Blackwell Encyclopedia of Health, Illness, Behavior, and Society* (pp. 2129–2214). Wiley-Blackwell: Chichester, UK. https://doi.org/10.1002/9781118410868.wbehibs395

Ball, K., Salmon, J., Giles-Corti, B., & Crawford, D. (2006). How can socio-economic differences in physical activity among women be explained? A qualitative study. *Women & Health*, 43(1), 93–113. https://doi.org/10.1300/J013v43n01_06

Casey, M. M., Eime, R. M., Harvey, J. T., Sawyer, N. A., Craike, M. J., Symons, C. M., & Payne, W. R. (2017). The influence of a Healthy Welcoming Environment on participation in club sport by adolescent girls: A longitudinal study. *BMC Sports Science, Medicine & Rehabilitation*, 9(1), 12. https://doi.org/10.1186/s13102-017-0076-y

Casper, J. M., Bocarro, J. N., Kanters, M. A., & Floyd, M. F. (2011). 'Just let me play!' – Understanding constraints that limit adolescent sport participation. *Journal of Physical Activity & Health*, 8, S32–S39. Retrieved from http://ezproxy.lib.swin.edu.au/login?url=http://search.ebscohost.com/login.aspx?direct=true&db=s3h&AN=58478878&site=ehost-live&scope=site

Cohen, A., & Welty Peachey, J. (2015). The making of a social entrepreneur: From participant to cause champion within a sport-for-development context. *Sport Management Review*, 18(1), 111–125. https://doi.org/10.1016/j.smr.2014.04.002

Eime, R. M., Charity, M. J., Harvey, J. T., & Payne, W. R. (2015). Participation in sport and physical activity: Associations with socio-economic status and geographical remoteness. *BMC Public Health*, 15(1), 434. https://doi.org/10.1186/s12889-015-1796-0

Eime, R. M., Harvey, J. T., Craike, M. J., Symons, C. M., & Payne, W. R. (2013). Family support and ease of access link socio-economic status and sports club membership in adolescent girls: A mediation study. *International Journal of Behavioral Nutrition and Physical Activity*, 10(50), 1–12. https://doi.org/10.1186/1479-5868-10-50

Eime, R. M., Casey, M. M., Harvey, J. T., Sawyer, N. A., Symons, C. M., & Payne, W. R. (2015). Socioecological factors potentially associated with participation in physical activity and sport: A longitudinal study of adolescent girls. *Journal of Science and Medicine in Sport*, 18(6), 684–690. https://doi.org/10.1016/j.jsams.2014.09.012

Eime, R. M., Harvey, J., Charity, M. J., Casey, M. M., Westerbeek, H., & Payne, W. R. (2017). The relationship of sport participation to provision of sports facilities and socio-economic status: A geographical analysis. *Australian and New Zealand Journal of Public Health*. Canberra: ACT. https://doi.org/10.1111/1753-6405.12647

Federico, B., Falese, L., Marandola, D., & Capelli, G. (2013). Socioeconomic differences in sport and physical activity among Italian adults. *Journal of Sports Sciences*, 31(4), 451–458. https://doi.org/10.1080/02640414.2012.736630

Filo, K., Funk, D., & Jordan, J. (2014). Exploring activity-contingent volunteerism: A preliminary investigation of Back on My Feet volunteers. *European Sport Management Quarterly*, 14(4), 397–421. https://doi.org/10.1080/16184742.2014.929158

Gallant, D., Sherry, E., & Nicholson, M. (2015). Recreation or rehabilitation? Managing sport for development programs with prison populations. *Sport Management Review*, 18(1), 45–56. https://doi.org/10.1016/j.smr.2014.07.005

Galobardes, B., Shaw, M., Lawlor, D. A., Lynch, J.W., & Davey Smith, G. (2006). Indicators of socioeconomic position (part 1). *Journal of Epidemiology and Community Health*, 60(1), 7–12. https://doi.org/10.1136/jech.2004.023531

Glanz, K., Rimer, B., & Lewis, F. (2008). *Health Behaviour and Health Education: Theory, Research and Practice*. San Francisco: John Wiley & Sons.

Hamilton, A., Foster, C., & Richards, J. (2016). A systematic review of the mental health impacts of sport and physical activity programmes for adolescents in post-conflict settings. *Journal of Sport for Development*, 4(6), 44–59. Retrieved from https://jsfd.org/2016/08/23/a-systematic-review-of-the-mental-health-impacts-of-sport-and-physical-activity-programmes-for-adolescents-in-post-conflict-settings/

Johnston, L. D., Delva, J., & O'Malley, P. M. (2007). Sports participation and physical education in American secondary schools: Current levels and racial/ethnic and socioeconomic disparities. *American Journal of Preventive Medicine*, 33(4), S195–S208. https://doi.org/10.1016/j.amepre.2007.07.015

Lim, S. Y., Warner, S., Dixon, M., Berg, B., Kim, C., & Newhouse-Bailey, M. (2011). Sport participation across national contexts: A multilevel investigation of individual and systemic influences on adult sport participation. *European Sport Management Quarterly*, 11(3), 197–224. https://doi.org/10.1080/16184742.2011.579993

Meek, R., & Lewis, G. E. (2014). Promoting well-being and desistance through sport and physical activity: The opportunities and barriers experienced by women in English prisons. *Women & Criminal Justice*, 24(2), 151–172. https://doi.org/10.1080/08974454.2013.842516

Missy Wright, E., Griffes, K. R., & Gould, D. R. (2017). A qualitative examination of adolescent girls' sport participation in a low-income, urban environment. *Women in Sport and Physical Activity*, 25(2), 77–88. https://doi.org/10.1123/wspaj.2016-0002

Oxford, S., & Spaaij, R. (2017). Critical pedagogy and power relations in sport for development and peace: lessons from Colombia. *Third World Thematics: A TWQ Journal*, 2(1), 102–116. https://doi.org/10.1080/23802014.2017.1297687

Pan, S. Y., Cameron, C., DesMeules, M., Morrison, H., Craig, C. L., & Jiang, X. (2009). Individual, social, environmental, and physical environmental correlates with physical activity among Canadians: A cross-sectional study. *BMC Public Health*, 9(21) https://doi.org/10.1186/1471-2458-9-21

Raw, K. (2018). *Sport for Social Cohesion: Exploring Management and Impacts*. Melbourne, Australia: Swinburne University of Technology.

Sherry, E. (2010). (Re)engaging marginalized groups through sport: The Homeless World Cup. *International Review for the Sociology of Sport*, 45(1), 59–71. https://doi.org/10.1177/1012690209356988

Slater, A., & Tiggemann, M. (2010). 'Uncool to do sport': A focus group study of adolescent girls' reasons for withdrawing from physical activity. *Psychology of Sport and Exercise*, 11(6), 619–626. https://doi.org/10.1016/j.psychsport.2010.07.006

Spaaij, R. (2015). Refugee youth, belonging and community sport. *Leisure Studies*, 34(3), 303–318. https://doi.org/10.1080/02614367.2014.893006

Steenhuis, I. H. M., Nooy, S. B. C., Moes, M. J. G., & Schuit, A. J. (2009). Financial barriers and pricing strategies related to participation in sports activities: The perceptions of people of low income. *Journal of Physical Activity & Health*, 6(6), 716–721. https://doi.org/10.1123/jpah.6.6.716

Stokols, D. (1996). Translating social ecological theory into guidelines for community health promotion. *American Journal of Health Promotion*, 10(4), 282–297.

Street Soccer USA. (2019). *Street Soccer USA: Mission – Model – Impact*. Retrieved from www.streetsoccerusa.org/mission-model-impact/

The Squeaky Wheel. (2014). *Good Wheel – The Huddle Program*. Retrieved from www.thesqueakywheel.com.au/blog/good-wheel-the-huddle-program

Toftegaard-Støckel, J., Nielsen, G. A., Ibsen, B., & Andersen, L. B. (2011). Parental, socio and cultural factors associated with adolescents' sports participation in four Danish municipalities. *Scandinavian Journal of Medicine & Science in Sports*, 21(4), 606–611. https://doi.org/10.1111/j.1600-0838.2010.01093.x

11

EMPOWERING WOMEN AND GIRLS THROUGH SPORT

Emma Seal

Introduction

Sport is increasingly being regarded as a powerful tool in international development, with many different organisations delivering sport programs and initiatives in order to achieve broader development aims. Sport for development (SFD) is the term that is used to describe the intentional use of sport and physical activity to achieve non-sport outcomes and affect positive change in the lives of people and communities. Education, health, gender equity, social cohesion and conflict resolution are some of the areas that sport has been applied to in order to bring about change (see Hayhurst, Kay & Chawansky, 2016; Sherry, Schulenkorf, & Phillips, 2016). Further, a growing number of SFD interventions focus on women and girls that aim to use sport and physical activity to promote girls' and women's development.

The purpose of this chapter is twofold: first, it will address the nascence of work that critically explores women's and girls' experiences in SFD programming by providing a case study of the Girl's Empowerment through Cricket (GET) programme that is delivered in Papua New Guinea (PNG). The initiative specifically aimed to empower young women and girls by increasing their critical awareness of PNG's sociocultural issues related to health, gender inequality and domestic violence. Second, the chapter will propose a theory or reading of empowerment that can be used by researchers to conceptualise programme outcomes in highly constrained sociocultural contexts. Consequently, the research lens focuses specifically on women and girls in low- and middle-income countries (LMICs) and how empowerment can be productively understood in such settings. Throughout the chapter, the abbreviations high-income countries (HICs) and low- and middle-income countries (LMICs) will be used to capture national differences along economic, political and developmental lines.

Development interventions, either implicitly or explicitly, utilise theories of change that make 'cause-and-effect' assumptions about the relationship between their activities and intended outcomes (Kabeer, 2010). Often, a much-described outcome of SFD programme interventions is the empowerment of participants, particularly in the context of programmes that are geared towards women and girls. Commonly, the term 'empowerment' is generously used without full consideration of what it actually means to be empowered and how this plays out in women's and girls' lives. Furthermore, a clear theoretical basis for understanding and describing empowerment – or a demonstration of the tangible ways in which shifts in empowerment have manifested – is lacking (Seal & Sherry, 2018). Therefore, this chapter advances a conceptualisation of empowerment that is theoretically informed, but pragmatically recognises the complexities of using sport as a vehicle for development in LMICs. Using the GET programme case study, the chapter will highlight how the proposed empowerment theory can be implemented and will share strategies for achieving meaningful change in the lives of women and girls in similar settings.

Additionally, the chapter draws from the work of scholars that operate outside of traditional sport and management literature – namely international development or development studies – to help bolster the approaches that are applied in SFD.

Literature review

Sport for women's and girls' development

To begin, it is important to discuss current practice and the wider academic landscape, before outlining the theoretical approach this chapter argues for and providing an in-depth overview of the GET programme case study with the approach in action. In SFD work and programming, there is increasing emphasis being placed on interventions focusing on women and girls with the hope of inciting broader social change, as well as growth in the number of programmes using sport to promote health. In the academic literature, this has been labelled as the 'girling' of development (Hayhurst, 2011), and refers to a pattern of investing in adolescent girls, typically those aged 8–18, and also adult women. These types of interventions are also commonly referred to as sport, gender and development (SGD) programmes.

International (e.g. United Nations (UN), International Olympic Committee) and national governing bodies undeniably support the use of sport for development ambitions, which helps to explain the proliferation of programmes globally. The SGD movement is substantiated by a wide range of non-government organisations (NGOs), sport federations, transnational corporations (TNCs) and UN agencies that broadly aim to contribute to international development, as outlined by the UN Sustainable Development Goals. As an indication of the volume of interventions, a study by Hancock, Lyras and Ha (2013) conducted a scoping review of the number of active SFD programmes targeting women and girls. The exercise highlighted that, in 2010, there were 440 programmes in existence specifically aimed at women and girls (Hancock, Lyras, & Ha, 2013). Arguably, that number would have risen even further since. SGD programmes focus on fostering a diverse range of outcomes for women and girls, including individual development (e.g. skill development), health and disease prevention, promotion of gender equality, social inclusion, peace-building, economic development and post-disaster relief. Another commonly cited aim that is fundamentally relevant for this chapter is the empowerment of women and girls (Chawansky & Schlenker, 2016).

One example of SGD programming that has received significant attention has been termed the Girl Effect movement (Hayhurst, 2011; 2013; McDonald, 2015), and it has grown into a global initiative. The movement encapsulates some of the key messages that are promoted when sport is purportedly used as a vehicle for empowering women and girls and helps to demonstrate the principles that underpin the development of SGD-orientated interventions. The Girl Effect movement originated from a campaign initiated by the Nike Foundation in 2005, which emphasised the importance of investing in women and girls in order to facilitate social change. Indeed, recent studies in SGD have tended to analyse the outcomes of programming through this lens, reporting that sport participation allows women and girls to challenge their traditional domestic duties, confront gender norms, boost their self-confidence and increase their ability to undertake responsibility for their own decision-making. While these outcomes appear desirable on the surface, often the research underpinning such claims is lacking theoretical rigour and imposes Eurocentric ideas about what empowerment means onto women and girls in LMICs (Samie, Johnson, Huffman, & Hillyer, 2015). Consequently, a growing body of research has started to carefully examine the increased presence of women and girls in SFD, which will now be outlined in more detail.

Use and limitations of sport as a tool for empowerment

Parallel to the rise of SFD programmes targeting women and girls, there has been a similar increase in the volume of academic research that critically explores the way SFD programmes position women and girls, what outcomes the programmes are designed to achieve and how they are implemented (see Darnell & Hayhurst, 2012; Sherry, Schulenkorf, Seal, Nicholson, & Hoye, 2017; Kay, 2009).

In the context of SGD for girls' and women's empowerment, the major criticism that has been levelled at both programming and research is the assumption that women and girls are free to make choices about their own behaviour and lifestyles without questioning the wider structural relations. Furthermore, when these types of assumptions are made, the responsibility for change is then placed on the shoulders of those women and girls, with little consideration for the role of men and boys in achieving gender equality (McDonald, 2015; Mwaanga & Prince, 2016). This critique helps to highlight the challenge of using sport as a tool for the empowerment of women and girls, particularly in highly constrained contexts. The major challenge in these circumstances is being able to articulate a theory of empowerment that remains cognisant of wider power relations, but also attends to outcomes emerging at the micro level, which could produce subtler changes in social relations and interactions. Ultimately, this involves invoking a reading of empowerment that is both pragmatic and relational. Chawansky (2011) has argued for more nuanced approaches to understanding how gender is understood in SFD. Furthermore, there has been a broader demand for researchers in the field to provide specific examples of agency emerging in LMICs (Lindsey, Kay, Jeanes, & Banda, 2017).

The following section will outline a conceptualisation of empowerment to aid understanding the empowerment-related outcomes emerging in SFD programming. There are no blueprints for social transformation – that is, for women and girls becoming more empowered – because of the diversity of contexts and cultures. However, it is imperative to establish and implement a theory of change that is grounded in an understanding of local realities and the constraints that women and girls experience in such environments (Kabeer, 2010). The implications for development planners and SFD managers will then be discussed to help highlight how they can play an active role in creating an enabling environment for the empowerment of women and girls. It is important to remember that the concept of empowerment should not only be considered during or at the end of an SFD project, when a retrospective piece of research or evaluation is taking place; rather, it should be considered from the programme inception and design phase.

Advancing a theory of empowerment for women and girls

New theoretical horizons: understanding empowerment, structure and agency

In order to advance how empowerment is interpreted and accounted for during the planning, implementation and evaluation/research cycles of SFD projects, it is fruitful to look beyond existing SFD literature and to cross-disciplinary boundaries, particularly because the concept of empowerment is often not robustly described or analysed in the SFD literature. In the body of literature that focuses on gender and international development, there has been much discussion around issues of gender, agency and empowerment by prominent scholars in this field (see Kabeer, 2010; Parpart, 2014). To describe what is meant by empowerment, it is useful, first, to describe what is meant by power. Power can be conceptualised in terms of people's capacity to influence others, make strategic life choices and control resources. The reading of empowerment proposed in this chapter, and further described below, highlights that it should be understood in a relational way. Pham (2003) argued that there is an overwhelming tendency in development and political theory to centre agency on freedom and conscious self- and world-transformation. However, this disregards the reality of individuals' lives and the social relations that constitute them. Ultimately, empowerment and social change takes time, and the focus should not be on actions that (re)present empowerment, but on the tentative moves people take towards it. Becoming empowered refers to a change in these traditional power relations – i.e. gendered norms – or related social dynamics.

The concept of power is related to notions of structure and agency. Structure is the organised set of social institutions and patterns of relationships that, together, comprise society. Social structure is both a product and a direct determinant of social interaction;

it can impose invisible constraints on human action that can produce forms of inequality. Agency refers to the role of human actors and their efforts to reproduce, modify or transform structural inequality (Kabeer, 2010). In SFD work, structure and agency have largely been described in deterministic ways, whereby agency is equated with the ability of individuals to exercise voice and control in their lives, set against wider structures of power. These approaches apply hierarchical, top-down understandings of power, where a dialectical relationship is assumed – for example oppressor/oppressed, empowered/disempowered. However, these approaches to expressing the relationship between structure, agency and power do not account for the processes in between, or the situational nature of power relations. In order to further develop this work, it is important to understand empowerment in a more nuanced way.

The approach being advocated for here was discussed by Parpart (2010) and is helpful for SFD work, particularly in highly constrained environments. Parpart (2010) highlighted the need to recognise agency, empowerment and choice as nuanced, situated and multi-levelled processes. Parpart (2010, p. 22) argued for a broader understanding of empowerment, where the focus is on 'the partial, tentative moves that people often take as they attempt to move toward understanding and subverting injustices, recognising that "injustice" is affected by local contexts, particularly in dangerous and highly constrained circumstances'. When looked at through this lens, the concepts of agency and empowerment are processual, and analysis should focus not on the end product – empowered awareness and action – but, rather, should focus on how disruptions are made to traditional gendered relations present in SFD contexts. In recognising these partial moves to empowerment, Kabeer (2010) articulated three ways to express change: the *power within*, the *power to* and the *power with*. The *power within* refers to changes in the way women view themselves, the *power to* refers to women's increased ability to make strategic life choices and exercise influence in their local community, and the *power with* refers to women coming together to reflect, question and act on their status in society.

Overall, the following factors should be considered when attempting to understand empowerment outcomes in the context of SGD work:

a   Articulate a specific theoretical framework and analytical approach, for example the conceptualisation of empowerment described here.
b   When designing interventions, be gender-aware and ensure that the approach is informed by the localised issues that are most pertinent for women and girls and expressed by those who have the most knowledge of these factors.
c   Implement a nuanced approach to understanding structure/agency that can account for micro-level changes to traditional relations, and
d   Adopt an approach that recognises the wide variety of ways in which being 'empowered' can be enacted and observed, rather than focusing solely on transforming current constraints (i.e. the end product). The deep-rooted nature of the sociocultural constraints that women face means change to their individual circumstances or position in society is unlikely to be a one-off event, but a gradual and evolving process

(Kabeer, 2010)

The case study that will help bring some of these concepts to life will now be outlined. The first sections provide an overview of the status of women in PNG society and the GET programme to generate some contextual insights. The final section will connect the theory of empowerment described here with the empirical data and discuss wider implications for SFD programmes and research.

CASE STUDY

Situating the case study: Pursuing empowerment of women and girls through an SFD programme in Papua New Guinea

Background context – Papua New Guinea (PNG)

Papua New Guinea is a unique country, with over 200 discrete cultural groups and around 800 distinct languages and dialects; it is extremely culturally and linguistically diverse. The place of women and girls in society is complex and highly constrained. Historically, it is a nation of tribal societies organised on the basis of kinship (Tivinarlik & Wanat, 2006), a system that prescribes how people living together should interact with one another. Each tribe, language group and culture acts to influence individuals to behave in distinct ways, and the majority of communities are patriarchal (Prideaux, 2008). There are extremely rigid gender roles for women and girls, with the majority undertaking domestic duties in the home with limited opportunities beyond that.

Gender inequality is a widespread issue and leaves women and girls particularly vulnerable to abuse, exploitation, and violence (Hinton & Earnest, 2010). A 2014 study by UN Women highlighted that more than 90% of women and girls in Port Moresby have experienced some form of violence or harassment. Violence against women is characterised by domestic and family violence, rape and gang rape, and the torture of women suspected of sorcery (Amnesty International, 2006; Hinton & Earnest, 2010). In the majority of communities, there is a patrilineal line of inheritance, which denies land rights to women and limits their access to resources. Consequently, women and girls inhabit a weak position in society with limited protection offered by formal and informal justice systems. Women and girls in Melanesia are beginning to advocate more strongly for their rights and are drawing more attention to oppressive practices and patriarchal dominance (Hinton & Earnest, 2010). However, these are very tentative steps and women remain highly vulnerable across PNG. The prevalence of gendered inequality is also reflected at higher levels of leadership. PNG has a national parliament with 111 members; since the country's independence in 1975, only seven women have ever been elected to parliament. This context provides an insight into the complex sociocultural, political and economic situation of women and girls and demonstrates the scale of change required. It also exemplifies why SFD programmes aimed at empowering women and girls in this type of environment require tailored planning and need to be realistic about the outcomes that are emerging and cautious about claims that are made.

The programme

The Girl's Empowerment through Cricket (GET) programme was funded as part of the Australian Government's Pacific Sports Partnership scheme, managed via a partnership between Cricket PNG, the International Cricket Council (ICC), and the Australian Sports Commission. The GET programme has been discussed elsewhere (see Seal & Sherry, 2018); however, we describe it again here and connect it to broader implications for SFD program developers and managers when it comes to designing for empowerment. Cricket PNG, the national governing body for cricket, helped to develop the programme, in collaboration with the ICC, and has sole responsibility for program design, delivery and working with associated programme partners. Most Cricket PNG staff members are Indigenous Papua New Guineans, which helps to build local capacity and also ensures that the GET programme activities are locally relevant and appropriate. The programme commenced in 2015 and is delivered in partnership with community high schools located in Port Moresby. The target group is young women aged 12 to 18 and each school term programme delivery takes place in three or four different schools with one class per school. The number of participants varies according to the school class size, but approximately 30 students are involved from each school per term.

The programme is divided into cricket activities and education sessions; each week the participants take part in one cricket and one education session. The sessions cover a broad range of areas including self-defence, domestic violence, non-communicable disease (NCD) prevention, and health and lifestyle education. During the education sessions, participants are encouraged to critically reflect on the issues and content discussed. At the end of programme delivery, the schools involved that term are brought together for a cricket carnival; parents, teachers and education partners are also invited to share the experience and celebrate with programme participants.

As well as providing opportunities for participants, the programme also fosters opportunities for the development officers – the deliverers of the cricket sessions – and the programme managers – those in leadership positions making decisions about programme design and delivery. All GET programme staff members are local, Indigenous women, which demonstrates Cricket PNG's commitment to facilitating new development platforms for women. Women have little access to job opportunities outside of becoming market vendors or undertaking domestic duties, therefore, being involved with the programme is unique and facilitates individual capacity building.

The research

The research conducted in PNG contributed to a broader programme evaluation of the GET programme's outcomes and impacts over a two-year period. The evaluation was underpinned by participatory action research (PAR) principles with a focus on planning and conducting the research process in partnership with the individuals whose lives, worlds, and experiences are being examined (Seal & Sherry, 2018; Sherry, Schulenkorf, Seal, Nicholson, & Hoye, 2017). The data collection tools included the use of interviews, observation and reflective journaling (journals were completed by the participants after each education session). In total, ten interviews were conducted with programme participants and eight interviews were conducted with GET programme staff. A total of twenty-five young women also took part in the reflective journaling component.

Case study outcomes: mobilising the theory of empowerment

Disruption of traditional gender relations

Gender relations refers to interpersonal relationships, expectations and the order of social life between men and women. From an analytical perspective, when attempting to understand empowerment outcomes, it is important to examine what impact the programme has on the young women in spaces outside GET sessions when interacting with others. The GET programme offered participants the opportunity to challenge traditional gendered expectations and disrupt conventional binaries concerning what roles men and women fulfil and what is considered appropriate behaviour. Cricket is a male-dominated activity in PNG and widely perceived to be a masculine sport. Active cricket participation by the women and girls involved in the GET programme enabled them to challenge existing stereotypes and foster new perceptions about what women and girls can do. As expressed by a participant:

> I didn't know or expect that cricket could do this much for me, before I thought that cricket was only for a man, but women are part of the game and I am proud of that, it will help others to think differently about things.
>
> *(Participant 1)*

When connected with the theory of empowerment previously outlined, it is important to note that these outcomes represent partial steps towards a wider process of social change. Without making such initial moves, wider change will not ensue.

Implications for SFD programming

The GET programme was able to foster this outcome because it was designed to be relevant for the local context and to elicit meaningful change for women and girls in this environment. Practically, this involved active participation from GET programme staff members to develop the programme content and overall programme objectives, which meant they were aligned with the most pertinent issues affecting women and girls. Consequently, the use of cricket (as opposed to other sports) actively facilitated the disruption of traditional lines of thinking and provided a platform for the participants to enact new identities (i.e. as cricket players).

Observing 'power within'

The *power within* refers to changes in the way women view themselves (Kabeer, 2010). It emerged strongly from the participants' accounts that there were changes in the way that women and girls perceived their rights, responsibilities and roles within PNG society. Empowerment is multi-levelled, therefore it is important to recognise the different ways in which shifts in power can occur, even if these are not explicitly expressed. The quotes below help to demonstrate how participants experienced a shift in their internal sense of agency.

> I have discovered that any sport can be played by a woman even though it might be male dominated because we have the same rights.
> *(Participant 2)*

> From being involved in the programme I felt that I can do men's normal work because all of us have a right to be educated and get what is usually a man's job, for example a mechanic, technician or electrician.
> *(Participant 3)*

These examples help to demonstrate how the education sessions facilitated a consciousness-raising experience for the girls, providing them with access to new knowledge resources. Consequently, they were able to think more critically about their position in PNG society, particularly in relation to women's rights, domestic violence and traditional gender roles.

Previous research in SFD literature (Chawansky, 2011; Forde & Frisby, 2015; Hayhurst, 2013) has critiqued programmes that place emphasis on women and girls being the singular agents for change. However, before applying such criticism, it is important to consider the context in which the programme is situated. In 2006, a study by Amnesty International highlighted that women in PNG were largely unaware that domestic violence constitutes abuse because it is such a deeply entrenched aspect of daily life. Thus, a first step towards achieving structural change is to start with women's and girls' own perceptions and engender critical pedagogies.

Implications for SFD programming and management

The GET programme was able to foster empowerment outcomes because full consideration was given to the position and status of women and girls in PNG society. The education sessions were delivered by local community organisations that best understood the most pressing sociocultural challenges. The sessions were designed to encourage participant reflexivity and were built on a foundation of Indigenous knowledge and practice, which has been identified as imperative for ethical SFD work (Darnell & Hayhurst, 2014). When developing SFD programmes in similar contexts, it is important to consider how best to include educational elements and to ensure these are driven by local organisations, where possible. Furthermore, the type of education should engage critical pedagogies that encourage self-reflexivity amongst participants in order to foster changes to the 'power within' and, ultimately, facilitate empowerment outcomes. Rauscher and Cooky (2016) argued that programmes that do not tackle inequality at a variety of levels will be unable to work on social change beyond the interpersonal level. Therefore, in the context of SFD, working with community organisations that actively lobby for social justice is important to connect participants with such lines of thinking and provide ongoing resources – beyond the life of the SFD programme.

Observing 'power to'

The *power to* refers to women's increased ability to make strategic life choices and exercise influence in their local community. Arguably, this type of change will take longer to happen. However, there were some indications in the participants' accounts of these outcomes emerging. For instance, some of the girls talked about how they discussed new knowledge with family and friends in an attempt to impact their behaviour:

> When we were taught about domestic violence, I informed my friends about it in class and I also encouraged my uncle who usually beats up his wife to change and I've seen some changes in my friends and also in my uncle.
>
> *(Participant 4)*

The excerpt above highlights how some of the participants were able to affect change in their local communities and within their own families. Additionally, the GET programme development officers were also able to disrupt traditional power relations and exert more influence. It was clear from participant narratives that undertaking these roles helped to facilitate their sense of self-efficacy and build their leadership capacity. For example, development officer 1 noted, 'the main things I have learned from this role is how to manage others and how to build good relationships with other people'. The women involved in these positions viewed themselves as role models for the GET programme participants, which enabled them to exert greater influence outside of their existing interpersonal relationships.

Implications for SFD programming and management

The GET programme was able to foster empowerment to make life choices ad exercise influence outcomes for participants because the education sessions were able to trigger a strong response and generated a high level of engagement. Furthermore, the GET programme staff members operated as role models for the girl participants. Observing women occupying new and different roles in society had a positive impact on participants and on the staff members themselves. It is important when designing SFD programmes in similar, highly constrained sociocultural environments that programme staff members have strong local roots in order to act as effective role models. Ultimately, this can instigate productive – empowering – change for some.

Development of network resources

One of the key emerging themes was the girls' (participants) and women's (development officers/programme managers) development of new social networks as a consequence of being involved in the programme. The development of such networks included the building of new interpersonal relationships and friendships, which afforded access to new resources. It emerged from the participants' accounts that the cricket carnival organised at the end of the programme – which brought different schools together – created an environment that fostered the development of new friendships that were maintained after the event. Furthermore, the development officers and programme managers continued to act as mentors for some of the programme participants by staying in contact and offering them ongoing cricket coaching. These networks would not have otherwise existed, and they help to facilitate the beginnings of growing consciousness, subversions and eventual challenges to gendered sociocultural orders (Parpart, 2010). The programme produced different effects and interactions within local communities, reflecting Kabeer's (2010) concept of 'power with', which argues that women coming together to reflect, to question and to act on their subordinate status can be a powerful force for change.

While the GET programme is currently delivered solely to women, it is important to ensure that men also engage in education on themes such as domestic violence and gender equality. Men's attitudes and behaviour are an equally important consideration when attempting to impact gender equality outcomes and this factor is imperative as the programme grows and evolves.

Implications for SFD programming and management

The GET programme was able to foster the development of network outcomes because the programme was designed with opportunities to bring all of the participants together and engage in events that fostered the development of ongoing relationships and networks. Furthermore, the GET programme staff continued to operate as mentors for the programme participants. Such networks provide access to new social resources for those involved and ongoing sources of support. These tools are important to help *build* communities and generate new connections.

Conclusion

This chapter has focused on the experiences of women and girls involved in the GET programme as either participants or Cricket PNG staff. The outcomes have been viewed through the lens of empowerment, and a relational theory of empowerment has been outlined in order to account for the participants' day-to-day experiences and interactions that constitute their lives. Parpart's (2010) conceptualisation of empowerment has been described and utilised in order to examine the empirical data and highlight how focus should be placed on an individual's sense of agency and the partial, tentative moves that can be taken towards this, rather than always focusing on an end product, such as affecting change to the social structure. It is difficult to transcend the argument that SFD programmes are unable to address the structural constraints that operate in women's lives (Hayhurst, 2013). However, structure and agency should not be understood in isolation; challenging current structural relations requires change at the interactional level and the disruption of existing norms.

On a practical level, when creating SFD interventions for empowerment in relation to gender (in)equality the following considerations should be made:

a   During the programme design and development stages, consideration should be given to the role and status of women and girls and the sociocultural issues they face, because these will differ between contexts.
b   Women should be involved in project planning and opportunities as programme staff, or as leaders, should be generated. This will help build the capacity of women in-country and also provide role models for the participants.
c   Partnerships with activist, local community organisations should be created to work with participants and ensure that local knowledge drives the development agenda.
d   Select a sport that women do not traditionally have access to, in order to contest gendered expectations.
e   The role of boys and men in the programme should be considered as the programme evolves.

Further research is required to explore the long-term impacts of the GET initiative and whether these effects penetrate wider communities. Additionally, it is imperative to consider the position and role of men and boys in these types of programme, and to expand research practices to include a wider variety of people, outside of those directly involved and not just the participants. It is also important to continue considering how empowerment is conceptualised and applied in the context of SGD and to adopt critical perspectives that can examine how women and girls are positioned in such programmes.

Notes

Thank you to the International Cricket Council (ICC) for providing funding for this research. The work of Associate Professor Emma Sherry as part of the evaluation team should also be noted.

References

Amnesty International. (2006). *Papua New Guinea: Violence Against women not Inevitable, Never Acceptable*. London, United Kingdom: Amnesty International.

Chawansky, M. (2011). New social movements, old gender games? Locating girls in the sport for development and peace movement. In A. Snyder & S. Stobbe (eds), *Critical Aspects of Gender in Conflict Resolution, Peacebuilding, and Social Movements* (pp. 121–134). London, United Kingdom: Emerald.

Chawansky, M., & Schlenker, M. (2016). Beyond girl power and the girl effect: The girling of sport for development and peace. In L. Hayhurst, T. Kay, & M. Chawansky (eds), *Beyond Sport for Development and Peace: Transnational Perspectives on Theory, Policy and Practice* (pp. 94–105). London, United Kingdom: Routledge.

Darnell, S. C. (2010). Power, politics and "sport for development and peace": Investigating the utility of sport for international development. *Sociology of Sport Journal*, 27(1), 54–75. doi:doi:10.1123/ssj.27. 1. 54

Darnell, S. C., & Hayhurst, L. (2012). Hegemony, postcolonialism, and sport-for-development: A response to Lindsey and Grattan. *International Journal of Sport Policy & Politics*, 4(1), 111–124. doi:10.1080/19406940.2011.627363

Darnell S. C., & Hayhurst, L. (2014). De-colonising sport-for-development: Critical insights from post-colonial feminist theory. In N. Schulenkorf & D. Adair (eds), *Global Sport for Development* (pp. 33–61). London, United Kingdom: Palgrave Macmillan.

Forde, S. D., & Frisby, W. (2015). Just be empowered: How girls are represented in a sport for development and peace HIV/AIDS prevention manual. *Sport in Society*, 18(8), 882–894. doi:10.1080/17430437.2014.997579

Hancock, M., Lyras, A., & Ha, J. (2013). Sport for development programmes for girls and women: A global assessment. *Journal of Sport for Development*, 1(1), 15–24.

Hayhurst, L. (2011). Corporatising sport, gender and development: Postcolonial IR feminisms, transnational private governance and global corporate social engagement. *Third World Quarterly*, 32(3), 531–549. doi:10.1080/01436597.2011.573944

Hayhurst, L. (2013). Girls as the 'new' agents of social change? Exploring the girl effect through sport, gender, and development programs in Uganda. *Sociological Research Online*, 18(2), 192–203. doi:10.5153/sro.2959

Hayhurst, L., Kay, T., & Chawansky, M. (2016). *Beyond Sport for Development and Peace: Transnational Perspectives on Theory, Policy and Practice*. London, United Kingdom: Routledge.

Hinton, R., & Earnest, J. (2010). The right to health: Overcoming inequalities and barriers to women's health in Papua New Guinea. *Women's Studies International Forum*, 33(3), 180–187. doi:10.1016/j.wsif.2009. 12. 006

Kabeer, N. (2010). Women's empowerment, development interventions and the management of information flows. *Institute of Development Studies*, 41(6), 105–113.

Kay, T. (2009). Developing through sport: evidencing sport impacts on young people. *Sport in Society: Culture, Commerce, Media, Politics*, 12, 1177–1191. doi:10.1080/17430430903137837

Levermore, R., & Beacom, A. (2009). *Sport and International Development*. London, United Kingdom: Palgrave Macmillan.

Lindsey, L., Kay, T., Jeanes, R., & Banda, D. (2017). *Localizing Global Sport for Development*. Oxford, United Kingdom: Oxford University Press.

McDonald, M. G. (2015). Imagining neoliberal feminisms? Thinking critically about the US diplomacy campaign, 'Empowering women and girls through sports.' *Sport in Society*, 18 (8), 909–922. doi:10.10180/17430437.2014.997580

Mwaanga, O., & Prince, S. (2016). Negotiating a liberative pedagogy in sport development and peace: Understanding consciousness raising through the Go Sisters programme in Zambia. *Sport, Education and Society*, 21(4), 588–604.

Parpart, J. L. (2010, July). *Choosing Silence: Rethinking Voice, Agency and Empowerment.* (Working Paper No. 297). East Lansing: Michigan State University

Parpart, J. L. (2014). Exploring the transformative potential of gender mainstreaming in international development institutions. *Journal of international Development*, 26(3), 382–395.

Pham, Q. N. (2003). Enduring bonds: Politics and life outside freedom as autonomy. *Alternatives: Global, Local, Political*, 38(1), 29–48.

Prideaux, M. (2008, December). *Leadership in Papua New Guinea: An Exploratory Study of Age Barriers and Leadership Styles.* Paper presented at the Australian and New Zealand Academy of Management Conference, Auckland, New Zealand.

Rauscher, L., & Cooky, C. (2016). Ready for anything the world gives her? A critical look at sports-based positive youth development for girls. *Sex Roles*, 74(7), 288–298. doi:10.1007/s11199-014-0400-x

Sherry, E., Schulenkorf, N., & Phillips, P. (2016). *Managing Sport Development: An International Approach.* Abingdon, United Kingdom: Routledge.

Sherry, E., Schulenkorf, N., Seal, E., Nicholson, M., & Hoye, R. (2017). Sport-for-development: Inclusive, reflexive and meaningful research in low- and middle- income settings. Sport Management Review, 20(1), 69–80. doi:10.1016/j.smr.2016.10.010

Seal, E., & Sherry, E. (2018). Exploring empowerment and gender relations in a sport for development program in Papua New Guinea. *Sociology of Sport Journal*, 35(3), 247–257.

Samie, F. S., Johnson, A. J., Huffman, A. M., & Hillyer, S. J. (2015). Voices of empowerment: Women from the Global South re/negotiating empowerment and the global sports mentoring program. *Sport in Society: Cultures, Commerce, Media, Politics*, 18, 923–937. doi:10.1080/17430437.2014.997582

Tivinarlik, A., & Wanat, C.L. (2006). Leadership styles of New Ireland high school administrators: A Papua New Guinea study. *Anthropology and Education Quarterly*, 37(1), 1–20. doi:10.1525/aeq.2006.37.1.1

UNWomen. (2014). Making Port Moresby safer for women and girls: A scoping study. Retrieved from www.unwomen.org/~/media/field%20office%20eseasia/docs/publications/2014/8/making%20port%20moresby%20safer%20for%20women%20and%20girls%202014.ashx

12

DEVELOPING SPORT FOR WOMEN AND GIRLS

Education

Ruth Jeanes

Introduction

This chapter examines the use of sport as a tool to support the education of women and girls. The challenges women and girls face accessing education across the globe are well established with the Millennium Development Goals and subsequent Sustainable Development Goals both prioritising gender equity and access to education as important targets. Various reports continue to document the lower educational levels of girls and women, predominantly within low- to middle-income countries (LMIC) and the negative impact this has on society more broadly (Wodon, Montenegro, Nguyen & Onagoruwa, 2018). International development policymakers and practitioners acknowledge that developing alternative mechanisms to support the education of girls and women is extremely important (Bellamy, 2004). Consequently, practitioners within sport for development (SFD) have explored how sport can be used as a potential vehicle for the delivery of education to girls and women, particularly within LMICs. Some form of education underpins the majority of SFD programmes, whether that be through the development of life skills (Svensson & Woods, 2017), conflict resolution skills (Schulenkorf, Sugden & Sugden, 2016), improving health knowledge (Jeanes, 2013), or promoting understanding of gender equality (Lyras & Hums, 2009).

Education delivered through sport can occur through programmes that seek to teach particular skills through participation in sport using embodied learning (Ansell, 2009). For example, young women participating in a soccer programme learn about the physical capabilities of their bodies whilst challenging gender stereotypes (Meier, 2005), or have the opportunity to develop their skills in the areas of leadership, teamwork, cooperation and negotiation through their participation in sports teams. Sports participation can be a useful mechanism to teach some of these life skills to young people (Fraser-Thomas, Côté & Deakin, 2005). This form of programme could also involve young women educating others about their capabilities and skills simply by participating visibly in sport in their local communities (Saavedra, 2009). Alternatively, education is delivered separately to sports participation, but sport is used as an attractor. Sport can provide the initial hook to encourage women to attend sessions, as well as support the development of networks and relationships that are crucial for a productive learning environment. Within this format, detailed educational sessions are usually delivered alongside sporting opportunities, with sport used as a tool to encourage ongoing attendance (Kay, 2010). Most SFD initiatives utilise a combination of explicit education using sport as a hook and embodied learning, or learning through sport.

This chapter examines sport and educational programmes to provide an overview of various initiatives that have sought to use sport as an educational platform for women and girls. The first part of the chapter outlines a selection of programmes, detailing their format and intended outcomes. This section considers educational programmes within both high-income countries (HICs) and LMICs and examines some of the diverse foci of initiatives across different contexts. The chapter then moves on to consider some of the critiques of education delivered through sport, before discussing practical actions and recommendations. The chapter concludes with a case study that illustrates the application of sport by a non-government organisation (NGO) in Zambia to support the education of girls and women.

Women, girls, education and sport for development in the LMICs

With the Millennium Development Goals and subsequently the Sustainable Development Goals both focusing on achieving gender equity and promoting quality education, it is unsurprising that a number of LMIC SFD initiatives use sport to target girls and young women as a mechanism for delivering or improving access to education. Hancock, Lyras and Ha (2013) conducted a database search that found 1,033 SFD programmes, with 440 of these specifically targeting girls and women. Of these, the authors suggest that, commonly, programme content focuses on health education, social inclusion and personal development. Most programmes combine HIC sports such as soccer and basketball, Indigenous games and movement forms, as well as educational components. Although not extensive, a growing body of research examining these women and girl-focused initiatives provides a valuable overview of the use of sport in this context. Several studies have examined the Zambian-based Go Sisters empowerment through sport programme (Hayhurst, MacNeill & Frisby, 2010; Lindsey, Kay, Jeanes & Banda, 2017; Mwaanga & Prince, 2016), which is examined in detail in the case study at the end of this chapter. Other programmes discussed in the academic literature include a girls' empowerment programme in Uganda, outlined in Hayhurst's (2014) research, where an NGO sought to use sport to address violence again women, increase their education, and challenge damaging gender relations within local communities. The programme employed staff to deliver martial arts activities and gender training sessions that 'assist girls' skill development in the realms of domestic violence, sexual relations and conflict management' (Hayhurst, 2014 p. 303). Hershow, et al. (2015) outline a girls-only soccer programme in South Africa that used bi-weekly session to provide HIV/AIDS education. Women community leaders were trained as coaches to deliver the activities. The programmes illustrate the general approach to delivering education through sport within LMICs: sport is used as a connection point, as a platform to then deliver key educational messages, but also – in the case of Hayhurst's (2014) study – sport becomes a site for embodied learning where girls can gain confidence through developing physical skills that they can use to protect themselves against violence within their community.

The studies suggest that initiatives such as these can be successful at reaching thousands of girls and young women (Hayhurst, 2013; Mwaanga & Prince, 2016). Existing research suggests potential outcomes included increases in health-related knowledge amongst girls and young women (Hershow, et al., 2015), increases in confidence and feelings of empowerment (Hayhurst, 2015; Jeanes, 2013) and the establishment of support networks that were important in helping young women negotiate ongoing challenges. Hayhurst (2015) and Jeanes (2013) both suggest that programmes can facilitate some levels of economic independence for young women by affording them opportunity to establish entrepreneurial activity, such as selling nut butter or clothing at local markets. A small number of studies suggest that girls' participation has assisted in making girls more visible within their local communities and – particularly when they are participating in masculinised sports such as football – young women can begin to challenge perceptions of women's capabilities amongst community members (Jeanes, Magee, Kay & Banda, 2013; Meier & Saavedra, 2009).

Many programmes of this type tend to be women and girl-only initiatives, often with the intention that this allows NGOs and deliverers to provide a safe space for women and girls, even if only for a temporary period (Spaaij & Schulenkorf, 2014). This is important for many women who value the opportunity to participate in physical activity and educational activities without fear of violence or abuse (Oxford, 2017).

Education and sport for girls and women in HICs

The following section considers education and sport through an HIC lens. While SFD education initiatives are commonplace within HICs, they rarely focus on girls or young women. Sport has been used as tool to support disengaged young people to reconnect with education (Sandford, Armour & Warmington, 2006), engage in education and training (Spaaij, Magee & Jeanes, 2013), and to educate young people about health and social issues such as drug abuse, mental illness and gang related violence (Kelly, 2011). These programmes are notable for their tendency to work with boys and young men, illustrating the connections between sport and masculinity and the belief that sport is a particularly attractive hook to engage young men (Magee, Spaaij & Jeanes, 2015). While practitioners in HICs rarely designed programmes exclusively for male participants, studies suggest that they struggle to recruit young women (Spaaij, Magee & Jeanes, 2013). There are, however, some examples of HIC education and sport initiatives working exclusively with girls and young women. Kay (2006) outlines the Widening Access through Sport initiative, a programme focusing on working with young Muslim women, providing a safe space to gain access to physical activity and sport and participate in an education programme to support access to higher education. Kay (2006, p. 370) suggests that the outcomes of this project were modest, with young women able to 'participate in sport in a controlled environment that conforms to their preferred practice of Islam'; however, she notes more significant gains for some women whose greater awareness led to them actively seeking to pursue higher education. Hayhurst, Giles and Wright (2016) discuss programmes targeting Indigenous women living in Australia and Canada. In both countries, programmes offered young women space to participate in sports and physical activities of their choice, while also providing self-development and education opportunities. Young women participants considered that their engagement in the programme helped them challenge racist and sexist stereotypes within their communities.

Reflecting the social issues prevalent in each context, the focus in HICs on girls, sport and education has generally been on supporting women and girls to become and remain active. This is often a secondary outcome for LMIC-based initiatives. The lower participation rates of girls in sport and the considerable drop out that takes place during girls' teenage years have been of concern to health and sport policymakers for several decades (Sabo, 2009). This, in part, has been attributed to poor experiences in school-based physical education (PE), leading to a plethora of studies considering how to improve the PE curriculum for girls and make it more relevant and appealing to them (Azzarito, Solmon & Harrison, 2006; Ennis, 1999; Enright & O'Sullivan, 2010; Mitchell, Gray & Inchley, 2015). These studies have demonstrated the importance of collaborative curricula, where girls codesign activities with teachers. When involved in the codesign of curricula, girls have the chance to participate in physical activities that they enjoy and that have relevance to their wider lives (Oliver & Lalik, 2004). Girls engaged more readily in physical education when teachers afforded them the opportunity to shape their educational experiences (Enright & O'Sullivan, 2010). Similar to studies within LMICs (Spaaij & Jeanes, 2013), this literature highlights the importance of educators using critical and creative pedagogies that raise girls' critical consciousness, helps them to consider why they disengage with physical activity and supports them to come up with solutions to encourage greater participation (Ennis, 1999).

Critiquing education through sport

Whilst recognising the value of sport initiatives for providing women and girls with education, there has been critique of the pedagogies used, curriculum content and some of the intended outcomes (Hayhurst, 2014). The majority of this research has focused on programmes delivered in LMICs, applying a feminist postcolonial lens to highlight the ways in which education is frequently underpinned by HIC assumptions of what is valuable knowledge and what outcomes girls should achieve (Chawansky, 2011; Forde & Frisby, 2015; Hayhurst, 2014; Hayhurst, Giles & Wright, 2016). Several studies (see, for example, Forde & Frisby, 2015; Hayhurst, 2014) have highlighted that the focus of projects on individual success, self-improvement and building self-esteem are more reflective of HIC neoliberalism rather than the collective norms and values that underpin many LMIC communities.

Forde and Frisby (2015) provide one of the few analyses of the curriculum used within LMIC girls' education initiatives, outlining some of the problematic ways the curriculum represents gender and sexuality. They suggest that simplistic constructions of gender are used to portray all girls as weak, vulnerable and passive but, through their engagement with the education programme, they will become confident, assertive and empowered. As Forde and Frisby (2015, p. 890) explain, this is problematic because 'much more than the girls' behaviour needs to change for them to live in spaces that are physically, psychologically, and socially safe'.

An ongoing critique of education programmes therefore, is that while they may transform girls' and women's attitudes towards themselves and their broader society, they do little to effect change across broader social structures (Hayhurst, Giles & Wright, 2016). Forde and Frisby (2015) highlight that,

> By focusing on the individual, these initiatives implore subjects to govern themselves and take responsibility for their own well-being regardless of their circumstances. In terms of gender, programmes that promote this form of neoliberal self-governance neglect the broader historical, political, social and cultural factors that produce and maintain gendered and social inequalities, and instead attempt to address unequal relations by encouraging girls to manage their behaviour and avoid risk.
>
> *(p. 883)*

This is evident in many African projects that focus on safe sexual practices. The education delivered within these tends to emphasise that girls should seek to abstain from sexual relationships or limit sexual partners and negotiate safe sex, actions that may not be possible for many young women (Jeanes, 2013). In educating this way, initiatives also perpetuate heteronormative conceptions of sexuality, with the assumption that all girls and women are engaging in heterosexual relationships (Chawansky, 2011). The rigidity of many of the curricula used to inform education through sport programmes, combined with a lack of awareness of local cultural nuances, can result in programmes having limited impact beyond the engagement of girls in regular sports and activities. The lack of relevance of some curricula, and therefore connection with the real-life circumstances of women and girls, limits the broader value of programmes (Forde & Frisby, 2015).

Furthermore, as Hayhurst and colleagues (2016) highlight, using sport and education to prepare girls for a neoliberal agenda that priorities employability as a key outcome can be counterproductive when little is being done to adjust the wider structures that contribute to ongoing unemployment and poverty within LMICs. While young women may develop important employment skills and gain higher levels of education, they still face a lack of employment opportunities, limited networks to help them gain employment and systemic prejudice that preferences the employment of males (Lindsey, et al., 2016). Hayhurst (2014, p. 310) reinforces the importance of recognising the limitations of what education and sport initiatives can achieve, highlighting the 'dangers of shifting too much responsibility onto targeted beneficiaries such as girls who must already negotiate immense gender and power imbalances'. Other studies have questioned whether projects are unintentionally exposing girls to further oppression by encouraging them to challenge well-established gender relations within their communities (Meier & Saavedra, 2009). Women and girls who attempt to exert themselves within arenas that they have traditionally experienced repression can face considerable resistance and an increased risk of violence (Chawansky, 2011; Meier & Saavedra, 2009).

Beyond the curriculum it is important to consider the pedagogies used to deliver sport and education programmes. There has been some critique that HIC volunteers deliver education programmes with little understanding of the broader cultural context and, along with the curriculum, perpetuate HIC ideals and values (Darnell, 2007). Additionally, while Indigenous deliverers have a far greater understanding of the cultural context they are working within, they may not have the skills to deliver more critical, reflective forms of education. Often, leaders deliver educational components using didactic, rote-learning methods that are commonplace within schools (Spaaij & Jeanes, 2013). These methods, while communicating knowledge, do little to support girls and young women in utilising this information in their lives. While there are examples of deliverers using critical and liberating pedagogies (Mwaanga & Prince, 2016), SFD policy and programming continues to give limited consideration to how education is delivered (Rossi & Jeanes, 2016; Spaaij & Jeanes, 2013).

There is significant opportunity for further research in this area. In general, existing studies have provided snapshots of single projects and their outcomes. These studies provide rich and detailed insights into the experiences of some women and girls and have provided a robust critique of practice. However, further research could offer greater insights into the curricula and pedagogies utilised within SFD and how these may support or constrain social change. More detailed, ideally longitudinal, research is required to begin to better assess the outcomes and ongoing impact of education initiatives. Mwaanga and Prince's (2016) study of the Go Sisters programme is one of the few to examine the value of education over any length of time and offers valuable insights into the growth of the programme and progression of the young women participants. More broadly, the relationship between education initiatives and social change – particularly exploring how education delivered through sport may begin to address systemic inequalities – is essential to move outcomes beyond individual impact and to better understand how initiatives targeting women and girls can more effectively connect with and influence the broader community.

Recommendations for practice

The studies reviewed in this chapter have a number of implications for practitioners and those involved in the design of education through sport initiatives for girls and young women. These are summarised below.

- Considering how outcomes will be achieved is important. If practitioners are expecting certain outcomes to occur through participation in sport, then careful consideration needs to be given to how sports opportunities are developed and managed to facilitate particular outcomes. It is unlikely outcomes will occur through sports participation alone.
- The notion of sport as a hook to engage young people in educational opportunities may be less effective when working with women and girls as it relies on them having some affiliation with sport and previous access. Tailoring the sport opportunity to encompass a broad array of movement forms – for example, dance – may be necessary to ensure they are appealing to young women and girls.
- Consideration needs to be given to what curriculum is used within programmes to ensure it is culturally sensitive and appropriate for women and girls, that it reflects the realities of their lives and does not reinforce or reproduce repressive stereotypes. Involving participants in the codesign of curriculum is a valuable way of creating an authentic and meaningful learning environment.
- Educating girls and women in isolation is unlikely to be effective if programmes are aiming to foster broader structural change and challenge the position of women within society. It is important programme deliverers consider how to educate others within the community, including boys, men and wider families to promote a wider impact.
- Who will deliver education to girls and women is important. Relatable women role models can have significant impact in attracting and retaining women and girls. Educators also need to be supported to deliver education using particular pedagogies, such as critical pedagogy, that may not be familiar to them, if they are seeking to support wider change and empowerment.
- It is important to recognise broader structural factors that may constrain girls and women's participation and the potential for sport and education programmes to achieve impact. Considering ways to help girls and women navigate structural barriers can be an important part of programme planning. Examples of this could be providing transport for women to ensure they can safely get to and from activities, through to offering participants educational scholarship.

Conclusion

The chapter has provided an overview of research examining the use of sport as a platform to support the education of girls and young women. Although there is not an extensive range of education and sport focused studies, what is available suggests that sport can play an important role in supporting the education of girls and young women and in facilitating education about gender inequality within communities. The chapter points to some of the tensions in this process, including the challenges of externally imposed and inappropriate curriculums, pedagogies that do little to facilitate broader learning and, more generally, the difficulties of facilitating broader social change through relatively small-scale programmes. Existing literature highlights the need for locally designed, culturally specific curricula, for deliverers who are relatable to participants and who understand the local contexts, and the importance of engaging the wider community in education opportunities.

> **CASE STUDY**
>
> ### Go Sisters, an SFD programme
>
> The case study discusses a sport for development initiative, Go Sisters, delivered in Zambia. This programme uses sport to empower disadvantaged young women. Zambian women and girls face considerable structural disadvantage in what continues to be a patriarchal society, particularly for young women who live in poverty (Jeanes, et al., 2013). While HIV/AIDS infection rates have considerably reduced over the last ten years, women and girls are still twice as likely as men and boys to become infected (Mwaanga & Prince, 2016). A variety of social conditions has created this dangerous discrepancy, including gender relations that make it difficult for women to say no to men or negotiate safe sex, the need for some women to engage in prostitution to ensure their economic survival and a normalised approach to sexual violence against women in some areas (Mwaanga & Prince, 2016). More broadly, families living in poverty consider girls' education a low priority. What money is available is usually spent on paying for the education of boy children. Whilst some girls may be able to access preliminary forms of education at volunteer-run community schools, they are usually unable to continue to high school to gain any formal education due to limited access to funding and limited opportunity to develop the literacy, numeracy and critical skills required to survive in high school.
>
> The Go Sisters initiative has been running for several decades, organised and managed by Zambian NGO, Edusport (Edusport, 2016). Operating via a peer leader model, the project recruits girls and young women across compound communities – high-density communities or 'shanty' towns – and provides training and support for them to work with young women in their local areas, delivering sports opportunities and health and broader life skills education. The programme also provides educational scholarships that pay the school fees of girls who engage and show commitment to the programme. It has been very successful at engaging young women in regular sport participation, increasing the visibility of women within public spaces and allowing young women to gain HIV/AIDS-related information. Some of the young women have also completed schooling to a certifiable level, with a small number continuing on to further education opportunities. A key impact of the Go Sisters programme is the establishment of an ongoing support network and friendship group for young women that can be invaluable in helping them negotiate often-challenging circumstances in their lives (Jeanes, et al., 2013).

Delivered by women peer leaders – who are from the same communities as participants and are therefore relatable to the girls – the educational component draws on critical pedagogy, seeking to support girls to challenge, question and consider the circumstances influencing their lives and work together to change them. Although over the years the programme has had to work with several externally-imposed curricula due to funding requirements, the NGO staff and peer leaders have constantly sought to adapt educational approaches and content to ensure that they are culturally and socially relevant to the young women that they are working with. An Ubuntu cultural philosophy – that Mwaanga & Mwansa (2014) suggests departs from HIC individualism and emphasises the importance of the collective and community – underpins the programme. A key aspect of the Go Sisters programme is the NGO's recognition of the broader structural barriers limiting girls' access to education. Alongside engaging with young women, staff additionally work with boys, young men and members of the wider family to educate them about the programme and the importance of gender equity more broadly. Edusport recognises that supporting girls and women alone is not enough to engender broader structural changes within communities; instead, it acknowledges that changing the attitudes and behaviour of men and boys towards women and girls is an important element of facilitating their empowerment.

The programme has worked with thousands of girls over the years (Edusport, 2016), with various studies suggesting participants experience multiple benefits, including greater visibility within their communities (Jeanes, et al., 2013; Mwaanga & Prince, 2016). Some young women have accessed certifiable education and ultimately employment. Others have used the networks established through the programme to begin their own entrepreneurial endeavours, such as making and selling clothing at local markets. A small number have had the opportunity to engage in elite sport and travel within and outside of Zambia (Jeanes, et al., 2013; Lindsey, et al., 2016).

While the outcomes of the programme are largely positive, staff and peer leaders face ongoing constraints. Reflecting some of the issues raised earlier in the chapter, for many young women changes can be slow to occur. They are able to participate in sport and critically inspired education, but do not necessarily have the agency or broader support to change their home circumstances and many continue to experience constraint, violence and abuse. For those with a level of support, participation still may not lead to significant changes in their situations. Some women struggled to gain significant employment due to the limited opportunities available within their communities and employers' continued preference for employing men. For young women who accessed scholarships, completing school and gaining qualifications was often difficult because they have undertaken most of their early education at community schools with unqualified teachers and are ill equipped to make the jump to more formal and exam-intensive education in high schools. More broadly, an increased critical awareness can lead to young women feeling discontented about their lack of ability to significantly change their circumstances (Lindsey, et al., 2016). Some young women also reported that families and communities found it difficult to accept more empowered, outspoken, less compliant versions of themselves and talked of the need to navigate a fine line between enacting traditional and repressive notions of Zambian femininity within their home environments and performing newer forms of empowered identity.

The case study illustrated that educating girls and women through sport is fraught with tensions and complexities. Localised approaches to education are essential, coupled with pedagogies that support transformative learning. The need for education programmes to consider broader contexts is highlighted in this example, with the education of boys and families shown to be essential for longer-term programme outcomes. Even with this, the case study illustrates that broader structural change is slow to occur, and that education initiatives need to be developed in a way that can make them sustainable over many years to continually challenge the wider social structures that prevent gender equity.

References

Ansell, N. (2009). Embodied learning: responding to AIDS in Lesotho's education sector. *Children's Geographies*, 7(1), 21–36.

Azzarito, L., Solmon, M. A., & Harrison Jr., L. (2006). "… If I had a choice, I would…." A feminist poststructuralist perspective on girls in physical education. *Research Quarterly for Exercise and Sport*, 77(2), 222–239.

Bellamy, C. (2004) *The State of the World's Children 2004: Girls, Education and Development.* New York: UNICEF.

Chawansky, M. (2011). New social movements, old gender games?: Locating girls in the sport for development and peace movement. In A. C. Snyder & S. P. Stobbe (eds), *Critical Aspects of Gender in Conflict Resolution, Peacebuilding, and Social Movements* (pp. 121–134). Emerald Group Publishing Limited.

Darnell, S. C. (2007). Playing with race: Right to play and the production of whiteness in 'development through sport'. *Sport in Society*, 10(4), 560–579.

Edusport (2016). *Go Sisters*. Retrieved from www.Edusport.no/prosjekter/go-sisters

Ennis, C. D. (1999). Creating a culturally relevant curriculum for disengaged girls. *Sport, Education and Society*, 4(1), 31–49.

Enright, E., & O'Sullivan, M. (2010). "Can I do it in my pyjamas?" Negotiating a physical education curriculum with teenage girls. *European Physical Education Review*, 16(3), 203–222.

Forde, S. D., & Frisby, W. (2015). Just be empowered: How girls are represented in a sport for development and peace HIV/AIDS prevention manual. *Sport in Society*, 18(8), 882–894.

Fraser-Thomas, J. L., Côté, J., & Deakin, J. (2005). Youth sport programs: An avenue to foster positive youth development. *Physical Education & Sport Pedagogy*, 10(1), 19–40.

Hancock, M., Lyras, A., & Ha, J. P. (2013). Sport for development programs for girls and women: A global assessment. *Journal of Sport for Development*, 1(1), 15–24.

Hayhurst, L. M. (2013). Girls as the "new" agents of social change? Exploring the "girl effect" through sport, gender and development programs in Uganda. *Sociological Research Online*, 18(2), 1–12.

Hayhurst, L. M. (2014). The "girl effect" and martial arts: Social entrepreneurship and sport, gender and development in Uganda. *Gender, Place & Culture*, 21(3), 297–315.

Hayhurst, L. M., Giles, A. R., & Radforth, W. M. (2015). "I want to come here to prove them wrong": using a post-colonial feminist participatory action research (PFPAR) approach to studying sport, gender and development programmes for urban Indigenous young women. *Sport in Society*, 18(8), 952–967.

Hayhurst, L. M., Giles, A. R., & Wright, J. (2016). Biopedagogies and Indigenous knowledge: Examining sport for development and peace for urban Indigenous young women in Canada and Australia. *Sport, Education and Society*, 21(4), 549–569.

Hayhurst, L., MacNeill, M., & Frisby, W. (2010). A postcolonial feminist approach to gender, development and Edusport. In B. Houlihan & M. Green (eds), *Routledge Handbook of Sports Development* (pp. 369–382). Oxon: Routledge.

Hershow, R. B., Gannett, K., Merrill, J., Kaufman, E. B., Barkley, C., DeCelles, J., & Harrison, A. (2015). Using soccer to build confidence and increase HCT uptake among adolescent girls: A mixed-methods study of an HIV prevention programme in South Africa. *Sport in Society*, 18(8), 1009–1022.

Jeanes, R. (2013). Educating through sport? Examining HIV/AIDS education and sport-for-development through the perspectives of Zambian young people. *Sport, Education and Society*, 18(3), 388–406.

Jeanes, R., Magee, J., Kay, T., & Banda, D. (2013). Sport for development in Zambia: The new or not so new colonisation? In C. Hallinan & B. Judd (eds), *Native Games: Indigenous Peoples and Sports in the Post-Colonial World* (pp. 127–145). Bingley: Emerald.

Kay, T. (2006). Daughters of Islam: Family influences on Muslim young women's participation in sport. *International Review for the Sociology of Sport*, 41(3–4), 357–373.

Kay, T. (2010). Development through sport? Sport in support of female empowerment in Delhi, India. In B. Houlihan & M. Green (eds), *Routledge Handbook of Sports Development* (pp. 324–338). Oxon: Routledge.

Kelly, L. (2011). Social inclusion through sports-based interventions? *Critical Social Policy*, 31(1), 126–150.

Lindsey, I., Kay, T., Jeanes, R., & Banda, D. (2016). *Localizing Global Sport for Development*. Manchester: Manchester University Press.

Lyras, A., & Hums, M. A. (2009). Sport and social change: The case for gender equality. *Journal of Physical Education, Recreation & Dance*, 80(1), 7–21.

Magee, J., Spaaij, R., & Jeanes, R. (2015). 'It's Recovery United for me': Promises and pitfalls of football as part of mental health recovery. *Sociology of Sport Journal*, 32(4), 357–376.

Meier, M. (2005). *Gender Equity, Sport and Development*. Bienne: Swiss Academy for Development.

Meier, M., & Saavedra, M. (2009). Esther Phiri and the Moutawakel effect in Zambia: An analysis of the use of female role models in sport-for-development. *Sport in Society*, 12(9), 1158–1176.

Mitchell, F., Gray, S., & Inchley, J. (2015). "This choice thing really works…" Changes in experiences and engagement of adolescent girls in physical education classes, during a school-based physical activity programme. *Physical Education and Sport Pedagogy*, 20(6), 593–611.

Mwaanga, O., & Mwansa, K. (2013). Indigenous discourses in sport for development and peace: A case study of the Ubuntu cultural philosophy in Edusport Foundation, Zambia. In N. Schulenkorf & D. Adair (eds), *Global Sport-for-Development* (pp. 115–133). London: Palgrave Macmillan.

Mwaanga, O., & Prince, S. (2016). Negotiating a liberative pedagogy in sport development and peace: Understanding consciousness raising through the Go Sisters programme in Zambia. *Sport, Education and Society*, 21(4), 588–604.

Oliver, K. L., & Lalik, R. (2004). Critical inquiry on the body in girls' physical education classes: A critical poststructural perspective. *Journal of Teaching in Physical Education*, 23(2), 162–195.

Oxford, S. (2017). The social, cultural, and historical complexities that shape and constrain (gendered) space in an SDP organisation in Colombia. *Journal of Sport for Development*, 6 (10), 1–11.

Rossi, T., & Jeanes, R. (2016). Education, pedagogy and sport for development: Addressing seldom asked questions. *Sport, Education and Society*, 21(4), 483–494.

Saavedra, M. (2009). Dilemmas and opportunities in gender and sport-in-development. In R. Levermore & A. Beacom (eds), *Sport and International Development* (pp. 124–155). London: Palgrave Macmillan.

Sabo, D. (2009). The gender gap in youth sports: Too many urban girls are being left behind. *Journal of Physical Education, Recreation & Dance*, 80(8), 35–40.

Sandford, R. A., Armour, K. M., & Warmington, P. C. (2006). Re-engaging disaffected youth through physical activity programmes. *British Educational Research Journal*, 32(2), 251–271.

Schulenkorf, N., Sugden, J., & Sugden, J. (2016). Sport for conflict resolution and peace building. In E. Sherry, N. Schulenkorf & P. Phillips (eds) *Managing Sport Development: An International Approach*, (pp. 148–158). Oxon: Routledge.

Spaaij, R., & Jeanes, R. (2013). Education for social change? A Freirean critique of sport for development and peace. *Physical Education and Sport Pedagogy*, 18(4), 442–457.

Spaaij, R., & Schulenkorf, N. (2014). Cultivating safe space: Lessons for sport-for-development projects and events. *Journal of Sport Management*, 28(6), 633–645.

Spaaij, R., Magee, J., & Jeanes, R. (2013). Urban youth, worklessness and sport: A comparison of sports-based employability programmes in Rotterdam and Stoke-on-Trent. *Urban Studies*, 50(8), 1608–1624.

Svensson, P. G., & Woods, H. (2017). A systematic overview of sport for development and peace organisations. *Journal of Sport for Development*, 5(9), 36–48.

Wodon, Q., Montenegro, C., Nguyen, H., & Onagoruwa, A. (2018). Missed opportunities: The high cost of not educating girls. *The Cost of Not Educating Girls Notes Series*. Washington, DC: The World Bank.

13

GENDER, SPORT, AND LIVELIHOODS

Rochelle Stewart-Withers

Introduction

The United Nations Office of Sport, Development and Peace (UNOSDP) argued the nexus between sport and its Sustainable Development Goals (SDG) are a 'compelling incentive and unmissable opportunity for joint efforts and actions' (UNOSDP, 2018, p. 2). As such, sport has been linked to the various SDGs, for example, Goal 1: No poverty, and Goal 8: Decent work and economic growth. The idea of livelihoods is highly relevant to the overarching SDG focus on 'no one left behind', by ending poverty and decent work.

With this in mind, the purpose of this chapter is to articulate an understanding of the role of sport in creating livelihoods for communities and to consider critically the social and cultural issues impacting on sport and livelihoods, thereby developing an understanding of sport and its utility in different contexts. Understanding the role of sport in creating livelihoods that benefit women and girls, in concert with a consideration of the social and cultural issues that facilitate or constrain women's and girls' participation, helps to illuminate the issue of sport and livelihoods. This speaks also to the SDG Goal 5: Gender Equality. Achieving gender equality through the empowerment of women and girls is especially important as sport does not sit in isolation 'from the cultural values and societal norms of society' (Petry & Kroner, 2019, p. 260), many of which discriminate against and exclude women and girls. The same can be said for livelihoods.

This chapter begins with an articulation of a nuanced understanding of livelihoods, specifically with the idea that livelihoods need to be sustainable. Distinctions are broadly made between the concepts of employment, work and livelihoods, to show why and how researching the notion of livelihoods is a useful and enlightening approach. The next section interrogates the role of sport in livelihoods creation for communities, especially for women. Given that the 'pervasive ideology', which discriminates against women in society generally, 'is replicated and reinforced in sport' (Kay, 2014, p. 90), it is important to not to assume that sport for development and peace (SDP), or sport for development (SFD) initiatives – even those with livelihoods aspirations – will automatically succeed. There are many social, cultural, context-specific elements at play that can impact on sport and livelihoods opportunities, especially for women and girls. The key area of concerns discussed in this chapter are women's triple role, women's status, resource access and restrictions surrounding women's mobility. The chapter then presents opportunities for further research and notes practical actions and recommendations. A case study of rugby-generated remittances in Fiji that highlights what is possible concludes the chapter.

Conceptualising employment, work and livelihoods

There are various overlaps, and important distinctions that need to be made between the concepts of work, employment and livelihoods. Definitions that simply equate work with remuneration are seen as problematic (Snyder, 2007). Not all work is paid. Women's domestic work was – and still is – deemed economically valueless and invisible (Waring, 1999). Employment has tended to refer to productive or economic activities, or to the exchange of labour services for payment, in cash or in kind. Yet not all economic activity has counted as employment. Broadening the definitions of employment to include other types of economic activities, such as market stalls, has meant women's economic activities are now more likely to be captured (Chant, 2006). Being more inclusive of women's work has also resulted in a greater interest in understanding the nature of women participation in work and employment (Maskia with Joekes, 1996). While research progress has been made, ongoing issues remain with the quality and breadth of sex-disaggregated data surrounding formal and informal labour, work time, time use and wages (Chant, 2006).

In his seminal livelihoods work, Chambers (1995) argued that for many vulnerable populations, the concept of livelihoods offers a better means for capturing how they live their lives. A livelihoods analysis seeks to incorporate all dimensions of work – paid, unpaid, formal and informal – the types of capitals (assets) people might have or not have, along with their capabilities. So, what people do in response to change – how they cope with stresses and shocks, and make the most of livelihood opportunities and the resultant outcomes – is understood as the goals people pursue (Chambers & Conway, 1991).

Livelihoods framing sees equity of great importance, thus income distribution is considered, as is the understanding equity of distribution of capitals, capabilities and opportunities. Livelihoods analysis links macro-level processes – i.e. migration policy or economic reform – to micro-level outcomes and responses. Livelihoods in themselves are only useful, however, if they can be sustained. Sustainability considers environmental impacts alongside social sustainability, which takes into account maintaining and improving livelihoods, while enhancing capitals and capabilities on which livelihoods depend (Chambers, 1995; Chambers & Conway, 1991).

People are more likely to have sustained livelihoods when they have various capitals to draw upon, both in the short and longer term (Chambers & Conway, 1991). Households are resilient when they can grow their capitals and have diverse options (DIFD, 2001). Livelihoods thinking - by taking into account the informal and unpaid dimensions of work - recognises that the majority of people in low- to middle-income countries (LMICs) are excluded from formal labour markets, with no provisions being made by the state (Jeanes, Spaaij, Magee & Kay, 2019). Women in LMICs tend to be concentrated in this informal area of work (ILO, 2002; 2018). Understanding women's livelihoods situation in general is an important step for understanding more deeply some of the complexities that exist when thinking about the role of sport in creating livelihoods for communities. The next section examines the possibilities related to creating livelihoods for communities via sport.

Sport as a livelihood or livelihoods through sport

Since the inception of SFD as an area of academic research, scholars have highlighted the importance of clarifying the difference between sport development (SD) and sport for development (SFD), arguing the progression of sport sometimes comes at the expense of development goals (Kidd, 2008; Levermore, 2008). However, a more tightly linked relationship between SD and SFD – in the research context of examining sport as a livelihoods option – can sometimes exist. In some instances, employment and any ensuing benefits via the sporting field also require the development of the sport itself. In the case of Pacific Island rugby, professional, semi-professional and non-professional athletes rely heavily on the fact the sport of rugby will continue to grow both internationally and at home (Stewart-Withers, Sewabu & Richardson, 2017). In further developing the sport, the demand for the Pacific Island rugby athlete also grows. Pacific men – through securing an overseas professional rugby contract and/or representing their home country in rugby – have been able to find economic success, fulfilment and prestige in their lives (Guinness & Besnier, 2016). In this sense, the growth of the sport has widened avenues and increased opportunities, with some Pacific Island families and their wider communities being able to meet their social and economic goals. As such, many Pacific families see a sport like rugby as a feasible avenue for men to gain future financial security for themselves and the wider family (Field, 2013). For many families, remittances earned from rugby are the major source of income (Stewart-Withers, Sewabu & Richardson, 2017).

At the simplest level, sport's contribution to livelihoods creation relates to earning a living via sport, either as a professional or semi-professional athlete with contracts or sponsorship, or in the sporting space as a coach, sport administrator, clinical personal, such as a physiotherapist or manager. The sporting goods industry offers some opportunities; however, that sector has also been criticised for using child labour and for exploitation of workers in LMICs (ILO-IPEC, 2002). Livelihood creation also indirectly occurs when the benefits that accrue via engagement in sport lead to additional and better livelihoods choices – from sport-based initiatives and programmes that focus on job-skills training, leadership and empowerment, to rehabilitation or social enterprise (Dudfield, 2019). Sport-based initiatives can provide an avenue whereby participants have access to education, which then enables them to better compete in the labour market (Cunningham, 2015). SPD initiatives, because of their inherent intent to target and involve people, can address issues of social exclusion and open up opportunities (Kay, 2014).

Sport also contributes to livelihoods when individuals employed in a sport-related position share their resources with other family or community members, most likely in the form of cash remittances, as assets or covering costs. There are also flow-on effects for communities when sport-generated remittances become donations and pay for community costs, such as a new roof on a school. Communities also benefit when sports earnings are used to set up small business, which then employ others (Stewart-Withers, Sewabu & Richardson, 2017).

However, care needs to be taken in terms of amplifying the role of sport in creating employment. Sport – both SD and SFD – faces challenges, in that LMICs do not have the infrastructure, sponsorship levels or funding seen in high-income countries (HICs). Governments with limited budgets often look to spend money on what they think are more pressing issues, such as health and education. Moreover, as pointed out by Coalter (2013), the lack of sport infrastructure is just one element among many that impact on successful outcomes in sport for employment programming. A peer leader in a South African initiative that focused on improving job prospects reported that while the SFD project had added to 'his employability by giving him an increased sense of self-efficacy, improved time management, problem solving skills and programme related administrative skills and report writing'; however, as he did not belong to a particular political group, the ANC, it was unlikely this increased capacity would lead to employment (Coalter & Taylor, 2010 cited in Coalter, 2013, p. 44). Of greater bearing in this instance was the broader political context.

Even in HICs, regardless of the 'laws mandating gender equality in the workplace' (Cunningham, 2015, p.135), women have lower levels of workforce participation comparative to men; they earn less and hold fewer management or leaderships roles, both generally and in sport. Therefore, even if the aspirations might be sound, participation by itself, even in SFD projects that focus on vocational training or entrepreneurship, does not automatically result in jobs or opportunities for participants. Moreover, even if there are jobs and opportunities, they will not necessarily be offered to women. Jobs might also be 'short term, casual and ad hoc' (Jeanes et al., 2019, p. 158), which is noteworthy, as 'contractual, steady, regular, well paid work or occupations have been argued to be the most empowering for women' (Masika with Joekes, 1996, p. 3).

Context specific social and cultural elements at play

The challenges and disadvantage women everywhere face in sport – as participants or as staff – are well documented (Coakley, 2017; Kay, 2009). Sport is stated to be a social domain created and governed predominantly by and for men, and, while girls and women comprise 50% of the population, they continue to be underrepresented in leadership, face more barriers to participating and are far less valued and visible in sport and active recreation (Coakley, 2017; Cunningham, 2015). These same dynamics are also evident in SFD (Brady, 2005; Hayhurst, 2013; Jeanes & Magee, 2014; Petry & Kroner, 2019; Saavedra, 2009). Hence, the inclusion of women in sport is a site of struggle and even more so for women and girls from LMICs.

When it comes to work and livelihoods, women are also disadvantaged (Sweetman, 2009). Thus, while on one hand interventions using sport to improve livelihoods are hugely important and highly desirable, sport as a means to challenge norms – to empower girls and women and thus promote gender equality – may be even more valuable. Especially if by challenging norms women have increased capacity to establish themselves and participate in their chosen livelihood, and even more so if this results in increased status and bargaining power. Achieving equality, however, is not an easy task, as there are various social and cultural norms that restrict women's access to paid work or livelihood engagement. These same norms may also mean women do not have a say over, or a share in, any of the benefits that come from paid work or livelihood engagement.

One major challenge that has implications for livelihoods is women's 'double day' or 'triple role', sometimes referred to as women's 'triple burden'. These phrases refer to the vital role women's labour plays in household maintenance and their labour contribution toward household costs (Chant, 2006). Moser (1989) asserts that women have triple roles, which include their productive (income-generating), reproductive (unpaid) and community (unpaid) work. Moser (1993) highlights the importance of women's practical gender needs (PGNs) – defined as a response to an immediate need that women identify within their socially defined roles – which do not challenge the status quo. PGNs include, for example, water supplies, health care, the need to generate income, and then strategic gender needs (SGNs). SGNs, by contrast, attempt to challenge the status quo because they are focused on the needs that women have identified that are related to their subordinate position in society. SGNs attempted to address issues of power, control, and decision-making, including the issues of legal and human rights or domestic violence (Moser, 1993). When thinking about SFD projects, understanding women's traditional roles is vital, as women may already be over-committed time-wise and may struggle to participate in activities, even if the focus is on upskilling for employability. Women and girls may not have time to be involved in sport or leisure activities, and any free time they do have, outside of domestic work, may be used for resting (Petry & Kroner, 2019). Furthermore, regardless of time, women simply may not be allowed to participate.

For women who are employed, high daily demands outside the workplace may mean they are less able to advance in their work situation. Even in HICs this can be an issue, as research has shown. For example, research with young Pacific Islander women in New Zealand found that domestic commitments, coupled with lack of financial means and no transport, meant they struggled to participate in school-facilitated, extra-curricular sporting activities, as parents working two or three jobs relied on them to take care of younger siblings before and after school and to complete household chores, such as laundry and cooking meals (Greene, 2015).

In most countries, women tend to earn less than men (ILO, 2012), and women are also frequently seen as secondary household earners. Regardless of their lower income, women tend to spend a higher proportion of earnings on the household and family (Chant, 2006; Kabeer, 1994). Positively, this can have increased benefits for girls, for example, as households have access to more and better quality food, or are able to play for school fees, meaning girls stay in school.

Cultural mores can hinder interactions between women and men. For example, women living in purdah – the religious and social practice of female seclusion prevalent in some Muslim and Hindu communities in South Asia (Kabeer, 1990) – can have their mobility restricted, which places severe limits on their ability to participate in employment or livelihoods options. Such constraints make them economically dependent and restrict them to the domestic sphere. Poorer women tend to observe purdah less due to the fact they need to engage in wage or self-employment (Kabeer, 1990). When women are restricted to the domestic sphere, the only livelihoods options become those that are home-based. While home-based income generation activities allow women the ability to manage their responsibility for caring for children, the sick and the old, it also makes them more vulnerable in that they received no work-related benefits and have little recourse if they are exploited (Maskia with Joekes, 1996).

Cultural restrictions that control women's movements also mean women have less opportunity to access urban centres where better markets may exist or where formal banking and credit systems are established – aspects that support livelihoods. Not recognising women as having legal status also means they can be dependent on male relatives to sign on their behalf, for instance, to set up a bank account or gain access to credit. Low literacy levels also impede legal and financial literacy (Kabeer, 1994; Chant, 2006).

While not definitive, Table 13.1 summarises various aspects that may impact women's livelihoods opportunities, impact opportunities while engaged in livelihoods and restrict benefits that ought to occur as result of livelihoods, and, which, therefore, require consideration when thinking about the role of sport in creating livelihoods for communities.

Opportunities for further research

As seen above, a number of social and cultural issues need to be accounted for when thinking about sport and livelihoods, all of which provide opportunities for further research. However, given the complexities of the issues, there appear to be two key areas of overarching concern. First, there is a need for more case studies that make better use of frameworks such as livelihoods and gender analysis. Second, more in-depth research that seeks to understand the mechanisms by which sport might promote gender equality and empowerment (Petry & Kroner, 2019).

TABLE 13.1 Some aspects which may impact women's livelihood opportunities

Triple role, time poor	Results in: - Less opportunity to reskill. - Less free time to participate in new initiatives. - Reduced ability to travel. - Women also draw on daughters' labour to assist them, sometimes removing them from school.
Occupational stereotyping	Results in: - Restricts work types available. - Women and girls also engage in self–limiting thinking and behaviours.
Gender discrimination	Results in: - Lower wages. - Fewer and poorer opportunities and choices. - Poorer experiences. - Reduced access to resources. - Inability to control resources.
Mobility	Restricted because: - Women have more home and local responsibilities than men. Cultural restrictions can also prohibit women's movements, meaning they are restricted to the domestic sphere. In some countries, women are not allowed to travel on public transport unless accompanied by a male relative, or even if they are entitled to, they still face harassment.
Spatial elements	- With the separation of workplace and home, women need a safe way to get to and from work; they also require childcare. - Home-based work can make women more vulnerable in that they received no work-related benefits and have little recourse if they are exploited. They can have little independence or control over their work. They work in often an isolated ways, with little opportunity to discuss experiences or rights with others. Home-based work is often done after the primary role of housework or parenting, during free time. Women end up with even less time for leisure.
Lack of education and training	Results in: - Lower earnings. - Lower returns from participation, which then acts as a disincentive to further invest in women.
Positioned as secondary earners	Results in: - Contributions by women are undervalued or are not recognised.
Low status	Restricts women's: - Ownership of land, property, stock or other assets. - Access to savings and credit schemes due to lack of collateral. When women do take out loans i.e. microfinance, they frequently have to turn over the money to male relatives, while still being accountable for repayments. Results in: - Inability to control revenue from livelihoods.

(*Continued*)

TABLE 13.1 (cont.)

Triple role, time poor	Results in: - Less opportunity to reskill. - Less free time to participate in new initiatives. - Reduced ability to travel. - Women also draw on daughters' labour to assist them, sometimes removing them from school.
Low literacy levels	Restricts women's: - Ability to fill out forms and understand what is required. Places women at risk of being taken advantage of. - Ability to access information regarding rights and employment opportunities.
Rural/Urban	Most formal banking and credit unions are found in urban environments. For rural women it will be harder to be involved in formal saving schemes.
Reduced access to credit	Women are less likely to own assets such as land. This hinders their ability to get credit as they have no collateral.
Legislation	The lack of legislation or systems that enforce legislation breeches means women are vulnerable. They can face sexual harassment and exploitation, in terms of hours and wages.
Few workplace benefits	Results in: No sick leave or superannuation. Ongoing education and training are all issues of concern.
Safety	Safety is about getting to work and being safe while at work. Basic requirements, such as having safe access to toilets, are issues women in low-income countries struggle with.

Making better use of livelihoods and gender analysis frameworks

A clear opportunity exists to think about the role of SFD initiatives with livelihoods aspirations utilising livelihoods, capitals and gender analysis. Generating positive livelihood outcomes for both women and men requires an in-depth understanding of their lives. It is imperative to understand the various capitals that exist within communities and households, and also to understand who has access to, and control of, these resources. Using bottom-up, participatory approaches and undertaking gender analysis will give a more detailed appreciation of women's position in any given community and will also provide a clearer picture of household and community dynamics (Kumar, 2002). In the context of the global development agenda – to end poverty and to achieve gender equality – the importance of sport-livelihood justice cannot be overlooked. Involvement in sport-related livelihoods strategies should enhance people's lives, and benefits should be distributed fairly. Whether enhancement is possible will only be known if clear needs assessments and ongoing analysis, including monitoring and evaluation (M&E), are undertaken.

It is important to also understand the value actually attributed to sport within communities. If sport is not valued, or does not feature highly, then the idea that sport can be tapped into as a vehicle for improving livelihoods may face opposition. In many cultures, sport and leisure activities are not part of daily life, and governments struggle to fund the arts and sport, which are often seen to be luxuries. Women's triple roles may hinder their participation and any spare time they may have will be used for things other than sport. In some cultures, it is usual to see girls in public spaces, whereas in other cultures it is not. For example, in Iran, girls are prohibited from playing on public sport grounds (Petry & Kroner, 2019). Resistance surrounding girls' participation can sometimes be overcome once parents understand educational and other benefits (Coalter, 2013); however, this does not address macro-level discriminatory policy and law, such as that illustrated with the Iranian example.

Empowering livelihoods

Given that women's livelihoods are intrinsically linked with issues of inclusion and exclusion, an area that warrants further research is understanding the mechanisms of exclusion (Petry & Kroner, 2019). For employment options to materialise in relation to sport requires challenging the systems, structures and attitudes that discriminate against women in society (Dudfield, 2019). Chant (2006) argues paid jobs and livelihoods creation can certainly lead to improved circumstances for women, even empowerment; however, much depends on the nature of employment or the livelihood, the working conditions and the wider societal systems and structures, which include, for example, good affordable childcare, support from wider family and the community including men, or access to safe affordable transport to get to and from work. Thus, whether a woman is a paid athlete or is acquiring new job skills from participating in an SFD, her position and experience do not sit in isolation from a society's social, cultural, political and economic frameworks, all of which have particular implications for women. SFD interventions alone cannot address market and structural issues that impact employment (Coalter, 2013), particularly given that many SFD initiatives tend to focus on the individual, and seek to achieve programme-level outcomes (Dudfield, 2019).

Practicalities and recommendations

In keeping with SGD Goal 17 Partnerships for the goals, Lindsey and Bitugu (2019) highlight the emphasis in SFD to work in partnership, noting the value of partnerships for policy and strategic development – in terms of funding and resource provision – as well as for implementation and delivery. These partnerships exist between bilaterals, multilaterals, international non-government organisations (INGOs), civil society organisations, the private sector, governments – both local and central – and communities. Academics as researchers are also partners in the process. Given the huge complexities partnerships come with – for example, relating to power and capacities – scholars argue for the need to be more 'discerning and prioritise the development of particular partnerships which offer the greatest likelihood of productive benefit' (Lindsey & Bitugu, 2019, p. 87).

There is also growing recognition of the importance of how we work. Using the case of homelessness, Sherry and Osborne (2019, p. 382) argue the importance of 'multidisciplinary or interdisciplinary approaches to programming and research in order to deal with the complexity'. Hapeta, Stewart-Withers and Palmer (2019) highlight the need for Indigenous-informed theory and approaches to research in SFD and sport management. Collison, Darnell, Giulianotti and Howe, (2018), citing Burnett (2008) and Nicholls, Giles and Sethna (2011), discuss the need for monitoring and evaluation (M&E) as a way to empower local voices; they also advocate the use of participatory methodologies, in which there is a growing interest (see also Lindsey & Bitugu, 2019, p. 88). The value of bottom-up people centred approaches – whether in terms of programme design, implementation or M&E – is a commonly found theme running through academic work on the topic.

There are certainly some instances where an SFD initiative in support of livelihoods have had a level of success. The success of such programmes is due to the inclusion of relevant partnerships, interdisciplinary and multi-stakeholder collaboration, nuanced consideration of livelihoods, and data collection that uses culturally appropriate methodologies (Stewart-Withers, Sewabu & Richardson, 2016). One such example is presented in the case study of rugby-generated remittances and SFD in Fiji at the end of this chapter.

Conclusion

The option to play and enjoy recreation and sport in a safe and healthy context is a human right embedded in numerous global conventions such as the Convention on the Elimination of All Forms of Discrimination Against Women (CEDAW) (UN, 2007). The UN Secretary General on the post-2015 Agenda recognised that sport has a significant role to play in the 2030 Agenda (United Nations General Assembly, 2015). Dudfield (2019, p. 120) rightly points out, however, 'that addressing inequalities within sport will be an important indicator of the level to which sport-based approaches can actually contribute to the leave no one behind agenda integral to the SDGs', including ending poverty and access to decent work. Keeping in mind that increased access to employment – formal and informal and, thus, income – does not readily translate into improved status or empowerment for those at the margins. Gains also need to be made in other – legal, social and political – spheres. Understanding women's experiences of inequity in terms of employment, work and livelihoods is important for understanding the ability of SFD programmes to address some of these disparities and bring about benefits for all, and not just a few.

Current SFD scholarship highlights the need for nuanced ways of working and thinking through these issues, as well as the need to develop relevant partnerships, for interdisciplinary and multi-stakeholder collaborations and for gathering and sharing information with communities using culturally appropriate and participatory methodologies (Hayhurst, Giles & Radforth, 2015).

CASE STUDY

Rugby Union and livelihoods in Fiji

Rugby in Fiji is an example where both aspects of SD and SFD are interconnected. Based on the findings of a multidisciplinary, intersectorial research project (Stewart-Withers, Sewabu & Richardson, 2014), the New Zealand's Ministry of Foreign Affairs and Trade set up a rugby athlete development pilot project, an SFD initiative, in Fiji. The intention of the SFD project was not only to increase the value of sport-generated remittances to the Pacific by protecting athletes, but also to better support the professional, pastoral needs and longer term livelihoods aspirations of Pacific athletes within the context of their families and their communities (Stewart-Withers, Sewabu & Richardson, 2017).

This SFD project was deemed to also be important because of the way the rugby-generated remittances can also improve the lives of women and girls. For example, being able to purchase household appliances, such as a washing machine, reduced women's workloads. More cash to pay for consumables meant household food choices increased, with more protein-based products included. Food preparation time decreased. The ability to afford better and more consistent electricity and water supplies meant less time was also spent on household's chores. Women and girls were able to afford hygiene and menstrual products, which had implications for girls' school attendance. As women care for the sick, the ability to afford medicines and health care meant family were less likely to become really unwell, which had positive implications for women's time use. Women tend to pay for school fees, uniforms, stationery and books, and the ability to meet these costs meant women were less likely to use money needed for other necessities, such as the food budget. Rugby-generated remittances has delivered positive outcomes for women and girls in terms of reducing the pressures of their triple role and meeting their basic needs.

Remittances also created more employment opportunities. Women could cover the start-up costs of a small business, without getting into debt. The SFD project has meant women now have better access to training opportunities, such as business plan development or financial literacy. Business success means greater opportunity to employ other women, whether in the business or within the household to cover household duties or childcare.

It is often women who bear the brunt when the household comes under financial stress. Rugby-related remittances have enabled families, including women, to increase their savings, which has enabled them to gain a credit rating, service a debt and afford insurance, and also reduced the need to take high-interest loans or sell assets or livestock in the event of the unexpected, such as illness, funeral costs, crop failure or natural disasters, such as cyclones.

Moreover, women often carry the burden of family contributions to church, community or cultural events. Women report no longer feeling panicked about how they are to make their family's contribution without depleting their asset base, that is without the need to kill small livestock, or produce time-consuming woven mats. Instead, women were able buy from other women and experienced increased self-esteem and family status due to being able to contribute.

Rugby as a livelihoods option has enabled women to improve their existing businesses, to renovate and make their homes safer, to relocate to urban settings to capitalise on better schools, health facilities and employment opportunities and to go overseas to see family. Overall, it was found that households, and especially women, ended up with greater choices and opportunities and reduced vulnerability as a result of their participation in the programme.

References

Brady, M. (2005). Creating safe spaces and building social assets for young women in the developing world: A new role for sports. *Women's Studies Quarterly*, 33(1&2), 35–49.

Burnett, C. (2008). Participatory action research (PAR) in monitoring and evaluation of sport-for-development programmes: Sport and physical activity. *African Journal for Physical Health Education, Recreation and Dance*, 14(3), 225–239.

Chambers R. (1995). *Poverty and Livelihoods: Whose Reality Counts?* IDS Discussion Paper No 347. Brighton: IDS.

Chambers, R. & Conway, G. R. (1991). *Sustainable Rural Livelihoods: Practical Concepts for the 21st Century*. IDS Discussion Paper No 296. Brighton: IDS.

Chant, S. (2006). Re-thinking the "feminization of poverty" in relation to aggregate gender indices. *Journal of Human Development*, 7(2), 201–220.

Coakley, J. (2017). *Sports in Society: Issues and Controversies*, 12th edn. New York: McGraw Hill Education.

Coalter, F. (2013). *Sport for Development: What Game are We Playing?* London, UK: Routledge.

Collison, H., Darnell, S., Giulianotti, R. & Howe, D. (2018). Introduction. In H. Collison, S. Darnell, R. Giulianotti & D. Howe (eds), *Routledge Handbook of Sport for Development and Peace* (pp. 1–9). Abingdon: Routledge.

Cunningham, G. B. (2015). *Diversity and Inclusion in Sport Organisations*, 3rd edn. Oxon, UK; New York, USA: Holcomb Hathaway Publishers.

DIFD (2001) *Sustainable Livelihoods Framework*. Retrieved from http://nzaidtools.nzaid.govt.nz/sustainable-livelihoods-approach/sustainable-livelihoods-framework

Dudfield, O. (2019). SDP and the sustainable development goals. In H. Collison, S. Darnell, R. Giulianotti & D. Howe (eds), *Routledge Handbook of Sport for Development and Peace* (pp. 116–127). Abingdon: Routledge.

Field, M. (2013). Polynesian men: A global sports commodity. Retrieved from www.stuff.co.nz/sport/8718872/ Polynesian-men-a-global-sports-commodity

Greene, M. (2015). *"Get into Groups": Young Pacific Island Women and Empowerment through Physical Education*. Unpublished Master's thesis, Massey University, Palmerston North, NZ. Retrieved from https://mro.massey.ac.nz/bitstream/handle/10179/7249/02_whole.pdf?sequence=2&isAllowed=y

Guinness, D. & Besnier, N. (2016). Nation, nationalism and sport: Fijian rugby in the local-global nexus. *Anthropology Quarterly*, 89(4), 1109–1141.

Hapeta, J., Stewart-Withers, R. & Palmer, F. (2019). Sport for social change with Aotearoa New Zealand youth: Navigating the theory-research-practice nexus through Indigenous principles. *Journal of Sport Management: Special Issue: Sport for Social Change*, 33(5), 481–492.

Hayhurst, L. M. (2013). Girls as the "new" agents of social change? Exploring the "girl effect" through sport, gender and development programs in Uganda. *Sociological Research Online*, 18(2), 1–12.

Hayhurst, L. M., Giles, A. R. & Radforth, W. M. (2015). "I want to come here to prove them wrong": Using a post-colonial feminist participatory action research (PFPAR) approach to studying sport, gender and development programmes for urban Indigenous young women. *Sport in Society*, 18(8), 952–967.

ILO (International Labour Office). (2002). *Decent Work and the Informal Economy*. 90th Session, Report VI, Geneva: ILO. Retrieved from www.ilo.org/public/libdoc/ilo/2002/102B09_133_engl.pdf

ILO (International Labour Office). (2018). *Trends for Women 2018 Global Snapshot*. Retrieved from www.ilo.org/wcmsp5/groups/public/—dgreports/—dcomm/—publ/documents/publication/wcms_619577.pdf

ILO-IPEC (International Labour Office – International Programme on the Elimination of Child Labour). (2002). *Red Card Initiative*. Retrieved from www.ilo.org/ipec/CampaigncndadvocacyRedCardtoChildLabour/lang—en/index.htm

Jeanes, R. & Magee, J. (2014). Promoting gender empowerment through sport? Exploring the experiences of Zambian female footballers. In N. Schulenkorf & D. Adair (eds), *Global Sport-for-Development: Critical Perspectives* (pp. 134–154). Basingstoke: Palgrave Macmillan.

Jeanes, R., Spaaij, R., Magee, J., & Kay, T. (2019). SDP and social exclusion. In H. Collison, S. Darnell, R. Giulianotti & D. Howe (eds), *Routledge Handbook of Sport for Development and Peace* (pp. 152–161). Abingdon: Routledge.

Kabeer, N. (1990) Poverty, purdah and women's survival strategies in rural Bangladesh. In H. Bernstein, B. Crow, M. Mackintosh & C. Martin (eds), *The Food Question. Profits Versus People?* (pp. 134–148). London: Earthscan.

Kabeer, N. (1994). *Reverse Realities. Gender Hierarchies in Development Thought*. London, New York: Verso.

Kay, T. (2009). Developing through sport: Evidencing sport impacts on young people. *Sport in Society*, 12(9), 1177–1191.

Kay, T. (2014). Gender, sport and social exclusion. In M. Collins with T. Kay (eds), *Sport and Social Exclusion* (pp. 90–106). London: Routledge.

Kidd, B. (2008). A new social movement: Sport for development and peace. *Sport in Society*, 11(4), 370–380.

Kirk, D. (2012). *Empowering Girls and Women through Physical Education and Sport – Advocacy Brief*. Bangkok: UNESCO.

Kumar, S. (2002). Does "participation" in common pool resource management help the poor? A social cost-benefit analysis of joint forest management in Jharkhand, India. *World Development*, 30(5), 763–782.

Levermore, R. (2008). Sport a new engine of development? *Progress in Development Studies*, 8(2), 183–190.

Lindsey, I. & Bitugu, B. B. (2019). Partnerships in and around SDP. In H. Collison, S. Darnell, R. Giulianotti & D. Howe (eds), *Routledge Handbook of Sport for Development and Peace* (pp. 80–90). Abingdon: Routledge.

Maskia R. with Joekes, S. (1996). *Employment and Sustainable Livelihoods: A Gender Perspective*. BRIDGE Report No 37. Retrieved from www.bridge.ids.ac.uk/sites/bridge.ids.ac.uk/files/reports/re37c.pdf

Moser, C. (1989). Gender planning in the Third World: Meeting practical and strategic gender needs. *World Development*, 17(11), 1799–1825.

Moser, C. (1993). *Gender Planning and Development: Theory, Practice and Training*. London and New York: Routledge.

Nicholls, S., Giles, A. R., & Sethna, C. (2011). Perpetuating the 'lack of evidence' discourse in sport for development: Privileged voices, unheard stories and subjugated knowledge. *International Review for the Sociology of Sport*, 46(3), 249–264.

Petry, K. & Kroner, F. (2019). SDP and gender. In H. Collison, S. Darnell, R. Giulianotti & D. Howe (eds), *Routledge Handbook of Sport for Development and Peace* (pp. 255–264). Abingdon: Routledge.

Saavedra, M. (2009). Dilemmas and opportunities in gender and sport-in-development. In R. Levermore & A. Beacom (eds), *Sport and International Development* (pp. 124–155). New York: Palgrave Macmillan.

Sherry, E., & Osborne, A. (2018). SDP and homelessness. In H. Collison, S. Darnell, R. Giulianotti & D. Howe (eds), *Routledge Handbook of Sport for Development and Peace* (pp. 374–384). Routledge.

Snyder, M. (2007). Gender, the economy and the workplace: Issues for the women's movement. In L. E. Lucas (ed.), *Unpacking Globalization: Markets, Gender, and Work* (pp. 11–20). Lanham: Lexington Books.

Stewart-Withers, R., Sewabu, K., & Richardson, S. (2014). *Increasing the Value of Sports-generated Remittances into the Pacific: A Research into a Pacific-wide Sport-for-Development Activity—Fieldwork Report*. Unpublished.

Stewart-Withers, R., Sewabu, K. & Richardson, S. (2016). Talanoa: A contemporary qualitative methodology for sport management. *Sport Management Review: Special Issue: Contemporary Qualitative Approaches to Sport Management Research*, 20(1), 55–68. doi:10.1016/j.smr.2016.11.001

Stewart-Withers, R., Sewabu, K. & Richardson, S. (2017). Rugby union driven migration as a means for sustainable livelihoods creation: A case study of iTaukei, indigenous Fijian. *Journal of Sport for Development*, 5(9), 1–20.

Sweetman, C. (2009) Introduction. *Gender & Development*, 17(2), 179–188.

United Nations. (2007). *Women 2000 and Beyond. Women Gender Equality and Sport*. Retrieved from www.un.org/womenwatch/daw/public/Women%20and%20Sport.pdf

United Nations General Assembly (UNGA). (2015). *Transforming our World: The 2030 Agenda for Sustainable Development*. Retrieved from www.un.org/ga/search/view_doc.asp?symbol=A/RES/70/1&Lang=E

United Nations Office of Sport, Development and Peace (UNOSDP). (2018). *Sport and the Sustainable Development Goals: An Overview Outlining the Contribution of Sport to the SDGs*. Retrieved from www.un.org/sport/sites/www.un.org.sport/files/ckfiles/files/Sport_for_SDGs_finalversion9.pdf

Waring, M. (1999). *Counting for Nothing – What Men Value and What Women are Worth*. Toronto: University of Toronto Press.

14

PROMOTING HEALTH FOR WOMEN AND GIRLS THROUGH SPORT

Katie Rowe and Emma Sherry

Introduction

Governments around the world often promote and invest in sport under an assumption that sport provides a vehicle through which population health benefits can be achieved (Hoekstra, et al., 2018; Nicholson, Hoye & Houlihan, 2010). In fact, health is one of the most common justifications for investment in, and prioritisation of, sport, alongside socialisation, economic development, community development and national pride (Chalip, 2006). The primary mechanism through which sport is understood to contribute positively to population health is via enhanced opportunities for physical activity (WHO, 2018). It is assumed that if people participate in sport, they are more likely to engage in greater amounts of physical activity at a higher intensity and therefore receive indirect physical and mental health benefits. Moreover, opportunities to socialise and interact with others, and to set and achieve personal goals, can also make for health enhancing environments (Rowe & Siefken, 2016). However, it is important to note that unless sport is strategically managed in ways that purposefully prioritise and promote health, it cannot be assumed that sport is inherently health promoting and that by encouraging sport participation, population health will be improved (Chalip, 2006; Edwards & Rowe, 2019).

While in most cases sport can be safe activity to engage people in increased physical health, sport participation can also increase one's risk of being injured (Mitchell, Curtis, & Foster, 2017) and may also create an environment that encourages negative health behaviours, such as alcohol consumption, performance enhancing drug use and eating disorders (Coakley, Hallinan, & MacDonald, 2011). While sport can be an effective vehicle for promoting health, it is important that strategic action is taken to ensure that sport systems, programmes and initiatives are designed and delivered in ways that promote health, if health is the primary reason for funding, promoting and delivering a sport programme or activity.

In this chapter, issues in relation to promoting sport as a vehicle for health are examined. Specifically, we consider complexities associated with assumptions that sport promotes health. We explore the ways in which sport can be strategically managed towards the achievement of health outcomes, specifically focusing on the health of women and girls. Additionally, future research opportunities around health and sport participation for women and girls are highlighted. From a practical perspective, a marketing campaign called This Girl Can is examined, with a focus on its implementation in English (Sport England) and Australian (VicHealth) contexts. In this case, an emphasis is placed on understanding how the This Girl Can campaign sought to encourage women and girls to engage in forms of sport and active recreation in ways that make them feel empowered and supported, rather than self-conscious and judged. However, complexities associated with measuring and providing evidence of health outcomes of such a campaign emerge, and these are also highlighted.

A sport health nexus?

Health has been defined by the World Health Organization (WHO) as 'a state of complete physical, mental and social well-being, and not merely the absence of disease' (WHO, 1948, p. 100). In this regard, health is considered a multidimensional concept that encapsulates dimensions beyond one's physical health status to also include mental/psychological and social dimensions of health. Within this definition, physical health focuses on the absence of physical disease and having the energy to perform daily tasks (including moderate to vigorous intensity activity); mental health relates to the absence of mental disorders and the ability to negotiate daily challenges and social interactions in life without major issues; and social health emphasises the ability to interact with other people in the social environment and engage in satisfying personal relationships (WHO, 1948).

The health benefits of regular participation in physical activity have long been established (Hardman & Stensel, 2009; Haskell, et al., 2007; Warburton, Nicol, & Bredin, 2006; WHO, 2010). The WHO (2010) developed a set of global guidelines outlining the frequency, duration and intensity of physical activity required by different population groups to achieve benefits for health. This framework is used by governments to develop national physical activity guidelines and inform national health policies. The WHO has also specifically identified sport as a vehicle through which regular participation in physical activity can be achieved and promoted. In 2018, the WHO released a Global Action Plan on Physical Activity 2018–2030, in which sport was identified as a priority area presenting relevant opportunities to encourage people to increase their levels of physical activity: 'Strengthening access to, and the promotion of participation in, sports and active recreation, across all ages and abilities, is an important element of increasing population levels of physical activity' (WHO, 2018, p. 17). This highlights that relationships between sport, physical activity and health are understood to exist.

However, 'evidence to support sport's positive impact on individual and community health is inconclusive, resulting in a need to further interrogate the agenda of sport for health' (Edwards & Rowe, 2019, p. 4). When applying the multidimensional definition of health outlined earlier, it can be argued that sport has the potential to enhance population health on multiple levels by encouraging people to engage in enjoyable forms of physical activity, but also by connecting individuals with others who share a similar interest in sport and providing them with opportunities to set and achieve personal goals (Rowe & Siefken, 2016). The links between sport and physical activity seem clear, with many forms of sport, such as basketball, tennis, soccer, and swimming, clearly providing participants with opportunities to engage in forms of moderate to vigorous intensity physical activity. But what about those sports that do not involve a substantial amount of physical activity, such as lawn bowls or archery? And what about forms of sport that are played in hyper-competitive environments, in which the primary focus is not on engaging in physical activity and giving everyone a fair opportunity to participate but rather, is on ensuring the best athletes takes the field/court on the day, leaving others to feel left out and subsequently miss opportunities for activity? Are these likely to lead to healthy outcomes for participants?

Eime and colleagues conducted systematic reviews of the psychological and social health benefits of sport participation for adults (2013a) and children and adolescents (2013b). In the review of literature that focused on adults, a range of psychological and social health benefits associated with sport participation were identified, with enhanced wellbeing, reduced distress and stress and benefits attributable to participation in physical activity, commonly reported in the literature. Interestingly, club-based and team-based sports were more often associated with improved health outcomes when compared with individual activities, due to the social nature of such participation settings (Eime, Young, Harvey, Charity, & Payne, 2013a). In the review that focused on children and adolescents, various psychological and social health benefits of sport participation were also identified, with improved self-esteem, social interaction, and fewer depressive symptoms being the most frequently reported benefits (Eime, Young, Charity, & Payne, 2013b). Importantly, the authors note that sport 'may be associated with improved psychosocial health above and beyond improvements attributable to participation in physical activity' (Eime, et al., 2013b, p. 1), highlighting that there may be something particularly health enhancing about sport as a form of physical activity.

Important links between sport and health were identified in both systematic reviews, focusing on children, adolescents, and adults; however, the authors (Eime, et al., 2013a; 2013b) reflect that it is difficult to derive causal links between sport and health, based on evidence contained in the identified studies, given such studies were largely cross-sectional in nature. As an outcome of these two systematic literature reviews, two conceptual models of Health through Sport (one for adults and one for children and adolescents) were proposed. The authors maintain that community sport participation should be promoted as a form of leisure time physical activity for children, adolescents and adults in efforts to improve the physical, psychological and social health of the population, and also to reduce the impact of obesity. However, importantly, they called for further research to be conducted to establish causal links between participation in sport and psychosocial health, in particular, further highlighting gaps in the extant literature.

Based on the evidence provided above, it is understood that sport has the potential to promote physical activity and health. Yet, we know that not all sport systems and organisations function with health as a primary objective, nor in ways that prioritise health. Governments often use health as a justification for investment in sport (Chalip, 2006; Hoekstra, et al., 2018; Nicholson, et al., 2010), yet often prioritise elite sport outcomes through their sport policies and funding (Jolly, 2013), with health remaining an assumed associated benefit of sport investment that is rarely rigorously measured. In this regard, while using health as a justification for investment in sport aligns more closely with sport for development (SFD) agendas, governments often engineer their sport systems in ways that align more closely with traditional views of sort development (SD). Hence, disconnections between SFD and SD become problematic in this context (Rowe & Siefken, 2016).

From a SD perspective, many sport systems have been designed in ways that aim to attract participants and establish sporting pathways to ensure talented athletes are provided with opportunities to achieve elite-level success (Sotiriadou, Shilbury, & Quick, 2008). This means that sport organisations are often ill equipped to strategically facilitate population health outcomes particularly when they are encouraged and incentivised to achieve performance outcomes as their primary objective (Casey, Payne, Eime, & Brown, 2009; Casey, Payne, & Eime, 2012; Edwards & Rowe, 2019). In sport systems that rely on the goodwill of volunteers, this can mean that efforts to work towards the achievement of health objectives, alongside performance objectives, can present operational and resourcing challenges. Moreover, the allure of revenue provided by junk food, soft drink and alcohol companies can be difficult for community sport organisations to turn down (Batty & Gee, 2019).

When we consider definitions of sport, commonly agreed attributes of sport include that it is playlike in nature, involves elements of competition, is based on physical prowess, involves skill and strategy, has an uncertain outcome, specific rules, uses specialised equipment and/or facilities, and involves formal sporting leagues based on competition, cooperation and conflict (Shilbury, Phillips, Karg, & Rowe, 2016). Such characteristics of sport are relevant in the context of traditional SD settings; however, in SFD contexts, broader definitions of sport are often applied that see the promotion of less-structured activities, which tend to be focused more on development outcomes and less on formalised competition and rules (Rowe & Siefken, 2016). In fact, national governments and sport governing bodies seem to be coming to a realisation that broader definitions of sport are more relevant in efforts to achieve non-sport outcomes, such as improved population health. In this regard, in efforts to promote sport as a vehicle for achieving health enhancement for women and girls, a broader conceptualisation definition of sport seems logical.

Scholars have argued that the value of sport, specifically as a vehicle for achieving health outcomes, depends largely on the way in which it is managed (Berg, Warner, & Das, 2015; Chalip, 2006; Edwards, 2015; Edwards & Rowe, 2019; Eime, et al., 2015; Henderson, 2009; Rowe, Shilbury, Ferkins, & Hinckson, 2013). In order for sport to be promoted as health enhancing, it needs to be managed with health objectives in mind. Edwards and Rowe (2019) reflected that investing in and promoting sport does not automatically lead to positive population health outcomes. The authors argued that in order for sport to be managed in ways that promotes and delivers health outcomes, sport managers should embrace the following key principles: sport should be accessible, aligned with community needs, and encourage participant leadership and empowerment; sport should be adaptable and evolving to ensure sport culture values health; and sport organisations should leverage partnerships for health to promote organisational sustainability.

In relation to sport delivery meeting community needs and encouraging participant leadership and empowerment, this is about ensuring that sport programming is community led and co-designed by participants in ways that ensure participants feel considered, included and supported. As an example, Stronach, Maxwell and Pearce (2019) reported on the importance of agency and empowerment for Indigenous Australian women in efforts to achieve health outcomes through sport. The authors note that 'Indigenous-women's only [sport participation] opportunities, partnerships with health agencies and sports organisations, culturally safe spaces, and Indigenous women acting as role models' (Stronach, et al., 2019, p. 5) are key ways in which Indigenous women's health can be enhanced through participating in sport. This highlights that simply promoting generic sport participation opportunities alone is insufficient for promoting health through sport, and specific action should be taken to ensure sport participation environments are conductive to promoting health. These specific actions also need to take into account the target population, such as women and girls, multicultural communities or people with a disability.

In efforts to ensure sport is adaptable and evolving to deliver sport through models that value health, Edwards and Rowe (2019, p. 2) note that this is about 'broadening definitions of sport and bringing together the concepts of development of sport and development through sport/SFD to establish more holistic views of sport management and delivery'. In Australia, we have seen sport organisations develop programmes that focus on innovative, non-traditional ways to engage women and girls in sport through less-structured activity formats. In particular, sport organisations looking to bring together fitness and sport-focused activities to develop creative new, and often non-competitive, programme ideas, such as SwingFit (golf), Cardio Tennis, She Rides (cycling) and Rock Up Netball, which are designed to break down traditional structural barriers to participation for women and focus on aspects of fun, fitness and developing skills and confidence. In the US and UK, flag football is an example of a sport that has been introduced in different contexts in efforts to attract women into sport in non-traditional ways.

The final point in relation to managing sport for health relates to sport organisations leveraging partnerships for health (Edwards & Rowe, 2019), which seems critical in light of earlier observations that sport systems, organisations, administrators and volunteers are not always equipped to work towards and deliver specific health outcomes through sport. Importantly, sport organisations can partner with health agencies, non-profit and non-government organisations, government departments and private health providers, to harness relevant health-focussed expertise that can ensure health outcomes are achieved through sport.

Targeting specific participant groups: women and girls

With health posited as a key justification for government investment in sport, logically, an emphasis is often placed on identifying less active and/or less engaged groups and prioritising such groups through various forms of sport programming. Different population groups, including those from diverse cultural backgrounds, the LGBT+ community, people with a disability, older adults, and Indigenous peoples, are often identified as being are less likely to engage in forms of sport, active recreation and physical activity. Various initiatives, in the form of programmes, grants, and events, are often developed to address inequalities in participation opportunities and to promote and encourage participation by individuals within these groups. In addition to the groups identified above, women and girls are often prioritised in strategic attempts to promote physical activity and sport participation among underrepresented groups.

While evidence is mixed, generally, it is accepted that women and girls are less likely than men and boys to participate in organised forms of sport and physical activity (Commonwealth of Australia, 2017; Women's Sport and Fitness Foundation, 2008). As was highlighted in Chapter 3, a substantial drop-off is observed in girls' participation through the teenage years, which sees many girls who were previously engaged in sport drop out and either move into less structured forms of activity (such as walking, going to the gym) or disengaging from activity all together. In Chapter 4, it was also explained that for women who have children and assume primary care responsibilities, there is often a range of additional barriers to sport and physical activity participation, making it more difficult to maintain regular engagement.

Women and girls often report a range of barriers to participation in sport; some align with barriers to physical activity participation and others relate especially to sport. Many of these barriers have been examined in earlier chapters, with a focus on barriers faced by specific groups of women and/or girls. In efforts to specifically target health through sport participation, it is important to ensure that women and girls are presented with positive messages about sport and physical activity, and that they are made to feel welcome and encouraged to participate in sport environments, and that they are supported to overcome such barriers. As was noted earlier, if managed appropriately, sport has the potential to contribute to physical, mental and social health benefits for women and girls. However, with such a substantial drop-off occurring through the teenage years, it should not be assumed that sport environments and sport offerings are welcoming for women and girls through the adolescent and adult years. More needs to be done to ensure that sport for women and girls remains a priority for sport organisations and that management actions focus on creating supportive environments for women and girls, which will lead to both sport participation and positive health outcomes.

Future research

Future research opportunities exist, particularly in relation to identifying direct, causal links between sport participation and health benefits, including physical, mental and social health. While indirect links are commonly reported, and benefits are often assumed, a stronger evidence base is needed to demonstrate how sport promotes health, what health outcomes are delivered through sport and under what conditions such benefits are strongest. There is a 'need to further interrogate the agenda of sport for health and better understand how sport managers can engage with this agenda in meaningful ways' (Edwards & Rowe, 2019, p. 4). This call to action is relevant to the sport sector broadly; however, in the context of promoting women's and girls' participation in sport for health benefits, it is particularly pertinent.

If women and girls are less likely to participate in sport than men and boys, does this matter for health outcomes if women and girls remain physically active via active recreation or fitness activities? Or are there particular health benefits delivered through a sport context that women and girls may miss out on if they turn away from organised sport and towards more individualised forms of activity? Such evidence will help to clarify whether governments and other stakeholder groups are wise to continue to promote sport specifically as a vehicle for health for women and girls. It would also serve to clarify whether definitions of sport should be expanded to ensure that managers are working towards a broader activity agenda, or whether promotion of physical activity, more broadly, is a more strategic way to promote health for women and girls. The following case study examines a campaign that targeted women's and girls' participation in sport and activity and highlights some of the issues explored in this chapter.

CASE STUDY

This Girl Can

The case study presented focuses on a campaign called This Girl Can, which was initially launched in 2015 by Sport England, with financial support provided by the British National Lottery – a common means of financial support for English sport programmes and organisations. The campaign was developed in response to a range of research-based barriers to sport and physical activity participation reported by women and girls, in particular: fear of judgement, lack of confidence and lack of time. The campaign was designed to encourage women to lead healthier and more active lives through regular engagement in sport and active recreation (Sport England, 2019a). The campaign uses imagery and messaging that encourages women and girls to get active, in whichever way they choose. Importantly, women and girls are encouraged to feel empowered to be themselves when participating in sport and physical activity.

The campaign disrupts typical imagery and messaging women and girls receive in relation to sport and physical activity participation, whereby women and girls are often made to feel unwelcome or inadequate if they do not display traditionally accepted physical characteristics of an active woman: thin, fit, white, athletic body shape. The imagery of the campaign shows everyday women of different shapes, sizes, abilities and ethnicities engaged in various forms of sport and active recreation through promotional videos and static imagery. Some of the campaign slogans and images have included the following:

- 'I kick balls. Deal with it' (image: women with a soccer ball)
- 'I'm slow but I'm lapping everyone on the couch' (image: plus size women in casual clothes on a bike)
- 'I jiggle therefore I am' (image: plus size woman running)
- 'I kick right in the stereotypes' (image: women wearing a hijab and boxing gloves, kicking a boxing bag)

The campaign website hosts promotional videos and stories of everyday women getting active in ways that make them feel good about themselves. It also provides links to information about how women and girls can get active in their local communities. Wheelchair basketball, school runs, spinning, sailing, basketball, group exercise, roller derby, dance fitness, yoga and badminton, are just a few examples of the types of activities listed, with the campaign website providing information and links to help women connect to local programmes and initiatives. Sport England claims that this initiative has encouraged close to three million women to get more active (Sport England, 2019b).

Following the success of This Girl Can in England, VicHealth, an Australian state government health promotion agency, entered into a licence agreement with Sport England to launch This Girl Can in state of Victoria. In addition to launching a campaign containing similar positive imagery and messaging to promote sport and active recreation participation for women and girls, VicHealth also partnered with various state sport organisations to ensure that programmes and activities were specifically designed and delivered to meet the needs of women and girls. For example, VicHealth partnered with the state governing bodies of Australian Rules football, basketball, cricket, cycling, hockey, netball and tennis. These partnerships were in addition to partnerships with professional and other sport organisations such as Melbourne City Football Club, the Richmond Football Club and the Victorian Institute of Sport, among others. The partnerships were formed in an effort to ensure messaging and programming would be designed to meet the needs of women and girls across a range of sport contexts and settings.

From these partnerships, new programmes were launched, and existing programmes were expanded or adapted to offer accessible, targeted programming for women and girls. For example, Bowling with Babies (see www.bowlsvic.org.au/bowling-with-babies) was designed to engage new mums in the sport of lawn bowls. Rock Up Netball (see www.rockupnetball.com.au), a sport programme that provides opportunities to participate in the netball in flexible, non-threatening environments wearing casual clothes, without the pressure of more structured competitive seasons, was expanded and promoted. VicHealth also recruited a number of This Girls Can ambassadors – everyday women of various, shapes, sizes, ethnicities, and abilities (see https://thisgirlcan.com.au/meet-the-girls/) – to act as the faces of the campaign and tell their stories of engaging in activities they enjoy and overcoming barriers to participation.

A clear objective of these campaigns is promoting health for women and girls through regular participation in sport, active recreation and physical activity. While the impact of both campaigns ultimately appears to be positive, with each campaign reporting increase in the number of women engaging in sport and active recreation as result of the campaign, the true impact and reach of the campaigns are difficult to ascertain, particularly with respect to the health impacts. These campaigns have been deemed a success based on increases in the number of women who self-report that they engaged in forms of sport, active recreation and physical activity. There is no doubt that initiatives such as This Girl Can have the potential to make a positive impact on the health of women and girls, and also impact organisations by encouraging them to think about innovative ways to their cultures and programme offerings to ensure they are inclusive of, and appealing for, women and girls. However, gaps remain in understanding their true impact of such campaigns on the health of women and girls when specific measures of physical activity changes and health outcomes remain absent from programme evaluation protocols. This presents an area for future development across the sport and active recreation sector.

References

Batty, R., & Gee, S. (2019). Fast food, fizz, & funding: Balancing the scales of regional sport organisation sponsorship. *Sport Management Review*, 22(1), 167–179. http://dx.doi.org/10.1016/j.smr.2018.06.014.

Berg, B. K., Warner, S., & Das, B. M. (2015). What about sport? A public health perspective on leisure-time physical activity. *Sport Management Review*, 18(1), 20–31.

Casey, M. M., Payne, W.R., & Eime, R. M. (2012). Organisational readiness and capacity building strategies of sporting organisations to promote health. *Sport Management Review*, 15(1), 109–124.

Casey, M. M., Payne, W. R., Eime, R. M., & Brown, S. J. (2009). Sustaining health promotion programs within sport and recreation organisations. *Journal of Science & Medicine in Sport*, 12(1), 113–118.

Chalip, L. (2006). Toward a distinctive sport management discipline. *Journal of Sport Management*, 20(1), 1–21.

Coakley, J., Hallinan, C., & McDonald, B. (2011). *Sport in Society: Sociological Issues and Controversies*. NSW: McGraw-Hill.

Commonwealth of Australia. (2017). *Ausplay focus: Women and girl's participation*. Retrieved from www.clearinghouseforsport.gov.au/__data/assets/pdf_file/0011/782345/ASC_AusPlay_Focus_on_Women_and_Girls_Participation_Final.pdf

Edwards, M. B. (2015). The role of sport in community capacity building: An examination of sport for development research and practice. *Sport Management Review*, 18(1), 6–19.

Edwards, M. B., & Rowe, K. (2019). Managing sport for health: An introduction to the special issue. *Sport Management Review*, 22(1), 1–4. https://doi.org/10.1016/j.smr.2018.12.006

Eime, R. M., Young, J. A., Harvey, J. T., Charity, M. J., & Payne, W. R. (2013a). A systematic review of the psychological and social benefits of participation in sport for adults: Informing development of a conceptual model of health through sport. *International Journal of Behavioral Nutrition & Physical Activity*, 10(135).

Eime, R. M., Young, J. A., Harvey, J. T., Charity, M. J., & Payne, W. R. (2013b). A systematic review of the psychological and social benefits of participation in sport for children and adolescents: Informing development of a conceptual model of health through sport. *International Journal of Behavioral Nutrition & Physical Activity*, 10(98).

Eime, R. M., Sawyer, N., Harvey, J. T., Casey, M. M., Westerbeek, H., & Payne, W. R. (2015). Integrating public health and sport management: Sport participation trends 2001–2010. *Sport Management Review*, 18(2), 207–217.

Hardman, A. E., & Stensel, D. J. (2009). *PA and Health: The Evidence Explained*, 2nd edn. New York: Routledge.

Haskell, W., Lee, I., Pate, R., Powell, K., Blair, S., Franklin, B., ... Bauman, A. (2007). Physical activity and public health: Updated recommendation for adults from the American College of Sports Medicine and the American Heart Association. *Medicine and Science in Sports & Exercise*, 39(8), 1423–1434.

Henderson, K. A. (2009). A paradox of sport management and physical activity interventions. *Sport Management Review*, 12(2), 57–65.

Hoekstra, F., Roberts, L., van Lindert, C., Martin Ginis, K. A., van der Woude, L. H., & McColl, M. A. (2018). National approaches to promote sports and physical activity in adults with disabilities: Examples from the Netherlands and Canada. *Disability and Rehabilitation*, 41(10), 1–10. http://dx.doi.org/10.1080/09638288.2017.1423402.

Jolly, R. (2013). *Sports Funding: Federal Balancing Act*. Canberra: Commonwealth of Australia.

Mitchell, R., Curtis, K., & Foster, K. (2017). A 10-year review of the characteristics and health outcomes of injury-related hospitalisations of children in Australia. Retrieved from www.paediatricinjuryoutcomes.org.au/wp-content/uploads/2017/06/Australian-child-injury-report_FINAL-070617.pdf

Nicholson, M., Hoye, R., & Houlihan, B. (eds). (2010). *Participation in Sport: International Policy Perspectives*. London: Routledge.

Rowe, K., & Siefken, K. (2016). Sport and health promotion. In E. Sherry, N. Schulenkorf & P. Phillips (eds), *Managing Sport Development: An International Approach* (pp. 121–134). Oxon: Routledge.

Rowe, K., Shilbury, D., Ferkins, L., & Hinckson, E. (2013). Sport development and physical activity promotion: An integrated model to enhance collaboration and understanding. *Sport Management Review*, 16(3), 364–377.

Shilbury, D., Phillips, P., Karg, A., & Rowe, K. (2016). *Sport Management in Australia: An Organisational Overview*, 5th edn. Crows Nest: Allen & Unwin.

Sotiriadou, K., Shilbury, D., & Quick, S. (2008). The attraction, retention/transition, and nurturing process of sport development: Some Australian evidence. *Journal of Sport Management*, 22 (3), 247–272. https://doi.org/10.1123/jsm.22.3.247

Sport England. (2019a). *This Girl Can*. Retrieved from www.sportengland.org/our-work/women/this-girl-can/

Sport England. (2019b). *About us*. This Girl Can, Sport England. Retrieved from www.thisgirlcan.co.uk/about-us/

Stronach, M., Maxwell, H., & Pearce, S. (2019). Indigenous Australian women promoting health through sport. *Sport Management Review*, 22(1), 5–20. http://dx.doi.org/10.1016/j.smr.2018.04.007

Warburton, D. E. R., Nicol, C.W., & Bredin, S.S.D. (2006). Health benefits of PA: The evidence. *Canadian Medical Association Journal*, 174(6), 801–809.

Women's Sport and Fitness Foundation. (2008). *Barriers to Sports Participation for Women and Girls.* Retrieved from www.womeninsport.org/wp-content/uploads/2017/10/Barriers-to-sports-participation-for-women-and-girls.pdf?x99836

World Health Organization (WHO). (1948). Preamble to the Constitution of the World Health Organization as adopted by the International Health Conference, New York, 19 June – 22 July 1946; signed on 22 July 1946 by the representatives of 61 States (Official Records of the World Health Organization, no. 2, p. 100) and entered into force on 7 April (1948).

World Health Organization (WHO). (2010). *Global Recommendations on Physical Activity and Health.* Retrieved from https://apps.who.int/iris/bitstream/handle/10665/44399/9789241599979_eng.pdf?sequence=1

World Health Organization (WHO). (2018). *Global Action Plan on Physical Activity 2018–2030. More active people for a healthier world.* Retrieved from https://apps.who.int/iris/bitstream/handle/10665/272722/9789241514187-eng.pdf

15

HIGH-PERFORMANCE ATHLETES

Lisa Gowthorp

Introduction

High-performance or elite sport is the pinnacle for athletes who strive to compete on an international or professional sporting stage. This chapter will examine the various components required for developing successful high-performance female athletes, while focusing on some examples from the Australian high-performance sport system. In particular, the chapter will examine the following considerations: athlete service provision, such as sport science, sport medicine, coaching; talent development and talent transfer; increasing opportunities for female athlete in professional sport leagues; and current concerns in the development of high-performance female athletes.

High-performance athlete development

Developing high-performance athletes is a process that involves the use of sport science, sport medicine, quality coaching and talent identification, all undertaken in a sport specific high-performance daily training environment (Sotiriadou & Shilbury, 2013). In addition, high-performance athlete development requires significant funding that is often obtained as result of successful international athletic performances (e.g. Federal Government funding). Therefore, unearthing talented athletes is a priority for many National Sporting Organisations (NSOs) who are ultimately responsible for achieving international sporting success. NSOs spend valuable resources on developing identified talent and design their athlete pathway in order to attract, retain and nurture identified talent (Wuylleman, Reints, & De Knop, 2013).

An athlete pathway outlines how a participant in the sport can advance from one development stage to another. Sotiriadou and Shilbury (2013, p. 148) suggest that 'the wellbeing of a sport at the junior level ... is a precondition for elite professional growth and development'. On the other hand, various studies suggest success at the junior level in sport does not always predict future senior success (Franck & Weibull, 2012; Hollings, Mallett, & Hume, 2014). In order to strategically plan for the development and transition of junior athletes into successful senior athletes, an athlete pathway framework called FTEM was developed by the Australian Institute of Sport (AIS) to guide athlete development strategies in the Australian context. The core elements of the FTEM framework align with Long Term Athlete Development (LTAD) principles and models applied in North American and other global contexts; however, the FTEM framework tends to place a greater focus on high-performance athlete development.

FTEM stands for Foundations, Talent, Elite and Mastery and is applied in Australian sport as a guide for NSOs in developing and refining their athlete pathways. The FTEM framework is specifically designed to be applied at the individual, sport and system level (Gulbin, et al., 2013). The Foundations stage is predominantly focused on development, refinement and foundations of movement in the early years – childhood. The remaining three stages are focused on high-performance athlete development and talent identification. The structure of the athlete pathway may vary depending upon the sport. Importantly, the FTEM is designed to be applicable to both male and female athletes. Figure 15.1 indicates the FTEM Framework (Gulbin, et al., 2013).

The value of the FTEM framework is that it provides flexibility in regard to an athlete's transition through the framework. Many athlete development models, such as the LTAD model (Balyi & Hamilton, 2004), are chronologically prescriptive in nature

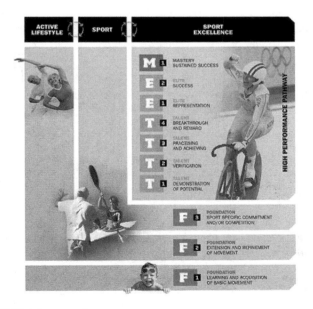

FIGURE 15.1 FTEM framework
Source: Gulbin, et al., 2013

and assume athlete development is a linear progression. The FTEM framework has no fixed age boundaries and is inclusive of non-linear movements with variable entry and exit points within the developmental pathway. Therefore, it is possible to 'leapfrog' several phases, which is important in high performance athlete development (Gulbin, et al., 2013). Athletes may also transfer from one sport into another, and potentially commence at a higher level in the new sport, due to their past experiences and athletic abilities. This is known as talent transfer. Naomi Flood is an example of an athlete who successfully transferred sports, moving from Ironwomen/surf lifesaving into sprint kayak in 2009, and successfully achieving elite status competing at the London 2012 Olympic Games in the K2–500m event. For athletes such as Naomi and others, the FTEM framework ensures previous training, fitness and skills are recognised in a new sport, where they continued training at the highest level.

Talent identification and development

NSOs establish sport development pathways to ensure individuals have access to opportunities designed to help them progress from sport participants to elite athletes. This is achieved through the use of talent identification, talent development and high-performance athlete development strategies. Programmes also put in place to strategically encourage athletes to transfer from one sport to another, with the view to assisting athletes to realise their athletic potential and to enhance performance outcomes in specific sports or countries. For example, UK Sport implemented two programmes including Girls4Gold (canoeing) and Target Tokyo 2020 (shotgun, rifle, pistol). Each of these programmes aimed to attract established athletes into the sports of canoeing and shooting, in an effort to achieve so-called 'soft medals' at the Olympic Games. In other words, the aim was to attract athletes into sport and events with fewer competitors (i.e. fewer nations competing). Talent transfer programmes often target female athletes and encourage them to transfer into male dominated sports, such as shooting events, combat sports and rugby 7s. Nations are increasingly targeting women's events in pursuit of international sporting success, which has given rise to increasing representation of women in Olympic Games; at the Rio 2016 Olympic Games, over 45% of athletes were women (Weatherford, Block, & Wagner, 2018). Talent search and transfer programmes encourage female athletes who have a sport background (i.e. are fit and athletic) to be tested for their potential to achieve in a new/different sport.

In Australia, the Western Australian Institute of Sport (WAIS) advertised a Talent Search Day with the aim of uncovering the state's next sporting champion in rowing and track cycling (WAIS, 2017). The advertisement was seeking participants aged 14–17 years, with no experience in rowing or track cycling to undertake specific testing in relation to these sports. Participants were tested using physical, psychological and skill measures, including fitness assessments (sprints, bike watt power, strength), anthropometric measures (height, limb length, flexibility etc), and psychological assessment (performance profiling and mental toughness). The choice of measures used to evaluate athletes' performance highlights the importance important role of sport science in the identification and development of female athletes.

Sport Science Sport Medicine (SSSM) and the Daily Training Environment (DTE)

Sport Science and Sport Medicine (SSSM) services are a crucial element in athlete development and include the following disciplines: physiotherapy, soft tissue therapy, strength and conditioning, recovery, nutrition and dietetics, physiology, biomechanics, performance analysis, skill acquisition and decision making, psychology and sport medicine (Fricker, 2013). Additionally, vocational guidance and support are often provided to athletes as NSOs encourage athletes to think about life after sport, as there are very few athletes that make a professional living from sport in Australia. SSSM services are provided in the Daily Training Environment (DTE), where athletes train and receive the support they require. The DTE provides similar support and services for both men and women athletes. Table 15.1 provides a brief

TABLE 15.1 SSSM definitions

Discipline	Definition
Physiotherapy	Physiotherapists' primary role is to advise, prescribe and monitor athletes' programmes for the rehabilitation of injury. They diagnose and manage athletes' musculoskeletal conditions in collaboration with sport medicine specialists. Physiotherapists also play a role in developing athlete programmes for the prevention of injury.
Soft tissue therapy	Soft tissue therapy includes massage, myotherapy, acupressure, myofascial and trigger point therapies, as well as acupuncture and dry needling. A soft tissue therapist can diagnose and manage a range of soft tissue complaints but works closely with the physiotherapist or sport doctor.
Strength & conditioning	Strength and Conditioning practitioners work on the principles of physiology through the understanding of musculoskeletal mechanics and development. It includes physical conditioning through individually designed programmes associated with elements of strength, speed, power, agility, balance, core strength and skeletal support. Exercises programmes are often conducted in a gymnasium, using a variety of equipment, machines and free weights.
Recovery	Recovery is about recuperation: the management of fatigue and the adaptations to training. Based on the science of physiology, recovery practices include hot and cold baths or showers, the use of high-pressured jets in spas, stretching and massage. In addition, further applications may include managing jet lag, sleep improvement and the management of training related muscle soreness.
Nutrition & Dietetics	Sports dieticians use science as a foundation for prescribing healthy eating plans to athletes, to maximise performance and recovery. In addition, the role investigates nutritional supplements and dietary strategies for enhanced performance, training and competition. Advice on nutrition for healthy weight management is also provided. Sports dieticians often travel with athletes and provide all meals and fluids intake throughout the trip.

(Continued)

TABLE 15.1 (cont.)

Discipline	Definition
Physiology	Physiology is focussed on the chemistry of exercise, to evaluate the effects of training on athletes' bodies. The effects are presented in terms of oxygen consumption (VO2Max), lactic acid production, heart rates, body temperature and fluid balances to name a few. Estimates of muscle mass, body fat and measures of height and limb length all contribute to an understanding of the impact of exercise and the accumulated effects of training. The results of the analysis inform the coach on how an athletes training programme may be structured.
Biomechanics	Biomechanics is the physics of human movement, measuring forces involved with jumping, landing, pushing etc. Cameras are used to understand path of motion of particular segments of the body during sport performance. Sensors detect and measure velocity and acceleration of athletes' movements. The biomechanist uses this information to inform coaches and athletes of minute details that may improve an athlete's performance.
Performance analysis	Performance analysis provides video analysis of performance for real-time analysis by the coach and or athlete. Various software packages record motion and images, and then allow for segments of information to be collected. This may include player analysis, competition analysis and performance parameters in terms of skill, accuracy, decision-making and tracking changes over time.
Skill Acquisition	Skill Acquisition is used to assess how athletes combine their sensory awareness and motor skills to perform in their sport. Much of the practice is performance using interactive visual stimulation and determines how athletes develop particular skills, how they are retained, refined and executed under pressure during competition. Athletes can only effectively execute skills if good decisions are made at the appropriate times, for instance, in basketball, knowing when and where to pass the ball. These decision-making skills are simulated, and athletes practice in a virtual game.
Psychology	Psychology in sport is fundamental to successful performance. Psychology is concerned with performance enhancement and focuses on mental imagery, mental routines, settling anxiety in competition, eliminating distractions, controlling emotions and minimising fatigue. A second area within psychology is associated with the clinical concerns such as issues with injury, disordered eating, confidence, stress and anxiety, social issues etc. There is the need for a more holistic approach to the care of an athlete's mental wellbeing, and psychologists work closely with the coach and the athlete to develop trust and confidence in these relationships.
Sport and Exercise Medicine	Sport and exercise medical practitioners receive professional training in general medicine, followed by specialist training in sport clinical centres of excellence, focusing on athlete injuries, surgeries etc. It is also important that the doctor understands the implications of doping and is aware of banned substances.

Source: Adapted from Fricker, 2013

definition of the SSSM services. While there are typically no specific variations in service provision for women and men, recent studies have highlighted the physiological and psychological differences that exist between male and female athletes (Forsyth & Roberts, 2018; Hanold, 2018; Schultz, 2018) that may impact the future delivery of these services in the context of the DTE of athletes.

Applied research in high-performance sport is critical and therefore the relationship between service providers, coaches and high-performance managers is crucial (Fricker, 2013). As a high-performance sport manager, coordinating service delivery and ensuring all services are strategically aligned and delivered with efficiency is crucial to the success of the programme and individual high-performance athletes (Reid, Stewart, & Thorne, 2004). For example, the programme manager of the AIS gymnastics programme would coordinate weekly service team meetings involving the head coach, doctor, physiotherapist, strength and conditioning coach, psychologist, nutritionist, and athlete career and education advisor (ACE). A typical week for a female high-performance gymnast involves training up to six to seven hours per day. This includes all apparatus (beam, bars, floor, vault), flexibility, strength, trampoline work and ballet. A typical week would also include one to two strength and conditioning sessions in the gym, one to two massages, one to three physiotherapy sessions, one recovery session, one nutrition session (skinfolds) and one study session. The complexity of the programme highlights the need for the SSSM service team to meet regularly to discuss each athlete in the programme, identifying key performance issues regarding the athlete's body or mental state (e.g. weight, a strength, or injury). The service team then works together to ensure key concerns are addressed, while ensuring the health and safety of the athlete.

Sport psychology

Principles of sport psychology can assist athletes to prepare their minds for the execution of elite performances. The mindset that enables the female athlete to perform under pressure is not obtained in the moments prior to a race, but requires work over time to develop the cognitive, emotional and behavioural skills that are relevant to performing successfully. Research on peak performance has identified that female athletes are in their peak psychological state when little or no conscious thought is required to efficiently execute a skill (Anderson, Hanrahan, & Mallett, 2014).

The peak performance mindset is misunderstood across many elite sports, and few teams comprehensively invest in resources to build and strengthen the psychological ability of athletes and teams. A gender bias, alongside a lack of understanding of psychology, embedded in many sport organisations generates incorrect assumptions about both the experience of psychological factors and the impact of mindset on performance and athlete development. False beliefs are widely prevalent that women may respond differently to men under the pressure of a competitive environment, or that there is one specific psychological state necessary for every athlete to achieve. However, when it comes to attaining automaticity, it is critical that an athlete discovers the optimal mindset that is relevant to the individual and the requirements of their sport (Anderson, Hanrahan, & Mallett, 2014).

Specific concerns regarding female high-performance athlete development

Historically, sport has been a male-dominated and male-controlled domain (Brown & Stone, 2016; Forsyth & Roberts, 2018), and as a result training programmes, dietary guidelines, psychological interventions, injury prevention and rehabilitation programmes are largely based on research that has been conducted on male athletes. Despite the growth of female athletes' representation in high-performance sport, research on how a 'woman's body responds to exercise still falls short of that carried out on men' (Forsyth & Roberts, 2018, p. 1). Therefore, there are specific considerations that the SSSM team and coaches must acknowledge and support when working with female athletes.

Current scientific research focusing on the female athlete has identified specific concerns particularly in relation to aspects of female anatomy and physiology (Donaldson, 2003; Rumball & Lebrun, 2004). A common medical condition experienced by female athletes is the Female Athlete Triad (FATr), which is 'a condition with the potential of long-term adverse effects on health and sports performance in female athletes' (Mukherjee, et al., 2016, p. 545). FATr refers to an interrelationship between energy availability, menstrual function and bone mineral density. In other words, there is a relationship between high-intensity training, food consumed (or lack of) and the impact of menstruating (or lack of), with a reduction in the bone density of female athletes as a result. The risk of developing FATr is increased as female athletes train to achieve elite sport success while also working to maintain a lean physique (i.e eating fewer calories than required to meet training demands). Young female athletes participating in competitive sports that have an aesthetic component (e.g. artistic gymnastics) and require leanness are at a higher risk in developing this condition (Reinking & Alexander, 2005). The diagnosis of FATr includes three criteria:

1. Disordered eating which includes a wide range of behaviours used to lose weight.
2. Amenorrhea is defined as an absence of a menstrual cycle for more than three cycles in a row.
3. Osteoporosis is where a bone mineral density score is less than 2.5 standard deviations below the mean for the age.

(Waldrop, 2005)

Athletes with FATr will generally show early warning signs such as fatigue, depressed mood, preoccupation with food, insomnia, irritability and perhaps a higher rate of stress fractures (Waldrop, 2005). Screening should be a component of all pre-participation physicals, where questions around menstrual history, dietary behaviours, exercise habits and injury can be asked. If athletes are not screened, the role of the coach in detecting early warning signs of FATr is important. However, a study conducted by Mukherjee, et al. (2016) found that only 42% of male coaches and 72% of female coaches were comfortable in discussing menstrual history with their female athletes. Furthermore, 38% of coaches believed menstrual irregularity is a natural outcome of elite sport, and – despite 70% of coaches being comfortable in talking about diet-related matters to their female athletes – only 28% of respondents were aware of their athletes' eating habits (Mukherjee, et al., 2016). These findings suggest it is imperative for high-performance managers to educate coaches on the implications of poor dietary habits, prolonged energy deficiency and irregular menstrual cycles in female athletes. Establishing a dedicated SSSM team around female athletes should ensure any signs of FATr are identified; however, the role of the coach is vital in reporting and communicating these signs to the SSSM team.

Another concern regarding female athletes is that they are more susceptible to experiencing concussion and anterior cruciate ligament (ACL) injuries than men, due to physiological factors, such as body structure, hormones and even neck strength in terms of concussion (Frank, et al., 2017). Statistics show that women will incur 'two to six times the number of non-impact ACL injuries compared to men when matched for age, sport, and level of competition' (Harber, 2015, p. 2). Researchers highlight that the unique changes to reproductive hormones in female athletes can impact ligament/tendon laxity which adds to the risk of musculoskeletal injury (Smith & Smith, 2002; Wolf, et al., 2015). Males and females are inherently different in a biological sense (Forsyth & Roberts, 2018). As the number of female athletes involved in elite level competition continues to increase, the need emerges for further research to be conducted into specific training requirements and injury preventing strategies for them. Existing research examining female athletes has proven valuable. For example, Mandelbaum, et al. (2005) determined that the implementation of a neuromuscular training intervention for women decreased anterior ligament injury rates by 88% in female soccer players, highlighting that specific forms of training are required to support female athletes' development and injury prevention.

Australian Rules football is the most popular traditional male football code in the Australian context. In 2017, the governing body for the sport, Australian Football League (AFL), introduced a women's competition, known as AFLW, with eight teams competing in its inaugural season. Tracking of injuries over the first two seasons has highlighted concussion and ruptured ACLs as key injury concerns for female players. There were 14 concussion recorded in the 2017 season, and 16 concussions in the 2018 season, over a seven-round season (total of 28 matches, plus finals). To compare rates of concussion and ACL injury between the men's and women's competitions, the data is converted to a measure of incident rates per 1,000 player hours. Torn ACL injuries in the AFLW athletes was 6.47 per 1,000 player hours, compared with 0.7 ACL injuries per 1,000 player hours for male athletes in the AFL. In relation to concussion, AFLW athletes experienced 3.2 concussions per 1,000 player hours, compared with 1.5 concussions per 1,000 player hours for male athletes in the AFL (AFL, 2018).

Importantly, it was identified that female athletes in the AFLW were new to the high-performance sport environment, with many in their first season of elite competition. Few ALFW athletes had previously engaged in specific fitness training or 'prehabilitation' programmes in the past (AFL, 2018), arguably putting them at higher risk of sustaining injuries. The lack of ALFW athletes' prehabilitation or conditioning highlights inequities in female athlete development pathways as many were inexperienced at the elite level due to inadequate opportunities, meaning they had not benefitted from the years of conditioning that most male athletes have had prior to competing at a professional level. For example, in the men's competition, athletes would have commenced in an athlete pathway at a young age and developed skills, strength, power and fitness over many years to cope with the demands of the game. The prehabilitation or conditioning is what prepares the body for demanding physical requirements of elite sport and, unfortunately for the AFLW, athletes were added to teams with minimal experience in elite competitions and with a lack of experience in high intensity training. Added to that, the 'semi-professional' nature of the AFLW, meant many players continued to work full time while training to compete at the elite level, which likely impacted the ability to commit to pre-season prehabilitation programmes. The above complexities highlight some of the key challenges facing the advancement of female athletes in high performance sport contexts.

Coaching high performance athletes

The success of any high-performance programme can be largely attributed to the coach and ultimately the coach-athlete relationship (Jowett, 2003). The coach and athlete have to develop a respectful and committed partnership, agree on the coaching philosophy and both have a similar work ethic (Collins, Trower, & Cruikshank, 2013). The aim of the coach is to produce athletes who perform 'intrinsically and unconsciously at the gold medal performance level' (Collins, et al., 2013, p. 212) and to develop athletes who can sustain gold medal performances over time (e.g. two or more Olympic cycles). Therefore, sport performance success relies on the physical and mental development of athletes, a role primarily undertaken by the athlete's coach.

As the number of female athletes in high-performance sport increases, researchers have examined the various differences between coaching female and male athletes. Steidinger (2014), a sport psychologist, believes emotional connections, empathy, positive peer group collaboration and camaraderie are all essential components to enhance female athlete development. A survey of elite female soccer players highlighted that females want to ask questions and understand why something should be done (Fasting & Pfister, 2000). Furthermore, the research identified that if a coach yells at female athletes, most will not listen to what they have to say. The female athlete's motivation revolves around them buying-in to decisions and developing good communication with their coaches (Fasting & Pfister, 2000). One coaching style, known as an athlete-centred approach, sees the coach 'support player autonomy by implementing various strategies intended to enhance each player's decision making ability' (de Souza & Oslin, 2013, p. 24). The benefits of the athlete-centred approach include increased player engagement, increased communication, increased competence and increased motivation. Further research suggests different coaching styles are evident between high-performances coaches: women are more rational and personal in their communication styles, whereas men tend to be more assertive and direct (Stewart & Owens, 2011). However, demonstrating empathy in a high-performance sport environment can be difficult for some coaches, particularly male coaches. Steidinger (2014) suggested that when coaching female athletes, talking and communicating is very important as females are more social and verbal than male athletes.

Future considerations

It is an exciting time for female high-performance athletes, with growth in professional women's sport leagues and increasing opportunities in Olympic event disciplines for women (e.g. rugby 7s, boxing). Research surrounding the development of high-performance female athletes is still emerging, especially in relation to contact and combat sports. We have yet to see the impact of these sports on women's bodies and minds. Sports Medicine Australia (SMA) identified a gap in this knowledge and delivered a symposium entitled *Keeping Female Athletes Fit to Play and Ready for the Podium* (May, 2019). The symposium was designed for those working with female athletes and focus on the unique challenges and demands faced by them. At the symposium, researchers presented information on training workloads, performance, injuries and illness to help advance knowledge and understanding of key issues for high-performance female athletes and on athlete development for women and girls. The results of such symposium should stimulate action to create safe pathways for professional female athletes, with SSSM support staff better understanding the physical and psychological requirements for female high-performance athlete development. To conclude, ongoing research into the female athlete, and more specifically female high-performance athlete development, will further enhance the ever-growing opportunities available for women and girls in high performance sport and aim to provide role models for the next generation of emerging talent.

CASE STUDY

Talent identification and development in women's high-performance sport: A practitioner's perspective

Jason Gulbin PhD, Director – International Sport Advisory Services

While one should always avoid generalisations and absolutes, there can be tendencies in women's high-performance sport where the playbook reads slightly differently compared with that of the men. When confronted with a seemingly endless list of diverse, yet valid, ideas and approaches in high-performance sport, a really sobering question to focus one's prioritisation skills is 'where would you spend your last dollar?' Having limited resources in the area of talent identification, and the need to generate a result, I would – without hesitation – spend my last dollar on a women's programme rather than a men's programme. International talent identification (TID) programmes – especially those implementing mature age, talent transfer approaches – have achieved their best results with their women, rather than their men. The reality is that the depth of women's competition does not run as deep as the men's, providing a greater probability of success against future international competitors. Of course, men's TID programmes have been successful, but in comparison, the magnitude of success in women's TID programmes is compelling.

Irrespective of gender, it is advantageous to ensure that coaches have a high degree of emotional intelligence (EI). However, my observations would reinforce that the more successful coaches of women's teams or programmes have a tendency to have a high degree of EI, and are, specifically, excellent communicators – both talking and listening. Those coaches that seem to have the happy knack of getting consistently great performances from their women athletes are renowned for their ability to forge strong working relationships with their athletes. This can manifest in a number of ways; however, successful coaches of women athletes have what might be colloquially described as the 'gift of the gab' or an observable communication style and patience that can sometimes be lacking in the style of those coaching men. Sharp and direct feedback can be unsettling for athletes of both genders, yet women athletes appear to be less accepting of this communication style, in comparison with men. Again, these are insights and observations that do not necessarily hold up scientifically, but the message here is to reinforce the importance of selecting coaches appropriately for the needs of the target athlete group.

Right now, women's professional sport in Australia is experiencing unprecedented growth, providing excellent opportunities for both athletes and coaches. Since 2017, women's sport has expanded considerably in netball, soccer, rugby league and especially cricket (Big Bash League – WBBL) and Australia Rules football (AFLW). The most impactful aspect of these recent developments will be the future legacies of these additional opportunities for women and the sports system. Firstly, for many of these aforementioned sports, there is now a viable, high-performance pathway in place, which in previous years prematurely truncated players' involvement in sports such as AFL where the competition opportunities for women and girls ended at junior football. This will likely have the flow-on effect of more parents being willing to sign up their daughters in a game that can provide a lifelong participatory pathway, rather than looking for brand new sport opportunities in the sensitive adolescent periods. Furthermore, the growth in professional teams has led to new career coaching opportunities. This expansion in full-time coaching substantially enhances the coaching pathway, by providing increased employment options and the opportunity to continue with coaching as a legitimate vocation. The corollary of strengthened coaching professionalism in women's sport will most likely lead to enhanced coaching skills throughout all levels of the athlete pathway, as NSO alignment, peer-mentoring and greater numbers of coaching communicators positively shape future junior and senior women's sport experiences.

References

Anderson, R., Hanrahan, S. J., & Mallett, C. J. (2014). Investigating the optimal psychological state for peak performance in Australian elite athletes. *Journal of Applied Sport Psychology*, 26(3), 318–333.

Arnold, F. D., & Anderson, R. (2015). Leadership and management in elite sport: Factors perceived to influence performance. *International Journal of Sports Science & Coaching*, 10(2+3), 285–304.

Australian Football League (AFL). (2018). *AFLW Concussion and ACL Injuries*. Retrieved, 12.11.18, from www.afl.com.au/news/2018-09-26/aflw-concussion-acl-injuries-highlighted

Australian Football League (AFL). (2019). *Women's AFL Teams*. Retrieved, 10.01.19, from https://womens.afl/teams

Balyi, I., & Hamilton, A. (2004). *Long-term Athlete Development: Trainability in Childhood and Adolescence*. Victoria, BC: National Coaching Institute British Columbia & Advanced Training Performance.

Brown, C. S., & Stone, E. A. (2016). Gender stereotypes and discrimination: How sexism impacts development. *Advances in Child Development and Behaviour*, 22(1), 105–133.

Collins, D., Trower, J., & Cruikshank, A. (2013). Coaching high performance athletes and the high performance team. In P. Sotiriadou & V. De Bosscher (eds), *Managing High Performance Sport* (pp. 205–220). Oxon: Routledge.

Crawford, D. (2009). *The Future of Sport in Australia*. Barton: Commonwealth of Australia.

De Souza, A., & Oslin, J. (2013) A player-centred approach to coaching. *Journal of Physical Education, Recreation and Dance*, 79(6), 24–30.

Donaldson, M. L., (2003). The female athlete triad: A growing health concern. *Orthopaedic Nursing*, 22(5), 322–324.

Fasting, K., & Pfister, G. (2000). Female and male coaches in the eyes of female elite soccer players. *European Physical Education Review*, 6(1), 91–110.

Forsyth, J., & Roberts, C. M. (2018) *The Exercising Female – Science and its Application*. Oxon: Routledge.

Franck, A., & Weibull, F. (2012). Assessment of the transition from junior-to-senior sports in Swedish athletes AU – Stambulova, Natalia. *International Journal of Sport and Exercise Psychology*, 10(2), 79–95. doi:10.1080/1612197X.2012.645136

Frank, R., Romeo, A., Bush-Joseph, C., & Bach, B. (2017). Injuries to the female athlete in 2017: Part I: General considerations, concussions, stress fractures and the Female Athlete Triad. *Journal of Orthopaedics for Physician Assistants*, 5(10), e4.

Fricker, P. (2013). Support services in athletic development. In P. Sotiriadou & V. De Bosscher (eds), *Managing High Performance Sport* (pp. 183–204). Oxon: Routledge.

Gulbin, J. P., Croser, M. J., Morley, E. J., & Weissensteiner, J. R. (2013). An integrated framework for the optimisation of sport and athlete development: A practitioner approach. *Journal of Sports Sciences,* 31(12), 1319–1331. doi:10.1080/02640414.2013.781661

Hanold, M. (2018). *Contemporary World Issues: Women in Sports*. California: ABC-CLIO, LLC.

Harber, V. (2015). Coaching female athletes: Developing your performance environment. *Canadian Journal for Women in Coaching*, 15(2), 1–6.

Hollings, S. C., Mallett, C. J., & Hume, P. A. (2014). The transition from elite junior track-and-field athlete to successful senior sthlete: Why some do, why others don't. *International Journal of Sports Science & Coaching*, 9(3), 457–471. doi:10.1260/1747–9541.9.3.457

ICCE Women in Coaching (2014). *Gender and Coaching Report Card: London 2012 Olympics*. Paper presented at the 6th World Conference on Women and Sport. June 12–15, Helsinki. Retrieved from www.icce.ws/_assets/files/news/IWG/Leanne_Norman-Gender_Coaching_Report_Card.pdf

Jowett, S. (2003). When the 'honeymoon' is over: A case study of a coach-athlete dyad in crisis. *The Sport Psychologist*, 17(4), 444–460. doi:10.1123/tsp.17.4.444

MacNamara, Á., Button, A., & Collins, D. (2010). The role of psychological characteristics in facilitating the pathway to elite performance, part 1: Identifying mental skills and behaviors. *The Sport Psychologist*, 24(1), 52–73. doi:10.1123/tsp.24.1.52

Mandelbaum, B. R., Silvers, H. J., Watanabe, D. S., Knarr, J. F., Thomas, S. D., Griffin, L. Y., ... Garrett, W. (2005). Effectiveness of a neuromuscular and proprioceptive training program in preventing anterior cruciate ligament injuries in female athletes: 2-Year follow-up. *The American Journal of Sports Medicine*, 33(7), 1003–1010. doi:10.1177/0363546504272261

Mukherjee, S., Chand, V., Wong, X. X., Choong, P. P., Lau, V. S. M., Wang, S. C. L., ... Ng, K. W. (2016). Perceptions, awareness and knowledge of the Female Athlete Triad amongst coaches – Are we meeting the expectations for athlete safety? *International Journal of Sports Science & Coaching*, 11(4), 545–551. doi:10.1177/1747954116654781

Reid, C., Stewart, E., & Thorne, G. (2004). Multidisciplinary sport science teams in elite sport: Comprehensive servicing or conflict and confusion? *The Sport Psychologist*, 18(2), 204–217. doi:10.1123/tsp.18.2. 204

Reinking, M. F., & Alexander, L. E. (2005). Prevalence of disordered-eating behaviors in undergraduate female collegiate athletes and nonathletes. *Journal of Athletic Training*, 40(1), 47–51.

Rumball, J. S., & Lebrun, C. M. (2004). Preparticipation physical examination, selected issues for the female athlete. *Clinical Journal of Sports Medicine*, 14(3), 199–213.

Schultz, J. (2018). *Women's Sports – What Everyone Needs to Know*. Oxford University Press: Oxford.

Smith, F. W., & Smith, P. A. (2002). Musculoskeletal differences between males and females. *Sports Medicine and Arthroscopy Review*, 10(1), 98–100.

Sotiriadou, P., & Shilbury, D. (2013). Sport development in high performance sport. In P. Sotiriadou & V. De Bosscher (eds), *Managing High Performance Sport* (pp. 139–158). Oxon: Routledge.

Steidinger, J. (2014). *Sisterhood in Sports: How Female Athletes Collaborate and Compete*. Lanham, MD: Rowman & Littlefield.

Stewart, C., & Owens, L. (2011). Behavioural characteristics of 'favourite' coaches: Implications for coach education. *Physical Educator*, 68(2), 90–97.

Waldrop, J., (2005). Early identification and interventions for female athlete triad. *Journal of Pediatric Health Care*. July/August.

Weatherford, G., Block, B., & Wagner, F. (2018). The complexity of sport: Universal challenges and their impact on women in sport. *Women in Sport and Physical Activity Journal*, 26(2), 89–98.

Western Australian Institute of Sport (WAIS) (2017). WAIS talent search looking for next WA sporting heroes. Western Australian Institute of Sport. Retrieved, 22.10.18, from http://wais.org.au/other/news_detail.php?id=9598

Wolf, J. M., Cannada, L., Heest, A. E., O'Connor, M. I., & Ladd, A. L. (2015). Male and female differences in musculoskeletal disease. *Journal of the American Academy of Orthopaedic Surgeons*, 23(6), 339–347.

Wuylleman, P., Reints, A., & De Knop, P. (2013). A development and holistic perspective on athletic career development. In P. Sotiriadou & V. De Bosscher (eds), *Managing High Performance Sport* (pp. 159–182). Oxon: Routledge.

16

COACHES AND OFFICIALS

Donna de Haan and Stacy Warner

Introduction

Despite the notable strides that have been made in terms of participation in sport, women continue to be underrepresented in sport leadership roles such as coaching and officiating. The 2014 United Nations (UN) International Working Group on Women's Sport (IWG) noted that: 'Women are significantly under-represented in management, administration, coaching and officiating, particularly at the higher levels' (IWG, 2014 p. 6). This statement, part of the Helsinki Declaration, was made in the context of how sport can support the UN Millennium Development Goals.

Across today's sporting landscape, women's sport experiences typically occur in male-dominated contexts, which favour men and masculinity (Norman, 2016). Recent data indicates the men to women ratio in high-performance coaching over the last four consecutive Olympic cycles has been approximately 10:1. Among US high school sporting officials, only 11% are women, and even a greater disparity exists with officiating sports traditionally played by men (Nordstrom, Warner, & Barnes, 2016).

This data highlights a systemic absence of women in coaching and officiating leadership roles across sport. In this chapter we will discuss the impact this has on developing sport for women and girls. Specifically, this chapter aims to:

- Provide an understanding of the roles and responsibilities of coaches and officials in women and girls sport delivery
- Explore career development pathways for improving opportunities for women in coaching and officiating
- Present a critical reflection of the differences and similarities between athlete development and coach/official development (systems and structures) for women and girls.

We begin by discussing the gendered nature of coaching before turning our attention to women's experiences in sport officiating. We draw on relevant literature throughout the chapter and identify issues and opportunities for further research. We conclude by providing practical actions and recommendations to help facilitate coaching and officiating development for women and girls.

The gendered nature of coaching

Regardless of the level of participation or performance, coaches play an influential role in an individual's sport experience. Beyond developing technical skills, coaches also play the role of mentors (Banks, 2006), managers and leaders (Gilbert & Trudel, 2004) and moral educators (Bergmann Drewe, 2000). Indeed, Becker (2009) argued that it is the coach's responsibility to tactically, physically, technically and psychologically train athletes and to consider their social wellbeing. Thus, it is a varied, demanding and powerful role that requires coaches to understand their athletes.

Considering the influential nature of their role, combined with their position of power, Norman (2016) suggests that coaches are important social change agents with the opportunity to implement visions and values of equity, equality and inclusion. Within sport for development (SFD), Philips and Schulenkorf (2016) also identify coaches as change agents who may use sport to establish or facilitate engagement between individuals and communities that are socially, culturally or ethically divided.

However, coaches often draw on their personal athletic experience as an important source of knowledge (Blackett, Evans, & Piggott, 2018). Thus, coaches may be reproducing the gender and social power discourse they have experienced. Coaches may transmit their notions about gender and try to discipline their athletes into those ideas (Claringbould, Knoppers, & Jacobs, 2015). This knowledge becomes generative, rather than transformative, by athletes who later coach. For coaches to act as social change agents therefore requires the disruption of dominant gendered discourses within coaching.

Coach education

Anderson (2007) explains that coaches play a significant role in reproducing sport social exclusions, which results from how they are educated and developed. Some emerging research explores the gendering of coaching education (e.g. Norman, 2016). This work highlights that coach education materials emphasise differences between men and women athletes, often positioning men athletes as 'ideal' and women athletes as 'other'. As LaVoi, Becker and Maxwell (2007) explain, socially constructed differences have established men as the universal ideological norm and women as 'other'. This has been one of the most powerful techniques employed to maintain male hegemony in sport.

In general, coaching education tends to emphasise physical differences between men and women, predominantly because it is based on a biomedical framework that views gender as a physical binary (Alsarve, 2018; LaVoi, et al., 2007). De Haan and Knoppers (2019) discussed their observations in relation to a rowing coaching handbook chapter (O'Brien, n.d.). In line with the biomedical framework, content in the chapter focused on physical differentiation between the sexes such as anatomical differences, menstrual 'problems', osteoporosis, muscular strength and endurance. Identified issues also extended beyond physical issues and considered 'societal problems' specifically relating to family commitments, and 'emotional problems'. In their analysis, de Haan and Knoppers (2019) noted that no comparative chapters outlining 'men's issues' were observed, implying that men athletes do not experience societal or emotional problems, thereby reinforcing men as dominant and women as 'other'.

In sport for development (SFD) in general, a similar binary gender divide reinforces traditional masculinities and marginalises girls and women (Forde & Frisby, 2015). Research on SFD gender issues and coaching is lacking, but recently, researchers have begun examining women coaches' experiences. In low-income countries (LIC) (i.e. countries in Africa, Asia, Latin America), collectively known as the Global South, women coaches were expected to adapt to masculine sport culture while retaining a traditional 'feminine' approach (Meier, 2015). An SFD study in the Caribbean found that a government coach training programme and sport governing body encouraged women coaches to change their clothing style and avoid 'manly' dressing (Schmidt Zipp, 2017). The concern was that these women coaches would be perceived as lesbians and be rejected in their communities. Research found that coaching education leaders directed coaches and trainees to conform to traditional gender norms (Schmidt Zipp, 2017).

As Philips and Schulenkorf (2016) discussed, coaching is diverse and multifaceted. Coaches may be full- or part-time, work in a specific sport or across multiple sports, and work with beginners or elite athletes. Thus, coach education is diverse. Norman (2016) investigated coaches' ideas about gender after their completion of a formal gender equity course. She found that although these coaches understood the influence of structural inequities, they continued to hold stereotypical hierarchical views of gender. LaVoi, et al. (2007) conducted a content analysis of best-selling books on coaching girls, and concluded that these texts were written from a perspective of inflated gender differences, and represented a simplified, stereotyped account of coaching girls.

Coach-athlete relationship

There is emerging evidence showing how different athletes respond to or receive coaching, and research that suggests gender can create power imbalances between (men) coaches and their (women) athletes, which in turn may impact on the coaching quality and style. To not consider gender within the coach-athlete relationship as involving more than just biological sex, to ignore the potential power imbalances between coach and athlete according to gender, or to ignore what it means to be a man or woman, removes the social actors within the relationship from the social context, thereby excluding the 'bigger picture' in which these individuals compete or coach (de Haan & Norman, 2018).

Norman and French (2013) found that gendered ideologies regarding women athletes' abilities and the views men coaches' subsequently held, negatively impacted the coach-athlete relationship. Women athletes want their relationship with their coach to be more power-equal, in which coaches communicate positively and understand who the athlete is – beyond the training or competition arena. This is salient to how they train and perform (Norman & French, 2013). Longshore and Sachs (2015) contend that women athletes will often request the rationale behind coaching decisions and will often want to be more involved with the decision-making process than men athletes. Indeed, de Haan and Norman (2018) noted that women athletes believed their men coaches often felt threatened by their questions, a situation which could change the power dynamics within the relationship. A breakdown in communication has been identified as a contributing coach-athlete relationship failure for women (Kristiansen, et al., 2012).

In the SFD context, coaches who can act as mentors are vital for fostering positive development outcomes. Meier (2015) identified SFD coaches as 'in between' mentors. Unlike elite athletes who might inspire young SFD participants via media outlets, coaches who also act as mentors have regular interaction with their athlete mentees. This unique positioning can help them build close relationships with mentees while also demonstrating attainable skills and behaviours (Meier, 2015).

Developing women coaches

Despite research that has attempted to understand and explain why women coaches remain underrepresented – especially at elite levels – there are still no definite answers. The majority of advancements in women's access to sport over the last 40 years can be characterised as liberal feminism. Fundamentally, liberal feminism advocates women's greater sport involvement by opportunities to join existing institutions and structures (de Haan & Dumbell, 2019). For example, the passage of Title IX in 1972 offered women, among many other rights and protections, equal opportunity to participate in school-sponsored athletics (Yiamouyiannis & Osborne, 2012). Equality in sport has been focused on participation, with an anecdotal belief that with more women playing, there will be enough women willing and able for leadership roles (de Haan & Dumbell, 2019). However, a causational link between participation and representation does not exist. Since Title IX passed, US women's high school sport participation has increased by more than 900%, yet the number of women in head coaching positions has decreased by 50% (Acosta & Carpenter, 2010).

Critics argue that adding women to existing masculine structures does little to challenge the gendered culture of sport. In the last decade, there has been an emerging body of research focusing on pathways, systems and structures to support and develop women coaches. Norman (2008) highlighted various UK sporting governing bodies' failures to provide adequate coach development and education for women due to the gendered culture. The result of the lack of support and infrastructure prevented women progressing their coaching career. Norman (2008) described this as a 'bottleneck' effect, whereby as women advance, they were excluded from positions of power. Greenhill, Auld, Cuskelly and Hooper (2009) noted similar cultural barriers in Australian sport organisations. Specifically, they noted that organisational strategies, prevailing hegemonic masculinity and systematic barriers sustained male coaching dominance and marginalisation of women coaches.

Focussing specifically on coaches' working conditions, Allen and Shaw (2013) concluded that organisational structures and values that facilitated quality interpersonal relationships, offered flexible working conditions, promoted continuous professional development and offered clear development pathways, contributed to women coaches feeling supported and valued and having enthusiasm for working for the organisation. Unfortunately, however, coaching pathways are not designed to facilitate progression to the highest echelons, creating a narrow bottleneck whereby the higher women coaches climb, the more constricted the pathways and opportunities become.

The SFD community has been calling for more opportunities for women in coaching since the Brighton Declaration in 1994 (IWG, 2014). Yet, the scarcity of women coaches remains (Zipp & Nauright, 2018; Meier, 2015). Even when women coaches are included in SFD programmes, they often face enormous pressure to balance their 'deviant' gender roles as coaches with traditional heterosexual feminine norms (Meier, 2015). The presence of women coaches and coaches who promote positive gender attitudes can profoundly influence how participants engage with SFD programming.

Sport officiating

Similar to women coaches, women who attempt sport officiating also face many of these same pressures and career bottlenecks. Unlike coaches, though, there is a shortage of qualified referees, which could have a detrimental impact on the number and quality of sporting competitions. As a result, researchers have sought to identify the barriers to officiating and to address how to better recruit and retain officials (e.g. Ridinger, et al., 2017; Warner, Tingle, & Kellett, 2013). Furthermore, researchers have recognised that women may face additional barriers and understanding women's sport officiating experience is important (e.g. Nordstrom, Warner & Barnes, 2016; Schaeperkoetter, 2016; Tingle, Warner, & Sartore-Baldwin, 2014).

Much of the early work on sport officiating was focused on the psychological barriers and perceptions that keep individuals from entering and staying in the profession. Such psychological barriers were thought to keep individuals from positively viewing sport officiating as a way to extend one's athletic career. Specifically, the perceived stress and abuse from officiating has been assumed to deter individuals from seeking and continuing in a sport officiating career. While this is not surprising – given the amount of media attention that often follows a professional referee missing a call or the harsh remarks parents and fans direct at amateur youth sport referees – recent research has demonstrated these concerns only explain a small portion of why more individuals are not officiating.

Sport officials often reframe the fan abuse and do not consider it a factor that might lead them to consider leaving the role (Kellett & Shilbury, 2007). While abuse may inhibit some from initially entering into the sport officiating role, it has not been found to be a key factor in why officials choose to leave. Rather, researchers have suggested that umpires view it as serious leisure pursuit and recognise the stress and fan abuse as a part of the game (Phillips & Fairley, 2014). Consequently, researchers and sport managers have begun to place a greater emphasis on both the on-the-field and off-the-field factors that are impacting officials. Because many sport officials view themselves as athletes, it is common for current officials to discover officiating as an avenue to remain involved in sport (Phillips & Fairley, 2014; Warner, et al., 2013). This has resulted in not just the psychological factors being identified and emphasised, but also the sociological and organisational factors (Ridinger, et al., 2017; Warner, et al., 2013). Viewing sport officiating as a leisure pursuit (not as an occupation or career) is important and has increased knowledge on how to better retain and recruit referees.

Arguably the most significant factor that has emerged from this officiating as a leisure pursuit perspective has been the value and importance placed on the sense of community among officials. That is, scholars have concluded that the community that is often among officials is fundamental to both officials' recruitment and retention. Officiating provides an avenue for individuals to stay connected to sport and remain involved with a strong community of interest (Warner, 2016). A burgeoning line of research continues to demonstrate that sport is one of the few remaining avenues in today's society where individuals can find and belong to community, which is fundamental to one's health and well-being (Warner, 2016; 2018). Recognising this innate desire to be involved and a part of a community is vital to promoting sport officiating as a leisure pursuit or career path for those with an interest in sport. For example, the opportunity to stay a part of the sport and a love of the game have been found to be fundamental in the recruitment of new officials (Ridinger, et al., 2017; Warner, et al., 2013). Further, Kellett and Shilbury (2007) noted how the social worlds – often formed around reframing abuse – was central to an individual's decision to continue officiating. Rather than viewing fan abuse as a negative aspect of the job, sport officials accepted it as part of the job and emphasised more the socialising with other umpires as being key to their continuation.

Later work from Kellett and Warner (2011) more explicitly identified how these social worlds or officiating communities form. The researchers noted factors that both foster and inhibit a community from forming. Those factors included lack of administration consideration, inequity (specifically related to remuneration and resources), competition and common interest (specifically in the sport, interactions within football community, and/or within social spaces), they impacted this sense of community that was deemed essential for officials to continue in profession. Interestingly, both Kellett and Shilbury (2007) and Kellett and Warner's (2011) studies only included male umpires as research participants. When considering the lack of women sport officials, however, the importance placed on the social worlds and community likely explains why more women are not entering and staying in officiating. Although the research on sport officiating communities demonstrates why officials likely stay involved, it may also highlight why new officials – and women specifically – may be hesitant to join. Without an insider within the sport community willing to help someone new navigate the social worlds and understand the social protocols, it may be especially difficult for an individual to enter into and become a part of an existing sport officiating community. The majority of the research into the topic of sport officiating has continually emphasised the importance of a mentor encouraging someone to try refereeing and provides them access to the community. This is important to the recruitment of new officials and likely highly crucial to seeing more women officials enter into the officiating role.

Women referee experiences and workplace incivility

Although little research exists on women sport officials, the research that does exist is quite consistent. For example, in an autoethnographic study of a woman basketball official, the author concluded her 'femaleness' was a salient part of her officiating experiences (Schaeperkoetter, 2016). The author described instances where she was treated differently than her male counterparts and learned to deal with demeaning actions from players and coaches. She also highlighted the difficulty of trying to enter into the strong, already-bonded community of older, more experienced officials.

To give another example: a study of eight women basketball officials revealed these officials experienced a lack of mutual respect from male counterparts, encountered a perceived inequity of policies, a lack of role modelling and mentoring for and from women officials, and experienced more gendered abuse than did their male counterparts (Tingle, et al., 2014). This gendered experience especially held true in sport traditionally considered male dominated sports. In a study involving eight US football officials, researchers reported:

> all the participants noted that their officiating experiences were different than their male counterparts. These collective experiences were defined as gendered experiences … the participants and data highlighted that the challenges, resistance and stereotypes were more subtle but nonetheless impactful on their experience.
>
> (Nordstrom, et al., 2016, p. 267)

Subtle, less overt discrimination has been defined as workplace incivility, and sport researchers have highlighted that this workplace incivility is being perceived and experienced by women sport officials. Clearly, if more women are going to enter into officiating and be retained in the role, it is vital that they be encouraged to do so, that they have a mentor and a welcoming community, and that they enter into a more civil environment.

Sport development (SD), sport for development (SFD) and officials

Because officiating can be an extension of an athlete's career, research has helped to understand the officiating experience via an SD lens. Warner, et al.'s (2013) work used the SD framework (Green, 2005) to demonstrate referee recruitment, retention, and advancement. At the referee recruitment stage, staying part of the game, and the competition and challenge of refereeing were on-the-field attractors, while the remuneration and socialisation in the community were the off-the-field factors that attracted officials. Again, this last factor – socialisation in the community – likely explains why few women are involved in sport officiating.

An initial first step to remedy the lack of women sport officials would be to place more emphasis on the recruitment of referees. Given the promising and steady growth of women's sport participation, a greater emphasis needs to be placed on targeting these women athletes as future potential referees. Because sport officiating is a great way to extend one's athletic career and provides an avenue to fine-tune and master athletic skills, ideally more women athletes would be pursuing it. Considering sport officiating as a part of SD – i.e. a way to further progress and advance one's athletic career – should encourage more to enter the role.

Further, in terms of SD, youth-level referees and umpires are fundamental to sport systems and athlete development. At the youth level specifically, sport officiating can provide direct guidance and coaching that can help ensure an athlete understands and advances in the sport. For example, if a young basketball player dribbles, picks up the ball, then dribbles again, a referee will typically just deal with the infraction immediately. A high-level, well-trained basketball official, on the other hand, will recognise this as a teaching and coaching opportunity. Instead of simply dealing with the issue, they might blow the whistle, briefly stop the game to explain to the young player that when he or she stopped dribbling and picked up the ball they must pass or shoot. They would go on to explain that if they dribble again, it is a called a 'double dribble' and the other team will get the ball. It may seem simple and straightforward, but a well-trained basketball official can have a huge impact on SD systems and, as a result, also on young players' retention in the sport.

Sport officials also can have an important impact in SFD. Because the goal of SFD is to use sport as a tool to bring about positive change, sport officials can play a role in supporting such outcomes. To give an example, an SFD programme may have a goal of promoting peace or positive social behaviour among its participants. In an intense contest, tempers can flare, and play can become more aggressive. A well-trained sport official would recognise this and do his or her best make calls that would steer players towards less aggressive play to aid in diffusing the situation. A high-level sport official has the ability to stay calm and redirect negative behaviour. For SFD programmes that place an emphasis on gender equity and improving diversity, sporting officials who are from minority groups can have an immediate positive impact; having an underrepresented individual – i.e. a woman in sport – in a power and authoritarian role, such as that of a sport official, can send an important message to participants. Furthermore, minority or underrepresented sport officials can – and should – be important role models to have involved SFD programmes. If sport is for all, those in power should be reflective of all individuals, regardless of gender. Thus, the role that sport officials play in both SD and SFD should not be overlooked.

Summary

Sport has long been male dominated. Women athletes, coaches, officials and leaders have to navigate their careers within organisational structures that have been built by men for men. Coach education, practices and methods have primarily been developed by men coaches for men athletes. While women's sport access and participation are increasing, women remain underrepresented in leadership roles like coaching and officiating. For sport officials, we are only beginning to recognise that the global shortage of referees is likely due to the oversight of women and women's sport.

The current inequality in sport indicates there are improvement opportunities. Organisations can develop structures and values that can help improve the recruitment and retention of women coaches and officials. Coach educators can develop resources that better support the needs of individual athletes. Better marketing and an improved understanding of the potential barriers keeping women from entering and seeing officiating as a viable career path are fundamental. A better understanding of the importance placed on the social worlds and community in officiating is key as women are reporting that this lack of community is fundamental to their decision to leave the profession. While women may face additional barriers, sport managers must continue to recruit men and women officials and provide an environment that can better retain all officials. Everyone should look beyond the intended behaviours or outcomes of coaching and officiating and focus on critiquing the gendered context. Our sport systems depend on this, and SD and SFD programmes will benefit from a more diverse pool of qualified coaches and referees.

CASE STUDY

UEFA Women's EURO

Most advancements in women's sport over the last 40 years can be characterised as liberal feminism, but the 'just add women' approach does not challenge the male hegemonic structure. Women's football is an example.

In 2017, the UEFA Women's EURO attracted a record audience (over 13 million) and became the host nation's most watched sports event that year. Of the 16 participating nations, six were led by women, including tournament champions The Netherlands, and all 33 officials involved were women. Within the global context of women's football, numerous nations have won the Olympics, World Cup and Euros since 2000 and all but one of these winning teams were coached by women. Numerically this reads like a success story. However, the number of women coaches and officials in men's football is

> miniscule and despite successes in women's football, these women coaches and officials routinely report experiencing discrimination, marginalisation, and injustices. This limits not only their own career retention and progression, but the career trajectory of other women, and the game in general.

References

Acosta, R. V., & Carpenter, L. J. (2010). Women in intercollegiate sport: A longitudinal, national study – thirty-three year update – 1977–2010. Unpublished manuscript. Retrieved from www.acostacarpenter.org/

Allen, J. B., & Shaw, S. (2013). An interdisciplinary approach to examining the working conditions of women coaches. *International Journal of Sports Science & Coaching*, 8(1), 1–17.

Alsarve, D. (2018). Addressing gender equality: Enactments of gender and hegemony in the educational textbooks used in Swedish sports coaching and educational programmes. *Sport, Education and Society*, 23(9), 840–852.

Anderson, E. (2007). Coaching identity and social exclusion. In Denison, J. (ed.), *Coaching Knowledges: Understanding the Dynamics of Sport Performance* (pp. 24–50). London: A & C Black.

Banks, J. (2006). The role of the coach. In Goodman, N. (ed.), *Beginning Coaching*, 4th edn (pp. 1–26). Canberra: Australian Sports Commission.

Becker, A. (2009). It's not what they do, it's how they do it: Athlete experiences of great coaching. *International Journal of Sports Science & Coaching*, 4(1), 93–119.

Bergmann Drewe, S. (2000). Coaches, ethics and autonomy. *Sport, Education & Society*, 5(2), 147–162.

Blackett, A. D., Evans, A.B., & Piggott, D. (2018). 'They have to toe the line': a Foucauldian analysis of the socialisation of former elite athletes into academy coaching roles. *Sports Coaching Review*, 8(1), 83–102. doi:10.1080/21640629.2018.1436502

Claringbould, I., Knoppers, A., & Jacobs, F. (2015). Young athletes and their coaches: Disciplinary processes and habitus development. *Leisure Studies*, 34(3), 319–334.

De Haan, D., & Dumbell, L. (2019). From the battlefield to the board room: the place of gender in sex-integrated sport. In Lough, N. & Geurin, A. N. (eds), *Routledge Handbook of the Business of Women's Sport* (pp. 134–150). London: Routledge

De Haan, D., & Knoppers, A. (2019). Gendered discourses in coaching high-performance sport. *International Review for the Sociology of Sport*. Advanced online publication. doi:10.1177/1012690219829692

De Haan, D. & Norman, L. (2018). Mind the gap: The presence of capital and power in the female athlete – male coach relationship within elite rowing. *Sports Coaching Review*. Advanced online publication. doi:10.1080/21640629.2019.1567160

Forde, S. D., & Frisby, W. (2015). Just be empowered: How girls are represented in a sport for development and peace HIV/AIDS prevention manual. *Sport in Society*, 18(8), 882–894.

Green, B. C. (2005). Building sport programs to optimize athlete recruitment, retention, and transition: Toward a normative theory of sport development. *Journal of Sport Management*, 19(3), 233–253.

Greenhill, J., Auld, C., Cuskelly, G., & Hooper, S. (2009). The impact of organisational factors on career pathways for female coaches. *Sport Management Review* 12(4), 229–240.

Gilbert, W., & Trudel, P. (2004). Role of the coach: how model youth team sport coaches frame their roles. *The Sports Psychologist*, 18(1), 21–43.

IWG. (2014). *Legacy Document of IWG Conference on Women and Sport Helsinki/Finland, June 12–15, 2014*. Retrieved from www.fisu.net/medias/fichiers/lead_the_change_ be_the_ change.pdf
Kellett, P., & Shilbury, D. (2007). Umpire participation: Is abuse really the issue? *Sport Management Review*, 10(3), 209–229. https://doi.org/10.1016/S1441-3523(07) 70012-70018
Kellett, P., & Warner, S. (2011). Creating communities that lead to retention: The social worlds and communities of umpires. *European Sport Management Quarterly*, 11(5), 471–494. https://doi.org/10.1080/16184742.2011.624109
Kristiansen, E., Tomten, S. E., Hanstad, D. V., & Roberts, G. C. (2012). Coaching communication issues with elite female athletes: Two Norwegian case studies. *Scandinavian Journal of Medicine & Science in Sports*, 22(16), 156–167.
LaVoi, N. M., Becker, M., & Maxwell, H. D. (2007). 'Coaching girls': A content analysis of best-selling popular press coaching books. *Women in Sport and Physical Activity Journal*, 15(4), 7–20.
Longshore, K., & Sachs, M. (2015). Mindfulness training for coaches: A mixed-method exploratory study. *Journal of Clinical Sport Psychology*, 9(2), 116–137.
Meier, M. (2015). The value of female sporting role models. *Sport in Society*, 18(8), 968–982.
Nordstrom, H., Warner, S., & Barnes, J. C. (2016). Behind the stripes: Female football officials' experiences. *International Journal of Sport Management and Marketing*, (3/4/5/6), 259–279. https://doi.org/10.1504/IJSMM.2016.077934
Norman, L. (2008). The UK coaching system is failing women coaches. *International Journal of Sports Science & Coaching*, 3(4), 447–467.
Norman, L. (2016). The impact of an "equal opportunities" ideological framework on coaches' knowledge and practice. *International Review for the Sociology of Sport*, 51(8), 975–1004.
Norman, L., & French, J. (2013). Understanding how high performance women athletes experience the coach-athlete relationship. *International Journal of Coaching Science*, 7(1), 3–24.
O'Brien, M. (n.d.). Problems of high performance female athletes. In *FISA Coaching Education Manual: Level 4*. Retrieved, 20 October 2018, from www.worldrowing.com/mm// Document/General/General/12/18/65/3Chapter5_English.pdf
Phillips, P., & Fairley, S. (2014). Umpiring: A serious leisure choice. *Journal of Leisure Research*, 46(2), 184–202. https://doi.org/10.1080/00222216.2014.11950319
Philips, P., & Schulenkorf, N. (2016). Coaches, officials and change agents. In Sherry, E., Schulenkorf, N., & Philips, P. (eds), *Managing Sport Development: An International Approach* (pp. 107–118). Oxon: Routledge.
Ridinger, L., Kim, K. R., Warner, S., & Tingle, J. K. (2017). Development of the referee retention scale. *Journal of Sport Management*, 31(5), 514–527. doi:10.1123/jsm.2017-0065
Schaeperkoetter, C. C. (2016). Basketball officiating as a gendered arena: An autoethnography. *Sport Management Review*, 20(1), 128–141. doi:10.1016/j.smr.2016.05.001
Schmidt Zipp, S. (2017, July 3). *Changing the Game or Dropping the Ball?: Sport as a Human Capability Development for At Risk Youth in Barbados and St. Lucia*. Rotterdam: Erasmus University. Retrieved from http://hdl.handle.net/1765/100422
Tingle, J. K., Warner, S., & Sartore-Baldwin, M. L. (2014). The experience of former women officials and the impact on the sporting community. *Sex Roles*, 71(1–2), 7–20. https://doi.org/10.1007/s11199-014-0366-8
Warner, S. (2016). Sport and sense of community theory. In Cunningham, G. B., Fink, J., & Doherty, A. (eds), *Routledge Handbook of Theory in Sport Management* (pp. 189–198). New York, NY: Routledge.
Warner, S. (2018). Sport as medicine: How F3 is building healthier men and communities. *Sport Management Review*, 22(1), 38–52. doi:10.1016/j.smr.2018.06.006

Warner, S., Tingle, J. K., & Kellett, P. (2013). Officiating attrition: The experiences of former referees via a sport development lens. Retrieved from http://digitalcommons.trinity.edu/busadmin_faculty/3/

Yiamouyiannis, A., & Osborne, B. (2012). Addressing gender inequities in collegiate sport: Examining female leadership representation within NCAA sport governance. *SAGE Open*, 2(2), 1–13. https://doi.org/10.1177/2158244012449340

Zipp, S., & Nauright, J. (2018). Levelling the playing field: Human capability approach and lived realities for sport and gender in the West Indies. *Journal of Sport for Development*, 6(10), 38–50.

17
ATHLETE PROTECTION AND DUTY OF CARE

Popi Sotiriadou and Pamela Wicker

Introduction

The focus of this chapter is on female athlete protection and duty of care. The chapter aims to crystalize an understanding of female sexual harassment and bullying in sport, as well as eating disorders and trends in uses of performance-enhancing substances by elite female athletes. It also aims to raise awareness and report on current research and trends in relation to these four topics. The chapter stresses the importance of these issues in the sport development of women and girls as participants and athletes and outlines the ramifications of inactivity or lack of protection and duty of care to the individual athletes and their health or success in sport, the culture of sports they play and the sport organisations they represent, as well as broader perceptions about female athletes and the role of sport in society. The findings reported in this chapter are the result of a literature review on sexual harassment, bullying, eating disorders and performance-enhancing recreational drugs based on research sourced from key databases. The search was not limited to a specific timeframe. However, as noted in the findings, this stream of research only started in the 1990s in sport contexts.

Sport organisations and anyone within these organisations who has an official capacity to organise and manage sport programmes and events have a duty to make such activities as safe as possible for participants. This duty is referred to as the duty of care. Sport participation is an inherently 'risky business' and high-performance managers, coaches, referees, or sport development officers are required to carry out their duty of care. Research by Mountjoy, et al. (2016) also shows that from an organisational perspective, the impacts of lack of duty of care and athlete protection represent asset depreciation. The cost-benefit analysis of harassment and abuse versus prevention or awareness and transparency has yet to be demonstrated. However, preliminary studies have shown that the economic impact of such incidents to athletes and sport organisations – for example, loss of sponsorships, reputation, medals, talent and poor publicity – is also considerable.

Mountjoy, Rhind, Tiivas and Leglise (2015) designed a framework for younger elite athletes to assist sport organisations in the creation of a safe sporting environment to ensure that young athletes can flourish and reach their athletic potential through an enjoyable experience. In this framework, they identified threats at three levels: organisational (systematic doping, cultures that normalise abuse), relational (e.g. sexual harassment and bullying), and individual (e.g. eating disorder). Duty of care, then, must also consider all levels. For example, the alarming rates and frequency of sexual harassment, bullying and eating disorders are indicative of the failure of existing sport strategies, policies and systems in place to protect female athletes. The consequences of this inability to offer duty of care can be detrimental to women's and girls' development in sport, sports themselves and society. This chapter discusses all three levels of duty of care (per Mountjoy, et al., 2015) with a specific focus on women and girl athletes and examines how sport systems, policies, and strategies work to protect female athletes.

Literature review

To understand the social and regulatory challenges of athlete protection and duty of care for women and girl sport participants, we conducted a literature review on four key areas including sexual harassment, bullying, disordered eating and performance-enhancing and recreational drugs based on research sourced from key databases.

Sexual harassment

Sexual harassment can be defined as any 'unwanted behaviour on the basis of sex' (Brackenridge, 2000, p. 187). It includes several forms of behaviour, such as sexual violence, abuse, locker room sex talk, and demeaning treatment of women and girls (Brackenridge & Fasting, 2002). As these forms of behaviour differ in their severity, sexual harassment was conceptualised along a continuum from mild sexual harassment (e.g. sexual discrimination) to severe harassment (e.g. sexual abuse) (Brackenridge, 2000). Importantly, especially mild forms of harassment are subjectively perceived by athletes and such perceptions and norms may vary between countries and cultural contexts.

Numerous scholars have studied the prevalence of sexual harassment in several countries and sports contexts. Summarising the body of research, the share of women athletes reporting experiences of any form of sexual harassment ranges from approximately 5% to 50%, depending on the study and context. For example, in a Turkish study, 56% of women elite athletes reported experiences of sexual harassment (Gündüz, Sunay, & Koz, 2008). In Norway, 21% of women elite athletes reported unwanted physical contact and 16% were victims of unwanted repeated sexually suggestive glances, comments, jokes etc. (Fasting, Brackenridge,

& Sundgot-Borgen, 2000). In the Czech Republic, 14% of women elite athletes reported unwanted physical contact (Fasting & Knorre, 2005).

Since understanding risk factors is important for designing intervention strategies, previous research identified a number of factors at all levels (Brackenridge, 2000; Cense & Brackenridge, 2001). At the *organisational level*, some sports are particularly susceptible to sexual harassment because coaching requires physical contact. Hence, the amount of touching and physical handling required for instruction and coaching is considered a risk factor (Brackenridge, 2000). Further risk factors are the opportunity for trips away, the amount of driving required and the frequency of training camps and trips (Cense & Brackenridge, 2001). The role of the type of sport remains unclear, with some scholars showing women athletes in men's sports experienced more sexual harassment (Fasting, Brackenridge, & Sundgot-Borgen, 2004), while others found no difference between sports (Ohlert, Seidler, Rau, Rulofs, & Allroggen, 2018).

Scholars have argued that some beliefs about sport have facilitated the occurrence of sexual harassment. For example, sport is regarded as a domain where men have traditionally experienced levels of privilege over women. However, the empirical evidence is inconsistent: Some scholars reported a higher prevalence of sexual harassment in sport (Fasting, Brackenridge, & Sundgot-Borgen, 2003), some a lower prevalence (Fasting, Brackenridge, & Knorre, 2010), and some no differences between sport and other sectors (Volkwein, Schnell, Sherwood, & Livezey, 1997), suggesting that generalisations are difficult. Furthermore, sport organisations are considered to be apolitical (Brackenridge, 1994), hindering the response of organisations and interventions from public agencies, such as the police (Brackenridge & Fasting, 2002). The occurrence in private settings, such as locker rooms or training halls, further complicate appropriate actions (Brackenridge & Fasting, 2002).

At the *relational level*, the coach–athlete relationship is under scrutiny, specifically when male coaches coach female athletes. In this regard, differences in power between the coach and the athlete represent important factors (Stirling & Kerr, 2009), which can yield differences in perceptions in terms of what is acceptable and what is not. Existing research shows that the person with more power – the coach – tends to find some forms of behaviour acceptable, while the person with less power – the athlete – perceives such behaviours as uncomfortable, inappropriate, irritating or insulting (Brackenridge, 2000). Moreover, coaches are considered trustworthy persons and the closeness of an athlete–coach relationship is similar to that between children and parents (Brackenridge, 2000). Further risk factors at this level include physical strength of the coach, high reputation, trust of parents, chances to be alone with athlete and car use to transport athletes (Cense & Brackenridge, 2001). Athletes also fear the consequences of disclosure, such as censure from teammates, disbelief from sports administrators and lack of consideration for competitions by the coach (Brackenridge, 2000), which have been reported by athletes disclosing sexual harassment (Fasting, Brackenridge, & Walseth, 2002).

At the *individual level*, risk factors include the status in career – beginners are able to easily exit the sport or training group, while the exit option is more costly for sub-elite and elite athletes who have already invested a lot in their sport (Brackenridge &

Kirby, 1997). Moreover, the likelihood of being sexually harassed was found to increase with increasing performance level (Fasting, et al., 2010). Risks were found to be greater for younger women athletes and athletes with physical or learning disabilities and difficulty communicating (Brackenridge, 2000), low self-esteem, low levels of awareness, medical problems and dependence on and devotion to the coach (Cense & Brackenridge, 2001).

Collectively, the literature suggests that duty of care is necessary at all three levels by paying particular attention to sports requiring physical contact and to the athlete–coach relationship. Communication about what is (un)acceptable behaviour is necessary in an effort to create sporting environments preventing sexual harassment. In addition, sport organisations should provide both monitoring and reporting systems that facilitate disclosure without negative personal consequences for athletes. In many cases, such policies and systems are already in place and only need to be reinforced.

Bullying

The literature distinguishes different forms of bullying, such as physical bullying (e.g. hitting, kicking), emotional bullying (i.e actions causing mental harm), social bullying (e.g. isolation from social groups) and cyber bullying (i.e electronic device is used to exert emotional bullying) (Bachand, 2017). Given the rise of social media platforms, especially the latter form of bullying has increased in magnitude over the last years (Tofler, 2016). Differences between sexual harassment and bullying are blurred, because sexual assault is also be considered a form of bullying, hazing and mobbing (Diamond, Callahan, Chain, & Solomon, 2016). Bullying research is complicated by the fact that many forms of bullying are commonly accepted behaviours because of the competitive and aggressive nature and culture of many sports (Kerr, Jewett, MacPherson, & Stirling, 2016).

Existing bullying research has focused on collegiate athletes and schoolchildren (Diamond, et al., 2016) and to a lesser extent on elite athletes. At the *organisational level*, the role of the type of sport is not clear: While some scholars found higher rates of bullying in team sports and contact sports (Waldron & Kowalski, 2009), others detected higher rates in individual sports and cheerleading (Gershel, Katz-Sidlow, Small, & Zandieh, 2003). At the *relational level*, weaker connections with peers on teams increase the chances of being a victim of bullying (Evans, Adler, MacDonald, & Côté, 2016).

At the *individual level*, gender and race are risk factors, with female athletes and women and girls from racial minorities being more likely to be a victim of bullying (Kentel & McHugh, 2015; O'Neill, Calder, & Allen, 2014). Similar to sexual harassment, athletes with higher performance levels are more likely to be victims of bullying (Kerr, et al., 2016; Waldron & Kowalski, 2009). Other risk factors encompass seniority on the team, younger age, personality, commitment and work ethic (Kerr, et al., 2016).

The empirical evidence supports the individual character of bullying, meaning that duty of care can be carried out by creating an appreciative sporting environment and, if incidents occur, an effective reporting system that does not disadvantage victim athletes.

Disordered eating

The literature distinguishes several forms of disordered eating, such as bulimia nervosa and anorexia nervosa, which can also result from sexual harassment (Sundgot-Borgen, Fasting, Brackenridge, Torstveit, & Berglund, 2003) and bullying (Bratland-Sanda & Sundgot-Borgen, 2013; Farrow & Fox, 2011). Disordered eating is of concern, as it negatively affects performance and is harmful to athlete health (Thompson & Sherman, 2014).

Eating disorders can be prevalent in both women and men and in all sports (Thompson & Sherman, 2014). They are diagnosed with both objective and subjective indicators. A body-mass-index (BMI) of <17.9 and <17.5 kg/m^2 for girls and boys, respectively, is an example for an objective indicator. Examples for subjective indicators include the drive for thinness and body dissatisfaction subscales from the eating disorders inventory (Martinsen, Bratland-Sanda, Eriksson, & Sundgot-Borgen, 2009). Overall, the literature reports prevalence rates of between 6% and 45% for female athletes, while the rates are lower for male athletes (between 0% and 9%) (Bratland-Sanda & Sundgot-Borgen, 2013).

At the *organisational level*, some studies argue that the leanness requirements and type of sport do not matter (Homan, Crowley, & Sim, 2018; Sanford-Martens, et al., 2005), while other studies report that athletes from lean sports are at higher risk (Coelho, et al., 2014). At the *relational* level, issues with peers, peer pressure and negative comments about body shape or weight by coaches constitute risk factors (Arthur-Cameselle, Sossin, & Quatromoni, 2017; Bratland-Sanda & Sundgot-Borgen, 2013).

At the *individual level*, gender is one risk factor, with adolescent girl athletes being at higher risk (Coelho, et al., 2014). Specific risk factors for women and girls include low self-worth, comorbid psychological disorders, performance pressure, team weigh-ins and injuries (Arthur-Cameselle, et al., 2017). Further risk factors, independent of gender, encompass body dissatisfaction, perfectionism, media influence, traumatic experiences, frequent weight regulation, dieting, pressure to lose weight, overtraining, and impression and extrinsic motivation (Bratland-Sanda & Sundgot-Borgen, 2013; Coelho, et al., 2014).

Overall, the high prevalence rates of eating disorders in female athletes indicate the need for athlete protection by designing measures at all levels. Given the prominent role of psychological factors among individual risk factors, sport organisations should offer some form of psychological support to exert their duty of care towards female athletes. Since sport psychologists are already on board in many sports, their role needs to be further clarified.

Performance-enhancing and recreational drug use

Performance-enhancing and recreational drug use involves the use of different types of substances that assist in improving performance and appearance, with most of them included in the prohibited list by the World Anti-Doping Agency (WADA).

Such substances are categorised into anabolic agents, peptide hormones and growth factors, beta-2 agonists, hormone and metabolic modulators, diuretics and masking agents, and stimulants (Angell, et al., 2012). Consumption of such drugs can have serious health consequences. For example, the use of anabolic steroids and stimulants (cocaine, amphetamines) is associated with various cardiovascular health issues, including stroke, myocardial infarction, heart failure, endocarditis, atrial fibrillation and sudden death (Angell, et al., 2012). Notably, eating disorders and performance enhancing drug use are also correlated (Piacentino, et al., 2017).

Studies have examined the prevalence of performance-enhancing and recreational drug use, with many of them making no distinction between female and male athletes. Overall, the share of athletes admitting drug use ranges from 8.4% (Campian, Flis, Teramoto, & Cushman, 2018), 14.5% (Özdemir, et al., 2005), 21.4% (Piacentino, et al., 2017) and 31.7% (Uvacsek, et al., 2011), depending on the country and context.

At the *relational level*, knowing someone who has used these drugs increases the likelihood of an athlete using them, therefore, it can be considered a risk factor (Campian, et al., 2018). At the *individual level*, some scholars found no differences between women's and men's usage (Campian, et al., 2018; Piacentino, et al., 2017), while others reported that men are more susceptible to performance-enhancing drug use (Dodge & Jaccard, 2006). Paradoxically, men also scored higher on the status of different substances and knowledge of adverse effects of performance-enhancing drug use (Orr, et al., 2018). Risk factors independent of gender include performance pressure, self-treating otherwise untreated mental illness, injuries and physical pain (Creado & Reardon, 2016). In addition, several anticipated benefits of drug use can represent risk factors, including material (e.g. prize money, sponsorships), social (e.g. recognition) and internalised benefits (e.g. satisfaction with own achievement) (Strelan & Boeckmann, 2003).

Research stresses again the role of individual factors, requiring individual measures for athlete protection by sport organisations. Sport organisations need to care especially for athletes with health, psychological and financial issues, and offer support schemes.

Identification of issues and opportunities for further research

Based on the findings in the literature review, the various cases reported of abuse of women athletes (see case study at the end of this chapter) and a lack for care of duty and protection, several opportunities for future research emerge. Specifically, it is not clear whether sexual harassment in sport is comparable to harassment in society. Therefore, comparing sexual harassment in the sport sector and other sectors of society can potentially pinpoint similarities and differences in power relationships and how they are enacted or manifest on sexual harassment. The boundaries between what is acceptable and unacceptable behaviour also appear to be blurred, and herein lies an opportunity to crystalize this understanding within specific cultural contexts. The literature suggests that sexual harassment and bullying are interlinked and more evidence-based research and comparisons between sport and other life domains may shed light in both topics. Last, an opportunity exists to explore eating disorder across younger athletes who appear to be at higher risk category (Thompson & Sherman, 2014) and to further identify differences in drivers for using performance-enhancing drugs in sport.

Actions taken and future recommendations

The findings reported in this chapter suggest that, to an extent, the lack of or not enforcing existing sport systems, policies and strategies that have been formulated to protect female athletes results in failure to offer duty of care. To illustrate, one of the factors hindering the prevention of sexual harassment in sport is the implementation of the policies that are already in place, including having sexual harassment officers, or, if insufficient, the development of new professional codes of conduct and ethics for sport coaches. For example, as a result of pressure from sport organisations, sport development officers, clubs and parents, the sport governing bodies in the UK began to fill the legal policy vacuum in the 1990s (Brackenridge & Fasting, 2002). In Canada, the national governing body of sport, Sport Canada, made funding of national and provincial sport organisations contingent on the presence of sexual harassment policies in the late 1990s. Two decades later most organisations have such policies, but only few have a harassment officer, which is a policy requirement (Donnelly, Kerr, Heron, & DiCarlo, 2016). In relation to sexual harassment policy, Marks, Mountjoy and Marcus (2011) made a case for sport organisations to design and offer more prevention strategies, more advice on the recognition and the management of suspected sexual harassment, and to highlight the role of the team doctor as a contact person. As Brackenridge (2000) argued, sport organisations should conduct systematic recruitment, screening, induction and monitoring of both voluntary and paid coaches. Furthermore, research recommends increasing public scrutiny (Bringer, Brackenridge, & Johnston, 2006) and enabling a climate for debating sexual harassment (Cense & Brackenridge, 2001).

Actions against bullying also demand greater overall prevention and awareness (O'Neill, Calder, & Allen, 2014) and studies stress the importance of prevention through active coaches and team bonding to address bullying (Kentel & McHugh, 2015). Similarly, the prevention and management of disordered eating and several prevention and educational programmes can be effective mechanisms. Early identification (e.g. through recognition of dietary markers, and use of self-report questionnaires or clinical interviews; more randomised clinical trials) and treatment (Bratland-Sanda & Sundgot-Borgen, 2013; Coelho, et al., 2014) also carry substantial weight in ensuring athletes do not reach to the point of requiring treatment. Team physicians, transparency and accountability between athletes and the medical care team also play a critical role in promoting knowledge on healthy nutrition among athletes, parents, coaches and athletic administrators (Joy, Kussman, & Nattiv, 2016). Similar to eating disorders, drug use in sport can be reduced by applying preventive measures, education of athletes about potential side effects of using drugs, motivational interviewing and pharmacologic interventions (Creado & Reardon, 2016; Özdemir, et al., 2005).

Conclusion

Bullying affects and causes damage to both individuals and sport systems (Tofler, 2016). This is because victimised athletes are hindered in their development and are less likely to reach their full potential. As is the case with victims of sexual harassment, athletes affected by bullying face social isolation and might withdraw from the sport. Continued bullying might also lead to mental health issues, such as depression, and ultimately suicide (Tofler, 2016). In addition, many athletes suffer performance detriments, opportunity costs, reduced medal chances and loss of sponsorships (Brackenridge, 2001). These consequences equally apply to victims of sexual harassment and eating disorders in sport.

Beyond the individual level, these incidents can negatively affect the perceived role of sport in society and in particular for women and girls. Athlete dropout or attrition due to their disaffection resulting from harassment or abuse represents not just a loss of potential medals, but also an opportunity cost for sport organisations, the talent pool of which may be depleted as a result (Mountjoy, et al., 2016). When sport is perceived as a non-safe space or activity for women and girls to engage in, their participation rates in sport will likely suffer. The ramification of sport being deemed unsafe for women and girls and being a male-dominated field, as well as women's biased portrayal through media (and more recently social media), affects society's perceptions and perpetuates existing barriers to women's participation in sport. Subsequently, lower numbers of females in sport participation compared to males and lower still engagement of females in leadership roles in sport (e.g. coaches, administrators, directors in sport organisations), are noted and women and girls are underrepresented. Identifying and discussing the risks associated with women in sport and enforcing existing policies and strategies in place is only a starting point in sustainable changes. Future studies are also necessary to unravel the complexities associated with female athlete protection and duty of care to inform further practice.

CASE STUDY

Bangladesh Weightlifting Federation – sexual assault allegation

This case study, which focuses on an alleged sexual assault incident that took place in Bangladesh on 13 September 2018 (and other recent examples included in this case study), illustrates that allegations of sexual harassment and assault made by women athletes are often reported, yet it is rare that punitive actions are taken against any of the accused. The alleged sexual assault of a young woman weightlifter revealed that the 17-year-old athlete was admitted to a mental hospital ten days following the alleged assault because of the mental traumas she suffered in the aftermath (Rahman, 2018). The athlete was allegedly sexually assaulted by Bangladesh Weightlifting Federation's (BWF's) office assistant Shohag Ali with the help of National Sports Council (NSC) staff member Abdul Malek and Unnoti (a female weightlifter). The athlete chose a career in sport to improve her family's financial position. In a twist of events, the family of the assaulted athlete did not file a case against Shohag because of financial constraints. Furthermore, in fear of the social stigma, the athlete elected not to pursue forensic testing. National Sports Award winner and prominent sports organiser, Qumrunnahar Dana, and former weightlifter and current coach, Shahria Sultan Suchi, have been heavily critical of the prevailing culture in Bangladesh wrestling (Rahman, 2018). However, the NSC, the country's sports regulatory body, is also considering the formation of its own probe committee (Rahman, 2018).

Elite women gymnasts have similarly experienced the devastating effects of sexual abuse. Of particular interest is the case of convicted sports medicine doctor Larry Nassar, who – in the biggest sexual abuse crisis in American sport history – was sentenced in 2018 for his sexual abuse of more than 150 young women athletes (Blaschke, 2018). Similar to the weightlifter's case in Bangladesh, federal law intending to protect girls and women failed to protect the interests and wellbeing of athletes and neither USA Gymnastics nor the US Olympic Committee acted to protect the interests of women and girl athletes (Blaschke, 2018). This failure to protect women and girl athletes from male predators is more prevalent than we would like to believe. What this inaction does, besides harming women and girl athletes, is further encourage the continued sexual assault of women in sport. Yasmin Brown presents yet another example. Her Taekwondo coach began abusing her in 2010, and neither USA Taekwondo nor the US Olympic Committee acted to remove the coach, who kept abusing her, as well as other girls (Blaschke, 2018). Such cases represent long-term, institutional male-dominance in sport organisations where policies and actions protect perpetrators rather than women and girl athletes, who seem to be losing the battle for their own safety and wellbeing (Blaschke, 2018).

References

Angell, P. J., Chester, N., Sculthorpe, N., Whyte, G., George, K., & Somauroo, J. (2012). Performance enhancing drug abuse and cardiovascular risk in athletes: implications for the clinician. *British Journal of Sports Medicine*, 46(1), i78–i84.

Arthur-Cameselle, J., Sossin, K., & Quatromoni, P. (2017). A qualitative analysis of factors related to eating disorder onset in female collegiate athletes and non-athletes. *Eating Disorders*, 25(3), 199–215.

Bachand, C. R. (2017). Bullying in sports: The definition depends on who you ask. *Sports Studies and Sports Psychology*, 9, 1–14.

Blaschke, A. (2018). Nassar abuse reflects more than 50 years of men's power over female athletes. Retrieved from http://theconversation.com/nassars-abuse-reflects-more-than-50-years-of-mens-power-over-female-athletes-90722

Brackenridge, C. H. (1994). Fair play or fair game: Child sexual abuse in sport organisations. *International Review for the Sociology of Sport*, 29(3), 287–299.

Brackenridge, C. H. (2000). Harassment, sexual abuse, ad safety of the female athlete. *Clinics in Sports Medicine*, 19(2), 187–198.

Brackenridge, C. H. (2001). *Spoilsports: Understanding and Preventing Sexual Exploitation in Sport*. London, UK: Routledge.

Brackenridge, C., & Fasting, K. (2002). Sexual harassment and abuse in sport: The research context. *Journal of Sexual Aggression: An International, Interdisciplinary Forum for Research, Theory and Practice*, 8(2), 3–15.

Brackenridge, C. H., & Kirby, S. (1997). Playing safe? Assessing the risk of sexual abuse to young elite athletes. *International Review for the Sociology of Sport*, 32(4), 407–418.

Bratland-Sanda, S., & Sundgot-Borgen, J. (2013). Eating disorders in athletes: Overview of prevalence, risk factors and recommendations for prevention and treatment. *European Journal of Sport Science*, 13(5), 499–508.

Bringer, J. D., Brackenridge, C. H., & Johnston, L. H. (2006). Swimming coaches' perceptions of sexual exploitation in sport: A preliminary model of role conflict and role ambiguity. *The Sport Psychologist*, 20, 465–479.

Campian, M. D., Flis, A. E., Teramoto, M., & Cushman, D. M. (2018). Self-reported use and attitudes toward performance-enhancing drugs in ultramarathon running. *Wilderness & Environmental Medicine*, 29(3), 330–337.

Cense, M., & Brackenridge, C. (2001). Temporal and developmental risk factors for sexual harassment and abuse in sport. *European Physical Education Review*, 7(1), 61–79.

Coelho, J. S., Wilson, S., Winslade, A., Thaler, L., Israel, M., & Steiger, H. (2014). Over-evaluation of thoughts about food: Differences across eating-disorder subtypes and a preliminary examination of treatment effects. *International Journal of Eating Disorders*, 47(3), 302–309.

Creado, S., & Reardon, C. (2016). The sports psychiatrist and performance-enhancing drugs. *International Review of Psychiatry*, 28(6), 564–571.

Diamond, A. B., Callahan, S. T., Chain, K. F., & Solomon, G. S. (2016). Qualitative review of hazing in collegiate and school sports: consequences from a lack of culture, knowledge and responsiveness. *British Journal of Sports Medicine*, 50(3), 149–153.

Dodge, T. L., & Jaccard, J. J. (2006). The effect of high school sports participation on the use of performance-enhancing substances in young adulthood. *Journal of Adolescent Health*, 39(3), 367–373.

Donnelly, P., Kerr, G., Heron, A., & DiCarlo, D. (2016). Protecting youth in sport: An examination of harassment policies. *International Journal of Sport Policy and Politics*, 8(1), 33–50.

Evans, B., Adler, A., MacDonald, D., & Côté, J. (2016). Bullying victimization and perpetration among adolescent sport teammates. *Pediatric Exercise Science*, 28(2), 296–303.

Farrow, C. V., & Fox, C. L. (2011). Gender differences in the relationships between bullying at school and unhealthy eating and shape-related attitudes and behaviours. *British Journal of Educational Psychology*, 81(3), 409–420.

Fasting, K., & Knorre, N. (2005). *Women in Sport in the Czech Republic: The Experiences of Female Athletes*. Oslo: Norwegian School of Sport Sciences.

Fasting, K., Brackenridge, C., & Knorre, N. (2010). Performance level and sexual harassment prevalence among female athletes in the Czech Republic. *Women in Sport and Physical Activity Journal*, 19(1), 26–32.

Fasting, K., Brackenridge, C., & Sundgot-Borgen, J. (2000). *Women, Elite-Sport and Sexual Harassment*. Oslo: The Norwegian Olympic and Paralympic Committee and Confederation of Sports.

Fasting, K., Brackenridge, C., & Sundgot-Borgen, J. (2003). Experiences of sexual harassment and abuse among Norwegian elite female athletes and nonathletes. *Research Quarterly for Exercise and Sport*, 74(1), 84–97.

Fasting, K., Brackenridge, C., & Sundgot-Borgen, J. (2004). Prevalence of sexual harassment among Norwegian female elite athletes in relation to sport type. *International Review for the Sociology of Sport*, 39(4), 373–386.

Fasting, K., Brackenridge, C., & Walseth, K. (2002). Consequences of sexual harassment in sport for female athletes. *Journal of Sexual Aggression*, 8(2), 37–48.

Gershel, J. C., Katz-Sidlow, R. J., Small, E., & Zandieh, S. (2003). Hazing of suburban middle school and high school athletes. *Journal of Adolescent Health*, 32(5), 333–335.

Gündüz, N., Sunay, H., & Koz, M. (2008). Incidents of sexual harassment in Turkey on elite sportswomen. *The Sport Journal*. Retrieved from https://thesportjournal.org/article/incidents-of-sexual-harassment-in-turkey-on-elite-sportswomen/

Homan, K. J., Crowley, S. L., & Sim, L. A. (2018). Motivation for sport participation and eating disorder risk among female collegiate athletes. *Eating Disorders*, 27(4), 369–383.

Joy, E., Kussman, A., & Nattiv, A. (2016). 2016 update on eating disorders in athletes: A comprehensive narrative review with a focus on clinical assessment and management. *British Journal of Sports Medicine*, 50(3), 154–162.

Kentel, J. L., & McHugh, T. L. F. (2015). "Mean mugging": An exploration of young Aboriginal women's experiences of bullying in team sports. *Journal of Sport and Exercise Psychology*, 37(4), 367–378.

Kerr, G., Jewett, R., MacPherson, E., & Stirling, A. (2016). Student-athletes' experiences of bullying on intercollegiate teams. *Journal for the Study of Sports and Athletes in Education*, 10(2), 132–149.

La Gerche, A., & Brosnan, M. J. (2018). Drugs in sport – a change is needed, but what? *Heart, Lung and Circulation*, 27(9), 1099–1104.

Marks, S., Mountjoy, M., & Marcus, M. (2011). Sexual harassment and abuse in sport: the role of the team doctor. *British Journal of Sports Medicine*, 46(13), 905–908.

Martinsen, M., Bratland-Sanda, S., Eriksson, A.K., & Sundgot-Borgen, J. (2010). Dieting to win or to be thin? A study of dieting and disordered eating among adolescent elite athletes and non-athlete controls. *British Journal of Sports Medicine*, 44(1), 70–76.

Mountjoy, M., Rhind, D.J.A., Tiivas, A., & Leglise, M. (2015). Safeguarding the child athlete in sport: A review, a framework and recommendations for the IOC youth athlete development model. *British Journal of Sports Medicine*, 49(13), 883–886.

Mountjoy, M., Brackenridge, C., Arrington, M., Blauwet, C., Carska-Sheppard, A., Fasting, K., et al. (2016). International Olympic Committee consensus statement: Harassment and abuse (non-accidental violence) in sport. *British Journal of Sports Medicine*, 50(17), 1019–1029.

Ohlert, J., Seidler, C., Rau, T., Rulofs, B., & Allroggen, M. (2018). Sexual violence in organized sport in Germany. *German Journal of Exercise and Sport Research*, 48(1), 59–68.

O'Neill, M., Calder, A., & Allen, B. (2014). Tall poppies: Bullying behaviors faced by Australian high-performance school-age athletes. *Journal of School Violence*, 13(2), 210–227.

Orr, R., Grassmayr, M., Macniven, R., Grunseit, A., Halaki, M., & Bauman, A. (2018). Australian athletes' knowledge of the WADA Prohibited Substances List and performance enhancing substances. *International Journal of Drug Policy*, 56, 40–45.

Özdemir, L., Nur, N., Bagcivan, I., Bulut, O., Sümer, H., & Tezeren, G. (2005). Doping and performance enhancing drug use in athletes living in Sivas, mid-Anatolia: A brief report. *Journal of Sports Science & Medicine*, 4(3), 248–252.

Piacentino, D., Kotzalidis, G. D., Longo, L., Pavan, A., Stivali, L., Stivali, G., … & Girardi, P. (2017). Body image and eating disorders are common among professional and amateur athletes using performance and image enhancing drugs: A cross-sectional study. *Journal of Psychoactive Drugs*, 49(5), 373–384.

Rahman, A. (2018). Threatened by an abusive culture. *The Daily Star*. Retrieved from www.thedailystar.net/sports/allegations-surface-sexual-harassment-on-female-a thlete-1665412

Sanford-Martens, T. C., Davidson, M. M., Yakushko, O. F., Martens, M. P., & Hinton, P. (2007). Clinical and subclinical eating disorders: An examination of college athletes. *Journal of Applied Sport Psychology*, 17(1), 79–86.

Stirling, A. E., & Kerr, G. A. (2009). Abused athletes' perceptions of the coach-athlete relationship. *Sport in Society*, 12(2), 227–239.

Strelan, P., & Boeckmann, R. J. (2003). A new model for understanding performance-enhancing drug use by elite athletes. *Journal of Applied Sport Psychology*, 15(2), 176–183.

Sundgot-Borgen, J., Fasting, K., Brackenridge, C., Torstveit, M. K., & Berglund, B. (2003). Sexual harassment and eating disorders in female elite athletes – A controlled study. *Scandinavian Journal of Medicine & Science in Sports*, 13(5), 330–335.

Thompson, R. A., & Sherman, R. (2014). Reflections on athletes and eating disorders. *Psychology of Sport and Exercise*, 15(6), 729–734.

Tofler, I. R. (2016). Bullying, hazing, and workplace harassment: The nexus in professional sports as exemplified by the first NFL Wells report. *International Review of Psychiatry*, 28(6), 623–628.

Uvacsek, M., Nepusz, T., Naughton, D. P., Mazanov, J., Ránky, M. Z., & Petróczi, A. (2011). Self-admitted behavior and perceived use of performance-enhancing vs psychoactive drugs among competitive athletes. *Scandinavian Journal of Medicine & Science in Sports*, 21(2), 224–234.

Volkwein, K. A., Schnell, F. I., Sherwood, D., & Livezey, A. (1997). Sexual harassment in sport: Perceptions and experiences of American female student-athletes. *International Review for the Sociology of Sport*, 32(3), 283–295.

Waldron, J. J., & Kowalski, C. L. (2009). Crossing the line: Rites of passage, team aspects, and ambiguity of hazing. *Research Quarterly for Exercise and Sport*, 80(2), 291–302.

18

REGULATING HIGH TESTOSTERONE IN INTERNATIONAL WOMEN'S SPORT

Madeleine Pape

Introduction

The regulation of elite women athletes with naturally high levels of testosterone has become one of the most divisive and broadly debated issues in contemporary women's sport. Sometimes described as gender verification or sex testing, such practices aim to identify women athletes with differences of sexual development, or women born with sexual and reproductive anatomy and/or chromosomal patterns that do not fit neatly within the familiar categories of male and female (ISNA, 2018). Sports governing bodies like the International Olympic Committee (IOC) approach this kind of variation as a problem for the female athlete category, alleging in particular that women with naturally elevated testosterone levels enjoy physiological advantages over their competitors that amount to being 'unfair' (IOC, 2012). As will be explored in this chapter, however, there is considerable scientific and ethical debate about the legitimacy of excluding women on the basis of their hormonal profile, since testosterone behaves in complex ways in the body and may not be the most decisive factor when it comes to athletic ability (Karkazis, Jordan-Young, Davis, & Camporesi, 2012; Pape, 2019; Pieper, 2016).

Efforts to identify and prohibit the participation of women with intersex traits are not new: since at least the late 1960s, the IOC and other prominent international sports governing bodies have deployed a variety of testing regimes with the aim of restricting women's competition to athletes they deem to be biologically female. This task has proven elusive, with biological sex and its relationship to athletic ability consistently proving too complex to regulate (Bohuon, 2015; Henne, 2014; Kane, 1995). Given the absence of parallel efforts to regulate men's athletic participation, many feminist scholars and activists have argued that such efforts are better understood as imposing restrictive notions of femininity onto women athletes and their bodies (Cavanagh & Sykes, 2006; Henne, 2014; Jordan-Young & Karkazis, 2012;

Kane, 1995; Wackwitz, 2003). The regulation of gender eligibility is thus neither good for women nor just, given that such practices target and stigmatise a minority of women with non-binary sexual development.

In recent years, these critiques have expanded to draw attention to the role of race and nation in the regulation of women athletes, particularly in the sport of track-and-field. This is because those women athletes in track-and-field who have been publicly accused in the media over the past decade of having naturally high testosterone have primarily been women of colour from the Global South. The term Global South is used in this chapter to denote nations that are resource-constrained compared to nations with higher levels of economic development (the Global North), often reflecting the legacies of European-driven colonial exploitation. However, it is acknowledged that the term is somewhat problematic and has been critiqued for simplifying enormous variation in the distribution of wealth across Southern and Northern hemisphere nations (Hayhurst & Giles, 2013). The overrepresentation of women of colour from the Global South among those singled out for scrutiny warrants critical examination, since their achievements in track-and-field events are not particularly exceptional when compared to dominant male athletes or current women's world record holders (Karkazis, et al., 2012). It appears instead that race and nation are mediating constructions of 'biological femininity' in international sport, with particular implications for the development of women's sport in contexts outside of the Global North.

The goal of this chapter is to extend the feminist case against the regulation of women with high testosterone by critically examining the geopolitical dimensions of such practices. The chapter focuses on debates surrounding the Hyperandrogenism Regulations introduced by International Association of Athletics Federations (IAAF) in 2011, which were later revised in 2018 (IAAF, 2011, 2018). Reflecting long-standing collaboration with the IAAF on this issue, the IOC also introduced parallel regulations in 2012, applying to all women's Olympic sports (Henne 2014; IOC, 2012). The 2011 IAAF regulations were in place until 2015, when an Indian sprinter, Dutee Chand, brought an appeal to the Court of Arbitration for Sport (CAS). The adjudicating panel suspended the regulations for two years due to what it perceived as a lack of scientific evidence to support the IAAF's claim that women with high testosterone enjoy a considerable advantage over their competitors (CAS, 2015). However, in 2018, the IAAF introduced revised regulations based on research alleged to demonstrate a correlation between testosterone levels and the performance of female athletes, specifically in middle distance events. The responsibility for resisting this regime has continued to fall on the shoulders of women of colour from Global South nations (Henne & Pape, 2018), with these more recent regulations appealed in 2019 by double Olympic champion in the 800m, Caster Semenya, and a black woman from South Africa. While acknowledging that the regulations were discriminatory, this time the CAS ruled in the IAAF's favour (CAS, 2019).

This chapter reviews these scientific and ethical debates and builds on recent scholarship by exploring how race and nation are also implicated in the regulation of women with high testosterone. It begins with an overview of the contested history of efforts to regulate the female athlete category, set against a longer story of how race and nation have figured in the both the scientific and sporting pursuit of binary sex. The chapter then turns to a case study of the IAAF's 2011 Hyperandrogenism Regulations, drawing on interview and textual data to show how the bodies of women athletes of colour from Global South nations were constructed as the legitimate targets of this regime. The chapter concludes by considering opportunities for further research and the practical implications of this case for the global development of women's and girls' sport.

Feminist and postcolonial perspectives on gender eligibility regulation

Deconstructing binary sex in sport and science

The deployment of scientific expertise by sports governing bodies reflects the intersection of two highly gendered institutions: sport and science (Pape, 2017). A central project for scholars in feminist science studies has been to reveal how scientific accounts of binary sex – or sex as two distinct categories, male and female – is not a reflection of 'nature', but rather ignores the complexities of biological variation. The commitment of researchers to 'discovering' binary sex informs their decisions throughout the research process – such as the questions deemed worth pursuing, the design of experiments and the interpretation and reporting of data (Fujimura, 2006; Haraway, 1988; Lorber, 1993; Richardson, 2012). In observing their data through a gendered lens, researchers may also attribute stereotypical ideas of masculinity and femininity to the biological phenomena they are observing. For example, biological accounts of reproductive physiology often attribute stereotypically masculine attributes to sperm (e.g. active, brave, penetrative, a decision-maker) while feminising the egg (e.g. as a passive recipient of sperm), thereby reinforcing hierarchical and essentialised notions of men/women and masculine/feminine (Martin, 1991).

Similar processes occur in the approach of medical professionals to infants and children with differences of sexual development. Irreversible surgeries to impose binary categories onto nonbinary bodies have been commonplace in many Global North countries (Fausto-Sterling, 2000; Hughes, Houk, Ahmed, & Lee, 2006). Such interventions are also accompanied by socialisation practices aimed at ensuring that the gender identity of children with differences of sexual development align with their assigned sex category (Rubin, 2012). Such practices have continued despite increasing activism by intersex organisations and communities aimed at exposing the associated trauma, violence and rights violations (Davis, 2015; Karkazis, 2008; Kessler, 1990). Though intended to naturalise the heteronormative alignment of binary sex and gender, the urgency with which medical practitioners intervene to 'fix' differences of sexual development reveals the very unnaturalness of such account (Fausto-Sterling, 2000).

Sport has emerged as a key institutional sphere where the difficulties and harms associated with imposing binary sex categories onto a far more complex reality have come to the fore. Formal testing practices, motivated by a desire to protect women's sport from 'male imposters' (Pieper 2016, p. 139), began with genital examinations in the late 1960s before moving to a chromosome-based testing regime that lasted over three decades. During this time, chromosomally 'certified' female competitors were required to present 'certificates of femininity' or 'femininity cards' in order to compete (Wackwitz, 2003). In the late 1990s, following decades of critique from geneticists and endocrinologists, the IOC and IAAF abandoned chromosome-based tests and looked to endogenous testosterone as an allegedly more accurate way to identify 'hypermuscular' women with a natural but 'unfair' athletic advantage (Pieper, 2016). In a departure from previous regimes when sex testing was mandatory, testing in the current 'hyperandrogenism era' is not mandated (Pape, in press). Rather, only those athletes deemed 'suspicious' by designated medical staff are required to undergo examination (IAAF, 2011), a situation that enables the uneven scrutiny of certain women (Henne & Pape, 2018; Karkazis, et al., 2012).

Although sports governing bodies like the IOC and IAAF have drawn on various scientific and medical experts in an effort to justify their testing procedures, the complexity of sexual variation has consistently undermined their efforts to scientifically define clear boundaries for the female athlete body (Henne, 2014; Kane, 1995; Lorber, 1993; Pieper 2016; Wackwitz, 2003). Sports governing bodies and their experts have also not been able to show that the characteristics they claim to be the basis of sex difference – genitals, chromosomes, and now testosterone – are decisively linked to athletic ability, which is also too complex to explain via singular biological traits, particularly given the variety of complex social factors that can influence an athlete's development and which vary by gender, class and nation (Karkazis, et al., 2012; Pape, 2017).

Race, nation, and biological femininity

Historical and contemporary practices of gender eligibility regulation for women athletes have also intersected with the politics of race and nation. As documented by Anaïs Bohuon (2015), this first took the form of an 'East/West Antagonism' as the Cold War divide infiltrated global sport and began to shape perceptions of the 'other' on the sporting field (see also Henne, 2014). Scrutiny of women athletes aligned with these geopolitical tensions, beginning at the 1936 Olympic Games in Berlin when two sprinters, American Helen Stephens and Polish Stella Walsh, were both accused of being men (Ritchie, Reynard & Lewis, 2008). German high jumper, Dora Ratjen, competed as a woman but was later revealed to identify as a man, prompting speculation that Nazi Germany had intentionally sought to 'cheat' (Berg, 2009). The East/West contours of debates over women's biological eligibility intensified in the 1950s and 1960s, when two Russian sisters, Irina and Tamara Press, amassed 26 World Records and six Olympic gold medals (Carlson, 2005). Intense speculation about these athletes prompted the introduction of compulsory gynaecological examinations at the 1966 European Athletics Championships. Analysis of US press coverage over this period shows that those women athletes portrayed as 'suspect' were consistently Eastern European, while similarly successful Western athletes were spared (Bohuon 2015; see also Henne 2015; Pieper 2016). Yet as geopolitical antagonisms shifted, so too did the dynamics of 'suspect' femininity, shifting over time toward a racialised 'North/South' narrative within which women athletes of colour from Global South nations have been constructed as the legitimate focus of scrutiny (Bohuon, 2015; Henne & Pape, 2018; Karkazis & Jordan-Young, 2018).

There are numerous similarities between the contemporary focus on Global South women of colour and the historical development of medical knowledge about differences of sexual development, which scholars have shown is inextricably linked to histories of colonial conquest and racial domination. From the early to mid-nineteenth century, Western medical practitioners capitalised on the access to racialised others – and particularly the bodies of women of colour in sub-Saharan Africa – that was enabled by colonial conquest, resulting in the construction of narratives of intersex 'abnormalities' that bolstered both binary sex and colonial white supremacy (Fausto-Sterling, 1995; Magubane, 2014). As documented by Magubane (2014), this same impulse to construct Black women's sexual anatomy as abnormal is found in nineteenth and twentieth century textbooks, with US medical texts from as recently as the 1980s alleging the overrepresentation of sex-based abnormalities among women of colour in non-western contexts. When viewed in their historical and global context, medical accounts of differences of sexual development have upheld not only binary ideas about sex/gender, but also the alleged purity of white femininity. Black feminist scholars, such as Patricia Hill Collins, have observed that the denial of 'pure' femininity to women of colour remains a broad contemporary tendency in Western nations (Collins, 1990).

International track-and-field has witnessed change over time in the racial and national dynamics of women's participation at the elite level. Unlike many Olympic sports, in track-and-field the dominance of white athletes from Western Euro-American countries has largely diminished in recent decades (IAAF, 2012; Smith & Wrynn, 2013). These changing demographics combine with the general precarity of women's competition, even in track-and-field, where women have only recently won the right to compete in a number of events. Thus, not only do race and nation shape medical knowledge of differences of sexual development, and perceptions of femininity more generally, but they may do so in particular ways in a sport where white women are no longer dominant (Karkazis & Jordan-Young, 2018). In sum, we see in both sport and science that gender, race and the legacies of colonialism intersect to shape perceptions of biological femininity. This warps the ability of different women athletes to be perceived as fully feminine, with implications for which women and girls can be recognised as legitimate champions at the international level (Nyong'o, 2010).

CASE STUDY

Contemporary politics of testosterone regulation in track-and-field

In this section, I turn to events surrounding the IAAF's 2011 Hyperandrogenism Regulations, which were in place until 2015, to explore how race and nation influence the development and implementation of gender eligibility rules for women athletes in the current hyperandrogenism era. I draw on a variety of primary and secondary sources, including: my own fieldwork and semi-structured interviews with 64 stakeholders in elite track-and-field; proceedings from the 2015 CAS appeal; and other published studies of the gendered and racialised politics of the gender eligibility regulation. My interviews were conducted with athletes, coaches, team staff, media personnel and athlete managers following the Rio de Janeiro 2016 Olympic Games, where significant debate unfolded regarding the legitimacy of the 2015 CAS decision to suspend the existing rules (see Henne & Pape, 2018; Pape, 2020).

Background: The North/South contours of controversy

The 2011 Regulations of the IAAF followed from the 2009 World Championships in track-and-field, which were marked by the controversial victory of Caster Semenya, then 18 years old, in the women's 800m competition. An announcement by the IAAF on the eve of the final that it was conducting tests to determine whether Semenya was '100 percent' a woman (Longman, 2016) led to unprecedented public scrutiny of her body and gender. The IAAF's reckless breach of confidentiality drew considerable critique, particularly in South Africa, where the organisation's actions were framed as racially motivated (Cooky, Dycus & Dworkin, 2013). The controversy prompted the IAAF to revise its procedure for investigating women athletes believed to have differences of sexual development, leading to the release of the Hyperandrogenism Regulations in 2011 (IAAF, 2011).

The regulations specified a limit of 10nmol/L for functional endogenous testosterone in women athletes. The Hyperandrogenism Regulations of the IOC specified a limit of 8nmol/L (IOC, 2012). Under the IAAF (2011) regulations, 'suspect' athletes were required to undertake initial blood testing, followed by a clinical examination if their testosterone levels were above the specified limit, the purpose of which was to assess the extent of 'virilisation' – visible signs of high testosterone exposure in the breasts, pubic hair, skin etc. This clinical assessment was taken to be equivalent to measuring the extent to which an athlete's testosterone levels were conferring an unfair athletic advantage. The IAAF regulations required that those women believed to be benefiting from high testosterone lower their levels before returning to competition. Importantly, in the absence of mandatory testing for all women athletes, the criteria for identifying athletes suspected of having high testosterone were vague and open-ended, with potential sources including any 'information received by the IAAF Medical Delegate or other responsible medical official' (IAAF, 2011, p. 3).

In 2015, Dutee Chand, an 18-year-old Indian sprinter who was barred from international track-and-field competition under the IAAF regulations, refused medical interventions and instead opted to appeal this regulatory regime at the Court of Arbitration for Sport (CAS) in Switzerland. Expert debate during the appeal focused primarily on the relationship between testosterone, sex difference and athletic ability, with Chand's legal team arguing that the regulations were 'based on flawed factual assumptions' about testosterone's role in athletic performance (CAS, 2015, p. 2). Ultimately, the CAS adjudicating panel ruled that while the IAAF regulations were not yet sufficiently supported by scientific evidence, such evidence could be generated by the IAAF. Thus, CAS suspended the regulations for two years and encouraged the IAAF to undertake new research to enable their reinstatement (CAS, 2015, p. 156). In other words, despite the inconclusiveness of the scientific debate before them, the CAS was generally supportive of a policy aimed at excluding women with high testosterone and shared the IAAF's belief that endogenous testosterone could be shown to decisively impact athletic ability.

In the season following the suspension of the IAAF regulations, Caster Semenya won Olympic gold in the women's 800m at the Rio di Janeiro 2016 Olympic Games. She was publicly accused by media commentators and track-and-field stakeholders of having elevated testosterone and an unfair advantage, as were the silver and bronze medallists, who were also women of colour from Sub-Saharan African nations. In a comment that highlighted the geopolitical dynamics of this outcome, Poland's Joanna Jozwik, who came fifth in the event behind Canada's Melissa Bishop, stated following the race, 'I'm glad I'm the first European, the second white' (Karkazis & Jordan-Young, 2018). In 2018, the IAAF announced a revised set of regulations, this time with a limit of 5nmol/L and applying only to those women's events where IAAF-affiliated researchers claimed to have established a correlation between testosterone levels and performance (IAAF, 2018). IAAF researchers claim a correlation between testosterone levels and performance in the women's hammer throw, pole vault, 400m, 400m hurdles and 800m. By contrast, the subsequent proposed (and then suspended) 'Eligibility Regulations for Female Classification' apply to the women's 400m, 400m hurdles, 800m, 1500m and mile (Bermon & Garnier, 2017; IAAF, 2018). At the time of the writing of this chapter, the CAS had endorsed these new eligibility regulations following an appeal by Semenya and Athletics South Africa. In a departure from its decision in the Chand case, this time, the CAS panel concluded that it was unable to assess the legitimacy of the scientific evidence before it, stating it was beyond the panel's scope as an adjudicating body.

Further excavating race and nation in the hyperandrogenism era

Since 2009, South African politicians, track-and-field officials and media have described the recent rule-making efforts of the IAAF as racist (Cooky, et al., 2013; Shalala, 2018). The IAAF has rejected such claims, yet my own research – and research by other feminist scholars – reveals that both the experts involved in drafting the 2011 (and subsequent) IAAF regulations and many track-and-field stakeholders believe that women of colour from Global South nations are the legitimate targets of these regulatory efforts. Among doctors affiliated with the IAAF, the dominant – unsubstantiated – narrative is that women with high testosterone are overrepresented in Global South nations (Karkazis & Jordan-Young, 2018). Among stakeholders, this belief is further sensationalised in the widespread rumour that high testosterone athletes from sub-Saharan African nations will soon be dominating women's track-and-field (Henne & Pape, 2018). In these discursive moves, women of colour from the Global South – and Sub-Saharan Africa in particular – are constructed as deviant and suspect, greatly increasing the chances that the successful athletes among them will be singled out for investigation under the regulations.

A study of the policymaking efforts of IAAF-affiliated medical doctors by Karkazis and Jordan-Young (2018) is particularly revealing. At an international sports conference in Glasgow in 2012, just a week prior to the London Olympic Games, they observed leading doctors for the IAAF and IOC associating high testosterone and 'unfair advantage' with women of colour located in the Global South, while linking pure biological femininity to whiteness (Karkazis & Jordan-Young, 2018, pp. 11–12, 20). At the same conference, a leading IAAF medical doctor stated that 'athletics is a whole world of sports, it's not purely the Caucasian sports. We have a lot of people coming from Africa, Asia, and ... a lot of these cases coming from these countries' (Karkazis & Jordan-Young, 2018, p. 21). Such statements lend support to the claim that changing demographics and the declining dominance of white women athletes are contributing to the panic around women with high testosterone in elite track-and-field.

My own research with Kathryn Henne (2018) shows that athletes and coaches from Global North nations are similarly concerned that 'certain tribes in Africa [have] larger populations of hyperandrogenous women', and that coaches and managers are 'going off [to Africa] looking for people with [intersex] conditions specifically to make money out of them [female athletes]' (Henne & Pape 2018, p. 219). Media commentators, too, may be more willing to accuse a female athlete of having high testosterone if she is from a country outside of the Global North. According to one journalist I interviewed:

> It's a hard truth of journalism that people are more careful where they think there's potential for legal action. Whether an athlete from an impoverished nation is going to take the trouble to sue a journalist in another country, or has the means to do that, is unlikely.... I think people are less diligent in that situation.

The association of high testosterone with women of colour from the Global South – which is legitimated by IAAF representatives, willingly taken up amongst track-and-field stakeholders in the Global North, and further enabled by the actions of certain media commentators – creates an environment where the achievements of such women are more likely to be cast as 'suspect', rather than afforded the respect and admiration enjoyed by successful women athletes from other countries.

There is some evidence that the lifelong embodied consequences for women athletes found to have higher than 'normal' levels of testosterone are disproportionately being borne by women of colour from Global South. One of the most alarming accounts is found in research published by IAAF-affiliated doctors themselves. In a 2013 article, they detail the treatment of four women athletes diagnosed with hyperandrogenism, all aged 21 or younger and from 'rural or mountainous regions of developing countries' (Fenichel, et al., 2013, p. 2), who allegedly consented to a gonadectomy, clitoral surgery and 'feminizing [sic] vaginoplasty' (pp. 3–4). None of these irreversible interventions, which can lead to permanent discomfort and pain, are linked to athletic ability or required under the IAAF regulations for an athlete to return to competition.

It was conceded by an IAAF witness during the 2015 Chand appeal 'that it was "questionable at best" whether young women in [such a] position can give informed consent for medical interventions' within the procedures outlined in the 2011 Regulations (CAS, 2015, p. 97). As Henne and I discuss (2018), the IAAF's Approved Specialist Reference Centres for diagnosing and developing 'treatment' plans for athletes are located in a select number of OECD countries, which likely compounds the difficulties of achieving truly informed consent for athletes with different linguistic or cultural backgrounds. In practice, athletes in this situation are forced to choose between limited options: comply with a treatment plan, never compete again, or go public and attempt an appeal with limited resources in a legal setting that is unlikely to find the actions of the IAAF problematic (Pape, 2017, 2019). Witnesses during the Chand appeal, for instance, described risks faced by 'outed' female athletes in countries like India with a culture of 'misogyny and violence against women' (CAS, 2015, p. 111) and 'cited examples of athletes being forced to undergo surgery without clear information about what the treatment involved' (CAS, 2015, p. 110). The CAS panel refused to recognise such implementation-related concerns as relevant to the legitimacy of the IAAF regulations.

The current regulatory efforts of the IAAF have important broader implications for the lived experiences of women athletes – especially those located in the Global South – and women with differences of sexual development more broadly. As recalled by one intersex advocate that I interviewed, who had been consulted by the IOC as they drafted their Hyperandrogenism Regulations:

> I [have] absolutely heard families discussing what [IAAF and IOC] decisions meant for their own understanding of their daughters or their wives … there's no question that psychologically, those decisions were having impacts on how [women with differences of sexual development] understood their own identities, how they understood their own legitimacy as women.

At a South African symposium on the Hyperandrogenism Regulations in September 2018, I heard representatives of the South African Women and Sport Foundation (SAWSF), a grassroots women's sports organisation, express fear

> that South African girls in rural areas would stop participating in track-and-field because of the scrutiny they might potentially encounter in the future. Thus, while the IAAF may seek to represent the participation of women with high testosterone as a purely scientific and elite issue, the stakes associated with their regulatory efforts are broad and include women's sports participation at the grassroots level.

Implications and opportunities

This examination of the IAAF's Hyperandrogenism Regulations, contextualised within the longer history of gender eligibility regulation efforts in international sport, points to a number of important implications for researchers and practitioners of sport development. To begin, there is as yet a limited body of empirical evidence demonstrating precisely how race and nation are relevant to the gendered regulatory regimes of international sport, making it difficult to hold sports governing bodies – and their Global North constituencies – accountable for the harms their actions may be causing to the development of women's sport and the lives of elite women athletes from the Global South. As argued elsewhere, it is critical that Global North researchers take up this challenge while supporting the efforts of researchers located outside of the academic 'metropole' to develop their own accounts of the gendered, racialised and imperialist contours of global sports governance (Henne & Pape, 2018; see also Connell, 2009; Santos, 2012). Rather than reveal a North/South divide, in which the 'North' has one perspective and the 'South' another, such research would likely highlight the tremendous diversity of experiences and perceptions of this issue (see, for example, Adjepong, in press; Cooky, et al., 2013; Magubane, 2014; Nyong'o, 2010).

From a sports practice perspective, education and awareness efforts are needed on two fronts, beginning first with educational efforts by both sports governing bodies and women's sports organisations. There remains a harmful lack of informed opinion and understanding of the complexities of sex difference and testosterone amongst the athletes, coaches, officials, media commentators, managers and other stakeholders engaged with the elite level of track-and-field (Pape, 2020). My research has shown that elite athletes and their coaches often have little-to-no understanding of the scientific complexities involved in relying on testosterone to define the female athlete category, and that team staff frequently avoid engaging athletes in informed discussion of the legitimacy of testosterone-based regulations. In a context where high-profile leaders of the sport have done little to address sensationalist and unsubstantiated claims about an imminent influx of women of colour with high testosterone, it is hardly surprising that white women competitors in the 800m have at times expressed fear and frustration (Karkazis & Jordan-Young, 2018). In track-and-field, and Olympic sports more broadly, governing bodies at the national and international levels are well positioned to minimise the potential for harm and promote cultural change by educating stakeholders about the complex scientific and ethical debates that surround these regulatory regimes. The International Working Group on Women and Sport (IWG) and Women's Sports Foundation (WSF) have already taken action to demand this kind of change from sports' governing bodies (see IWG, 2018; WSF, 2018).

Second, in the nations where successful women athletes are more likely to be constructed as 'suspect', it is critical that sports organisations at both national and subnational levels acquire an understanding of the procedures for appealing testosterone-based regulatory regimes, since international sports governing bodies provide little information about such options. The experiences of Dutee Chand and Caster Semenya should shed some light on the complex steps associated with lodging an appeal at the CAS or pursuing other avenues. The experiences of Chand and Semenya under the Hyperandrogenism Regulations also suggest that national federations must be better informed about athletes' rights to confidentiality and informed consent if singled out for investigation. It cannot be assumed, however, that national sports leaders will necessarily align themselves with, and seek to support, the rights of women athletes believed to have high testosterone. For this reason, grassroots women's sports organisations, like SAWSF, have an important role to play in promoting awareness at the local level and mobilising to hold sports leaders to account.

References

Adjepong, A. (in press). Voetsek! Get[ting] lost: African sportswomen in "the sporting black Diaspora". *International Review for the Sociology of Sport*. Advanced online publication. doi:10.1177/1012690219834486

Berg, S. (2009). How Dora the man competed in the woman's high jump. *Spiegel Online*, 15 September 2009. Retrieved from www.spiegel.de/international/germany/1936-berlin-olympics-how-dora-the-man-competed-in-the-woman-s-high-jump-a-649104.html

Bermon, S., & Garnier P. Y. (2017). Serum androgen levels and their relation to performance in track and field. *British Journal of Sports Medicine*, 51(17), 1309–1314.

Bohuon, A. (2015). Gender verifications in sport: From an East/West antagonism to a North/South antagonism. *The International Journal of the History of Sport*, 32(7), 965–979.

Cavanagh, S. L., & Sykes, H. (2006). Transsexual bodies at the Olympics: The International Olympic Committee's policy on transsexual athletes at the 2004 Athens Summer Games. *Body & Society*, 12(3), 75–102.

Collins, P. H. (1990). *Black Feminist Thought*. New York: Routledge.

Connell, R. (2009). *Southern Theory: The Global Dynamics of Knowledge in Social Science*. Cambridge: Polity.

Cooky, C., Dycus, R., & Dworkin, S. L. (2013). "What makes a woman a woman?" versus "our first lady of sport": A comparative analysis of United States and the South African media coverage of Caster Semenya. *Journal of Sport and Social Issues*, 37(1), 31–56.

Court of Arbitration for Sport (CAS). (2015). *CAS 2014/A/3759 Dutee Chand v. Athletics Federation of India & The International Association of Athletics Federations. Interim Arbitral Award*. Retrieved from www.tas-cas.org/fileadmin/user_upload/award_internet.pdf

Court of Arbitration for Sport (CAS). (2019). *Semenya, ASA and IAAF: Executive Summary*. Lausanne: Court of Arbitration for Sport.

Carlson, A. (2005). Essay: Suspect sex. *The Lancet*, 366(Special Issue), S39–S40.

Cavanagh, S. L., & Sykes, H. (2006). Transsexual bodies at the Olympics: The International Olympic Committee's policy on transsexual athletes at the 2004 Athens Summer Games. *Body & Society*, 12(3), 75–102.

Davis, G. (2015). *Contesting Intersex: The Dubious Diagnosis*. New York: NYU Press.

Fausto-Sterling, A. (1995). Gender, race, and nation: The comparative anatomy of 'Hottentot' women in Europe, 1815–1817. In J. Terry & J. Urla (eds), *Deviant Bodies: Critical Perspectives on Difference in Sex and Popular Culture* (pp. 19–48). Bloomington, IN: Indiana University Press.

Fausto-Sterling, A. (2000). *Sexing the Body: Gender Politics and the Construction of Sexuality*. New York: Basic Books.

Fenichel, P., Paris, F., Philibert, P., Hieronimus, S., Gaspari, L., Kurzenne, J.Y., … Sultan C. (2013). Molecular diagnosis of 5α-reductase deficiency in 4 elite young female athletes through hormonal screening for hyperandrogenism. *The Journal of Clinical Endocrinology and Metabolism*, 98(6), 1055–1059.

Fujimura, J. (2006). Sex genes: A critical sociomaterial approach to the politics and molecular genetics of sex determination. *Signs*, 32(1), 49–82.

Haraway, D. (1988). Situated knowledges: The science question in feminism and the privilege of partial perspective. *Feminist Studies*, 14(3), 575–599.

Hayhurst, L. M. C., & Giles, A. (2013). Private and moral authority, self-determination, and the domestic transfer objective: Foundations for understanding sport for development and peace in Aboriginal communities in Canada. *Sociology of Sport Journal*, 30(4), 504–519.

Henne, K. (2014). The 'science' of fair play in sport: Gender and the politics of testing. *Signs*, 39(3), 787–812.

Henne, K. E. (2015). *Testing for athlete citizenship: Regulating doping and sex in sport*. Rutgers University Press.

Henne, K., & Pape, M. (2018). Dilemmas of gender and global sports governance: An invitation to southern theory. *Sociology of Sport Journal*, 35(3), 216–225.

Hughes, A., Houk, C., Ahmed, S. F., & Lee, P.A. (2006). Consensus statement on management of intersex disorders. *Archives of Disease in Childhood*, 91(7), 554–563.

International Association of Athletics Federations (IAAF). (2011). *IAAF Regulations Governing Eligibility of Females with Hyperandrogenism to Compete in Women's Competition*. Monaco: IAAF.

International Association of Athletics Federations (IAAF). (2012). *IAAF 1912–2012: 100 Years of Athletics Excellence*. Monaco: IAAF.

International Association of Athletics Federations (IAAF). (2018). *IAAF Introduces New Eligibility Regulations for Female Classification*. 27 April, 2018. Retrieved from www.iaaf.org/news/press-release/eligibility-regulations-for-female-classifica

International Olympic Committee (IOC). (2012). *IOC Regulations on Female Hyperandrogenism*. Games of the XXX Olympiad in London, 2012. Retrieved from https://stillmed.olympic.org/Documents/Commissions_PDFfiles/Medical_commission/2012-06-22-IOC-Regulations-on-Female-Hyperandrogenism-eng.pdf

International Working Group on Women and Sport (IWG). (2018). *IWG official statement on the controversial new policy of the International Association of Athletics Federations, May 1, 2018*. Retrieved, from <www.iapesgw.org/images/docs/IWG–IAAF-Statement.pdf>

Intersex Society of North America (ISNA). (2018). *What is Intersex?* Retrieved from www.isna.org/faq/what_is_intersex

Jordan-Young, R., & Karkazis, K. (2012). Some of their parts: "Gender verification" and elite sports. *Anthropology News*, 53(6), S1–S41.

Kane, M. J. (1995). Resistance/transformation of the oppositional binary: Exposing sport as a continuum. *Journal of Sport and Social Issues*, 19(2), 191–218.

Karkazis, K. (2008). *Fixing Sex: Intersex, Medical Authority, and Lived Experience*. Durham, NC: Duke University Press.

Karkazis, K., & Jordan-Young, R. (2018). The powers of testosterone: Obscuring race and regional bias in the regulation of women athletes. *Feminist Formations*, 30(2), 1–39.

Karkazis, K., Jordan-Young, R., Davis, G., & Camporesi, S. (2012). Out of bounds? A critique of the new policies on hyperandrogenism in elite female athletes. *American Journal of Bioethics*, 12(1), 3–16.

Kessler, S. J. (1990). The medical construction of gender: Case management of intersexed infants. *Signs*, 16(1), 3–26.

Longman, J. (2016). Understanding the controversy over Caster Semenya. *The New York Times*, 18 August, 2016. Retrieved from www.nytimes.com/2016/08/20/sports/caster-semenya-800-meters.html

Lorber, J. (1993). Believing is seeing: Biology as ideology. *Gender & Society*, 7(4), 568–581.

Magubane, Z. (2014). Spectacles and scholarship: Caster Semenya, intersex studies, and the problem of race in feminist theory. *Signs*, 39(3), 761–785.

Martin, E. (1991). The egg and the sperm: How science has constructed a romance based on stereotypical male-female roles. *Signs: Journal of Women in Culture & Society*, 16(3), 485–501.

Morna, C. L. (2018). We can back SA's golden girl by challenging our stereotypes. *Mail & Guardian*, 4 May, 2018. Retrieved from https://mg.co.za/article/2018-05-04-00-we-can-back-sas-golden-girl-by-challenging-our-stereotypes

Nyong'o, T. (2010). The unforgivable transgression of being Caster Semenya. *Women & Performance: A Journal of Feminist Theory*, 20(1), 95–100.

Pape, M. (2017). The fairest of them all: Gender determining institutions and the science of sex testing.In V. Demos and M. T. Segal (eds) *Advances in Gender Research: Gender Panic, Gender Policy* (pp. 177–200). Bingley, UK: Emerald Publishing.

Pape, M. (2019). Gender segregation and trajectories of organizational change: Explaining the underrepresentation of women in sports leadership. *Gender and Society*.

Pape, M. (2020). Ignorance and the gender binary: Resisting complex epistemologies of sex and testosterone. In J. Sterling and M. McDonald (eds) *Sports, Society, Technology* (pp. 219–245). New York: Routledge.

Pape, M. (in press). Expertise, epistemologies of the body, and the institutional enactment of the binary. *Body & Society*. Advanced online publication. doi:10.1177/1357034X19865940

Pieper, L. P. (2016). *Sex Testing: Gender Policing in Women's Sports*. Champaign, IL: University of Illinois Press.

Richardson, S. S. (2012). Sexing the X: How the X became the 'female chromosome'. *Signs*, 37(4), 909–933.

Ritchie, T., Reynard, J., & Lewis, T. (2008). Intersex and the Olympic Games. *Journal of the Royal Society of Medicine*, 101(8), 395–399.

Rubin, D. (2012). An unnamed blank that craved a name: A genealogy of intersex as gender. *Signs*, 37(4), 883–908.

Santos, B. S. (2012). Public sphere and epistemologies of the South. *Africa Development*, 37(1), 43–67.

Shalala, A. (2018). IAAF female classification rules slammed as "blatantly racist". *ABC News*, 27 April, 2018. Retrieved from www.abc.net.au/news/2018-04-28/critics-say-iaaf-testosterone-rules-blatantly-racist/9706744

Smith, M. M., & Wrynn, A. M. (2013). *Women in the Olympic and Paralympic Games: An Analysis of Participation and Leadership Opportunities*. Ann Arbor, MI: SHARP Center for Women and Girls.

Spivak, G. C. (1988). Can the subaltern speak? In C. Nelson & L. Grossberg (eds) *Marxism and the Interpretation of Culture* (pp. 271–311). Chicago: University of Illinois Press.

Wackwitz, L. (2003). Verifying the myth: Olympic sex testing and the category woman. *Women's Studies International Forum*, 26(6), 553–560.

Women's Sports Foundation (WSF). (2018). *WSF Responds to IAAF's Proposed Eligibility Regulations for Female Classification*. Statement, April 26, 2018. Women's Sports Foundation. Retrieved from www.iapesgw.org/images/docs/Womens-Sports-Foundation-IAAF-statement.pdf

# 19

PROFESSIONAL WOMEN'S SPORT LEAGUES

Chelsey Taylor

Introduction

Professionalisation of women's sport has enhanced opportunities for women and girls to access talent development opportunities that were previously limited or non-existent. Increased investment in elite competitions and talent pathways for women and girls has led to a greater emphasis and need to invest into the grassroots development of women's sport. This chapter will examine how the professionalisation of women's sport, in particular, how the emergence of elite, professional women's sport leagues, has developed sport opportunities for women and girls.

The professionalisation of sport advanced as spectators began to pay money to watch sport; the commercial revenue opportunities began to increase, and athletes garnered the ability to be traded and further negotiate terms (Downward & Dawson, 2000; Smart, 2005). As sport events, leagues and associated professional teams generate revenue from broadcasting rights, sponsorships, match day tickets, memberships and other commercial initiatives, the time demands and performance expectations on athletes' increase. Professional sport can be defined as any sport that offers a form of remuneration or compensation to an athlete for their ability, skill or performance within the sport (Gladden & Sutton, 2014). In line with this definition, sporting codes and leagues have become increasingly business-focused in their operations moving from volunteer administration to complex, strategic organisations driven by commercial gain (Shilbury & Ferkins, 2011). A large proportion of men's professional leagues and teams have now reached a point where they are generating enough income to sustain highly lucrative player wages, and in the majority sports, elite male athletes do not require a secondary source of income; however, for the majority of elite female athletes this is not the case (Smart, 2005).

The professionalisation and focus of sporting organisations in developing commercially relevant leagues previously focused predominantly on male codes. Growing interest and investment from governments, corporates and spectators, coupled with a slight increase in media coverage, has helped enhance momentum on the professionalisation of women's sport (McLachlan, 2019). While there has been some improvement, significant differences remain in the remuneration, conditions and development of male and female athletes (Sherry & Taylor, 2019). Some successful women athletes, who excel in particular sports, are now in a position to generate substantial income through their sporting careers (e.g. tennis players), but many – perhaps the majority – continue to struggle to make ends meet, even as the professionalisation of women's sport continues to evolve and gain momentum. In many countries, we now see professional women's sport leagues, but the pay and conditions experienced by women athletes are far from equal to that of men's leagues and associated athletes. An example of a country that has experienced substantial advancement in relation to the professionalisation of women's sport over the past decade is Australia. In this chapter, a focus is placed on exploring the Australian women's sport landscape and some of the professional leagues that exist within this context.

Overview of the Australian women's professional sport landscape

The Australian professional women's sport landscape has experienced an 'evolution', with female athletes finally having a seat at the table and earning a wage from their athletic efforts (Willson et al., 2017). Professional leagues play an important role in the development of sport, participation and talent pathways, making them a focus area for exploring the professionalisation of women's sport. The professional women's leagues examined in this chapter have existed for varying lengths of time; each league has a variety of strategic purposes, from innovation and financial gain, through to developing participation and talent pathways for women and girls.

Basketball

Elite women's basketball in Australia is not new: the Women's National Basketball League (WNBL) was established in 1981 and is one of the most consistent leagues in the Australian women's sport landscape. In 2009, the average player wage was AU $5,000–$10,000, with no stipulated minimum wage (Basketball Australia, 2009). In 2019, the minimum wage for women basketballers in the WNBL has been set at AU $13,000, which is an increase of 73% from the 2018 minimum wage (Uluc, 2019), signalling a positive trajectory for payment of women basketballers. The Australian Basketballers Association, the athlete players association for basketball, negotiated a more favourable agreement with the WNBL to ensure players were receiving fairer conditions and remuneration in the sport. The agreement, which was negotiated in 2018, includes guaranteed contracts, restricted training periods and the inclusion of pregnancy and parenting policy (Uluc, 2019). The WNBL is focussing on strengthening commercial value including sponsorship packaging, marketing and new community engagement and sport development initiatives (WNBL, 2017), to ensure athletes contribute to benefit from the professionalisation of the WNBL.

Netball

Netball is the dominant participant sport for women and girls in Australia, with 5% of the total population and 9.6% of Australian women and girls participating in the sport of netball (Ausplay, 2019a). Netball has been traditionally played by women and girls and continues to be a sport dominated by women and girls, despite slight increases to participation by men and boys. The first national netball league was established in 1985, with various commercial and structural changes over time leading to the establishment of the Suncorp Super Netball League, in 2017 (Sherry & Taylor, 2019). Netball Australia, the national governing body for the sport of netball, continues to agree to increasingly attractive player contracts for athletes, which place an emphasis on improved pay and conditions (Netball Australia, 2016). Netball Australia's pay agreement in relation to Suncorp Super Netball players led to the first full-time wages being paid to women athletes who compete in an Australian women's sport league, with an average player wage of AU$52,000 per annum, and a minimum wage of AU$30,000 (Super Netball, 2018). Conditions of the contracts include additional remit for ambassador-related work, income protection in the case of injury or pregnancy and subsidy for private health insurance – an important but often overlooked condition in women's professional sport contracts (Super Netball, 2018). The wage increases and improved athlete conditions can be attributed to the collective bargaining agreement and negotiations of the Australian Netballer Players' Association, in conjunction with higher levels of sponsorship and broadcasting deals (Dabscheck, 2017).

Football (soccer)

Football dominates the professional sportscape globally, and the gender pay gap starts at the very top and trickles down to various local contexts. In Australia, the difference is player payments for national representative athletes in men's and women's teams is considerable. Currently, Australian players who play for the Matildas (the national women's team) will earn 10% of what their male counterparts do as representatives of the Socceroos (the national men's team), despite stronger performance demonstrated by the national women's team (Pockett, 2019). At the time this chapter was written, the Professional Footballers Association (PFA) is in the process of lobbying for equal rights and better conditions for Australian women athletes. A national women's football competition – the W-League – was established in Australia in 2007. Since its establishment, the wages for athletes in the W-League have ranged from AU$0 to AU$10,000 (Dabscheck, 2017). A new collective bargaining agreement was signed in 2017, which saw the average athlete salary increase from AU$7,000 to AU$15,500 with an extra AU$2,000 for the following season (Lulham, 2017). This brought the W-League into closer alignment with other Australian leagues, but still not close to parity with the Australian men's soccer league, the A-League.

Cricket

Cricket is a traditionally male-dominated sport in the Australian landscape. The national governing body for cricket in Australia, Cricket Australia, wanted to increase women's and girls' participation and engagement in the sport of cricket and, as a key component of this strategy, established a professional women's league – Women's Big Bash League (WBBL) – in 2015. Upon the launch of the WBBL, Cricket Australia's Executive General Manager, Operations was quoted as saying 'the major purpose of the WBBL is to inspire girls to play cricket' (Cricket Network, 2015, p. 5). The Australian Cricketers Association (ACA), in 2017, was a key voice in the establishment of the gender equity payment model; the negotiations also included upgrades to grassroots programmes and facilities (Ramsey, 2017a). The gender equity payment model was a large step in bridging the disparity between men's and women's remuneration in cricket. The gender equity payment model for WBBL players saw a rise from a minimum payment of AU$10,000 per season to AU$36,000 (Ramsey, 2017b). While the minimum wage for the WBBL and men's Big Bash League (BBL) is equal, the average men's wage in domestic professional cricket still remains higher. The case study at the end of this chapter will detail more about the role of the ACA in the negotiations and establishment of the new player agreements.

Australian Rules football

Australian Rules football is an Australian football code traditionally played by men; however, women have been competing in the sport in various ways since the early 1900s (Hess, 2011). In 2016, the national governing body for the sport, the Australian Football League (AFL) announced that an official women's league – the AFLW – would be launched in 2017. The AFLW issued licenses to a selection of teams in the long-established men's league to operate a women's team in the inaugural season. Grassroots participation initiatives, designed to stimulate girls' participation in football that were promised by the professional men's teams, were highlighted in the decision regarding which teams received licenses to operate a women's team. It was a requirement of license holders to support the establishment of grassroots participation through Next Generation Academies, the dedicated regional talent pathway and participation programmes (Pierik, 2017).

To sustain the investment and growth of the AFLW, a range of sponsorship deals and broadcast arrangements were made, with the majority of promotion and influence stemming from social media, critical for both the league and its clubs (Australian Football League, 2017). The AFL Players' Association played an integral part in the collective bargaining agreement for AFLW players, which ultimately determined the remuneration and conditions for women athletes in the league. In the inaugural season, AFLW players were contracted for a total of 24 weeks, with a minimum salary of AU$8,500 – the pro-rata equivalent to the first-year male athletes for an eight-week home-and-away season (Sewell, 2017). The establishment of the league has significantly increased women's participation, with 154% growth from the first three seasons (Sport Australia, 2019).

Influence on women's sport

While many of the abovementioned leagues are considered professional, as players are paid, this is a contentious point, given many of the women athletes are paid only small sums of money, which do not present a living wage and are not comparable to the rate of pay of men. Women athletes have taken several different strategies to subsidise income within their sport such as code-hopping and taking on development roles within the league itself (Dabscheck, 2017). Many have competed in multiple sport codes within the same year, or even season – something unique to the women's sport landscape – in an effort to supplement income and benefit from various development and representative opportunities. Elyse Perry is an example; Perry is an Australian athlete who simultaneously competes in the national level competitions of two sports, cricket (WBBL) and soccer (W-League). So-called code-hopping can have practical implications for women athletes. As wages for women athletes increase, so too will expectations and contractual arrangements likely become more complex, perhaps making it more difficult for athletes to compete at the highest level in more than one sport.

Despite recent advancements in the Australian landscape, the limited earning potential of women athletes impedes the viability of sport as a career option for the vast majority of women and girls. The role of players' associations is to provide athletes with a voice and various forms of support in relation to career development. Such support may include guidance on income, education and preparing athletes for retirement from the sport (Dabscheck, 1996). As the professionalisation of women's sport continues, the role of players' associations becomes increasingly critical to ensure the rights, financial arrangements and conditions of women athletes continue to improve (Dabscheck, 1996). The ability to generate income from elite sport is influencing the choice for participation of athletes on the talent pathway (Maynes, Mitchell, Schuwalow & Stewart, 2016). Sport leagues will need to distinguish the benefits of elite performance from other codes.

The establishment of professional women's leagues has beneficial flow-on effects for both talent pathways and the growth of grassroots participation for women and girls. Professional leagues necessitate the development of opportunities for young athletes to be discovered through talent pathways and dedicated talent development programmes. Such pathways do not exist without an elite pinnacle competition to aim for (Sotiriadou, 2009). National governing bodies are more likely to invest in women's development if the commercial viability of the professional women's competition depends on attracting the best and brightest talent into the sport. The growth patterns in the leagues described in this chapter, particularly in the sports of Australian Rules football and cricket, highlight the impact that a professional league can have on participation, with significant growth for women and girls participating in sport correlating with the establishment of the leagues. To ensure talented athletes are available to be selected in the elite, professional leagues, participation and development pathways for women and girls need to become more refined across different sports (Sotiriadou, 2009; Breitbarth & Harris, 2008).

Heroism of athletes and media exposure of sports are key elements to encouraging children and adults to play sport (Hogan & Norton, 2000; Cashman, 2006).

Grassroots participation is best harnessed through a dedicated sport development programme underpinned by a professional league, a phenomenon not unique to women's sport (Breitbarth & Harris, 2008). Supporting the literature, women's professional sport league creation is strategically driven by the goal of growing grassroots participation for the respective sport. Each league has had an immediate influence on the participation and development of grassroots sports, with most success seen when professional clubs influence and nurture community programmes (Breitbarth & Harris, 2008; Alonso & O'Shea, 2012). Sport development programmes are most successful at growing sport participation when used in conjunction with the professional sport leagues, teams or events. National sport organisations are using the professionalisation of women's sport and the establishment of professional women's leagues to sustain and grow participation bases and deepen the future talent pool. Those Australian sports that have had professional women's leagues in place for longer periods of time, namely the sports of netball, football (soccer) and basketball, experience higher rates of female participation when compared with the sports of Australian Rules football and cricket, which have traditionally focused on male participation and development, and have only recently invested in pathways and professional leagues for women and girls (Ausplay, 2019b). Trends in participation suggest that the longer a professional sport league has existed, the greater likelihood of maintaining grassroots participation throughout adult years.

A key issue with the development of professional leagues can become the balance of elite talent versus grassroots participation. The continuum from participation through to elite – demonstrated through Gulbin, Croser, Morley and Weissensteiner (2013) FTEM model: Foundations, Elite, Talent, Mastery (FTEM) – demonstrates the relationship between the establishment of professional elite women's leagues and the need for talent pathways. It is important to ensure the connection between grassroots participation and elite sport is maintained. Practically, equal levels of investment for grassroots support through the creation of talent pathways underpins the future success of professional women's leagues. Using cricket versus Australian Rules football as an example here, the pay deal and remuneration for AFLW is less than that of elite cricketers; however, the impact on grassroots participation and ability to specifically target women and girls through the implementation of the league has a greater influence on female participation (Ausplay, 2019c; Ausplay, 2019d). The establishment of elite leagues has empowered many women and girls with the awareness and opportunity to participate in grassroots sport, breaking stereotypes of women's and girls' participation in competitive, typically male sports (Kerr, 2019).

Issues and opportunities for research

Opportunities exist for future research to examine the impact of the growth of professional women's sport leagues on the overall economics of sport (Dabscheck, 2017).

The disparity between women's and men's wages provides a need to understand how the conditions and terms of employment affect athlete wellbeing and likelihood to perform as an elite athlete in a particular sport (Dabscheck, 2017; Sotiriadou, 2009). Additionally, the connection between the role of players' associations, leagues and the impact on the athletes, with a focus on women's sport, could provide the industry with a deeper understanding of the impact players' associations can have on the women athletes and their respective leagues and teams (Maynes, et al., 2016). Talent pathways are integral for the future of women's sport; further exploration is needed on the impact of financial and other contractual arrangements of different leagues on the sporting decisions of younger athletes throughout the talent pathways and across sports, including code-hopping (Sotiriadou, 2009; Breitbarth & Harris, 2008). Existing research can be deepened to understand the effect of the wage disparity and conditions as drivers for engagement in talent pathways. The exposure of young girls to strong women athletes and role models appears to have a practical influence on the growth of participation (Cashman, 2006). Further research can assist in understanding the link between women's professional leagues and the leagues' position in leveraging opportunities for long-term, sustainable grassroots participation. Opportunities exist to compare differences between women and men in motivations to participate in sport, specifically identifying the role that professional leagues play in shaping participation, perceptions and cultural norms in relation to sport (Kerr, 2019).

Practical actions

The rise of professional women's leagues has practical impacts for national governing bodies, players' associations and leagues. As the demands and pressures placed on women athletes increase, so too do the roles of professional players' associations and well-negotiated bargaining agreements. The case study on women's cricket that follows is a great example of a step taken in the direction of players' associations supporting athletes and fostering grassroots participation. There is a need for professional leagues and teams to work in consultation with athletes through players' associations to ensure fair and equitable arrangements are provided to support women athletes. This will include considerations such as maternity leave arrangements, pay increases, insurance, training and athlete appearance restrictions that facilitate study or outside work commitments, until women athletes receive full-time wages. The Netball Australia pay deal for athletes was one of the first agreements in Australian sport to consider such conditions. The agreement included set training times that allowed athletes to balance outside work and study commitments, and also included a maternity clause providing income protection. Cricket Australia and Netball Australia appear to be leading the way in the negotiations with women athletes, with other leagues starting to follow suit.

Sport governing bodies, leagues and players associations have an opportunity to work together to ensure the sustainability of professional women's leagues in the future. Collaboratively, they can further understand the development needs of women athletes. Players' associations should be used as a tool to help ensure the salary packages and pay deals for athletes continue to grow. This will have an impact on the development and growth of the talent pathways for women and girls. The players associations also have a large impact on the links between national team salary packaging and the league itself. Packaging between national teams and leagues provides opportunity for sports to gain a competitive advantage over leagues without a national talent pathway – for example, the connection between Super Netball League and the national netball team. Standalone leagues, such as the AFLW, will have to consider how to differentiate salary and terms of athlete agreements to sustain their talent pathway (Sotiriadou, 2009). The need for more depth in talent influences the allocation of government funding relating to both participation and high performance (Sport Australia, 2019), as well as how player association and leagues manage their negotiations.

This chapter has used Australian examples of netball, basketball, football, cricket and Australian Rules football to highlight the connection between women's professional leagues, women athletes and players' associations. Sports can leverage the positive momentum of women's professional sport to grow their grassroots participation base. The FTEM demonstrates the continuum of development from grassroots to elite sports and asserts the importance of balancing organisational focus and finances across the entirety of the sport (Gulbin, et al., 2013). Opportunity exists for other sports to build off the learnings of sports with existing talent pathways. The following case study provides an overview of the role the Australian Cricketers Association plays in the development of women's cricket and the negotiations with Cricket Australia to ensure equity within the sport.

CASE STUDY

Australian Women's Big Bash League

In 2015, the Women's Big Bash League (WBBL) was introduced into the Australian sport landscape. Professional women's cricket was not a new phenomenon, with elite women cricketers representing Australia different forms of cricket – One Day International cricket (ODI) and International Twenty-over Cricket (T20I) – on the global stage. However, this was the first professional league in Australia for women cricketers. When the WBBL was first introduced, a 9% growth in girls participating in youth cricket across Australia was recorded (Cricket Network, 2016). In 2019, women and girls make up 30% of overall cricket participants, up from 24% in 2015 (Cricket Network 2018; 2016). In 2015, Cricket Australia's CEO confirmed,

> The Women's Big Bash League also achieved impressive results in just its first season. We were able to demonstrate a viable pathway for girls and women to pick up a bat and ball and take up cricket as a professional sport.
> *(Cricket Network, 2016, p. 16)*

In the inaugural year of the WBBL, broadcasting rights were negotiated with one major Australian broadcast network; various sponsorship agreements were in place and the season ran in parallel with the men's BBL (Cricket Australia, 2015). Women cricketers were paid a minimum of $7,000 per season, which increased to $10,000 throughout the early years of the league (ABC, 2017). The agreement included different payment structures for those who play other forms of cricket for the national or state representative teams (Cricket Australia, 2015). For those cricketers not representing Australia, the conditions were limiting. Extensive training commitments and player appearances were not commensurate with the level of pay received by athletes. Previously, women cricketers were not adequately represented in previous contractual agreements, the Memorandum of Understanding (MOU); there was disconnect between the needs of women cricketers and cricket's administration (Nicholson, 2015). In 2017, the ACA entered into negotiations with Cricket Australia for the latest bargaining agreement, or in cricket's case, the MOU.

The role of the ACA in the negotiations is to ensure the fair and equitable treatment of athletes, including revenue sharing and contract terms for cricketers in Australia. The ACA comprises the current leaders in the men's and women's national cricket team and executive staff of the ACA who contribute to the negotiations. The ACA had several clear set objectives to achieve leading into the MOU negotiations with Cricket Australia. These objectives include, but are not limited to:

- A partnership based on revenue sharing
- Inclusiveness of women/girls and men/boys
- A gender equity payment model
- Higher investment into grassroots cricket
- Greater input into the cricketing schedule
- Greater collaboration on the retirement scheme

(ACA, 2018a)

The ACA represents all athletes, both male and female, in contract negotiations, ensuring athletes receive fair treatment, conditions and payment. As a result of the 2017 negotiations, a "ground-breaking' agreement was reached in the sport of cricket, taking the form of a 'gender equity payment model' (Ramsey, 2017a). The gender equity payment model sees a minimum AU$36,000 salary being paid to any cricketer playing in the WBBL, including provision of health insurance (Ramsey, 2017b). By comparison, AFLW players receive a minimum wage of AU$9,276, not including health insurance, for a seven-match home-and-away season. The W-League players (soccer) receive a minimum of AU$10,000, with no health insurance for a twelve-match season (SBS, 2017). In addition to the improved salary conditions for women cricketers, a grassroots investment fund was agreed to in the MOU. The fund is a joint contribution of ACA and Cricket Australia to support and invest in local cricket with the aim of inspiring generations of future cricketers (My Cricket Community, 2019).

The MOU is in place until 2022. There is a combined payment structure for those who are representing Australia nationally or in a state-based competition as well as the WBBL. The gender-based equity structure is a payment model that takes into consideration hours worked, premiums for Australian players and the commercialisation of the competition, which includes protected hours for those who are employed as part time domestic athletes (ACA, 2018b). The model has been established in conjunction with industrial relations and discrimination experts, reviewed by the Fair Work Commission (ACA, 2018b). The inclusion in the gender equity model include:

- Women's National Cricket League (WNCL) and WBBL prize money
- Match fees
- Retirement fund
- Marketing and performance pools
- Injury payments
- Visitor periods for player families and partners
- Payments for captain allowance

(ACA, 2018b)

The gender equity payment model and overall MOU for women cricketers and women athletes in general is a step forward in equity and development in sport. As noted earlier, the economic viability can play a role in the choices of athletes early on in the talent pathway (Maynes, et al., 2016). The MOU has triggered negotiations and increasingly competitive wages across several other women's leagues, adding to the tension between codes in the competition for talent from a smaller pool of female athletes (Dabscheck, 2017). The national and state teams provide a competitive advantage and opportunity for cricket athletes to be amongst some of the highest paid in Australia.

References

ABC. (2017). *Cricket Pay Deal Huge for Women as Australia's Female Cricketers get Massive Windfall*. Retrieved from www.abc.net.au/news/2017-08-03/cricket-pay-deal-lauded-womens-pay/8772186

ACA. (2018a). *Heads of Agreement Reached in MOU Negotiation*. Retrieved from www.auscricket.com.au/news-media/news-articles/heads-of-agreement-reached-in-mou-negotiation

ACA. (2018b). *ACA Agreement Infographic*. Retrieved from www.auscricket.com.au/media/749852/aca-agreement-infographic-final.pdf

Alonso, A. D., & O'Shea, M. (2012). 'You only get back what you put in': Perceptions of professional sport organizations as community anchors. *Community Development*, 43(5), 656–676.

Ausplay. (2019a). *Netball State of Play Report: Driving Participation and Engagement*. Retrieved from www.clearinghouseforsport.gov.au/__data/assets/pdf_file/0003/821991/State_of_Play_Report_-_Netball.pdf

Ausplay. (2019b). *Australia's top 20 Sports and Physical Activities Revealed.* Retrieved from www.sportaus.gov.au/media_centre/news/australias_top_20_sports_and_physical_activities_revealed

Ausplay. (2019c). *Cricket State of Play Report: Driving Participation and Engagement.* Retrieved from www.clearinghouseforsport.gov.au/__data/assets/pdf_file/0004/821983/State_of_Play_Report_-_Cricket.pdf

Ausplay. (2019d). *Australian Football State of Play Report: Driving Participation and Engagement.* Retrieved from www.clearinghouseforsport.gov.au/__data/assets/pdf_file/0010/821980/State_of_Play_Report_-_Australian_Football.pdf

Australian Football League. (2017). *2016 AFL Annual Report.* Retrieved from http://s.afl.com.au/staticfile/AFL%20Tenant/AFL/Files/Images/compressed_2016-AFL-Annual-Report%20(1).pdf

BasketballAustralia. (2009). *Making your Career in Basketball: A guide to the Australian Basketball Pathway.* Retrieved from http://websites.sportstg.com/get_file.cgi?id=502401

Breitbarth, T., & Harris, P. (2008). The role of corporate social responsibility in the football business: Towards the development of a conceptual model. *European Sport Management Quarterly*, 8(2), 179–206.

Cashman, R. (2006). *Olympic Legacy: The Bitter-Sweet Awakening.* Sydney: Walla Walla Press.

CricketAustralia. (2015). *Schedule, Broadcast, First Players Announced for Women's Big Bash League.* Retrieved from www.cricketaustralia.com.au/media/media-releases/schedule-broadcast-first-players-announced-for-womens-big-bash-league/2015-07-10

CricketNetwork. (2015). *Rebel Throws Support Behind Women's BBL.* Retrieved from www.cricket.com.au/news/rebel-new-name-rights-sponsor-womens-big-bash-league-wbbl01-meg-lanning-ellyse-perry-alyssa-healy/2015-11-25

CricketNetwork. (2016). *Cricket becomes Australia's No.1 Participation Sport.* Retrieved from www.cricket.com.au/news/cricket-australia-census-participation-numbers-women-men-children-james-sutherland/2016-08-23

CricketNetwork. (2018). *Cricket Participation Reaches New Heights.* Retrieved from www.cricket.com.au/news/cricket-australia-national-cricket-census-participation-ceo-james-sutherland/2018-09-06

Dabscheck, B. (1996). Playing the team game: Unions in Australian professional team sports. *Journal of Industrial Relations*, 38(4), 600–628.

Dabscheck, B. (2017). *Building Momentum: The Evolution of Women's Wages in Australian Professional Team Sports.* Retrieved from www.lawinsport.com/topics/features/item/building-momentum-the-evolution-of-women-s-wages-in-australian-professional-team-sports

Downward, P., & Dawson, A. (2000). *The Economics of Professional Team Sports.* London: Routledge.

Frawley, S., & Cush, A. (2011). Major sport events and participation legacy: The case of the 2003 Rugby World Cup. *Managing Leisure*, 16(1), 65–76.

Gearin, M. (2016). *Netball Pay Deal: Athletes Set to Earn Double the Previous Minimum wage.* Retrieved from www.abc.net.au/news/2016-09-14/new-landmark-pay-deal-for-australian-netballers/7842660

Gladden, J., & Sutton, W. (2014). Professional sport. In P. M. Pederson & L. Thibault (eds) *Contemporary Sport Management* (pp. 218–239). Champaign: Human Kinetics.

Gulbin J., Croser, M. J., Morley, E. J., & Weissensteiner, J. R. (2013). An integrated framework for the optimisation of sport and athlete development: a practitioner approach. *Journal of Sports Sciences*, 31(12), 1319–1331.

Hess, R. (2011). Playing with 'patriotic fire': Women and football in the Antipodes during the Great War. *The International Journal of the History of Sport*, 28(10), 1388–1408.

Hogan, K., & Norton, K. (2000). The 'price' of Olympic gold. *Journal of Science and Medicine in Sport*, 3(2), 203–218.

Kerr, J. (2019). The multifaceted nature of participation motivation in elite Canadian women rugby union players. *International Journal of Sport and Exercise Psychology*. Advanced online publication. doi:10.1080/1612197X.2019.1611904

Lulham, A. (2017). W-League players kick goal with landmark deal struck. *Daily Telegraph*. Retrieved from www.dailytelegraph.com.au/sport/swoop/wleague-players-kick-goal-with-landmark-deal-struck/news-story/84aa2191c160e8defad5717b2a440eb7

Maynes, G., Mitchell, H., Schuwalow, P., & Stewart, M. (2016). If you want to play sport professionally, which sport should you choose? In M. Barry, J. Skinner & T. Engelberg (eds) *Research Handbook of Employment Relations in Sport* (pp. 250–272). Cheltenham: Edward Elgar Publishing Limited.

McLachlan, F. (2019). It's boom time! (again): Progress narratives and women's sport in Australia. *Journal of Australian Studies*, 43(1), 7–21.

My Cricket Community. (2019). *Grassroots Community Fund*. Retrieved from www.community.cricket.com.au/clubs/facilities/grassroots-cricket-fund

NetballAustralia. (2016). *New National Netball League – What You Need to Know*. Retrieved from http://netball.com.au/new-national-netball-league-need-know/

Nicholson, A. (2015). *ACA Looks to a Women's MOU*. Retrieved from www.auscricket.com.au/news-media/news-articles/aca-looks-to-a-womens-mou

Pierik, J. (2017, August 14). AFL clubs weigh up new pathway program. *The Age*. Retrieved from www.theage.com.au/afl/afl-news/afl-clubs-weigh-up-new-pathway-program-20170814-gxvj0o.html

Pockett, D. (2019). *PFA Launches Campaign for Pay Equity in Men's and Women's Soccer on Eve of Women's World Cup*. ABC. Retrieved from www.abc.net.au/news/2019-06-04/pfa-steps-up-fight-for-world-cup-equity-for-matildas/11177058?pfmredir=sm

Ramsey, A. (2017a). *CA, ACA Agree Terms to End Pay Dispute*. Retrieved from www.cricket.com.au/news/pay-dispute-mou-deal-cricket-australia-aca-ca-bangladesh-tour-revenue/2017-08-03

Ramsey, A. (2017b). *Dust Settles as MOU Agreement Finalised*. Retrieved from www.cricket.com.au/news/james-sutherland-mou-finalised-strategy-australian-cricket-ceo-future/2017-09-07

SBS. (2017). *Explainer: How the New W-League Pay Deal Stacks Up to Other Sports*. Retrieved from https://theworldgame.sbs.com.au/explainer-how-the-new-w-league-pay-deal-stacks-up-to-other-sports

Sewell, E. (2017) AFL agrees to new deal that will see every AFLW player earn more in season two of competition. *Herald Sun*. Retrieved from www.heraldsun.com.au/sport/afl/aflw/afl-agrees-to-new-deal-that-will-see-every-aflw-player-earn-more-in-season-two-of-competition/news-story/b919a9cc29d0fa24f43a9f99dd7a2be4

Sherry, E., & Taylor, C. (2019). Professional women's sport in Australia. In N. Lough & A. Geurin, *Routledge Handbook of the Business of Women's Sport* (pp. 124–133). Oxon, Milton Park: Routledge.

Shilbury, D., & Ferkins, L. (2011). Professionalisation, sport governance and strategic capability. *Managing Leisure*, 16(2), 108–127.

Smart, B. (2005). *The Sport Star: Modern Sport and the Culture Economy of Sporting Celebrity*. Nottingham: Sage.

Sotiriadou, K. (2009). The Australian sport system and its stakeholders: Development of cooperative relationships. *Sport in Society*, 12(7), 842–860.

Sport Australia. (2019). *NSO Investment Announcements*. Retrieved from www.sportaus.gov.au/grants_and_funding/investment_announcements

Super Netball. (2017). *Season 2018 Revealed*. Retrieved from https://supernetball.com.au/2017/10/11/season-2018-revealed/

Super Netball. (2018). *Suncorp Super Netball Player Payment Rise In 2019*. Retrieved from https://supernetball.com.au/2018/06/20/suncorp-super-netball-player-payment-rise-in-2019/

Uluc, O. (2019). *WNBL and Australian Basketballers' Association Secure Increased Minimum Player Payment*. Retrieved from www.foxsports.com.au/basketball/wnbl/wnbl-and-australian-basketballers-association-secure-increased-minimum-player-payment/news-story/24f3890bd919315f9358f6da2b695771

Willson, M., Tye, M., Ely-Harper, K., & Leaver, M. (2017). Framing the women's AFL: Contested spaces and emerging narratives of hope and opportunity for women in sport. *Sport in Society*, 21(11), 1704–1720.

WNBL. (2017). *WNBL Media Guide 2017/18*. Retrieved from http://wnbl.com.au/assets/14766_baskaus_wnbl-media-guide_2017-18_final_high-res.pdf

20

DEVELOPING SPORT FOR WOMEN AND GIRLS

Media influence

Merryn Sherwood

Introduction

Traditional sports media products – newspapers, radio and television – have historically not covered women's sports. When they have, coverage has often seen women athletes and the sport they play trivialised and sexualised. Needless to say, this has potential detrimental effects on women's participation in sport, as a result of the negative effects these images have on women's body satisfaction and self-esteem. But in the twenty-first century, there are signs that legacy media coverage is changing and is focusing on women as athletes first. At the same time, the powerful reach of traditional media, also referred to as legacy media, has been disrupted by digital technology, and social and digital media have allowed new narratives to form. While the advent of social and digital media has lowered the barrier of entry for those wanting to create media content and has given both organisations and individuals the ability to change the traditional media paradigm around women athletes and women's sport, these platforms are also problematic in that they allow participants to post directly to the public, and the public to respond, without any filters. In this chapter, these important changes in the media landscape are discussed in relation to sport for women and girls.

Where are the women? Media representation

Decades of international sports media research has found that elite women athletes and women's sports receive less mainstream media coverage than men athletes and men's sports, in contexts such as the US, UK, New Zealand, and Poland (Cooky, Messner, & Hextrum, 2013; French, 2013; Godoy-Pressland, 2014; King, 2007; Zbigniew, Organista, & Mazur, 2019). The seminal work in the US has been led by Cooky and Messner, and their analysis of news broadcasts found that the percentage of media sports coverage of women's sport in the US has trended down over time

(Cooky, Messner, & Musto, 2015). In Australia, one study found that horse-racing received more television coverage than women's sports and women athletes (Lumby, Caple, & Greenwood, 2014). However it is not simply the lack of coverage of women's sports that has side-lined women athletes in sport media, but that when they are represented, they are often characterised by personality, rather than their athletic ability, and they are sometimes presented in a sexualised manner (Bernstein, 2002; Fink, 2015; Wensing & Bruce, 2003), and, more often than not, their achievements are trivialised. This trivialisation includes gendered language; an example is provided by UK columnist Simon Barnes's description of one of Lindsey Davenport's tennis matches as an 'embarrassing ladies-excuse-me of a match: two silly girls taking it in turns to give each other points' (Vincent, 2004, p. 442). Research that examines sports commentary has found significant differences in the way men's and women's sports are covered (Jones, Murrell, & Jackson, 1999). For example, analysis of the National Collegiate Athletic Association (NCAA) final four basketball tournament found that the men athletes were primarily described in terms of physicality and athleticism, whereas the women athletes were categorically evaluated in terms of a) positive consonance, b) personality, c) looks and appearance, and d) background (Billings, Halone, & Denham, 2002). Athletes that meet stereotypical ideas of feminine beauty and compete in feminine sports are also likely to gain more media coverage and that coverage is more likely to be more positive (Fink & Kensicki, 2002). When women are presented in images in sports media, it has often been with non-competitive images that may also be sexualised (Duncan, 1990; Messner, Duncan, & Cooky, 2003). Women's sport and women athletes have consistently been framed differently to men.

What happens if women aren't seen? Media influence on participation

Research indicates that this media coverage – both the overall lack and its trivialised nature – has a potential impact on women's participation in sport. More broadly, systematic reviews of media effects literature indicate that the stereotypical, slender, supermodel images of women presented across mass media have a negative effect on body image (Grabe, Ward, & Hyde, 2008; Holmstrom, 2004; Groesz, Levine, & Murnen, 2002). Work that examines the specific impact of images on women athletes indicates similar trends. Further, it is found that exposure to images of athletes in action – that is, athletes competing – has the opposite effect (Daniels, 2009; Smith, 2016). Daniels (2009) examined women's responses to both sexualised and non-sexualised images, and found that portrayals of women athletes in action – that is, performance athletes – triggered less self-objectification in women viewers, while sexualised depictions of women athletes prompted more self-objectification. Yet there is also research that indicates that while women themselves preferred images of women athletes in action, they were also wedded to the idea that 'sex sells' in women's sport. Kane, LaVoi and Fink (2013) found that women most closely identified with women in action images and highlighted that those were best to increase respect of sport; however, almost half of the respondents in the study picked a range of 'soft-porn' images as those that would be best to increase interest. That a significant proportion of women athletes believe that 'sex sells' is a good approach for women's sport, indicates the problematic nature of sexualised content and how the sexualisation of women has become institutionalised in a patriarchal society. While there remains little research to directly link media influence and sport participation, and the 'trickle-down' effect is largely extremely difficult to measure, the extensive body of literature establishes that women generally do not feel good about themselves after engaging with mass media generally, and women athletes report the same after engaging with a sport media that reduces them to stereotypes.

Are we there yet? No, but perhaps it's starting to change

Recently, however, there is evidence that the type of coverage has changed. Sports mega events, such as Olympic and Paralympic Games, and FIFA football World Cups, have often bucked the trend of regular daily news coverage (Delorme, 2014). Sometimes, this is because other dominant frames take priority; Wensing and Bruce (2003), for example, found that Cathy Freeman's symbolic role in national reconciliation during the Sydney 2000 Olympic Games displaced gender as the primary frame. But generally, since 2010, research into media coverage of women's sport is less likely to find outright examples that trivialise and sexualise athletes. Petty and Pope's (2019) examination of British media coverage of the FIFA Women's World Cup found that most major English newspapers covered it regularly for the duration of the tournament, positioned women's coverage on both front and back pages, and included photographs and descriptions that framed women's performance by athletic skill first. In a sense, the women's football coverage had taken on the same shape as that of the men's, even if it was not equal in terms of volume of coverage. A study of netball coverage in Australia noted that, while there were some examples of women athletes being presented as mother figures over athletes – which is a frame not often invoked for athletes who are men, even if they are a parent – generally, athlete-first coverage had been adopted (English, Calder, Pearce, & Kirby, 2019). A review of sports images in Australia also found very little evidence of sexualised stereotyping of women (Sherry, Osborne, & Nicholson, 2015). Even Cooky, Messner and Musto's (2015) long-term study found in its most recent update that the sexualisation of female athletes was scarce; however, they noted it had instead been replaced by not showing women at all. In order to examine how it is that the type of coverage has changed, but the volume has not, we need to examine the three factors that created an imbalanced media landscape to begin with.

What has changed? The routinised nature of sport news

Essentially, research that examines why sports media is so focused on male professional sport indicates it is a combination of the male-dominated nature of sports newsrooms, the ingrained assumptions about readership and/or viewership and specific work routines of sports departments (Sherwood, Osborne, Nicholson, & Sherry, 2017). At the turn of the twenty-first century, research indicated that the people in charge of media making decisions were mostly men, and those men still believed women's sport was less worthy than men's. A survey of US newspaper editors in 2002 found that nearly a third believed that women were 'naturally less athletic and less interested in sports than are men' (Hardin & Shain, 2005, pp. 71–72). An editor in Knoppers and Elling's (2004) study in The Netherlands stated:

> You select [sport news] using journalistic norms. That is why a men's tournament can be more important than a woman's event. The women's world championships in basketball just aren't as important as the men's championships. When you have to choose who gets seven minutes of air time and who gets four, then naturally the choice falls on the men.
>
> (p. 65)

Later in the twenty-first century, editors and journalists, in both France (Gee & Leberman, 2011) and Australia (Sherwood,, et al., 2017), have claimed newsworthiness was the major factor in deciding what to publish, regardless of gender. And Peeters and Elling's (2015) updated study on the way women's football has been reported in The Netherlands over time found that women's football has also been accepted as newsworthy, and is reported using similar professional norms to those used in men's sport.

These changes help explain how coverage of women's sport has become less trivialised and sexualised, but it is the routinised nature of sport news coverage that helps us to understand why men's sport still dominates the volume of coverage. Studies that have looked in detail at the construction of narratives around sport have found that it is almost exclusively focused on men's sport, but also that it is almost exclusively one type of coverage: match reviews and previews (Rowe, 2007). This is partly explained by the routinised nature of sports news. Journalists are assigned particular sports or teams in a system known as a 'beat' or 'round', and their job is to follow that particular round and file stories to meet regular deadlines. It is this system that prioritises news about those teams or sports, regardless of whether it is particularly newsworthy or not (Sherwood & Nicholson, 2017; Sherwood, et al., 2017). Men's professional sports organisations are usually the ones assigned to journalists to cover, and those organisations then help this cycle of news coverage by providing regular information subsidies – such as media releases and media conferences – that are neatly packaged pieces of information that readily become news (Sherwood & Nicholson, 2017; Theberge & Cronk, 1986). Men's sporting organisations have employed media relations managers to create and manage these information subsidies since the 1990s, which has further reinforced the hierarchy of coverage (Boyle & Haynes, 2006). Given that many of the elite women's leagues globally still see women athletes competing semi-professionally, they perhaps do not necessarily have the time or resources to engage in providing the same type of information subsidies as men's sport. Examining the daily working structure of sports news, it is easier to see how the ingrained, routinised nature of sports news coverage has proved difficult to change. Essentially sports coverage is stuck on a hamster wheel of its own making – where male professional sports are covered above anything else. However, in an age where the business model of mainstream media is in decline due to digital disruption, it also might be time to consider whether or not traditional media still has the most potential to influence women's and girls' participation in sport.

Social and digital media. What does it mean?

The development of digital and social media has meant the barriers of entry to creating media have been lowered dramatically. In the past, publishing media content was costly and required ownership of media; however, since the early 2000s, anyone with access to internet and a laptop could start a blog. The rapid development of smartphones and social media further increased this capacity from 2010, with social networks such as Facebook, Instagram and Twitter becoming key information-delivery sites. In some contexts, the majority of the public now go to social media to read news first, rather than media sites (Shearer, 2018).

Social and digital media have the ability to challenge the historical narrative around women in sport, particularly as they allow women athletes to present themselves on their own terms (Antunovic & Hardin, 2015; Bruce, 2016; Thorpe, Toffoletti, & Bruce, 2017). Legacy media is no longer the keeper of the 'gate' that determines what the public see. A common finding in analysis of sport blogs on non-mainstream sports, such as gymnastics, is that bloggers wanted to fill a gap not covered by mainstream media (Antunovic & Hardin, 2013; McCarthy, 2014). Analyses of social and digital media indicate how women – both those participating in alternative or non-mainstream sports (MacKay & Dallaire, 2012; Olive, 2015) and some of the world's most popular athletes (Toffoletti & Thorpe, 2018) – have used social and digital media to reframe traditional media discourses on gender. Importantly, social and digital media have also offered spaces for those even more marginalised communities, such as members of the LGBTIQ+ population. For example, analysis of US basketball player Brittany Griner's Instagram, including the public portrayal of her same-sex relationship with Glory Johnston, found it offered a chance to 'challenge the intersectional invisibility of Black lesbian sporting celebrities and discusses the implications of this visibility for similarly positioned LGB youth' (Chawansky, 2016). As well as athletes, sport organisations also have the ability to directly influence the viewability and framing of women's sports through their own social and digital platforms.

But there is also evidence that social media and digital media can reinforce previous stereotypes. Looking at ten popular sport blogs in 2008 in the US, Clavio and Eagleman (2011) found that women were not likely to appear often, but when they did, they were more likely to be depicted using a sexually suggestive photo. Coche's (2016) study on US Football Federation's (USSF) two Twitter accounts during major events found a gender gap between the tweets of the women's national team and the men's. Similar to the approach taken by traditional media, the teams' own organising body framed the women's team as less important than the men's, even though Coche's (2016) study was purposefully conducted at a time when women's soccer was supposed to be prominent. Research on athlete self-presentation on social media channels has indicated again that women themselves reinforce traditional stereotypes. In a study of eight popular Olympic athletes' self-presentation during 2013, Guerin-Eagleman and Burch (2016) found that the approach taken by women athletes in their sample was more likely to reflect the traditional practices of mainstream media outlets and that the athletes were more likely to post photos of themselves that depicted them in 'personal life' or where they were not in competitive mode (Geurin-Eagleman & Burch, 2016). Examination of the #fitspo hashtag (short for fitness inspiration) on the photo-sharing site Instagram, found it was dominated by one body type – thin and toned (Tiggemann & Zaccardo, 2018) – which has a potential negative effect on body image (Robinson, et al., 2017; Slater, Varsani, & Diedrichs, 2017). Therefore, while social media offers the chance for women to present themselves in a narrative of their own choosing directly to the public, it may still be a site in which problematic images presented in mainstream media are reinforced.

Another problematic area in social and digital media is the ability for the public to contact women directly, and initial research has found women are more likely to be attacked online (Sobieraj, 2018). A stark example of the negative impact on women in sport occurred in March 2019 when Australian broadcaster Channel 7 posted an action photo of AFLW player Tayla Harris, which it then removed because it attracted vile, sexist comments. While community support swelled – to the extent that Melbourne's most-circulated newspaper published a Tayla Harris poster and international news sites covered the story (Lewis, 2019) – the incident provides an example of how digital and social media are not always safe spaces for women.

Future research

As we approach the twentieth year of the twenty-first century, it is clear that the traditional media environment that has dominated the last half century of research has fragmented. It is in this context and environment that we need to consider how we undertake and understand research on women's sport and women athletes in the media, and also how this might impact on women's and girls' participation and involvement in sport. For example, the idea that 'you can't be what you can't see', is often invoked when lamenting the lack of traditional media coverage of female athletes and women's sport – but are print newspapers and television broadcasts still the most influential media? More research that examines where women and girls get their information about sport would be extremely valuable, so that efforts to direct change would be most effective. This is not to suggest that all traditional media research should cease, but we need better audience research to support it.

More attention could also be paid to sport organisations' media content and strategies. Sport organisations globally have now become their own publishers; research that examines how they create and manage content digital and social would offer key insights into the field. Comparisons of how sports organisations frame their men's and women's teams or athletes would be interesting; as Coche's (2016) study on the US national football teams Twitter found, women's teams may be side-lined even by their own governing body.

We also need to apply updated frameworks and methods to existing contexts. In particular, different feminist perspectives offer important insights into elite athletes' self-presentation strategies (Bruce, 2016; Thorpe, Toffoletti, & Bruce, 2017). In addition, more qualitative methods would be useful, as much of the research on women and media still focuses on content analysis; research that speaks directly to women and girls about their experiences of media coverage would add depth to this field.

Finally, research would also benefit from increasing diversity, particularly in terms of location and population. Much of the research is from the US, UK, Australia and New Zealand, and a wider international perspective on each context would be valuable. There is a need to focus more on media representations of groups that have received less attention in the literature, such as those within the LGBTIQ+ community and community sport participants.

Suggestions for action

It is fair to say that previous suggestions that place the emphasis on sport media to change the balance of their reporting have not been successful in changing the volume of coverage of women's sport and women athletes. Even direct action has not necessarily been successful: reflections on the introduction of Title IX – the US legislation that made it compulsory for women's college sports to receive the same funding and treatment as men's – indicated that journalists saw it had very little power to actually change their coverage (Antunovic, 2017). While we should not completely give up on influencing broader media narratives, given the potential declining power of legacy media, perhaps it is time to consider different forms of direct action that could be taken.

The twenty-first century now sees sport organisations in a previously unthinkable position. They do not need the media to communicate their message; instead, they have their own social and digital channels. Sport organisations themselves therefore now have the opportunity to more equally present their women's teams. This could take a range of forms, from allocating more equal media management resources to women's team, to increase the amount of content available through their own channels, through to overt actions designed to promote gender equality. For example, in 2017 Cricket Australia officially changed the name of its national teams to the Australian Men's Cricket Team and Australian Women's Cricket Team (ABC, 2017), challenging the assumption that the name the 'Australian cricket team' directly refers to the men.

Health promotion agencies may also play a role more directly influencing women's and girls' participation. A perfect example of this has been the Sport England This Girl Can, a campaign run in the United Kingdom, whose advertising featured a series of fun, upbeat videos that depicted regular women, of all shapes, sizes and ethnicities, taking part in exercise, and which was backed up by a network of programs to help women find opportunities to get active (Hills, 2017). The campaign has now extended to Australia (Whelan, 2019), run by Victorian health promotion agency VicHealth. We do not yet know if these direct actions by sport organisations or the use of social and digital media by health agencies to directly influence target populations have the potential to be more effective in changing women's and girls' sport participation than they are on influencing legacy media's coverage of women's sport. But, given that extensive academic research indicates traditional, legacy media coverage has not changed dramatically over time, it is worth exploring.

CASE STUDY

Changing traditional discourses through digital: *The Outer Sanctum* Podcast

The women behind *The Outer Sanctum* podcast always knew they had a different perspective on sport, but it took the introduction of digital technology for them to start sharing it.

The six Hawthorn (an Australian Rules football club) fans first started talking footy together on a Facebook messenger group chat. After an excerpt of that group chat was published in a book, an idea was floated to continue their partnership – why not start a podcast? For cofounder Emma Race, a radio producer who had recently taken a podcasting course, it was exactly the spark she needed. A week later Race set up recording equipment in her living room and sat down with sisters Lucy and Felicity and fellow footy fiends Alicia Sometimes, Nicole Hayes and Kate Seear, to record the first episode.

The podcast is not solely focused on women's sport, though it has devoted much of its coverage to the first AFLW league, but instead offers a female perspective on sport. Race said they wanted to be the voices they always wanted to hear:

> No one was talking about football the way we always had, not our partners or our friends. We'd known that for a really long time anecdotally. We felt underrepresented as fans, but I think we were hoping that someone else would start a show dissecting footy in the way we did. But it wasn't coming, and it had been a lifetime of waiting, and then podcasting made it seem really easy. It was the intersection of technology with timing of knowing that there was going to be a women's league coming which we were so excited about. We just thought, 'well we'll just have a go'.

The Outer Sanctum hit headlines shortly after its debut when the presenters collectively called out comments made by club president and AFL commentator Eddie McGuire. During a radio broadcast, McGuire had implied he would like to drown prominent football journalist Caroline Wilson. The *Outer Sanctum*'s condemnation of the comments and the misogynistic environment of professional sport led to widespread criticism and helped to force an apology from McGuire and others (ABC, 2016), though the presenters also found themselves the targets of that misogyny (Hayes, 2016).

Since then, the podcast has not just been covered by legacy media but has partnered with them. *The Outer Sanctum* joined Melbourne broadsheet newspaper *The Age* to cover the first AFLW season. Since 2017, the podcast has been produced by the ABC, Australia's national broadcaster. In partnering with traditional, legacy media, the podcast has created a public space for voices and issues previously on the periphery in sports media. In 2018, it won an award for best description of inclusive sport at the Sport Australia media awards.

> I can't imagine that there'll be anything else that happens in my working life that will ever be anything like the social change that we've created through *The Outer Sanctum*, so I feel really proud of it.

The Outer Sanctum is just one example of digital media products led by women in Australia that have subsequently found mainstream media homes. Another is *Ladies Who League*, initially a website and social media presence founded by rugby league fan Mary Konstantopoulos, which is now also an ABC podcast. Women's football website, *The Women's Game*, started by Ann Odong, was sold to niche publishing company NextMedia at the start of 2018. These are all successful examples of how social and digital media have the potential to bring new voices to the still largely male-dominated field of sports media.

References

ABC. (2016). Eddie McGuire apologises for comments about journalist Caroline Wilson drowning. *ABC News*. Retrieved from www.abc.net.au/news/2016-06-20/eddie-mcguire-apologises-caroline-wilson-drowning-comments/7524748

ABC. (2017). Southern Stars' name change "a big step towards gender equality" in cricket, captain Meg Lanning says. *ABC News*. Retrieved from www.abc.net.au/news/2017-06-08/southern-stars-name-change-a-big-step-towards-cricket-equality/8600716

Antunovic, D. (2017). "Just another story": Sports journalists' memories of Title IX and women's sport. *Communication & Sport*, 5(2), 205–225. https://doi.org/10.1177/2167479515603956

Antunovic, D., & Hardin, M. (2013). Women bloggers: Identity and the conceptualization of sports. *New Media & Society*, 15(8), 1374–1392. https://doi.org/10.1177/1461444812472323

Antunovic, D., & Hardin, M. (2015). Women and the blogosphere: Exploring feminist approaches to sport. *International Review for the Sociology of Sport*, 50(6), 661–677. https://doi.org/10.1177/1012690213493106

Bernstein, A. (2002). Is it time for a victory lap? *International Review for the Sociology of Sport*, 37(3–4), 415–428. https://doi.org/10.1177/101269020203700301

Billings, A.C., Halone, K.K., & Denham, B.E. (2002). 'Man, hat was a pretty shot': An analysis of gendered broadcast commentary surrounding the 2000 Men's and Women's NCAA Final Four Basketball Championships. *Mass Communication and Society*, 5(3), 295–315. https://doi.org/10.1207/s15327825mcs0503_4

Boyle, R., & Haynes, R. (2006). The football industry and public relations. In J. L'Etang & M. Pieczka (eds), *Public Relations. Critical Debates and Contemporary Practice* (pp. 221–240). Mahwah, NJ: London: Lawrence Erlbaum Associates.

Bruce, T. (2016). New rules for new times: Sportswomen and media representation in the Third Wave. *Sex Roles*, 74(7–8), 361–376. https://doi.org/10.1007/s11199-015-0497-6

Chawansky, M. (2016). Be who you are and be proud: Brittney Griner, intersectional invisibility and digital possibilities for lesbian sporting celebrity. *Leisure Studies*, 35(6), 771–782. https://doi.org/10.1080/02614367.2015.1128476

Clavio, G., & Eagleman, A. N. (2011). Gender and sexually suggestive images in sports blogs. *Journal of Sport Management*, 7(4), 295–304. https://doi.org/10.1123/jsm.25.4.295

Coche, R. (2016). Promoting women's soccer through social media: How the US federation used Twitter for the 2011 World Cup. *Soccer & Society*, 17(1), 90–108. https://doi.org/10.1080/14660970.2014.919279

Cooky, C., Messner, M. A., & Hextrum, R. H. (2013). Women play sport, but not on TV: A longitudinal study of televised news media. *Communication and Sport*, 1(3), 203–230. https://doi.org/10.1177/2167479513476947

Cooky, C., Messner, M. A., & Musto, M. (2015). "It's dude time!": A quarter century of excluding women's sports in televised news and highlight shows. *Communication & Sport*, 3(3), 261–287. https://doi.org/10.1177/2167479515588761

Daniels, E. A. (2009). Sex objects, athletes, and sexy athletes. *Journal of Adolescent Research*, 24(4), 399–422. https://doi.org/10.1177/0743558409336748

Delorme, N. (2014). Were women really underrepresented in media coverage of Summer Olympic Games (1984–2008)? An invitation to open a methodological discussion regarding sex equity in sports media. *Mass Communication and Society*, 17(1), 121–147. https://doi.org/10.1080/15205436.2013.816740

Duncan, M. C. (1990). Sports photographs and sexual difference: Images of women and men in the 1984 and 1988 Olympic Games. *Sociology of Sport Journal*, 7(1), 22–43.

English, P., Calder, A., Pearce, S., & Kirby, K. (2019). A new sporting horizon: A content analysis of Super Netball newspaper coverage. *Media International Australia*, 171(1), 110–124. https://doi.org/10.1177/1329878X18798696

Hardin, M., & Shain, S. (2005). Female sports journalists: Are we there yet? "No". *Newspaper Research Journal*, 26(4), 22–35.

Fink, J. S. (2015). Female athletes, women's sport, and the sport media commercial complex: Have we really 'come a long way, baby'? *Sport Management Review*, 18(3), 331–342. https://doi.org/10.1016/j.smr.2014.05.001

Fink, J. S., & Kensicki, L. J. (2002). An imperceptible difference: Visual and textual constructions of femininity in Sports Illustrated and Sports Illustrated for Women. *Mass Communication and Society*, 5(3), 317–339. https://doi.org/10.1207/s15327825mcs0503_5

French, S. (2013). Still not there: The continued invisibility of female athletes and sports in the New Zealand print media. *Media International Australia*, 148(1), 39–50.

Gee, B. L., & Leberman, S. I. (2011). Sports media decision making in France: How they choose what we get to see and read. *International Journal of Sport Communication*, 4(3), 321–343.

Geurin-Eagleman, A. N., & Burch, L. M. (2016). Communicating via photographs: A gendered analysis of Olympic athletes' visual self-presentation on Instagram. *Sport Management Review*, 19(2), 133–145. https://doi.org/10.1016/j.smr.2015.03.002

Godoy-Pressland, A. (2014). "Nothing to report": A semi-longitudinal investigation of the print media coverage of sportswomen in British Sunday newspapers. *Media, Culture and Society*, 36(5), 595–609. https://doi.org/10.1177/0163443714532977

Grabe, S., Ward, L.M., & Hyde, J.S. (2008). The role of the media in body image concerns among women: A meta-analysis of experimental and correlational studies. *Psychological Bulletin*, 134(3), 460–476. https://doi.org/10.1037/0033-2909.134.3.460

Groesz, L., Levine, M.P., & Murnen, S.K. (2002). The effect of experimental presentation of thin media images on body satisfaction: A meta-analytic review. *International Journal of Eating Disorders*, 31(1), 1–16. https://doi.org/10.1002/eat.10005

Hayes, N. (2016). From the outer sanctum: What it's like to be called "excrement" by Sam Newman. Retrieved from www.theguardian.com/sport/2016/aug/12/from-the-outer-sanctum-what-its-like-to-be-called-excrement-by-sam-newman

Hills, L. (2017). This Girl Can has really made a difference to women in sport. Retrieved from https://theconversation.com/this-girl-can-has-really-made-a-difference-to-women-in-sport-82191

Holmstrom, A. J. (2004). The effects of the media on body image: A meta-analysis. *Journal of Broadcasting & Electronic Media*, 48(2), 196–217. https://doi.org/10.1207/s15506878jobem4802

Jones, R., Murrell, A. J., & Jackson, J. (1999). Pretty versus powerful in the sports pages. *Journal of Sport & Social Issues*, 23(2), 183–192. https://doi.org/10.1177/0193723599232005

Kane, M. J., LaVoi, N. M., & Fink, J. S. (2013). Exploring elite female athletes' interpretations of sport media images. *Communication & Sport*, 1(3), 269–298. https://doi.org/10.1177/2167479512473585

King, C. (2007). Media portrayals of male and female athletes: A text and picture analysis of British national newspaper coverage of the Olympic Games since 1948. *International Review for the Sociology of Sport*, 42(2), 187–199. https://doi.org/10.1177/1012690207084751

Knoppers, A., & Elling, A. (2004). "We do not engage in promotional journalism." Discursive strategies used by sport journalists to describe the selection process. *International Review for the Sociology of Sport*, 39(1), 57–73.

Lewis, A. (2019). Tayla Harris: How "repulsive" social media comments sparked outrage in Australia. Retrieved from https://edition.cnn.com/2019/03/20/sport/tayla-harris-photo-aflw-trolls-australia-spt-int/index.html

Lumby, C., Caple, H., & Greenwood, K. (2014). *Towards a Level Playing Field: Sport and Gender in Australian Media*.

MacKay, S., & Dallaire, C. (2012). Skirtboarder net-a-narratives: Young women creating their own skateboarding (re)presentations. *International Review for the Sociology of Sport*, 48(2), 171–195. https://doi.org/10.1177/1012690211432661

McCarthy, B. (2014). A sports journalism of their own: An investigation into the motivations, behaviours, and media attitudes of fan sports bloggers. *Communication & Sport*, 2(1), 65–79. https://doi.org/10.1177/2167479512469943

Messner, M.A., Duncan, M.C., & Cooky, C. (2003). Silence, sports bras, and wrestling porn. *Journal of Sport & Social Issues*, 27(1), 38–51. https://doi.org/10.1177/0193732502239583

Olive, R. (2015). Reframing surfing: Physical culture in online spaces. *Media International Australia*, 155, 99–107.

Peeters, R., & Elling, A. (2015). The coming of age of women's football in the Dutch sports media, 1995–2013. *Soccer and Society*, 16(5–6), 620–638. https://doi.org/10.1080/14660970.2014.963313

Petty, K., & Pope, S. (2019). A new age for media coverage of women's sport? An analysis of English media coverage of the 2015 FIFA Women's World Cup. *Sociology*, 53(3), 486–502.

Robinson, L., Prichard, I., Nikolaidis, A., Drummond, C., Drummond, M., & Tiggemann, M. (2017). Idealised media images: The effect of fitspiration imagery on body satisfaction and exercise behaviour. *Body Image*, 22, 65–71. https://doi.org/10.1016/j.bodyim.2017.06.001

Rowe, D. (2007). Sports journalism: Still the 'toy department' of the news media? *Journalism*, 8(4), 385–405.

Shearer, E. (2018). Social media outpaces print newspapers in the U.S. as a news source. Retrieved from www.pewresearch.org/fact-tank/2018/12/10/social-media-outpaces-print-newspapers-in-the-u-s-as-a-news-source/

Sherry, E., Osborne, A., & Nicholson, M. (2015). Images of sports women: A review. *Sex Roles*, 74(7), 299–309. https://doi.org/10.1007/s11199-015-0493-x

Sherwood, M., & Nicholson, M. (2017). Who controls sport news? Media relations and information subsidies in Australian sport media. *Media International Australia*, 165(1), 146–156. https://doi.org/10.1177/1329878X17713340

Sherwood, M., Osborne, A., Nicholson, M., & Sherry, E. (2017). Newswork, news values, and audience considerations: Factors that facilitate media coverage of women's sports. *Communication & Sport*, 5(6), 647–668. https://doi.org/10.1177/2167479516645535

Slater, A., Varsani, N., & Diedrichs, P. C. (2017). #fitspo or #loveyourself? The impact of fitspiration and self-compassion Instagram images on women's body image, self-compassion, and mood. *Body Image*, 22, 87–96. https://doi.org/10.1016/j.bodyim.2017.06.004

Smith, L. R. (2016). What's the best exposure? Examining media representations of female athletes and the impact on collegiate athletes' self-objectification. *Communication and Sport*, 4(3), 282–302. https://doi.org/10.1177/2167479515577080

Sobieraj, S. (2018). Bitch, slut, skank, cunt: Patterned resistance to women's visibility in digital publics. *Information Communication and Society*, 21(11), 1700–1714. https://doi.org/10.1080/1369118X.2017.1348535

Theberge, N., & Cronk, A. (1986). Work routines in newspaper sports departments and the coverage of women's sport. *Sociology of Sport Journal*, 3(3), 195–203.

Thorpe, H., Toffoletti, K., & Bruce, T. (2017). Sportswomen and social media: Bringing Third-Wave feminism, postfeminism, and neoliberal feminism into conversation. *Journal of Sport and Social Issues*, 41(5), 359–383. https://doi.org/10.1177/0193723517730808

Tiggemann, M., & Zaccardo, M. (2018). 'Strong is the new skinny': A content analysis of #fitspiration images on Instagram. *Journal of Health Psychology*, 23(8), 1003–1011. https://doi.org/10.1177/1359105316639436

Toffoletti, K., & Thorpe, H. (2018). The athletic labour of femininity: The branding and consumption of global celebrity sportswomen on Instagram. *Journal of Consumer Culture*, 18(2), 298–316. https://doi.org/10.1177/1469540517747068

Vincent, J. (2004). Game, sex, and match: The construction of gender in British newspaper coverage of the 2000 Wimbledon Championships. *Sociology of Sport Journal*, 21, 435–456.

Wensing, E. H., & Bruce, T. (2003). Bending the rules: Media representations of gender during an international sporting event. *International Review for the Sociology of Sport*, 38(4), 387–396.

Whelan, M. (2019). Ballarat mum Sharon Dundas rocks up to show This Girl Can. Retrieved from www.thecourier.com.au/story/5956523/ballarat-mum-sharon-dundas-rocks-up-to-show-this-girl-can-video/

Zbigniew, D., Organista, N. & Mazur, Z. (2019). Still marginalized: Gender inequalities in the largest Polish daily's sports coverage. *Communications*, 44(1), 33–57.

INDEX

Note: Page locators in **bold** refer to tables.

access to sport 10, 141; CALD women 87, 88, 89; equal 9, 10, 23; 'low SES' communities 113, 115, 116; mothers 35, 38; older women 48, 50; women with disabilities 60
'active ageing' 45–46
Active Herts programme 50
adolescent girls *see* girls and adolescents
agency, structure and empowerment 124–126, 132
Allison, R. 24, 25
American Development Model (ADM) 8
Amnesty International 126, 129
Anderson, R. 177
Annetts, D. 74–75
anterior cruciate ligament (ACL) injuries 179
athlete-centred coaching approach 180–181
athlete protection and duty of care 197–208; actions and recommendations 203–204; Bangladesh Weightlifting Federation 204–205; bullying 200, 203, 204; disordered eating 201, 203; drug use 201–202, 203–204; future research 202; impacts of lack of 197–198, 204; Larry Nassar 205; literature review 198–202; sexual harassment 198–200, 202–203, 204–205; Yasemin Brown 205
Atkinson, J, 98
Auburn Tigers 92
Australia: Active Women and Girls for Health and Wellbeing programme 24; AFL for Muslim women 92–93; Ashleigh Barty case study 105–106; Ballarat women's and girls' cricket 27–28; Bowling with Babies 168; CALD women and sport 37, 85, 87–89, 90, 92–93; education system and participation pathways 11–12; FTEM model 1, 8, 173–174, 228; Good Wheel cycling programme 117–118; growth in women's sport 182; indigenous women and sport 95, 96–97, 97–98, 102, 103–104, 138, 165; Lakemba Sport and Recreation Club (LSRC) 87–89; LGBT+ inclusion, promoting 69–82; marriage equality campaign 69; media coverage of women's sport 237, 238, 241; mothers and participation in sport 37, 39, 168; older women participation trends 46; *The Outer Sanctum* Podcast 243–244; partnerships 127, 168; Pride in Sport Index 70; professional women's sport leagues 223–235; Rock Up Netball 168; soccer mums programme 41–42; Swim Sisters group 90; Talent Search Day 174; This Girl Can 62–63, 162, 168–169; volunteering mothers 37; Women's Big Bash League (WBBL) 230–232
Australian Cricketers Association (ACA) 226, 231, 232
Australian Football League Women's (AFLW) 13–14, 73, 241; injury risks

Index   249

179–180; *The Outer Sanctum* Podcast 243–244; pay and conditions 226, 228, 230, 231
Australian Institute of Sport (AIS) 173

Baby Ballers 39
Back on My Feet 116
Back to Netball (B2N) 39
Bahfen, N. 85, 86, 90, 92
Ballarat women's and girls' cricket 27–28
Bangladesh Weightlifting Federation 204–205
barriers to participation in sport 166; CALD women 86–87, 92; indigenous women 101; low-SES women 111–113, 116; mothers 34, 35, 36; older women 48; women with disabilities 60–62, 62–63; young and adolescent girls 20, 21–22
Barty, Ashleigh 105–106
basketball 25–26, 39, 224; officials 191, 192; walking 50; wheelchair 59, 60, 61, 63
binary sex, deconstructing 211–212
biomechanics **176**
Bitugu, B.B. 155, 156
Black and Minority Ethnic (BME) communities in UK 85
Blackwell, Alex 78
Blaschke, A. 205
Blinde, E.M. 60, 61
blogging 33, 39, 240
body awareness 34
body image 9, 20, 34; media and negative effects on 237, 241
Bowling with Babies 168
Brackenridge, C. 198, 199, 200, 201, 203, 204
British Columbia Wheelchair Sports Association (BCWSA) 63–65
Brown, Yasemin 205
bullying 200, 203, 204
Burch, L.M. 241

Canada: 'Actively Engaged' policy 9; indigenous women and sport 95, 96–97, 99, 102–103, 103–104, 138; sexual harassment policies 203; Sport for Life 8, 9; sport in school system 11; wheelchair sport, British Columbia 63–65
Canadian Association for the Advancement of Women and Sport and Physical Activity (CAAWS) 102, 103
Caperchione, C.M. 86, 89
CBS News 5
Chambers, R. 148, 149
Chand, Dutee 210, 214–215, 217, 219

charitable societies, disability sport 65
Cheng, J.E. 90
China, migrant women from 86
chromosome-based tests 212
clothing, accommodating 88
clubs, local and regional: female-friendly, positive environments 10–11, 23, 115; fostering inclusion 81, 87–89; role of 10
coaches 185–189; coach-athlete relationship 187–188, 199; coaching high-performance athletes 180–181; developing women 188–189; education 186–187; gendered nature of coaching 186–189; screening and monitoring 203; sexual harassment 199, 203, 205; skills for successful women's 182; UEFA women's EURO 193–194; underrepresentation of women 6, 185, 188–189, 193; volunteer mothers 37–38
Coche, R. 240–241, 242
code-hopping 227
Collins, P. Hill 213
Come Out to Play study 72
community, officials sense of 190–191
community sport 21, 26, 163–164; CALD women 84–85, 86, 87–89, 90–91; older adults 50, 51
competition, motivation of 51
conceptualising sport development 2–3
concussion 179
Conway, G.R. 148, 149
costs of participation in sport 11, 21–22, 89, 101
Court of Arbitration for Sport (CAS) 217; Chand appeal 210, 214–215, 217; Semenya appeal 210, 215
cricket: Ballarat women's and girls' 27–28; Girl's Empowerment through Cricket (GET) 126–131; LGBT+ inclusion in Australian women's 72, 73–79; national team names in Australia 242; professional women's 226, 228, 229, 230–232; Women's Big Bash League (WBBL) 226, 230–232
Cricket Australia (CA) 27, 73, 226, 229, 230, 231, 242
Cricket Network 226, 230
cultural facilitators 88
culturally and linguistically diverse (CALD) women and girls 83–94; Australian Rules Football case study 92–93; barriers to participation in sport 86–87, 92; future research 91; inclusive practices at LSRC 87–89; mothers with dependent children 36–37; motivations to participate in sport

85–86; new directions to enable and facilitate 90–91; older women 49; place of sport in lives of migrant women 84–85; policy approaches 89–90; understanding CALD women and girls 84–87; Widening Access through Sport initiative 137–138
curriculum: co-design of 138, 141; problematic issues 139
cyberbullying 200
cycling: Cycling Mums Australia 39; Good Wheel programme 117–118; talent identification 174

Dabscheck, B. 225, 227, 228, 229, 232
Daily Training Environment (DTE) 175, 177; high-performance athletes 177
Davenport, Lindsey 237
Denison, E. 72
Dickson, C. 59, 60
digital marketing for walking groups 52–54
digital media 236, 240–241; podcasts 243–244
disability, women and girls with a 57–68; barriers, recommendations to address 62–63; barriers to participation in sport 60–62; charitable societies 65; coaches and 186; feminist disability studies 58; funding 65; girls-only events 64, 65; motivations for participation in sport 58–60; research focused on male athletes 59; wheelchair sport case study 63–65
dropping out from sport 12–13, 20, 23, 138, 166, 204
drug use 201–202, 203–204
duty of care *see* athlete protection and duty of care

eating disorders 201, 203
economic independence 137, 157
education of women and girls 135–146; critiquing 138–140, 143–144; embodied learning 135–136; future research 140; Girl's Empowerment through Cricket (GET) sessions 127, 129–130; Go Sisters programme 140, 142–144; in HICs 137–138; learning through sport 135–136; in LMICs 136–137, 139–140; pedagogies to deliver programmes 140, 143; positive outcomes 137, 143; recommendations for practice 140–141; system providing pathways to sport participation 11–12
Edusport 142, 143
Edwards, M.B. 11, 45, 161, 163, 164, 165, 167

Eime, R.M. 19, 20, 21, 22, 23, 46, 47, 85, 111, 112, 113, 114, 163, 164
Elling, A. 238
employment *see* livelihoods, gender and sport
empowering women and girls 121–134; concepts of power, structure and agency 124–125, 132; education through sport and feelings of 137; employment and mechanisms for 155; future research 132; Girl's Empowerment through Cricket (GET) 126–128; Girl's Empowerment through Cricket (GET) outcomes 128–131; Go Sisters programme 142–144; literature review 122–124; practical actions for SFD interventions 132; a theory for empowerment 124–126; use and limitations of sport as a tool for 123–124
entry and exit points, multiple 8–9
Equal Play study 72

Fakier, F. 92
family: friendly programmes 39; planning a 9, 229
fan abuse 190
Fasting, K. 180, 198, 199, 200, 201, 203
Female Athlete Triad (FATr) 178
female-friendly environments 10–11, 23, 115
femininity: cards 212; 'pure' biological 213, 216; race, nation and biological 210, 212–213; restrictive notions of 60, 209–210, 211; young girls and concerns over 13
feminist disability studies 58
FIFA Women's World Cup 238
Fiji 149, 157–158
First Nations people 99
flag football 165
Flood, Naomi 174
Flying Bats 81
food and drink, culturally appropriate 88
football (soccer): Australian women's professional 225, 231; FIFA Women's World Cup 238; flag 165; lesbian involvement in women's 77–78; media coverage of women's 238, 239; Muslim women 85–86, 87–89; podcast 244; soccer mums programme 41–42; South African girls-only programme 136–137; Street Soccer USA 116; UEFA women's EURO 193–194; walking 49, 50
Forde, S.D. 129, 138, 139, 187
Frisby, W. 129, 136, 138, 139

FTEM (Foundations, Elite, Talent, Mastery) model 1, 8, 173–174, 228
fun and enjoyment, playing sport for 21, 22, 51, 59
funding disability sports 65

Gallant, D. 115
Garland-Thomson, R. 58, 65
gender eligibility regulation 210, 211–213
gender equality, Sustainable Development Goal 147
gender equity 1, 83; challenges to 9, 23; coaches' education in 187; MDGs, SDGs and promotion of 136; payment model 226, 231, 232
gender identity, inclusion based on 72–73
gender inequality 23; engaging men on 123, 131; in Papua New Guinea 126; practical actions for empowerment in relation to 132; in sports employment 150; using sport to challenge 151
gender, participation by 9
gender relations, disruption of traditional 128
gender segregation 11, 64–65, 88, 103, 136
gender stereotypes 22, 23, 48, 61, 80
gender verification 209, 211–212
Girl Effect movement 123
girls and adolescents 19–31; approaches to increase participation 24–26; cricket case study 27–28; optimal age of entry to sport 20; participation trends 19–21; sensitivity to girls' insecurities 12–13; sociological determinants for participation 21–23; transition from primary to secondary school 22–23
Girl's Empowerment through Cricket (GET) 126–128; disruption of traditional gender relations 128; education sessions 127, 129–130; outcomes 128–131
Girls Only Wheelchair Tennis programme 64
girls/women-only events 11, 21, 26, 27, 64–65, 88, 103, 136–137
Girls4Gold 174
Go Sisters programme 140, 142–144
Good Wheel cycling programme 117–118
Goodall, H. 98
Goolagong Cawley, Evonne 105–106
Grassroots Sites Netball Programme 102
Griffin, P. 71, 72
Griner, Brittany 240
Guagliano, J.M. 25–26
Guerin, B. 86
Guerin-Eagleman, A.N. 241
Gulbin, Jason 181–182

Ha, J. 122, 136
Hancock, M. 122, 136
Hanrahan, S.J. 177
Harris, Tayla 241
Harris, Toni 5–6
Hassan, Amna 92
Hayhurst, L. 97, 100, 101, 103, 121, 122, 123, 129, 132, 136, 137, 138, 139, 140
health: barriers to participation in sport 48; benefits for older people 47; sport for health movement 45–46; and wellbeing of mothers 34–35
Health Action Zones (HAZ) 89
health promotion through sport 161–171; connections between sport and health 162–165; elite sport prioritised over 164; future research 166–167; management of sport for 164–165; negative health outcomes and behaviours 161; partnerships 165, 168; psychological and social health benefits 163–164; targeting women and girls 166; This Girl Can campaign 24, 62–63, 162, 167–169, 242–243
Hershow, R.B. 136–137
Hickey, C. 72
high-performance athletes 7–8, 172–184; bullying of 200; coaching 180–181; concerns specific to women 178–180; Daily Training Environment (DTE) 175, 177; development 172–174; Female Athlete Triad (FATr) 178; FTEM model 173–174; future considerations 181; injuries to women 179–180; mothers with dependent children 35–36; prioritised over health promotion 164; sexual harassment risk 200; SMA symposium 181; sport psychology 177; Sport Science Sport Medicine (SSSM) 175–177, **175–176**; talent identification and development 174, 181–182, 227, 229; talent transfer 174, 182
Hillier, Lynne 77
HIV/AIDS education 136, 142
homeless women, developing sport for 116
homophobia in sport 71, 72; women's cricket 75–76, 77
hyperandrogenism, medical interventions for 211, 217
Hyperandrogenism Regulations 2011, IAAF 210, 213–219
Hyperandrogenism Regulations 2018, IAAF 210, 215
Hyperandrogenism Regulations 2012, IOC 214, 217–218

identity, sense of 33, 35–38, 39, 59
imagery 51, 80, 89, 167–168
India, migrant women from 87
indigenous women and girls 95–109; Ashleigh Barty case study 105–106; barriers to participation in sport 101; education programmes 138; effects of colonisation 95, 96, 104–105; enablers for participation in sport 99–101; future research 104; health promotion through sport 165; historical background 97–99; policy and future practice 103–104; sport and physical activity levels 96–97; sport programming 101–103
injuries 179–180
insecurities, addressing girls' 12–13
International Association of Athletics Federations (IAAF) 210, 212, 216, 217; Approved Specialist Reference Centres 217; Hyperandrogenism Regulations 2011 210, 213–219; Hyperandrogenism Regulations 2018 210, 215
International Olympic Committee (IOC) 209, 212; Hyperandrogenism Regulations 210, 214, 217–218
interpersonal determinants of participation 22, 113
intrapersonal determinants of participation 21–22, 112–113
Iran 155

Jeanes, R. 60, 87, 124, 135, 136, 137, 138, 139, 140, 142, 143, 149, 150, 151
Jordan-Young, R. 209, 213, 215, 216, 218

Kabeer, N. 122, 124, 125, 129, 131, 152
Karkazis, K. 209, 210, 211, 212, 213, 215, 216, 218
Kay, T. 121, 123, 124, 136, 137, 138, 148, 149, 150
Kellett, P. 8, 10, 189, 190
Kickett-Tucker, C. 100
Kitchener, K. 72
Knoppers, A. 186, 187, 239
Konstantopoulos, M. 244

Ladies Who League 244
Lakemba Sport and Recreation Club (LSRC) 87–89
language, inclusive 79–80
LaVoi, N.M. 37, 38, 186, 187, 237
leadership positions, women in 23, 150, 151, 204; CALD 88; GET programme and 127, 130; indigenous women 101; mothers in volunteer 37–38 *see also* coaches; officials
lesbians: championing contribution to cricket of 78–79; historical prejudice in cricket against 74–75; negative myths about 77; research on 71; stigma and discrimination in cricket 75–78
Lewis, B.S. 32, 34, 35
Lewis, G.E. 115
LGBT+ communities 69–82; affirming LGBTI+ athletes 80; building and supporting allies 80; focus on lesbians 71; gender identity, inclusion based on 72–73; inclusive language 79–80; institutional support 79; literature review 71–72; marketing and communications 80; recommendations and future research 79–81; social media 240; support and guidance 80–81; terminology 70–71; women's cricket case study 73–79
Lindsey, I. 140, 143, 144, 155, 156
livelihoods, gender and sport 147–160; concepts of employment, work and livelihoods 148; empowerment mechanisms 155; further research 152, 154–155; gender analysis frameworks 154–155; gender inequalities in 150, 151; limitations in creating employment 150; partnerships 155; recommendations 155–156; restrictions on women's opportunities 150–152, 153–154; rugby union remittances in Fiji 149, 157–158; SD, SFD and 149–150
London Sport 50, 51, 52–54
Long-Term Athlete Development (LTAD) model 8, 9, 173
low socio-economic and underserved communities 110–120; actions to address issues 114–116, 116–117; barriers to participation in sport 111–113, 116; defining 'low SES' 111; future research 114–115; Good Wheel cycling programme 117–118; homeless 116; literature review 110–113; prisoners 115; recommendations 116–117; reduced levels of participation 111–112; research challenges 113–114; socioecological model and understanding influences on physical activity 112–113
Lyras, A. 122, 135, 136

Magee, J. 87, 137, 149, 151
Mallett, C.J. 173, 177
Mandelbaum, B.R. 179

marketing: charitable societies 64, 65; to engage older women 51, 52–54; of female athletes 72; LGBT+ inclusion 80; This Girl Can campaign 24, 62–63, 162, 167–169, 242–243
masculinities 60, 137, 211
Masters sport 46, 49–50
maternity provisions 9, 229
McCallister, S.G. 60, 61
McGannon, K. 33, 34, 35, 36
McGuire, Eddie 243–244
media 236–247; campaigns 24; changes in legacy media coverage of women's sport 238, 240; future research 241–242; and government partnerships 62; legacy media coverage of women's sport 236–237, 240, 242, 243; negative influence on participation 237–238; *The Outer Sanctum* Podcast 243–244; recommendations 242–243; routinised nature of sport news 238–240; self-presentation on social 241; sexualised images of women athletes 237–238, 240; social and digital 240–241; sports commentary 237; volume of coverage of women's sport 239, 242
Meek, R. 115
menstrual history and irregularity 178–179
mentors 131, 188
Millennium Development Goals 135, 136, 185
Missy Wright, E. 111, 112, 113, 114, 115
mobility restrictions, women's 148, 152, **153**
modified sports 49, 50, 58, 165 *see also* wheelchair sport
Moser, C. 151
mothers with dependent children 32–44; actions to connect mothers to sport 39–40; body awareness 34; culture and ethnicity 36–37; elite athletes 35–36; further research 38–39; health and wellbeing 34–35; identity 35–38; involvement in LTPA and sport 33; recommendations 40, **40**; role models 36; sense of belonging 33–34; soccer mums case study 41–42; support networks 35, 37–38; volunteering 37–38
motivations for participation in sport: CALD women 85–86; girls and adolescents 21, 22, 23, 25, 26; girls and women with disabilities 58–60, 64; indigenous women 100–101; mothers with dependent children 33–38; older women 46–48
Mouncey, Hannah 73
Mountjoy, M. 197, 198, 203, 204

movement in and out of sport 8–9
Muir, K. 37, 83, 85, 87
Mukherjee, S. 179, 180
Mums Who Ball 39
Murray, Andy 80
Muslim women: Australian Rules Football case study 92–93; barriers to participation in sport 86–87, 92; challenging stereotypes 90; community sport 85, 86, 87–89, 90; fostering inclusion at a soccer club 87–89; future research 91; motivations for participation in sport 85–86; as role models 89, 90; Widening Access through Sport initiative 137–138
myths and perceptions of women in sport, challenging 6–7

Nassar, Larry 205
'natural' athletes 100
netball 225, 229; Back to Netball (B2N) 39; Grassroots Sites Netball Programme 102; media coverage in Australia 238; Rock Up Netball 168; sitting 50
Netherlands 238
Nordstrom, H. 185, 189, 191
Norman, L. 185, 186, 187, 188, 189
nutrition and dietetics **175**

Odong, Ann 244
Office for Women in Sport and Recreation (OWSR), Australia 61, 62
officials 189–194; fan abuse 190; recruitment of female referees 192; SD, SFD and 192–193; sense of community 190–191; UEFA women's EURO 193–194; women referee experiences 191; workplace incivility 191
older women 45–56; actions to address issues and service population 49–50; barriers to participation 48; culture and ethnicity 49; defining 'older adults' 46; designing and promoting programmes 50–52; digital marketing for walking groups 52–54; external partnerships 51–52; future research 49; motivations and benefits of sport participation 46–48; negotiating ageing process 47–48; sport for health movement 45–46; sport participation trends 46; volunteering 48–49
Olympic Games 174, 181, 212, 215, 238
organisational and environmental determinants of participation in sport 22–23, 113
'other,' women athletes as 186–187

Out in the Fields study 72
The Outer Sanctum Podcast 243–244

Pacific Island rugby 149, 157–158
Papua New Guinea: disruption of traditional gender relations 128; domestic violence 126, 129, 130; gender inequality 126; Girl's Empowerment through Cricket (GET) 127–128; Girl's Empowerment through Cricket (GET) outcomes 128–131
parental support 9, 22
Parpart, J.L. 124, 125, 131, 132
participation and inclusion in sport 2, 3; CALD women and girls 83–94; by gender 9; girls and adolescents 19–31; increases in women's 188; indigenous women and girls 95–109; LGBT+ communities 69–82; low socio-economic and underserved communities 110–120; media influence on 237–238; mothers with dependent children 32–44; older women 45–56; women and girls with a disability 57–68
participation opportunities and pathways 5–18; AFLW case study 13–14; challenges to 5–6; challenging myths and perceptions 6–7; future research 12; practical actions to address issues 12–13; role of education system in 11–12; sport organisations' roles in developing 7–11
partnerships 51–52, 62, 89, 102, 127, 132, 155, 156, 165, 168
Pawelski, J.O. 62
pay, women's 227, 230; basketball 224; cricket 226, 231, 232; netball 225, 229; soccer 225, 231
Pearce, S. 96, 102, 165, 238
Pearson, N. 24, 25
peer support 22, 51, 113
performance analysis **176**
performance-enhancing drugs 201–202, 203–204
Perreault, S. 58, 59
Perry, Elyse 227
Pfister, G. 7, 14, 47, 48, 83, 84, 180
physical education in schools: curriculum 138, 139, 141; decrease in girls' participation 23; improving girls' experience of 24, 138; LGBT+ students 72
physiology **176**
physiotherapy **175**
pickleball 50
players' associations, role of 226, 227, 229–230

podcasts 243–244
power: concept of 124–125; dynamics in coach-athlete relationship 187–188, 199; to 125, 130; with 125, 131; within 125, 129–130
practical gender needs (PGNs) 151
pregnancy: exercising in 34; support provisions 9, 224, 225
Press, Irina and Tamara 212
Pride in Sport Index 70
prisoners, developing sport for women 115
professional women's sport leagues 223–235; Australia 224–226; Australian Rules Football Women 226, 228, 230, 231; balance of elite versus grassroots participation 228; basketball 224; cricket 226, 228, 229; cricket case study 230–232; future research 228–229; growing grassroots participation 228; influence on women's sport 227–228; netball 225, 229; practical actions 229–230; professionalisation of women's sport 223–224; and role of players' associations 226, 227, 229–230; soccer 225; talent identification and development 227, 229
Proud 2 Play 80–81
psychology **176**; sport 58, 177, 201
purdah 152

Race, Emma 243
racism: against BME communities in community sport 85; bullying and 200; in constructions of biological femininity 213; IAAF Hyperandrogenism Regulations 215–216; against indigenous peoples 97, 103; in sport 37, 85, 86–87; sport an opportunity to challenge 83, 92, 138
recovery **175**
recreational drug use 201–202, 203–204
referees *see* officials
regional differences in participation in sport 20–21
retention of girls and young women 24, 26, 192
Ridge, D. 32, 34, 35
Rock Up Netball 168
role models: CALD women 89, 90; educators 141; girls and women with disabilities 59–60, 62–63, 64–65; importance to SFD programmes 130–131; indigenous women and girls 102; mothers 36
Roller Derby 81

Ruddell, J.L. 60, 61
rugby league podcast 244
rugby union, Pacific Island 149, 157–158
rule modifications 7
running 33, 34, 35
rural communities and access to sports facilities 113

safe sexual practices, projects for 139, 142
safe spaces 76, 117, 137, 138, 204, 241
Sawrikar, P. 83, 85, 87
Semenya, Caster 210, 214, 215, 219
sense of belonging 33–34, 39
sex: discrimination laws 6; testing 209, 211–212
sexism in sport 71, 72, 83, 92, 138
sexual harassment 198–200, 202–203; Bangladesh Weightlifting Federation 204–205; Larry Nassar 205; policies 203; prevalence of 198–199; Yasemin Brown 205
sexualised images of women athletes 237–238; on social media 240
Shilbury, D. 8, 164, 172, 190, 223
Shinew, K. 37, 60, 61
skill acquisition **176**
soccer *see* football (soccer)
social: health 47, 163–164; media 236, 240–241; networks 33–34, 39, 89, 131
socioecological model 21–23, 112–113, *112*
soft tissue therapy **175**
softball 102, 115
South Africa 136–137, 150, 214, 215
South African Women and Sport Foundation (SAWSF) 217–218
Spaaij, R. 23, 87, 110, 137, 138, 140, 149
specialised schools for sport 11
sport and exercise medicine **176**
Sport Australia 12, 46, 49, 103, 226, 230, 244
Sport Canada 8, 103, 203
sport development (SD) 2–3, 4; athlete protection and duty of care 197–208; coaches and officials 185–194; high-performance athletes 172–184; high testosterone regulation 209–222; media influence 236–247; Pacific Island rugby 149, 157–158; professional sport leagues 232–235
Sport England 46, 48, 49, 53; This Girl Can 24, 162, 167–168, 242–243
sport for development (SFD) 2–3, 3–4; coaches and 187, 188, 189; education 135–146; empowering women and girls through sport 121–134; health 161–171;
homeless populations 116; livelihoods 147–160; officials and 192–193; soccer mums programme 41–42
sport for health movement 45–46
Sport for Life 8, 9
sport, gender and development (SGD) programmes: concepts of power, structure and agency 124–125, 132; criticisms of 123–124; literature review 122–123
sport leagues, professional women's *see* professional women's sport leagues
sport psychology 58, 177, 201
Sport Science Sport Medicine (SSSM) 175–177, **175–176**
sporting goods industry 149
sports commentary 237
Sports Medicine Australia (SMA) 181
Spowart, L. 33, 34, 35
Stephens, Helen 212
stereotypes: challenging community perceptions 137, 138; gender 22, 23, 48, 61, 80; Muslim women 90; 'natural' athletes 100; older women 48; social and digital media and reinforcing of 240–241
strategic gender needs (SGNs) 151
Street Soccer USA 116
strength and conditioning **175**
Suncorp Super Netball League 225
support networks: education and development of 137; girls and women with disabilities 59–60, 61, 64; Go Sisters programme 142; mothers with dependent children 35, 37–38, 40, **40**; older women 47, 48, 51; SES and 113
surfing 33, 34, 35
Sustainable Development Goals 135, 136, 147, 155, 156
Swim Sisters group 90

Taekwondo 205
talent: identification and development 174, 181–182, 227, 229; transfer 174, 182
Target Tokyo 2020 174
Tatz, C. 98
team building exercises 89
Team Spirit: Aboriginal Girls in Sport 102–103
tennis: Ashleigh Barty case study 105–106; media representation 237; wheelchair 63, 64
terminology 1–2
testosterone in elite women athletes, regulating high 209–222; binary sex in sport and science 211–212; East/West

divide over women's biological eligibility 212–213; future research 218; links between testosterone levels and performance 215, 216, 218–219; medical interventions for hyperandrogenism 211, 217; need for education on issues 218–219; North/South divide over women's biological eligibility 213, 214–215, 215–217, 218; overrepresentation of women of colour from Global South 210, 213, 216; perspectives on gender eligibility regulation 211–213; race and nation in hyperandrogenism era 215–218; race, nation and biological femininity 212–213; in track-and-field 213–218
This Girl Can campaign 24, 62–63, 162, 167–169, 242–243
time, lack of 22, 151
Title IX 6, 188, 242
track-and-field 210, 213; politics of testosterone regulation 213–218
transgender athletes 70, 71, 79; lack of research on inclusion and 72–73 *see also* LGBT+ communities
transition from primary to secondary school 22–23
transphobia 73
'triple role' of women 151, **153**, 155

Uganda 136
unemployment 113, 139
United Kingdom (UK): Back to Netball (B2N) 39; Black and Minority Ethnic (BME) communities 85; digital marketing for walking groups 52–54; Health Action Zones (HAZ) 89; talent identification programmes 174; This Girl Can campaign 24, 167–168, 242–243; walking football 50
United Nations Office of Sport, Development and Peace (UNOSDP) 147
United States of America (US): American Development Model (ADM) 8; Back on My Feet 116; club system 10–11; family spending on children's sport 11; gender of high school sporting officials 185, 188; media coverage of women's sport in 236–237, 239, 240–241; mothers' volleyball league 40; sexual abuse of athletes 205; sport in school system 11; Street Soccer USA 116; Title IX 6, 188, 242
US Football Federation (USSF) 240–241

Vallerand, R.J. 58, 59
Vancouver Aboriginal Friendship Centre Society (VAFCS) 103
Veldman, S. 26
VicHealth 24, 41; This Girl Can 62–63, 162, 168–169, 243
Victorian Equal Opportunities and Human Rights Commission 81
volleyball 40
volunteering 23; mothers 37–38; older adults 48–49

W-League 225, 231
Waldrop, J. 178
walking: basketball 50; football 49, 50; groups, digital marketing for 52–54
Walsh, Stella 212
weightlifting 204–205
Western Australian Institute of Sport (WAIS) 174
wheelchair sport: basketball 59, 60, 61, 63; in British Columbia 63–65; tennis 63, 64
Widening Access through Sport initiative 137–138
women/girls-only events 11, 21, 26, 27, 64–65, 88, 103, 136–137
Women's Big Bash League (WBBL) 226, 230–232
The Women's Game 244
workplace incivility 191
World Health Organisation 45, 46, 162

Zambia 142–144